George Louis Faber

The fisheries of the Adriatic and the fish thereof

A report of the Austro-Hungarian sea-fisheries

George Louis Faber

The fisheries of the Adriatic and the fish thereof
A report of the Austro-Hungarian sea-fisheries

ISBN/EAN: 9783337274801

Printed in Europe, USA, Canada, Australia, Japan

Cover: Foto ©Andreas Hilbeck / pixelio.de

More available books at **www.hansebooks.com**

THE
FISHERIES OF THE ADRIATIC

AND

THE FISH THEREOF.

A Report of

THE AUSTRO-HUNGARIAN SEA-FISHERIES,

With a detailed description of the Marine Fauna of the Adriatic Gulf.

By G. L. FABER,

HER MAJESTY'S CONSUL, FIUME.

WITH EIGHTEEN WOODCUT ILLUSTRATIONS AFTER DRAWINGS BY LEO LITTROW,

AND NUMEROUS ENGRAVINGS ON STONE.

LONDON:
BERNARD QUARITCH, 15 PICCADILLY.
1883.

All rights reserved.

To CAPTAIN RICHARD F. BURTON,

Her Majesty's Consul for Trieste,

&c. &c. &c.

My Dear Colleague,

As the execution of this work—or Report, as I shall call it—is due to your conception, encouragement, and, in a main degree, to your patient advice to a novice, in an art in which you excel, I venture to hope you will accept its dedication as a slight tribute of my high regard and personal devotion.

Your grateful friend and admirer,

G. L. FABER.

Fiume, *September* 30, 1882.

INTRODUCTION.

HAVING enjoyed the privilege of perusing the following pages before publication, I have great pleasure in complying with the Author's request to introduce his work with a few remarks.

The circumstance that the year of the birth of this work coincides with that of the Great International Fisheries Exhibition in London, cannot fail to attract a greater amount of attention than any words of mine could secure. For, although it relates to a district, the Fauna and Fishing interests of which are in great measure foreign to those of the countries in whose language it is written, it will be favourably received as one of the contributions which help to accomplish the very objects aimed at by the promoters of the International Exhibition. It will be found to give much practical information applicable to conditions in this country, and, therefore, valuable to those who have British Fishing interests at heart. Pisciculturists will have their attention drawn to the plan practised by Italians, viz., to rear fry of marine fishes, such as Red and Grey Mullets, Flat-fishes, Eels, &c., in enclosed waters to a marketable size; a practice yielding direct and immediate profits, and advocated by myself for the last twenty years. To the great number of persons who annually leave these shores for the Mediterranean in quest of sport and recreation, the present work may serve as guide to a field which hitherto seems to have been much neglected by them. And, finally, the Zoologist will be glad of finding in it a general review of the Adriatic Fauna with its singularly varied character, and of the agencies by which its distribution has been determined.

I trust that the Author will be amply repaid for the sacrifices he has had to make in the production of this work, by seeing its usefulness extend far beyond the limits to which its contents relate.

ALBERT GÜNTHER.

BRITISH MUSEUM, 24 *March*, 1883.

TO THE READER.

S far as I am aware, no comprehensive work has hitherto been published on the Austro-Hungarian Sea-fisheries.[1] Count Antonio Marazzi, Vice-Consul for Trieste, addressed in 1873, to the Italian Ministry of Foreign Affairs, a report on the subject, from the point of view of the Italian fishermen engaged in the East Adriatic fisheries.[2] Valuable information on the same subject was also prepared by Dr. Syrski for the Vienna Exhibition of 1873, and published by the Marine Section of the Austrian Ministry of Commerce.[3] The following report, suggested by my learned colleague, Capt. R. F. Burton, Her Majesty's Consul for Trieste, is intended to treat the subject in a more general sense, and to pave the way for a comprehensive work.

The original plan has been considerably enlarged in the course of execution.

Inquiries into the nomenclature of fishes, local and popular, and their identification, have necessitated more serious studies of the fauna than was at first contemplated: this has led to a short description of the fauna and its chorology, which does not by any means aspire to scientific merits, and

---

[1] Dr. Carlo de Marchesetti's work, *La Pesca lungo le coste orientali dell' Adria*, has appeared since these pages were written, and I am indebted to this valuable contribution for a variety of information.

[2] *Bollettino Consolare* of July, 1873.

[3] *Special Catalog der im Pavillon der Oesterr. Handelsmarine und Maritimen Etablissements ausgestellten Gegenstände.*

b

is given only as what it really is,—a study or rather a report. It must accordingly claim the privileges due to a work of the kind. My only excuse in presenting it to the reader must be the excellence and value of the investigations of Dr. J. R. Lorenz on the horizontal chorology of animal life in the Quarnero,—a work, which, although familiar to many Austrian and German readers, is not so generally known to my countrymen as it deserves. Hence the reason of the prominence I have thought fit to give to his observations.

The nomenclature of fishes has led to a systematic list (including the fresh-water fauna of the water-shed of the northern and eastern shores of the Adriatic), and to a partial list of invertebrates, as far as they have any value or possess local names. A systematic list of invertebrates would have been beyond the scope of this volume.

The list of fishes is compiled with the greatest care, and with a view of obviating, if possible, the almost inevitable mistakes, or inaccuracies, to which an unassisted student is liable. The classification was adopted from the learned Dr. Albert Günther's "Catalogue of Fishes of the British Museum." It has since been rearranged on the system of Dr. A. Günther's subsequent work "An Introduction to the Study of Fishes."[1] The list of the fauna is compiled on the authority of Günther, Lorenz, Canestrini, Grube, Nardo, Perugia, and Plucar; and the fresh-water fishes on the authority of Günther, Heckel and Kner, Bonizzi, Canestrini, Nardo, and Ninni. A systematic list is now in course of publication by Prof. M. Stossich, of Fiume: it will be a very valuable contribution to the investigation of the Adriatic fauna.[2]

The Italian nomenclature has been published by Canestrini, Grube, Naccari, Nardo, Martens, Olivi, Perugia, Plucar, and others; this has been subjected to careful comparison and revision as regards those names which are in use on these shores, and others have been added from personal information and inquiry. I am indebted to Dr. C. de Marchesetti, Director

---

[1] Edinburgh: 1880.
[2] *Bol. della Soc. Adriat. di Scienze Nat.* Trieste: 1879-81. (*See* Appendix, p. 258.)

of the Trieste Museo Civico di Storia Naturale, for the identification of various fishes and for other valuable information he has been kind enough to furnish.

The Croatian names are entirely new; they have not hitherto been published, and I have been at great pains to collect them from a variety of sources too numerous to catalogue.[1]

I am indebted to Mr. H. Thierry and Mr. Bacarcić, of Fiume, for many of those in use on the Hungarian-Croatian littoral, and to Mr. C. I. Kovacević, late Harbour-master at Spalato, for those in use at his former post. Prof. Anton Korlević, Professor of Natural History at the Croatian Gymnasium at Fiume, has been good enough to revise the Croatian nomenclature, and Prof. Spiridion Brusina, Professor of Zoology at the University of Agram, has had the kindness *en dernier lieu* to correct and further extend the list. I am particularly indebted to these two gentlemen for their valuable aid.

In part of the text I have thought fit to introduce, where practicable, the more familiar English names of fishes, in order to render the text more intelligible.

The invaluable work of Forbes and Godwin-Austen, on the Natural History of the European Seas; "The Sea-fisheries," by E. W. H. Holdsworth, and "Die Bewirthschaftung des Meeres, mit Rücksicht auf den Adriat. Golf," by M. Anton Gareis, have in their turn furnished a variety of information. Nardo's work, "Sulla Coltura degli Animali acquatici nel Veneto Dominio," is my authority on the subject of the lagoon-fisheries.

In many instances I have quoted my authorities; but it would have been tedious to do so in every case, and I hope I may not be accused of

---

[1] Since writing these lines I have received, through the kindness of Prof. G. Kolombatović, his works entitled *Pesce della Acque di Spalato*. Spalato: 1881; and *Fische welche in den Gewässern von Spalato beobachtet und überhaupt im Adriatischen Meere registrirt wurden*. Spalato, 1882: to these volumes I am indebted for a variety of information concerning the fauna of Spalato and the local Croatian nomenclature.

plagiarism on that account; my study does not profess to be more than a compilation of details derived from a variety of sources.

This I have endeavoured to put together in a form such as I hope may recommend itself to the reader. Beginning with a topographical and climatic account of the Adriatic Gulf, the report—for such I must again call it—proceeds to give a description of the horizontal distribution of animal life in the Quarnero, and of the fauna generally; of the fisheries from an historical and legislative point of view; of the share taken in the Austrian fisheries by Italian fishermen; of the fishing districts and the produce of the fisheries, together with an account of the fishing craft and gear, such as nets, lines, and similar matters; the names applied to fishermen and different modes of fishing; the fish-market, and methods of cooking and curing fish; concluding with a systematic list of the fauna, with scientific, English, German, Italian, Croatian nomenclature, and with sundry details including statistics.

The plates and engravings will add much to the interest of this work. The latter are executed after drawings for which I am indebted to a friend, M. LEO LITTROW. They speak for themselves.

I am conscious of my shortcomings,—for the more one enters into the subject the more imperfect one's work appears,—and I must, therefore, again solicit the indulgence of the reader. My task is, however, fulfilled if I have the satisfaction of thinking that my report may lead to a more comprehensive work on the subject,—a work which at present is wanting.

In conclusion, I must express my thanks to Messrs. WYMAN & SONS for the trouble and care they have taken in preparing this book in its present shape.

FIUME, *September 30th*, 1882.

CONTENTS.

CHAPTER I.
THE FAUNA.

PAGE.

Preliminary.—Topographical.—Tides.—Currents.— Temperature.— Saltness.— Professors Wolf and Luksch; their investigations in the Adriatic Gulf.—Haunts of fishes.—Investigations of the fauna in the Adriatic.—Dr. J. R. Lorenz; his work on the Horizontal Chorology in the Quarnero.—Zone I.—Zone II.—Zone III.—Zone IV.—Zone V.—Zone VI.—Zone VII.—Vertebrates.—Sedentary class.—Shore fishes.—Littoral forms.— Rovers. — Squatters. — Forms of the declivity and shallows.—Rovers. — Squatters.—Forms of the deep-bed. — Squatters. — Migratory forms.—Recapitulation.—Invertebrates, Articulates, and Radiates.—Characteristic species of the various zones.—Extended and limited distribution.—Boreal forms.—*Pisces.*—Fresh-water fishes.—Fishes which frequent the brackish waters.—Sea-fishes. 1

CHAPTER II.
HISTORICAL.—LEGISLATION.—THE CHIOGGIOTTI.

Historical.—State of the coast, political and economic.—Inland markets; fluctuations of the trade.—Trawlers.—Statistics.—Ice.—Salt.—Italian fishermen.—Legislation.—Privileges of the Italian fishermen.—Titles from which the fishing rights were derived under the Republic of Venice.—Treaty between Austria and Italy.—The Chioggiotti; their craft engaged in the Austrian fisheries; proceeds of their share in the fisheries.—Count Marazzi.—Professor Ninni.—Individual profit of the Chioggiotti.—Consul Revest.—Distribution of the Italian fishing fleet on the Austrian coast; value of craft and gear employed.—Total value of craft and gear at Chioggia and Pelestrina.—The Italian fisheries.—Italian fishing craft; ditto engaged in the Austrian fisheries; ditto engaged in the foreign fisheries.—Value of the Chioggia fisheries.—Imports and exports of fish at Venice.—Venetian fisheries.—Craft and crew. 40

CHAPTER III.

FISHING DISTRICTS.—SEASON OF FISHING.—PRODUCE.

Fishing Districts.—Austria: Gorizia, Gradisca, Trieste.—Istria: Isola, Pirano, Salvore, Umago, Daila, Parenzo, Pola, Lussinpiccolo, Preluca.—Hungarian-Croatian littoral: Fiume, Buccari, Portoré, Segna.—Dalmatia; Zara, Sebenico, Spalato, Ragusa, Cattaro.—Dalmatian Archipelago.—Season of Fishing.—Descriptive part.—Produce. —Pisces.—Sharks, Rays, Sturgeons, Perch tribe, Sea-perches, Red Mullet, Sea-breams, Scorpions, Meagres, Sword-fish, Scabbard-fish, Hair-tail, Horse Mackerel, John Dory, Black-fish, Dolphins, Mackerel, Tunny, Star-gazers, Weevers, Anglers, Gurnards, Flying-Gurnards, Gobies, Dragonets, Band-fishes, Blennies, Spets, Atherines, Mullets, Sticklebacks, Trumpet-fish, Suck-fishes, Lophotes cepedianus, Ribbon-fishes, Coral-fishes, Wrasses, Cod tribe, Ophidium, Fierasfer, Sand-eels, Macrurus, Flat-fish tribe, Scopelidæ, Cyprinodon, Gar-pikes, Flying-fish, Salmon tribe, Herring tribe, Eel tribe, Pipe-fishes, Sea-horses, File-fishes, Sun-fishes, Lampreys, Lancelot.—Mollusks.— Cephalopods, Bivalves, Univalves, Tunicates. — Crustaceans. — Echinoderms. — Actiniæ.—Sponges.—Red Coral.... 62

CHAPTER IV.

THE FISHING CRAFT.

Description of craft.—Value of the same. 99

CHAPTER V.

THE NETS.

Process of making, tanning, and mounting. — Drift-nets ; Trammel-nets ; Circle-nets ; Seine-nets ; Trawling-nets ; Hand-nets.—Fish-weirs and Ponds.—Snares.— Basket-traps.—Store-pots, &c.—Value of the fishing gear. 104

CHAPTER VI.

LINE-FISHING.

Lines.—Hooks.—Implements of various kinds.—Prongs, &c.—Scares. —Bait. ... 130

CHAPTER VII.

NAMES APPLIED TO FISHERMEN AND VARIOUS MODES OF FISHING.—
SARDINE FISHERIES.—DIVISION OF PROFITS. ...   135

CHAPTER VIII.

THE FISH-MARKETS.

Description   141

CHAPTER IX.

METHODS OF CURING AND COOKING FISH.

Curing Pilchards, Anchovies, &c.—Preserving Pilchards, Tunny, Norway-lobster, &c. in oil.—Fishes which are smoked, or dried for exportation.—Ways of preparing various fishes and other produce of the sea for the table. 148

CHAPTER X.

STATISTICS.

Proceeds of the fisheries.—The Austrian fishing fleet; its distribution on the coast.—Yield of the Istrian, Hungarian-Croatian, and Dalmatian fisheries.—Recapitulation.—Share of the Italian boats.—Statistics of the Austrian sea-fisheries; ditto of the Hungarian sea-fisheries.—Total yield.—Craft belonging to the Hungarian-Croatian seaboard.— Imports and exports of fish.—Fish sold in the Fiume fish-market. 154

FAUNA OF THE ADRIATIC.

	PAGE.
Mammalia	177
Reptilia	178
Fishes	179

Special Lists of Fishes :

- A. Fresh-water Fishes ... 234
- B. British Fishes which are common to the Adriatic Fauna ... 236
- C. Five Fishes belonging exclusively to the Adriatic Fauna ... 237
- D. Thirty-one Fishes which are only quite accidentally met with in the Adriatic ... 237
- E. Fourteen Fishes which belong more especially to the Venetian Fauna ... 238
- F. Forty-eight Fishes which belong more especially to the Dalmatian Fauna ... 238
- G. Twenty-nine Fishes which have hitherto been caught only on the south coast of Dalmatia ... 239
- H. Fishes which belong to the class of Minutaja, or Misto, *i.e.*, Fishes which are thrown together, and sold as one class ... 239
- I. Table of the Fresh-water and Sea Fishes, showing the number of Species belonging to each Family ... 240

Invertebrata :

Mollusca ...	242
Crustacea ...	252
Echinodermata ...	255
Polypi ...	257
Mollusks of the Adriatic enumerated by Professor M. Stossich	258
Crustaceans of the Adriatic enumerated by Professor M. Stossich	259
Vermes of the Adriatic, enumerated by Professor M. Stossich	261

APPENDICES.

- I. Alphabetical Index to the Scientific Names ... 262
- II. Alphabetical Index to the English Names ... 265
- III. Reference Index to the Italian Local and Vulgar Names of the Adriatic Fauna on the Austro-Hungarian Seaboard and Venetian Estuary ... 269
  Key to the Pronunciation of Croatian Words ... 277
- IV. Reference Index to the Croatian Local and Vulgar Names of the Adriatic Fauna on the Austro-Hungarian Seaboard ... 278

INDEX TO THE SYSTEMATIC LIST OF FISHES.

Sub-Classes, Orders, Families, and Genera.

Sub-Class I.—PALÆICHTHYES.
  Order I.—CHONDROPTERYGII.
    Sub-Order I.—PLAGIOSTOMATA.
      A. SELACHOIDEI (*Sharks*).
Fam. I.—CARCHARIIDÆ .... *p.* 179
  Group I.—Carchariina.
    Gen. 4 Carcharias.
      1 Galeus.
  Group II.—Zygænina.
    Gen. 2 Zygæna.
  Group III.—Mustelina.
    Gen. 2 Mustelus.
Fam. II.—LAMNIDÆ .... *p.* 180
  Group I.—Lamnina.
    Gen. 2 Lamna.
      1 Carcharodon.
      2 Odontaspis.
      1 Alopecias.
  Group II.—Selachina.
    Gen. 1 Selache.

Fam. III.—NOTIDANIDÆ .... *p.* 181
  Gen. 3 Notidanus.

Fam. IV.—SCYLIIDÆ .... *p.* 181
  Gen. 3 Scyllium.
    1 Pristiurus.

Fam. V.—SPINACIDÆ .... *p.* 182
  Gen. 1 Centrina.
    2 Acanthias.
    1 Spinax.
    1 Echinorhinus.

Fam. VI.—RHINIDÆ .... *p.* 182
  Gen. 2 Rhina.

      B. BATOIDEI (*Rays*).

Fam. I.—TORPEDINIDÆ .... *p.* 183
  Gen. 3 Torpedo.

Fam. II.—RAJIDÆ .... *p.* 183
  Gen. 12 Raja.

Fam. III.—TRYGONIDÆ............ p. 185
  Gen. 3 Trygon.
    1 Pteroplatea.

Fam. IV.—MYLIOBATIDÆ............ p. 185
  Group I.—Myliobatina.
    Gen. 2 Myliobatis.
      1 Rhinoptera.

  Group II.—Ceralopterina.
    Gen. 1 Dicerobatis.

Order II.—GANOIDEI

  Sub-Order I.—CHONDROSTEI.
Fam. I.—ACIPENSERIDÆ (*Sturgeons*) .... p. 186
  Gen. 7 Acipenser.

Sub-Class II.—TELEOSTEI.
  Order I.—ACANTHOPTERYGII.
  Divis. I. — ACANTHOPTERYGII PERCIFORMES.

Fam. I.—PERCIDÆ (*Perch-tribe*)...... p. 187
  Group I.—Percina.
    Gen. 1 Perca.
      1 Labrax.
      1 Lucioperca.

  Group II.—Serranina.
    Gen. 1 Centropristis.
      1 Anthias.
      4 Serranus.
      1 Polyprion.

  Group III.—Apogonina.
    Gen. 1 Apogon.

Group IV.—Pristipomatidæ.
  Gen. 3 Dentex.
    3 Mæna.
    4 Smaris.

Fam. II.—MULLIDÆ (*Red Mullets*) p. 190
  Gen. 2 Mullus.

Fam. III.—SPARIDÆ (*Sea-breams*) ... p. 190
  Group I.—Cantharina.
    Gen. 3 Cantharus.
      2 Box.
      1 Oblata.

  Group II.—Sargina.
    Gen. 4 Sargus.
      1 Charax.

  Group III.—Pagrina.
    Gen. 3 Pagrus.
      5 Pagellus.
      1 Chrysophrys.

Fam. IV. SCORPÆNIDÆ (*Scorpions*) p. 193
  Gen. 1 Sebastes.
    2 Scorpæna.

Divis. II.—ACANTHOPTERYGII SCIÆNIFORMES.

Fam.—SCIÆNIDÆ (*Meagres*) .... p. 193
  Gen. 1 Umbrina.
    1 Sciæna.
    1 Corvina.

Divis. III.—ACANTHOPTERYGII XIPHIIFORMES.

Fam.—XIPHIIDÆ (*Sword-fishes*)...... p. 194
  Gen. 1 Xiphias.
    1 Histiophorus.

Divis. IV.—ACANTHOPTERYGII TRICHI-
URIFORMES.

Fam. — TRICHIURIDÆ (*Scabbard-fishes, Hair-tails*) .... *p.* 194
   Gen. 1 Lepidopus.
      1 Trichiurus.
      1 Thyrsites.

Divis. V.—ACANTHOPTERYGII COTTO-SCOMBRIFORMES.

Fam. I.—CARANGIDÆ (*Horse Mackerels, &c.*) .... *p.* 194
   Gen. 1 Trachurus.
      1 Caranx.
      1 Seriola.
      1 Naucrates.
      3 Lichia.
      1 Temnodon.
      1 Capros.

Fam. II.—CYTTIDÆ (*John Dorys*)... *p.* 196
   Gen. 2 Zeus.

Fam. III.—STROMATEIDÆ (*Black-fish*) .... *p.* 196
   Gen. 2 Stromateus.
      2 Centrolophus.

Fam. IV.—CORYPHÆNIDÆ (*Dolphins*) .... *p.* 196
   Gen. 2 Coryphæna.
      1 Brama.
      1 Schedophilus.
      1 Ausonia.

Fam. V.—SCOMBRIDÆ (*Mackerel, Tunny, &c.*) .... *p.* 197
   Gen. 3 Scomber.
      4 Thynnus.
      2 Pelamys.
      1 Auxis.
      2 Echeneis.

Fam. VI.—TRACHINIDÆ .... *p.* 198
   Group I.—Uranoscopina (*Star-gazers*).
      Gen. 1 Uranoscopus.
   Group II.—Trachinina (*Weevers*).
      Gen. 4 Trachinus.

Fam. VII.—PEDICULATI (*Anglers*) *p.* 199
   Gen. 2 Lophius.

Fam. VIII.—COTTIDÆ (*Bull-heads, Gurnards*) .... *p.* 199
   Gen. 1 Cottus.
      1 Lepidotrigla.
      6 Trigla.

Fam. IX.—CATAPHRACTI (*Flying Gurnards*) .... *p.* 201
   Gen. 1 Peristethus.
      1 Dactylopterus.

Divis. VI.—ACANTHOPTERYGII GOBII-FORMES.

Fam. I.—GOBIIDÆ (*Goby-tribe*) ...... *p.* 201
   Group I.—Gobiina (*Gobies*).
      Gen. 22 Gobius.
         2 Latrunculus.
   Group II.—Callionymina (*Dragonets*).
      Gen. 6 Callionymus.

Divis. VII.—ACANTHOPTERYGII BLENNII-FORMES.

Fam. I.—CEPOLIDÆ (*Band-fishes*)... *p.* 204
   Gen. 1 Cepola.

Fam. II.—BLENNIIDÆ (*Blennies*) ... *p.* 204
   Gen. 14 Blennius.
      1 Cristiceps.
      1 Tripterygium.

Divis. VIII.—ACANTHOPTERYGII MUGILI-
FORMES.

Fam. I.—SPHYRÆNIDÆ.............. *p*. 206
Gen. 1 Sphyræna.

Fam. II.—ATHERINIDÆ (*Atherines*,
or *Sand-smelts*)................... *p*. 206
Group.—Atherina.
Gen. 3 Atherina.

Fam. III.—MUGILIDÆ (*Mullets*) ... *p*. 206
Gen. 6 Mugil.

Divis. IX.—ACANTHOPTERYGII GASTRO-
STEIFORMES.

Fam.—GASTROSTEIDÆ (*Stickle-
backs*) .... *p*. 207
Gen. 2 Gastrosteus.

Divis. X.—ACANTHOPTERYGII CENTRIS-
CIFORMES.

Fam.—CENTRISCIDÆ (*Trumpet fish*) *p*. 207
Gen. 1 Centriscus.

Divis. XI.—ACANTHOPTERYGII GOBIESO-
CIFORMES.

Fam.—GOBIESOCIDÆ (*Suck-fishes*) *p*. 208
Gen. 6 Lepadogaster.
1 Leptopterygius.

Divis. XII.—ACANTHOPTERYGII LOPHO-
TIFORMES.

Fam.—LOPHOTIDÆ.................. *p*. 208
Gen. 1 Lophotes.

Divis. XIII.—ACANTHOPTERYGII TÆNII-
FORMES.

Fam.—TRACHYPTERIDÆ (*Ribbon-
fishes*) .... *p*. 208
Gen. 2 Trachypterus.

Order II.—ACANTHOPTERYGII PHA-
RYNGOGNATHI.

Fam. I.—POMACENTRIDÆ (*Coral-
fishes*) .... *p*. 209
Gen. 1 Heliastes.

Fam. II.—LABRIDÆ (Wrasses). ... *p*. 209
Group I.—Labrina.
Gen. 6 Labrus.
10 Crenilabrus.
1 Acantholabrus.
Group II.—Julidina.
Gen. 1 Novacula.
1 Julis.
2 Coris.

Order III.—ANACANTHINI.

Divis. I.—ANACANTHINI GADOIDEI.

Fam. I.—GADIDÆ (*Cod-tribe*) .... *p*. 212
Gen. 5 Gadus.
1 Merluccius.
2 Phycis.
1 Lota.
1 Hypsiptera.
3 Motella.

Fam. II.—OPHIDIIDÆ .... *p*. 214
Group. I.—Brotulina.
Gen. 1 Pteridium.
Group II.—Ophidiina.
Gen. 4 Ophidium.

Group III.—Fierasferina.
    Gen. 2 Fierasfer.
Group IV.—Ammodytina (*Sand-eels*, or *launces*).
    Gen. 1 Ammodytes.

Fam. III.—MACRURIDÆ .... *p.* 214
    Gen. 1 Macrurus.

Divis. II.—ANACANTHINI PLEURONECTOIDEI.

Fam.—PLEURONECTIDÆ (*Flat-fishes*)
    p. 214
    Gen. 2 Rhombus.
        1 Phrynorhombus.
        4 Arnoglossus.
        1 Citharus.
        2 Rhomboidichtys.
        2 Pleuronectes.
        9 Solea.
        1 Ammopleurops.

Order IV.—PHYSOSTOMI.

Fam. I.—SCOPELIDÆ .... *p.* 217
    Group.—Saurina.
    Gen. 1 Saurus.
        1 Aulopus.

Fam. II.—CYPRINIDÆ (*Carp-tribe*) *p.* 217
    Group I.—Cyprinina.
    Gen. 2 Cyprinus.
        3 Barbus.
        1 Aulopyge.
        2 Gobio.
    Group II —Leuciscina.
    Gen. 12 Leuciscus.
        2 Paraphoxinus.
        1 Tinca.
        4 Chondrostoma.

Group III.—Abramidina.
    Gen. 1 Abramis.
        2 Alburnus.
Group IV.—Cobitidina.
    Gen. 1 Nemachilus.
        1 Cobitis.

Fam. III.—CYPRINODONTIDÆ ... *p.* 223
    Group.—Cyprinodontidæ carnivoræ.
    Gen. 1 Cyprinodon.

Fam. IV.—SCOMBRESOCIDÆ (*Garpikes, &c.*) .... *p.* 223
    Gen. 1 Belone.
        1 Scombresox.
        2 Exocœtus.

Fam. V.—ESOCIDÆ (*Pikes*) .... *p.* 223
    Gen. 1 Esox.

Fam. VI.—SALMONIDÆ (*Salmons*) *p.* 224
    Group.—Salmonina.
    Gen. 6 Salmo.
        1 Thymallus.
        1 Argentina.

Fam. VII.—CLUPEIDÆ (*Herring-tribe*) .... *p.* 225
    Group I.—Engraulina.
    Gen. 1 Engraulis.
    Group II.—Clupeina.
    Gen. 5 Clupea.

Fam. VIII.—MURÆNIDÆ (*Eel-tribe*). *p.* 226
    Group I.—Anguillina.
    Gen. 2 Anguilla
        1 Conger.
        1 Myrus.
    Group II.—Ophichthyina.
    Gen. 3 Ophichthys.
    Group III.—Murænina.
    Gen. 2 Muræna.

Order V.—LOPHOBRANCHII.
Fam.—SYNGNATHIDÆ (*Pipe-fishes*) *p.* 227
Group I.—Syngnathina.
   Gen. 3 Siphonostoma.
      6 Syngnathus.
      2 Nerophis.
Group II.—Hippocampina (*Sea-horses*).
   Gen. 2 Hippocampus.

Order VI.—PLECTOGNATHI.
Fam. I.—SCLERODERMI (*File-fishes*) .... *p.* 229
Group I.—Balistina.
   Gen. 1 Balistes.

Fam. II.—GYMNODONTES (*Sun-fishes*) .... *p.* 229
Group I.—Molina.
   Gen. 2 Orthagoriscus.

Sub-Class III.—CYCLOSTOMATA.
Fam.—PETROMYZONTIDÆ (*Lampreys*) .... *p.* 230
   Gen. 3 Petromyzon.

Sub-Class IV.—LEPTOCARDII.
Fam.—CIRROSTOMI (*Lancelets*) ...... *p.* 231
   Gen. 1 Branchiostoma.

Recapitulation of fishes.

  4 Sub-Classes.
10 Orders.
57 Families.
161 Genera.
382 Species.

LIST OF ILLUSTRATIONS.

DRAWINGS ON STONE.

DIAGRAM OF THE TONNARE IN THE QUARNERO ....*to face page*	66
BOATS :—TOPPO ; ZOPPOLO	98
BATELLO DI MUGGIA ; BARCA DI MUGGIA.................................	99
BRAGAGNA	100
BRAZZERA DI CAPO D'ISTRIA ; GAETA	101
LEUTO ; TARTANA	102
BRAGOZZO...	103
CIMAROL	104
NETS :—VARIOUS KNOTS USED IN NETTING	105
MESHES OF THE MOST COMMON NETS................................	106
SALTARELLO..	109
TONNARA DI PRELUCA	111
TONNARA DI BUCCARICA	112
PALANDARA DA POSTA	113
PALANDARA DA TIRO	114
TRATTA	115
TRATTA	116
SCIABICA	117
COCCHIA	118
TARTANA	120
VALLE CHIUSA ARGINATA	124
VALLE A GRIGIUOLI	126
PARANGALA DISTESA ; PARANGALA GALLEGIANTE	131
SUNDRY FISHING GEAR...	133

LIST OF ILLUSTRATIONS.

WOOD ENGRAVINGS.

FIUME FROM THE WEST	*Frontispiece.*
ARBE (ISLAND), QUARNERO ....*to face page*	9
BRAGOZZI AT ANCHOR	17
CASTLE TERSATO, NEAR FIUME	25
LIGHTHOUSE OF PROMONTORE (ISTRIA)	33
BRAGOZZI AT ANCHOR, DRYING NETS	40
,, ,, LEAVING PORT	49
,, ,, RUNNING BEFORE THE WIND	57
TONNARA IN THE BAY OF PRELUCA	65
VOLOSCA HARBOUR (GULF OF FIUME)	73
ZOPPOLI AT BUCCARI	81
SCOGLIO S. MARCO, FROM THE ISLAND OF VEGLIA	89
BRAGOZZI FISHING	97
SEGNALE (BARREL-BUOY)	134
FIUME FROM THE EAST	141
SHIP-BUILDING OFF SCOGLIO S. MARCO	145
GULF OF BUCCARI AND CHANNEL OF MALTEMPO, FROM THE HEIGHTS OF BUCCARI	152
BUOY	175

BIBLIOGRAPHY

ON ICHTHYOLOGY IN CONNEXION WITH THE ADRIATIC.

BONAPARTE, C. L.—Fauna Italica.
—— Catalogo metodico.
BRUSINA, S. P.—Conch. Dalmat. Ined. 1865.
—— Contrib. pella Fauna dei Molluschi Dalmat. Vienna. 1866.
CANESTRINI, G.—Fauna italica.
CHIEREGHINI, S.—Descr. dei Crost. Test. e Pesci che abitano le lagune e golfo Veneto.
CLAUS, C.—Studien über Polypen und Quallen der Adria. Wien 1877.
DONATI.—Trattato de' Pesci marini dei Lidi di Venezia.
ECKHEL, G.—Commun. sopra le Spugne. Bot. Soc. Adriat. Sc. Nat. Trieste. 1875.
GAREIS, A.—Die Bewirthschaftung des Meeres mit Rücksicht auf den Adriat. Golf.
GIGLIOLI, E. H.—Catal. dei Pesci italiani. Cat. Esposizione di Pesca in Berlino. 1880.
GINNANI.—Testacea marina del Mare Adriat.
GRAVENHORST.—Tergestina.
GRUBE, A. E.—Ein Ausflug nach Triest und dem Quarnero. Berlin. 1861.
—— Die Insel Lussin. 1864.
—— Actinien, Echinodermen und Würmer des Adriat. und Mittelmeeres.
HECKEL, JACOB.—Cat. dei pesci della Dalmazia in Carrara. La Dalmazia, Zara, 1864.
—— Descr. di una nuova specie di Acipenser nel mare di Venezia. IX. Congresso di sc. Ital. 1847.
—— Die Störarten der Lagunen bei Venedig. Sitzungsber. der Acad. d. Wissensch. Wien. 1851.
—— Ichthyolog. Reisen. Sitzungsber. 1851-1852.

HELLER, C.—Horæ Dalmat. 1863-4.
—— Crust. Sud-Europas. 1863.
—— Amph. Adriat. Meeres. 1866.
—— Die Tunicaten, Zoophyten und Echino. dermen des Adriat. Meeres. Wien. 1874-7.
KOLOMBATOVIĆ, G.—Pesci delle Acque di Spalato. Spalato. 1881.
—— Osservazioni sul lavoro di M. Stossich· Spalato, 1880.
—— Fische welche in den Gewässern von Spalato beobachtet und überhaupt im Adriat. Meere registrirt wurden. Spalato. 1882.
LORENZ, J. R.—Physicalische Verhältnisse und Vertheilung der Organismen im Quarnerischen Golfe. Wien. 1863.
MARCHESETTI, DR. C. DE.—La pesca lungo le coste orientali dell' Adria. Tr. 1882.
MARENZELLER, E. — Adriatische Anelliden. Wien. 1874-5.
MARTENS.—Reise nach Venedig. Ulm. 1838.
MICHAELLIS, M.—Nuovi pesci del mare Adriat. Isis. 1829. Pag. 1011.
—— Scyphius cultirostris. Isis. 1830. Pag. 251.
NACCARI, F. L.—Ittiologia Adriatica. Pavia. 1822.
NARDO, G. D.— Prospetti sistematici degli Animali delle Prov. Venete. Ven. 1860.
—— Annot. d. 54 Crost. Ven. 1869.
—— Sinonimia moderna delle Specie, etc., descritte dall' Abate Stef. Chieroghini. Ven. 1847.
—— Prodromus observationum et disquisitionum Adriat. Icht. Ticini. 1827.
—— Del Prottostego. Annali della sc. del Regno Lombardo. Veneto. 1840.

NARDO, D. G.—Osservazioni Itt. Ann. d. sc. del Regno L.V. 1843.
—— De Proctostego. Pataviæ. 1827.
—— Annotazioni, etc., in Isis. 1833.
—— Considerazioni sui Pesci Mola. Ann. d. sc. del Regno L.V. 1859.
—— Osservazioni anat. intorno alla struttura delle cute del Xiphias. Firenze. 1841.
—— Descr. di un pesce raro. Giorn. di fisica. Pavia. 1827.
—— Memoria sopra tre nuove sp. di pesci. Giorn. di fisica. Pavia. 1824.
NINNI, DR. A. P.—Gli Anacantini del Mare Adriatico. Atti Soc. It. Sc. Nat. Vol. XXIII. 1880.
—— Materiali per la fauna Veneta. Atti reale Istituto Veneto. Tom. IV., Serie V.
OLIVI.—Zoologia Adriatica.
PERUGIA ALBERTO.—Catalogo dei Pesci dell' Adr.
—— Elenco dei Pesci dell' Adriat. Milano. 1881.
PLUCAR, E.—Der Fischplatz zu Trieste. Tr. 1846.
RENIER.—Osservazioni postume di Zool. Adriat.
SARS.—Bemaerkninger over det. Adriat. Havs Fauna sammenlignet med Nordhavets.

SCHMARDA, L. K.—Die maritime Production der Oesterr. Küstenlander (Oesterr. Revue).
—— Zur Naturgeschichte der Adria. Wien Staatsdruckerei. 1852.
STALIO.—Catal. Crost. Adriat. 1877.
STEINDACHNER, DR. F.—Icht. Notizen. Sitzungsber der Wiener Ak. 1880. Band. LXI.
—— Beiträge zur Kenntniss der Gobioiden. Sitzungsber der Wiener Ak. 1860. Band XLII.
STOSSICH, M.—Prospetto della Fauna del Mare Adriat. Parte I., II., III. (Bot. delle Sc. Adriat. d. Sc. Nat. Trieste. 1879–1881.
—— En. Mollusch. di Trieste. 1865.
TROIS, E. F.—Pesci del Adriat. Venezia. 1875.
—— Notizie sopra l'Echinorinus spinosus. Atti Ist. Veneto. Vol. III., Serie V.
—— Sulla Platessa vulgaris. Atti Ist. Ven. Vol. IV., Serie V.
—— Ricerche Zootomiche ed Ittiolog. sul Luvarus imperialis. Mem. dell' Ist. Ven. Vol. XX.
VOLPI.—Verzeichniss verschiedener Fische und Krebse des Adriat. Meerbusens. Trieste. 1796.

FRESH-WATER FISHES.

BONAPARTE, C. L.—Catalogo metodico.
BONIZZI, P.—Prosp. Sistem. e Catalogo dei Pesci nel Modenese.
CANESTRINI, G.—Fauna d' Italia. Part I.
—— Catalogo dei Pesci d' acqua dolce d' Italia.
DE-BETTA, ED.—Ittiol. Veronese.
DE-FILIPPI, F.—Cenni sui Pesci d'Acqua dolce della Lombard.
HECKEL & KNER.—Die Süsswasserfische der Oesterreichischen Monarchie. Leipzic. 1858.

NACCARI, F. L.—Ittiolog. Adriat.
NARDO, G. D.—Prodomus observ. et disquisit. Adriat. Ittiolog.
—— Prospetti sistem. degli Animali delle Prov. Venet.
—— Della coltura degli animali acquatici nel veneto dominio. Ven. 1864.
NINNI, A. P.—Cenni sui Pesci della Prov. di Treviso. Ven. 1863.
PERUGIA, ALB.—Catal. dei Pesci dell' Adriat.

CHAPTER I.

THE FAUNA.

Preliminary.—Topographical.—Tides.—Currents.—Temperature.—Saltness.—Professors Wolf and Luksch; their investigations in the Adriatic Gulf.—Haunts of fishes.—Investigations of the fauna in the Adriatic.—Dr. J. R. Lorenz; his work on the Horizontal Chorology in the Quarnero.—Zone I.—Zone II.—Zone III.—Zone IV.—Zone V.—Zone VI.—Zone VII.—Vertebrates.—Sedentary class.—Shore fishes.—Littoral forms.—Rovers.—Squatters.—Forms of the declivity and shallows.—Rovers.—Squatters.—Forms of the deep-bed.—Squatters.—Migratory forms.—Recapitulation.—Invertebrates, Articulates, and Radiates.—Characteristic species of the various zones.—Extended and limited distribution.—Boreal forms.—*Pisces.*—Fresh-water fishes.—Fishes which frequent the brackish waters.—Sea-fishes.

HE Adriatic Gulf (*Mare Superum, Mare Adriaticum*) derives its name, according to most authorities, from the Venetian town of Adria, near Rovigo, once situate on the sea-shore, and a place of some importance; whereas nowadays it is a small village, lying twelve miles inland. Other authorities, again, attribute its derivation to the Neapolitan town of Atri, in the Abruzzo Ulteriore, once known by the name of Adria, or Hadria, and situate on the coast, now four miles distant from the sea. Its southernmost limit is marked by the Cape S. Maria di Leuca, the Promontorium Solentinum of old, on the west; and the Cape Glossa, or Linguetta, on the Albanian coast, on the east. Its narrowest breadth is 54 miles (60 m. = 1°), between Otranto and Cape Linguetta; its greatest breadth 120 miles, between the mouths of the Tronto and Spalato; its average breadth is about 96 miles; its length 425 miles; and its surface has a total superficial area of 2,500 square geographical miles.

What is generally understood as the eastern shore extends from Epirus to Venice, and comprises the Austrian-Hungarian seaboard in a total length of 330 nautical miles in a straight line, and an extent of sea-coast of 2,840 miles, including the islands. It consists:—

1. Of the Dalmatian coast and islands, commencing somewhat north of Antivari, and extending to a point south of Carlopago, including the island of Pelagosa as the most distant island off the coast, and the islands of Arbe and Selve as the most northern limit.

2. Of the Hungarian-Croatian littoral, including Carlopago as southern and Fiume as northern limits.

3. The Austrian coast proper, including the peninsula of Istria, commencing at the northernmost head of the Quarnero Gulf, including the islands of the Quarnero, and the Trieste seaboard (*Küstenland*), extending as far as the Italian frontier, marked by the river Aussa and Cape Buso.

The eastern and western shores are essentially different from one another in their physical aspect. The western coast is exposed to the full fury of the S.E. (Scirocco) and N.E. (Bora) winds; the northern part is flat and low, and is studded with sand-banks and marshes; whereas further south it becomes iron-bound, and the entire coast is devoid of natural harbours. The eastern shore has, on the other hand, a very different character; a high coast-land much indented and studded with numerous islands and reefs (*scogli*),[1] which extend from Ragusa in the south to the Istrian shores in almost unbroken continuity,[2] thus forming a sort of natural rampart, or breakwater, against the fury of the winds and waves. The innumerable creeks and bays (*valli*),[3] inlets and channels, which thus abound along the coast, are so many natural harbours, with deep water and good anchorage-ground, so that the coast of Dalmatia and Istria has not without reason been termed " a natural harbour from beginning to end" (*tutto*

---

[1] This term is often misapplied on the coast to the islands generally, as, for instance, at Zara, where the inhabitants of the islands are called *Scogliani*.

[2] The only interruption is at the promontory of Planca (*Slav.* Ploča), the wave-lashed Promontorium Diomedis of old.

[3] The larger fjords are called *valloni*, and secondary basins (*mandracchio*) are artificially created, which extend out of the primary creeks in order to afford protection to small craft: these are known as Dražice (*Slav.*).

un porto), a circumstance which may account—though offering no excuse—for the covetousness with which the possession of this coast is viewed by the restless, ambitious, and ever-watchful neighbour to the west.

The eastern flank of Istria partakes of the characteristics of the Italian shores, being exposed alike to the fury of the Bora and the full force of the Scirocco, and is consequently much less hospitable than the western coast of the peninsula. There are other points of the Austrian-Hungarian seaboard, such as the Gulf of Trieste, the Channel of Maltempo or Morlacca (Quarnero), the Bocche di Segna further south, and the Bay of Vrulja (between Almissa and Macarsca on the Dalmatian coast), which are specially subject to the vehemence of the Bora, and thus form so many exceptions to the rule.

The tides[1] are inconsiderable, the normal rise and fall being only $1\frac{1}{2}$ foot, and only one ebb and flow in 24 hours; the spring tide is 2 feet in excess, thus giving a maximum of 5–6 feet. The greatest ebb is in February, the greatest flood in September; they are also affected by the winds, the Bora depressing, whilst the Scirocco swells, the waters. The currents (*Correnti*) are numerous, and keep the water in constant circulation, thus acting as modifiers of the effects of climate, and influencing by their agency the diffusion of submarine life.

There is a constant current along the eastern or Dalmatian coast in a northerly direction, returning along the western or Italian coast in a southerly direction; this current is necessarily subject to local influences, such as the interposition of islands, which neutralise its effects, without, however, seriously affecting its course. It does not affect the water in greater depths than 3 to 4 fathoms, and it is generally met with 6 or 10 miles from the shore, according to the formation of the coast. Beyond that point the sea is often very rough, without any visible cause, a phenomenon which has

---

[1] *It.* Marèa. At Venice, the tides, which are called there by the names of *Cerènte* and *Dosana*, do not, as a rule, exceed a few inches, excepting under the influence of a strong Scirocco wind, when the waters are known to rise 1–4 feet beyond the average limit, overflowing the dikes, inundating the town, and damaging the fishing-ponds (*valli*).

hitherto received no satisfactory explanation; these waves are called *Ligazzi*.

The mean temperature of the air is between 59° and 73° F., that of the water being between 66° and 71° F., and it has been found that, as a rule, the temperature of the water decreases from the coast-line outwards, as also from the surface downwards, this decrease being greater in summer than in winter. This rule is, however, somewhat modified by local influences, such as the influence of the land and the outward atmosphere, as also the prevalence of submarine sources. Thus, it has been ascertained that layers of water, which are in contact with the land, are subject to alterations of temperature altogether independent of this theory, having both a higher temperature in summer, and a lower temperature in winter, than similar layers of water further outwards.

Again, the surface waters are subject to the influence of the temperature of the atmosphere, hence the changes are more sudden than in lower depths; thus, in winter, the surface waters may become colder than the deeper layers, and even, as a rule, it will be found that the temperature in winter (February) is almost alike in all depths, the difference being only 1–2° F.; at the same time the temperature does not appear to fall below 45° F. in any zone, even in winter.

The greatest difference in the various zones is met with in summer, when the surface waters reach 77° F., and exceptionally, when under the direct influence of the sun's rays, or the proximity of the land, even more, whereas the lower zones retain much of their winter freshness. Thus in 10 fathoms the temperature never exceeds 72°, in 20 fathoms 66°, and in 30 fathoms 61°.

The mean temperature of the air in winter is from 40 to 32° F., which is that of the British Isles and both coasts of the British Channel; but the waters retain during winter much of the warmth acquired during the summer heats, and their temperature is higher than that of the air in autumn and winter; and lower in spring and summer.

The slower influence of changes of the temperature of the air on the lower zones has the effect that, excepting in summer, warmer layers of water are found under colder layers, contrary to the current theory, or, in other words, *the seasons are later in proportion to the greater depth of water.*

Thus, in winter, there is a continual increase of temperature downwards, or warmer layers under cold layers; in spring (March), above warmer, underneath colder, and below, again, warmer layers; in autumn, cold surface waters, underneath warmer layers, below these colder layers, and below these again warmer layers. This theory is rendered more intelligible by the aid of the following table:—

Depth	January.	February.	March.		April.	May.	June.	
Surface	7–8°	7–8°	7–8°	8–10°	12–15°	12–15°	16–19°	
10 fathoms	6½–7°	6½–7°	6½–7°		7–8°	10–12°	14°	14–16°
20 fathoms	7°*	7°*	7°		7°	7–8°	10–11°	11°	13°
30 fathoms	8–7½°	7½°	7¼°		6–7°	6–7°	7–8°	8–10°	10°	11°

Winter.　　　　　Spring.

Date.	July.	August.	September.		October.	November.	December.	
Surface	17–19°	17–19°	17–19°		15–10°*	12–10°	10–8°	8–7°
10 fathoms	16–17¼°	16–17¼°	14–12°	12°	12°	12–10°	8–7°	
20 fathoms	13–15°	15°	15°	15–12°*	12–10°*	10°*	10°	10–8°
30 fathoms	11–13°	11–13°	11–13°		11–13°	13–10°	10–9°	

Summer.　　　　　Autumn.
Temperature in ° Réaumur.

Professors J. Wolf and J. Luksch, of the Imperial and Royal Naval Academy of Fiume, have made some very interesting investigations on the subject of currents, temperature, and soundings in the Adriatic, which form

---

* Denotes the points at which warmer layers are to be found under colder layers.

the subject of four reports,[1] which may be recommended to the attention of those whom the subject may specially interest. Suffice it here briefly to recapitulate the principal conclusions.

1. The greatest influx of sweet water in the Adriatic is found on the Austro-Italian coast between Grado and Ravenna.

2. A current of sweet water flows from the north-west basin towards south-east; the further it proceeds south, the nearer it skirts the Italian shores, and the more it affects the deeper layers of water, thus bringing them into circulation.

3. A line drawn from Trieste to a point 20 miles south of Cape Promontore (the apex of the Istrian triangle) gives a uniform depth of 20–22 fathoms.

4. Increase of temperature towards the south-east; in the north higher temperature outwards, and in the south higher temperature nearer the shore (thus showing the influence of the proximity of the land).

5. Between Brindisi and Aulona the greatest depth is 270 fathoms (512 mètres), and the ground temperature $14°$ centigrade ($11°·2$ Réaumur). This temperature is not lower than, shortly before, on the same line nearer Brindisi, in 61 fathoms. The summer temperature of the water off Punta d'Ostro, in 100 fathoms, is $13°·4$ cent.; Ancona—Tremiti, 73 and 60 fathoms, $13°·2$–$13°·4$ cent.; Quarnerolo, 40–50 fathoms, $13°·1$ $12°·7$ $13°·1$ cent. The greater coolness of the water in the Quarnero is due to the influence of the ground-springs.

6. Lower temperature and higher degree of saltness on the eastern than on the western coast; increase of temperature the more one proceeds south.

7. In the Dalmatian channels lower degree of saltness and higher temperature in the upper layers than on the Albanian coast.

8. The Gulf of Fiume, the Segna Channel, and the Quarnerolo show the lowest temperature of water in the whole northern basin of the Adriatic, which fact is probably due to the abundance of fresh-water springs bursting

---

[1] "Berichte an die königliche Ungarische Seebehörde in Fiume, über Physicalische Untersuchungen im Adriatischen Meere." Fiume: 1878.

forth from the sea-bed. The water is also colder than at similar depths elsewhere; thus, on the Dalmatian coast, nowhere less than 13°·5 cent.; opposite Ragusa, in the high sea, in 125 fathoms, 13°·9 cent.; Lissa, in 60 fathoms, 14° cent.; Channel of Brazza, in 40 fathoms, 13°·8 cent.; whereas, in the Gulf of Fiume, in 30 fathoms, 12° cent., and even 11° cent.; off Arbe, in rather deeper water, 10° cent.; and near Segna, 9°·7 cent., this being the approximate temperature of the sweet-water springs at Fiume.

9. In the Gulf of Fiume and Channel of Segna the surface-waters have a smaller proportion of salt, owing to the Fiumara and other torrents; the greatest amount of saline matter is found in 30 fathoms, below which again there is a decrease, owing to the submarine springs. The increase from the surface downwards is very rapid.

10. The high sea contrasts with the foregoing conclusions (No. 9), by higher temperatures, and higher degree of saltness in deep waters.

11. In the Gulf of Trieste the highest temperatures are to be met with throughout, owing to the shallowness; lowest degree of saltness on the surface, and below 5 fathoms a relatively high degree of saltness, showing that the supply of sweet water from the Po and other water-courses does not mix with the sea water, but remains upon the surface.

12. The variations of the temperature in deep water, which is impervious to the direct effect of light or radiation, are necessarily slow, for the simple reason that such effect can only make itself felt by degrees. The fact, however, of such variations taking place on days when the sea has been calm for some time past, seems to point at the influences of *vertical currents*, on the theory of Dr. Carpenter, created by the evaporation of the surface waters, bringing forth an increased percentage of saltness, greater specific gravity, and consequent tendency downwards. This motion is further increased by the influence of the ground-springs, whose lighter waters naturally tend to the surface, thus creating a current upwards, and necessarily a corresponding current downwards, by which means the warmer surface waters are brought to the lower depths, thereby influencing their temperature.[1]

---

[1] The results of these valuable investigations have been recapitulated in a publication:

It has been shown what great variety the shores of the eastern coast present in their physical characteristics; owing to the protection afforded by the islands, and the innumerable creeks, inlets, and channels, fjords and bays. The same variety may be noticed in the formation of the bed of the Adriatic. Towards the middle it is composed chiefly of mud (*fango*), but near the coast it changes from shingle or sand to the limestone rock, which forms the steep declivity of its shores. The fissures and crevices furnish the favourite lurking-places and resorts of many of the *sedentary* class of fishes, on the waving fields of zostera, which afford protection to myriads of invertebrates, and over which many kinds of fish love to hover, either in search of food or in order to seek protection from pursuers.

There are no large sand-banks, but this is in some wise compensated for by their number. Between the shallow banks and the rocks are deep hollows, where the temperature of the water remains low. These afford a favourite resort to many kinds of fish, which there seek protection in summer from the hot rays of the sun.

Thus, each variety of fish has abundant choice for its particular predilection. Those of the *sedentary* class, which are bound to a particular locality, either by temperature, depth, comparative saltness of water, or nature of bed or food, and have their fixed habitations, or places of refuge, amongst the crevices of rocks, or amongst the zostera, tangles, or sea-weed, on the precipitous slopes forming the sea-coast, or the bed of the sea, or on the plateaux or sand-banks. Also those amongst the class of *shore fishes* which are always on the move in search of prey, shunning, as a rule, the light of day. Each kind has its particular fancy in the choice both of its lurking-places, where it rests by day, on the watch for any prey that may pass within reach, and for its hunting-grounds, which it frequents by night, some

---

" Physicalische Untersuchungen im Adriatischen und Sicilisch-Ionischen Meere während des Sommers, 1880." Von den Akademie Professoren Julius Wolf und Josef Luksch. Wien: Gerold. 1881. The maps appended to this work were exhibited at the Geographical Congress at Venice, 1881, for which the authors received the gold medal. A reference to this work is recommended to those whom the subject may specially interest.

ARBE.

preferring well-overgrown declivities or zostera meadows, whilst others seek the rocky shores, or the creviced precipices, according to the nature of their food, tarrying, nevertheless, in the vicinity of their favourite resorts, and hovering about within given limits, both horizontal and vertical.

The sea water proper of the Adriatic, in respect of the degree of saltness, is about the same as the Atlantic under the tropics, so that southern forms prosper.[1]

But it has been shown that, similar to the lochs of Scotland and the fjords of Norway, the salt water is often intermingled with fresh water, arising from the limestone springs, which abound especially in the Quarnero, so that the surface waters may be fresh, or nearly so, whilst the depths are as salt as in mid-ocean.

This circumstance alone accounts for the prosperity of single colonies of otherwise foreign, and even northern forms, though not affording an explanation of the question how they came there.

The depth of the Adriatic is for the most part moderate; the depth of the Quarnero varies from 20 to 40 fathoms, and only at points it reaches 60; proceeding south, it increases to 80 to 100 fathoms near the islands of Zuri, Incoronata, and Scoglio Pomo; from Pomo, the course of the greatest depths is south-east, and near the island of Meleda the bed has not been reached at 500 fathoms.

In the great variety of physical characteristics here enumerated we find so many factors in favour of a high development, and furnishing the requirements for the most opposite attributes of submarine animal life. Thus it is that the Adriatic offers an extensive field for the investigations of the student of natural history, and is justly appreciated on this account by naturalists from all parts of the world.

Nevertheless, the fauna of the Adriatic has not been subject to a thorough and systematic investigation like many other seas, such as the Ægean, the

---

[1] The affinity between the Mediterranean and Japanese faunas has been pointed out by Dr. Gunther, the number of genera common to these two faunas being larger than that of the genera common to the Mediterranean and the opposite American coasts.

shores of Nice, &c., &c., although partial researches have furnished a variety of valuable information which constitutes an important instalment towards the fulfilment of the more comprehensive task of an exhaustive work. Foremost amongst such researches must be mentioned the able and painstaking work of Dr. J. R. Lorenz[1] on the Quarnero.

These interesting investigations refer to the horizontal distribution of animal and vegetable life in the Quarnero, on the theory of Professor Forbes, demonstrating that marine animals and plants have their zones of depth, just as plants have their regions of altitude.

As no systematic account of the horizontal distribution, or *chorology*, of animal life in the Adriatic has yet been published, this must be considered a most valuable contribution to the inquiries on the subject of its fauna, on which subject so much remains to be done, and it may not be out of place here to give a short account of the general results of this work as regards the chorology in the Quarnero.

Dr. Lorenz has found the following distinct zones :—

ZONE I.—THE SUPER-LITTORAL ZONE, characterised by the one very poor species of Algæ, *Catenella;* and the fauna facies,[2] *Ligia Brandtii*, and other animals, which neither live in the water nor proceed more than a few feet from the immediate border of the sea.

ZONE II.—THE LITTORAL ZONE, divided into the EXPOSED LITTORAL ZONE, between high and low-water marks, and, when influenced by the wind, two feet above, or 1⅓ foot below the normal tide-marks—altogether a maximum range of 5½ feet. This is the region of green sea-weeds, characterised by the Algæ, *Ulvæ* (sloke plants), *Enteromorpha*, and *Cladophora* in

---

[1] "Physicalische Verhältnisse und Vertheilung der Organismen im Quarnerischen Golfe." Wien: 1863.

[2] *Facies* is the representative species of any particular zone, so that, as Professor Forbes observes, the *facies* of the inhabitants of any given region of depth is so marked, that the sight of a sufficient assemblage of them from some one locality can enable the naturalist to speak at once to the soundings within certain limits, without the aid of line or plummet.

brackish waters; in other places *Heteractis*, *Oscillaria*, and other kinds abound. On rocky shores the upper edge is covered with the periwinkle (*Litorina Basteroti*); *Ligia Brandtii* from above, and *Grapsus varius* from below, meet here; below this, several species of the littoral shell-fish limpets (*Patellæ*) adhere to the rocks near the water's edge, also *Chiton Polii*. About midway between the tide-marks appears the advance-guard of the *Balani* (barnacles), which grow on the rocks so as to belt the coast when the tide is out; the representative species is in this case *Chthamalus stellatus*. On spots retaining the moisture after the receding tide *Nereis cultrifera*, *Heterocirrus saxicola*, *Sipunculus verrucosus*, and *Mytilus minimus* are commonly to be seen.

Below these, again, as far as low-water mark, whole groups of *Mytilus minimus*, and, in hidden places attached to the rocks, the date-shell, (*Lithodomus lithophagus*), and the indolent *Actinia mesembryanthemum*, one of the few Red-Sea polyps[1] found in the Mediterranean region, and one of the most characteristic forms of this zone, never moving during the whole period of its exposure to the air, whereas species of *Trochus*,[2] which here first make their appearance, and *Grapsus varius*, a marginal crab, follow the receding tide, remaining exposed to the air at most for one or two consecutive hours.

Shores exposed to the breakers are overgrown with *Fucus vesiculosus*, and the genera are limited here to *Mytilus minimus*, *Trochi*, and *Grapsus varius* already mentioned. On shingle, sandy, or muddy shores, also when covered with sea-weed, and where the moisture is retained at low water, *Amphitoë penicillata* is characteristic, being found here in large numbers, besides *Gammarus Olivii*, in second order.

On muddy, but sheltered, flat shores we find species of the rag-worm (*Nereis*); where sand predominates, *Gebia littoralis*, an elegant green and sandy-coloured, marbled shore-crab, which swims backwards and forwards;

---

[1] A sea-anemone like masses of brilliant crimson, or bright green pulp, but, when covered by the water, expanding into many armed disks and displaying shapes and colours of exquisite beauty.—E. FORBES.

[2] *Trochus divaricatus*, the purple-striped top-shell, remains exposed to the air on moist shores.—E. F.

also *Arenicola branchialis*, a species of lug-worm, which, together with the *Nereis*, are caught by fishermen for bait.

ZONE III.—THE SUBMERGED LITTORAL ZONE, extending from low-water mark to a depth of 2 fathoms; average temperature of water 59° F., subject to rapid changes; characterised by forty species of Mollusks, ten Crustacea, six Annellides, four Echinoderms, four Polyps, three Amorphozoa.

This is the region of the corallines, more especially of the pretty calciferous sea-plant *Corallina officinalis*, which marks its appearance just below low-water mark; these are often overgrown by dense Cystoseira, forming the most prevalent and striking facies of this region. Another prevalent facies is that of the waving meadows of Zostera, or grass-wrack, which grows on sand or mud. This mass of vegetation is interwoven by Diatomaceæ, of which fifty-nine species, belonging to twenty-six genera, belong exclusively to this region. At a depth of 4 to 10 feet commence the Nullipores, coral-like vegetables, simulating minerals in figure and consistence, and furnishing a favourable spawning-ground for fishes; they grow in vast quantities, and assume many strange modifications of form, sometimes expanding into small cabbage-heads, but mostly assuming the appearance of coral. Nullipore ground is very necessary to the development of animal life, as it harbours a number of forms which are scattered by its destruction; hence the value attached to its preservation. On rocky shores are found several species of the Polyp Actinia, chiefly *A. viridis*; more rarely *A. aurantiaca*, *A. rhododactylos*, *A. bimaculata*: *Echinus lividus* adheres to the rocks, *Bonellia viridis* lies in crevices; *Purpura maculosa*, *Trochus fragarioides*, *T. tessellatus*, *Patella cærulea*, *Chiton siculus*, *Spondylus aculeatus* just below the surface on Algæ, as also the crustaceans *Grapsus varius* and *Palæmon squilla*.

On corallines are found *Conus mediterraneus*, *Murex cristatus*, and different species of *Trochus* (*T. Laugieri*), all shells of varying beauty. Here and there appears the Echinoderm *Asteracanthion glacialis*, common to the Boreal and Celtic regions, sometimes as much as 7 to 8 inches long, often left dry by the receding tide and anxiously clinging to the rocks. *Asteracanthion tenuispinus* is found less frequently.

Animal life increases where the rocks are covered with hard, brittle and useless sponges, which first make their appearance here, and are so far characteristic of this region as to form the facies of *littoral Spongieta*. They are of three species :—1. *Sarcotragus spinosulus* (which harbours some Annellides, such as *Lumbriconereis Nardonis, Polynoë squamata, P. elegans*); 2. *Geodia placenta* (which, besides the aforenamed Annellides, supports *Nereis Costæ* in large numbers, and *Saxicava arctica* and *S. Guerini* embedded in the sponge), resembling the *Tethya lyncurnium* in its texture, and 3. *Reniera calyx*.

On coasts sheltered from the full force of the prevalent winds, Bora and Scirocco, on the surface of rocks covered with Algæ, are found elegant Bryozoæ, such as the dark *Lepralia Heckelii* and a bright red *Cellepora*; adhering to the rocks, *Haliotis tuberculata*, a shell extending as far as Guernsey, which is its most northern limit, *Patella cærulea, P. vulgata, Chiton siculus, Fissurella gibba*; species of *Trochus, Murex; Arca barbata, A. lactea, Lima squamosa, Spondylus gadæropus*. Underneath the rocks several nudibranch sea-snails seek shelter, such as *Doris Villafranca*, a beautiful dark blue snail with golden, white, and light blue lines, also *D. argus* and *Elysia splendida*, a snail of exquisite beauty found and described by Dr. Grube,[1] and displaying the most brilliant colours (it is in many respects similar to *Acteon Hopei* of Verany).

Inside the rock swarms of *Lithodomus lithophagus*, also *Galeomma turtoni, Venerupis Irus* are to be found. The Crustaceans *Eriphia spinifrons* and species of *Sphæroma* likewise hide here, also a number of Annellides, such as *Sabella, Terrebella, Eunice*, soft sea-worms of various lengths which inhabit the rocks, *E. sanguinea*, for instance, attaining a length of 2 feet and more, *Polynoë*, and sporadically *Bouellia viridis*.

Nullipore ground affords protection to *Serpula aspera, Eupomatos uncinatus, Terrebella corallina, T. spiralis, Eulalia macroceros, Polynoë arcolata, P. clypeata*, &c., besides several Crustacea. Foremost amongst the latter are *Palæmon squilla, Galeomma turtoni, Chiton cajetanus*, together with

---

[1] "Ein Ausflug nach Triesle und dem Quarnero," p. 86. By Dr. A. E. Grube. Berlin : 1861.

Saxicava artica and the *Lima*, a kind of scallop, which constructs for itself a comfortable nest in and by means of the coral-like weeds. Such are the characteristic forms.

Where broken rocks rest upon sand or shingle, gravel or mud, grows the sponge *Ancorina verruca*. Under similar conditions is found an enormous limivorous Annellide of extreme beauty, *Sabella Spallanzanii*, which attains a length of as much as 16½ inches, and appears in groups, resembling submarine palms or tree-ferns.

Where the position is sheltered, and the shingle, being undisturbed, is covered with a fine coating of sea-weed, are found the shell-framing Annellide, *Spirorbis pusilla*, and the Crustaceans *Sphæroma serratum*, *Amphitoë Prevostii*, and *Gammarus Olivii*. This is the only locality in which appears the large black periwinkle (*Littorina litorea*).

Where there is dense vegetation, with or without sponges, the genera *Caprella* and *Idothea*, *Acantonyx lunulatus*, are characteristic; also the beautiful little univalves *Rissoa*, wonderfully varied in colour and form. Myriads of *Cerithea* are to be found amongst the grass-wrack, besides *Buccinum*, the bivalve *Modiola costulata*, species of *Trochus*, and a number of Annellides, foremost amongst which *Nerine vulgaris*.

Cystoseira or Sargassum-tangles harbours the characteristic facies of *Pisa Gibsii* and *Mitra Savignyi*, and on the branches of the tangles creeps the Annellide *Euphrosyne myrtosa*, amongst many other similar species.

On shingle and loose rocks, exposed to the heaviest roll of the waves, appear *Sipunculus nudus* (the *Syrinx* of Forbes), the bivalve *Mya arctica*, and *Heterocirrus saxicola*, a soft and very delicate Annellide discovered and described by Dr. Grube,[1] to whom it owes its name : it is found in narrow channels of the hard limestone, probably worked by its own industry.

On coarse sand appear *Venus decussata*, *V. aurea*, *Buccinum reticulatum*, *Cardium edule*; on fine sand, *C. tuberculatum*.

Where the sand, or mud, is covered with dense Zostera, animal life is still more numerous, and is characterised by several species of *Buccinum*, the

---

[1] "Ein Ausflug nach Triest," &c., pp. 47, 66.

Echinoderm *Asteriscus ciliatus, Phasianella pulla, Cerithium vulg., Trochus Biasoletti*, and *Cyclonassa nerithea*, a curious little whelk resembling a nerithea in shape, creeping on the sand and burrowing in it.

In shallow and sheltered creeks, whose muddy bed is covered with Valonia, is found a numerous variety of small Crustaceans, viz., *Gammarus scissimanus, Amphitoë guttata, Cymodoce pilosa, Sphæroma Jurinii.*

Loam or red clay bed is rare, and affords little attraction to animal or vegetable life; the characteristic species are *Gebia litoralis, Scobicularia piperita*, and species of *Sphæroma* and *Amphitoë*. This is a favourite site for the propagation of the sand-smelt (*Atherina hepsetus*) and various species of grey mullet (*Mugilidæ*); in the month of April the young fry is caught by the million in the Bay of Dobrigno, and transferred to the lagoons of Venice and the *valli chiuse* (fish-ponds), where they are reared as nourishment for other fishes.

On black muddy ground, composed of decaying animal and vegetable matter, and in the shallows of sheltered bays, the characteristic Annellides are *Cirratulus Lamarckii*, not found elsewhere, also species of *Clymene, Glycera alba*, hitherto known only in Norwegian and Danish waters; the Mollusks *Cerithium scabrum, Natica pulchella, Trochus canaliculatus, Venus nitens, V. læta, Psammobia vespertina*, &c., also prevail here.

ZONE IV.—THE SUB-LITTORAL ZONE, extending from 2–10 fathoms; average temperature 57 to 59° F., subject to slow changes; pressure at 6 fathoms 2·13 atmospheres; the variations of the temperature are only slightly less than those of the surface waters; effect of waves, slight. This is the region of the sea-flags, or tangles, lying beyond the lowest ebb, which are overgrown by dense Cystoseira. The number of Algæ is very much reduced, as also the prevalence of the different species, only forty-four species belonging to eighteen genera being found here. On the sea-shrubs live a quantity of Mollusks, Actiniæ, and Ascidians. Characteristic are four Crustaceans, one Annellide, ten Mollusks, two Echinoderms, one Polyp, and one sponge. The latter is the *Aplysina aërophoba*, a remarkable yellow sponge which grows on craggy rock-inclines, mostly covered by more, or less, dense

Cystoseira, shining like smooth yellow leather whilst immersed, but changing to dark green when exposed to the air; it is peculiarly characteristic of depths of 5 to 6 fathoms. The *Spongia Quarnerensis* is also found adhering to the tangles.

Here abound the Crustacean *Galathea squamifera* and the univalves *Aplysia depilans, Buccinum ascanias, Cerithium vulg. var. gracile*, and most characteristic of all are the Annellides *Lumbriconereis quadristriata* of Grube. In shallow waters on bare rock, or shingle, appear the bivalve *Pinna squamosa*, the Ascidians *Cynthia microcosmus* and *C. papillosa*, a large species in form somewhat like the common species, but of extreme beauty from the effect of its colour; its tough skin is thickly overset with disks of the brightest scarlet; it is known here by the name of *Limone di Mar*, or sea-lemon.

The Polyp *Actinia bellis* here attains its maximum development, the sea-urchin *Echinus brevispinosus* also appears, and amongst the rocks is found the common lobster, *Homarus marinus*.

On clean sand is found the elegant crab, *Gonoplax rhomboides*, also the bivalve *Cytherea chione*, and the Echinoderm *Astropecten aurantiacus*, which, however, only attains to its maximum of development in the next region. On clean clay beds appear *Venus verrucosa, Modiola barbata, Cardium exiguum*, different species of *Pectines* (*P. sulcatus, P. jacobæus, P. polymorphus*), and *Echinus microtuberculatus*.

The oyster, *Ostrea edulis var. cristata*, is rarely found in the Quarnero, but otherwise abounds in this region, chiefly at Val Cassione, on the island of Veglia.

Black clay supports a number of Foraminifers, such as *Miliola obesa, Rosalina varians*, and *Acervulina inhærens*.

The Zostera fields swarm with animal life, the most characteristic of this region; most prevalent amongst these are *Sicyonia sculpta, Palæmon rectirostris, Leucotoë denticulata*, and *Ilia nucleus;* also the Annellides *Serpula echinata*, and *Aspidosiphon Mülleri*.

Forms found in the littoral zones, such as *Idothea appendiculata, Lysianassa spinicornis, Trochus pyramidatus*, here attain their maximum of development.

HA
CA.

BRAGOZZI AT ANCHOR.

Cymodoce pilosa, C. truncata, Sphæroma Jurinii, Pectinaria auricoma, Nereis zostericola, and *Buccinum ascanius* do not descend below 6 fathoms.

The pipe, or needle-fishes (*Syngnathidæ*), the gar-pike (*Belone vulgaris*), and the wrasse (*Labrus turdus*) are also found here.

Squilla mantis, Maja squinado, Murex brandaris, Pecten jacobæus, and *Ostrea edulis* are forms which abound in this region, in the Gulfs of Trieste and of Venice. They are exceptional in the Quarnero, *var. cristata* being the only kind of oyster found in some parts of this gulf.

ZONE V.—This is the medium declivity and depth extending from 10 to 20 fathoms, mostly on steep inclines, rarely on flat beds.

Sweet surface waters have no effect here, and submarine springs do not issue forth in this region; specific gravity of water 1,027; intensity of the effect of the daylight on the decrease, rays of light yellowish and difference between night and day perceptible; pressure at 15 fathoms 3·67 atmospheres; no effect felt of the action of the waves; no drift currents, but the chief currents reach to the bottom of this zone; average temperature 56° F., difference of temperature between summer and winter, 18–20° F.

This zone corresponds closely with Professor Forbes' *Laminarian Zone*. The number of Algæ falls off considerably, particularly the typical forms of the Mediterranean and Adriatic flora, general forms only remaining. The lower declivity and the flat bed are both characterised by dense and high *Cystoseira* and *Nullipores*, which especially abound there; few *Diatomaceæ* remain. Characteristic forms:—eight Crustaceans, four Annellides, twenty-two Mollusks, eight Echinoderms, two Polyps, and two Sponges.

On bare rocks, free of, or with little vegetation, in crevices and fissures are found the Conger-eel (*Conger vulgaris*), the common lobster, the crabs *Palinurus vulg.*, and the smaller *Praniza cærulata;* in sponges, *Typton spongicula* and the Echinoderm *Ophiopsila aranea* of Forbes. The Annellides *Serpula contortuplicata* and *Terebella parviloba* adhere to stones. *Eunice norvegica, E. gallica, Meckelia annulata*, and *Polynöe cirrata*, a Boreal and Celtic Annellide, where it attains to higher development than here, are often found in the holes of stones, or amongst the coral-like Nullipores.

Cardium echinatum, C. lævigatum, the sea-urchins *Echinus brevispinosus,* and especially the enormous *E. melo,* which presents the characteristic facies, occupy rocks covered with loose gravel, or grit.

Polyps of the Gorgonia genus, such as *G. verrucosa, G. Bertoloni,* first appear in 15 fathoms, and increase in number with the depth.

Where Cystoseira grows on rock, or loose stones, or broken shells, the crustaceans *Pisa armata, Porcellana platycheles, Atelecyclus heterodon, Ethusa mascarone, Inachus thoracicus,* are particularly characteristic. They are joined by *Xantho floridus, X. rivolosus, Pagurus maculatus, Pilumnus hirtellus,* and *Galathea strigosa,* which here attain to their maximum. *Stenorhynchus phalangium* here commences to appear and increases with the depth; *Portunus longipipes* is on the decrease.

The characteristic Annellides are *Euphrosyne mediterranea, Eulalia viridis,* and *Polyophthalmus pictus,* the latter a remarkable one described by Quatrefrages (the *Nais picta* of Dugès).[1]

Under similar conditions appear the Mollusks: *Fusus rostratus, Cardium exiguum,* and *Turbo rugosus;* on the tangles, *Chiton Rissoë,* and *Fissurella græca;* on the branches *Doris tuberculata,* a Celtic form, *Aplysia marginata, Fusus syracusanus, Mitra ebenus, Cerithium pulchellum, C. minutum, Rissoa Bruguieri,* also the bivalve *Anatina pusilla.* Besides these many species of *Trochus, Cerithium,* and *Rissoa* are found, characteristic of the littoral zone; they disappear in the course of this region.

Where Sargassum grows scattered on gravel, or grit, and loose stones, life is still more varied. Inside the stones dwell *Saxicava Guerini, Anceus forficularis,* and attached to the outside of stones are *Serpula contortuplicata, S. aspera, Pomatoceros tricuspis,* and *Spirorbis pusilla,* which cease here. The Polyps *Cyathina striata, Actinia carciniopados,* and *A. bellis,* likewise appear in their company.

The Ascidian *Phallusia intestinalis,* whose mantle is invariably incrusted with *Modiola discrepans,* adheres to stones (Philippi cites this as the ordinary

---

[1] Quatrefrages, "Annales des Sciences Naturelles," iii. série, tome xiii., 1850, p. 8; and Grube, "Ein Ausflug," &c., p. 49.

appearance of this small bivalve); also *Tethya lyncurium*, a species of sponge rendered firm by containing numerous needles of flint throughout its substance, extending to Celtic waters.

The Crustaceans *Lambrus angulifrons, L. massena, Dromia vulgaris, Ethusa mascarone, Eurynome scutellata, Maja verrucosa*, are here characteristic.

Annellides are less abundant. The most characteristic are *Cerebratulus spectabilis, Meckelia annulata*, and a beautiful violet *Eunice*, new to the European fauna, discovered and described by Dr. Grube:[1] it is similar to the *E. violacea* of Oersted, though only half its size, viz., $2\frac{1}{2}$ inches long.

The characteristic species in this zone are the univalves *Fusus rostratus, Ovula spelta*, and *Dentalium entalis*, a Boreal species; the bivalve *Solen ensis*; the sea-urchin *Schizaster canaliferus*; the star-fishes, *Asteriscus verruculatus, Asteracanthion glacialis, Alecto mediterranea*; and the cucumbers *Holothuria tubulosa* and *Cucumaria doliolum*.

The Polyps *Gorgonia verrucosa* and *G. Bertoloni* rise amid the Cystoseira and Sargassum in the form of shrubs, whose withered branches are often entirely covered with the cherry-red-coloured *Sympodium coralloides*. These, again, are varied by *Tubularia larynx, T. ramosa, Lepralia tetragona*, and *Filograna implexa*, which either grow amongst the tangles, or are interwoven with, or cling to, their branches.

More numerous than elsewhere appear the snails *Doris cærulea*, of a beautiful violet tint, *Æolis Bellardii, Pleurobranchus* species, and *Tylodina citrina*, a species of a sulphur-yellow colour.

Clean gravel and coarse sand harbour most of the foregoing species, but in fewer numbers. The most characteristic form of this locality is *Venus verrucosa*, both as regards abundance and development. The bivalve *Tellina donacina* has a wide horizontal extension, and it is found here in the company of a quantity of Annellides, especially *Borlasia* species, *Meckelia annulata*, besides a beautiful green *Phyllodoce*.

On clay-bed covered with scattered Dictyomenia, the number of groups

---

[1] See "Ein Ausflug nach Trieste," &c., by Dr. A. E. Grube, p. 61. Berlin.

of the Ascidians *Phallusia cristata*, and more especially *P. mammillata* entwined with *Dictyomeniæ*, are most characteristic. Quantities of *Turritella communis* and *Aporrhais pes pelicani* here first make their appearance, whilst the bivalves *Corbula nucleus* and *Pecten inflexus* seem to be limited to this region, and form one of its principal facies. The Capanus, or Dry-rot-worm, *Teredo navalis*, the "calamitas navium," or the scourge of vessels, as it has been called, is found in sunken pieces of wood, and is especially prevalent at Sebenico. Lastly may be noticed the Annellides *Aphrodite hystrix*, *A. sericea*, the Crustacean *Portunus plicatus* and species of *Ophiolepis*.

Some species descend here from the former region, such as *Lambrus angulifrons*, *Portunus Rondeletii*, &c.; the Echinoderms *Asteracanthion glacialis*, *Astropecten aurantiacus*, *A. platyacanthus*, and *Echinus microtuberculatus*. But they disappear entirely in the course of this zone; *Astropecten aurantiacus* is at its height of development here.

Last of all may be mentioned on loam-beds the sponge *Esperia massa*, and other yellow and red sponges; also the Echinoderms *Echinaster sepositus*, *Ophioderma longicauda*, *Astropecten pentacanthus*, and *Cucumaria pentactes*: the latter has a northern extension.

ZONE VI., forming the lowest declivity of the shore-incline, and a great part of the bed of the Gulf, including a number of channels and larger bays, extending from 20 to 45 fathoms' depth, in which respect, as also to some extent also in character, it corresponds with Professor Forbes' *coralline zone*. Rocky precipice, whose base consists to a great extent of stone fragments and *débris;* bed chiefly loam, or clay; springs from the limestone rock below, influencing the degree of saltness, and the temperature of the water; influence of light reduced to a minimum, but the difference between day and night still perceptible; pressure at 30 fathoms, 6·35 atmospheres; absolute quiescence of waters; change of temperature slow, and the difference between the extremes 16–18° F.

The characteristic forms of the Mediterranean flora vanish, and there remain for the most part only general Atlantic, Celtic, and Scandinavian.

The vegetation decreases markedly below this point, and is only represented by some species of Dictyomeniæ, which reach down to 50 fathoms, and are characteristic of these depths. The characteristic fauna comprises three Crustaceans, two Annellides, fourteen Mollusks, three Echinoderms, three Polyps, and four Sponges.

At the bottom of the shore-incline, formed by stone *débris*, and more seawards, on loam or sand-beds, amongst the mostly distorted forms of Cystoseira, which still grow here and there, and heaps of broken fragments of shells, which have accumulated in course of time—the most characteristic forms are the Annellide *Onuphis tubicola*, the bivalves *Venus ovata, V. fasciata, Cardium oblongum, C. punctatum*, and the Polyp *Eschara cervicornis*. Besides these, some few characteristic species of the former region still appear, but are on the decrease.

On gravel and scattered fragments of shells, stone, or Nullipores, in 20–30 fathoms, forming the bed in a wide circle around the island of Lussin, and partly also that of Veglia, and also less prominently so in other parts, are quite characteristic: the Annellides *Serpula venusta, Vermilia clavigera, Eunice gallica, E. norvegica, Nereis Dumerilii*, and *Cerebratulus marginatus*, mostly Celtic forms; the Mollusks *Fusus lavatus, Turritella triplicata, Pleurotoma Philberti*, and *Turbo rugosus* in swarms; *Chiton lævis, Capulus hungaricus*, both Boreal forms, small elegant specimens of *Pecten* (*P. pusio, P. testæ, P. pellucidus, P. opercularis*); swarms of *Comatula* (*Alecto*) *mediterranea*, also well-developed and many-coloured varieties of the Boreal species *Ophiotrix fragilis, Astropecten pentacanthus*, and *Retipora reticulata*.

Forms characteristic of the whole region are found here, such as *Lysianassa humilis* in hollow sponges; the Annellide *Terebella pustulosa* on plants and sponges; the Mollusks *Turritella quadricarinata, Dentalium dentalis*, and two Boreal bivalves, *Venus fasciata* and *Cardium lævigatum*.

On uniform and extended loam-beds appear, in dispersed groups, the Crustaceans *Alpheus ruber, Galathea rugosa, Corystes dentatus*, and swarms of *Portunus plicatus*; also *Maldane glebifex*, an Annellide described by

Dr. Grube,[1] which, wrapped in 1-2 inch loam-sausages about the thickness of a finger, cover the bed by the million, and are easily taken for mere lumps of earth. On the same ground dwell *Terebella crocea*, *T. pustulosa*, *Sabella brevibarbis*, adhering to Ascidians, Dictyomeniæ, or fragments of shells, also swarms of *Aphrodite hystrix*, more rarely *A. aculeata;* besides these are found *Clymene digitata*, *Nereis Dumerilii*, *Lumbriconereis unicornis*, *Sigalion tetragonum*, *Chætopterus pergamentaceus*, *Protula protensa*, and *P. Rudolphii*, one of the most magnificent of its genus, adorned by the most brilliant colours (the *Serpula intestinum* of L.); *P. protensa*, though less brilliant in its colouring, is perhaps as beautiful, on account of the more tasteful and delicate diffusion of its tints.[2]

The Mollusks *Bullæa planciana*, swarms of *Aporrhais pes pelecani* and *Turritella ungulina*, more rarely *T. triplicata;* *Trochus granulatus;* here and there *Dolium galea*, the largest snail of the Adriatic; *Cassidaria echinophora*, *Tapes geographica*, *Cardium ciliare*, *Isocardia cor*, *Pectunculus pilosus*, a Boreal form, and *Nucula sulcata*, all abound here. Amongst the Echinoderms *Holothuria regalis* is characteristic by their abundance; *Ophiolepis ciliata* are numerous, but *Cladodactyla pentactes*, which has a wide northern extension, *Cucumaria tergestina*, *Echinaster sepositus*, *Asteriscus palmipes*, *Asteracanthion glacialis*, *Ophioderma longicauda*, are scarce.

The characteristic Polyps are *Mammillifera univittata*, *Alcyonium palmatum* in large quantities; *Pennatula phosphorea*, or sea-pens, and *Cyathina striata* on the shells of Turritella.

The Sponges found here are *Raspailia stelligera*, *Spongia adriatica*, *Cacospongia scalaris*, and *Esperia Lorenzii*.

The Norway Lobster (*Nephrops norvegicus*), found in swarms locally distributed over the deepest parts of the northern and central portion of the Gulf of Quarnero, must be considered a colony of an entirely foreign form, as it is not met with in any other part of the Adriatic. In its company appear, imbedded in and firmly adhering to the mud, *Virgularia*

---

[1] "Ein Ausflug," &c., by Dr. A. E. Grube, pp. 46, 62, 63, 65. Berlin: 1861.
[2] See Grube's work, "Ein Ausflug," &c., pp. 51, 63.

multiflora, a representative species of the Boreal form *Virgularia mirabilis*, a form hitherto strange to the Mediterranean fauna, and altogether to the Lusitanian province. In the same locality are found *Alcyonium palmatum* and *Pennatula phosphorea;* and the Crustacean, *Galathea rugosa*, is more prevalent and prosperous here than elsewhere.

In order to account for the insular appearance of this association of northern representative forms it is necessary to assume that, as elsewhere where analogous appearances of Boreal *outliers* occur, these forms had a further southern distribution during the Glacial Period, and that in course of time, owing to a raised temperature of the waters, particularly in summer time, their distribution became limited to the deeper and cooler regions, as long as the nature of the bed proved suitable, and the pressure of the water was not too great.

The Gulf of Fiume, the Quarnerolo, and the Channel of Punta Croce are depressions in the bed to which this theory applies. Further to the south they are shut in from the open sea by a ridge of higher ground, which accounts for their isolation, whilst the lower temperature which prevails on the bed of the Quarnero, and the difference in the composition of the water, due to the limestone springs, must explain why they prosper here, whereas they do not occur in the neighbouring Dalmatian waters.

Ulterior investigation may possibly bring to light fossil remains of northern forms of Gasteropods and Lamellibranchs, now extinct in these waters. The discovery would go far to explain the phenomenon which has caused this apparent freak of nature, and to furnish the proof of what at present must remain an assumption, viz., that changes of temperature have taken place, which have destroyed some forms of life, whilst others have been able to assimilate themselves to the new conditions.

Mr. R. Godwin-Austen, in the work, "The Natural History of the European Seas," commenced by Professor E. Forbes, but edited and continued by him, says (p. 157), "the *Nephrops norvegicus* has its numerical maximum in, and is a good characteristic Crustacean for, the Scandinavian region, but it occurs abundantly in Dublin Bay; it has not, however, according to Mr. W. Thompson, a general distribution—such as west and south, even throughout the Irish seas. We may feel sure, from its excellence as an edible species, that it has not been overlooked by fishermen, whilst its size, form, and proportions make it the most elegant Crustacean we have—a prize which no naturalist would overlook; yet, strange to say, it has not been recorded from the western coasts of France, nor do we meet with it till we reach the Mediterranean. It seems to be abundant in the Adriatic,[1] in which sea it may be noticed, that several other outlying forms of northern types have also been met with."

This is one of the many curiosities which abound in Natural History, affording abundant food for meditation to the student, and over which it is well worth his while to ponder.

On this head it is not out of place to recall to the reader Professor Forbes' reflections whilst dwelling on a similar, and not less interesting enigma, viz., that of the presence of certain littoral Mollusks on both sides of the Atlantic, and the problem how their migration from one side of the Atlantic to the other was effected, as it undoubtedly *was* effected in some manner which at best remains a mere conjecture. He says:—

" The student of history follows with intense interest the march of a conqueror or the migration of a nation.

" The traveller traces, with most breathless delight, every step of the progress of some mighty hero of ancient days.

" I have had my share of the pleasure when tracking the course of Alexander and his armies in Pisidia, and determining mile by mile the route of Manlius through Milias; on ground, too, to the modern geographer wholly new.

" Yet, absurd as it may seem to those who have not thought of such things before, there is a deeper interest in the march of a periwinkle and the progress of a limpet.

" It is easier to understand how the son of Philip made his way safely through the sea, on his famous march from Phaselis, than to comprehend

---

[1] In the Quarnero Gulf.

TERSATO, NEAR FIUME.

how the larva of a Patella crossed the fathomless gulf between Finmark and Greenland. It is a strong saying, but not said without a meaning, that the existence of Alexander may have been determined by the migration of the shell-fish. If I am right in my interpretation, we acquire a clue to the origin of the peculiar physical conformation of the world as it is, and to the disposition of those geographical arrangements upon which the development of nations and characters of men in a great measure depend."

ZONE VII. is that of the greatest depths, extending from 45 to 75 fathoms; limestone springs rise here and there; effect of light reduced to a minimum; pressure at 60 fathoms, 12·26 atmospheres; average temperature 52° F.; difference of extreme temperatures 5° F., and change very gradual.

The characteristic species are the Polyps *Aglaophænia myriophyllum*, and *Scrialaria lendigera*; the bivalves, *Pecten glaber*, *Avicula tarentina*, *Venus ovata*, and *Venus fasciata*, and the univalve, *Turritella quadricarinata*, which ends the short list.

VERTEBRATES.

The distribution of the Vertebrates is much more extended than that of the forms hitherto described; their division by horizontal regions is to a certain extent practicable, but the limits are not nearly so well defined as is the case with the Invertebrates.

They are divided into two very distinct classes, viz.: —

1. The SEDENTARY class of fishes, composed of those which are bound to given limits, both horizontal and vertical; these being determined by the temperature or composition of the water, the depth, the nature of the bed or the adjacent land, or the quality of their food. This class, which is also called *Shore fishes*, is subdivided into what I shall term :—

(*a*) The *Rovers*,[1] which hover about within given limits, suitable to their particular predilections.

---

[1] I consider these divisions the most appropriate rendering of what Dr. Lorenz terms (*a*), *Grundschwärmer;* (*b*), *Grundstete*.

(*b*) The *Squatters*,[1] which are bound to given localities, and have their fixed abodes.

2. The MIGRATORY or Pelagic class (*voyageurs*), which frequents the deep, without reference to the coast or formation of the bed.

CLASS I.—SEDENTARY FORMS.

1. *Littoral* forms in depths of 0-6 fathoms, or within the third and fourth zones.

(*a*) *Littoral Rovers.*—On the open coast-lands most species of *Blennies* and *Gobies* abound, such as the ocellated Blenny, or Butterfly-fish, a British species here common; *Bl. palmicornis*, *Bl. tentacularis*, and *Bl. pavo*, rarer; the black Goby, a British species, common, and *G. capito* rarer. These genera are numerously represented in these waters, the Gobies by no less than twenty-two species, of which only seven are known in British waters; and the Blennies by fourteen species, of which four belong to the British fauna. Some of them are brilliantly coloured.

Calm and sheltered rocky shores are frequented by *Lepadogasteres*, or Suck-fishes, amongst which are three British species: the Cornish Sucker and the Connemara Sucker are the most prevalent of this genus.

The Wrasses hover about the littoral tangles and grass-wrack; they are very numerous, and are represented by twenty distinct species, only four of which are known in British waters. This is the characteristic genus of the Mediterranean region.

Amongst the most prevalent species are *Labrus turdus*, *L. merula*, *Crenilabrus pavo*, *Cr. melops* (the Corkwing), *Cr. quinquemaculatus*, *Cr. griseus*, *Cr. rostratus*, *Coris Geoffredi*, and *Coris julis* (the Rainbow Wrasse). They are very brilliant, and the last-named is the brightest of the painted beauties, exceeding all Adriatic fishes in splendour of colour.

Shallow zostera fields, on clay or muddy beds, are the favourite resort of the Atherines (*Atherina hepsetus*).

---

[1] I consider these divisions the most appropriate rendering of what Dr. Lorenz terms (*a*), *Grundschwärmer*; (*b*), *Grundstete*.

Shoals of the Sea-bream tribe, particularly the young, rise here from the lower zone they usually frequent: they are to be found in sheltered bays, or creeks, where the bed is muddy, or covered with sea-weed, and are particularly characteristic of this zone.

The most prevalent kinds are:—*Box Salpa*, also the Gilthead, a British species, and one of the most esteemed of fishes: *Sargus annularis* and *Oblata melanura;* they are seen in shoals around the vessels at anchor, their broad silvery sides glancing in the water, in some striped with irregular bands of gold, in others marked with one or two dusky clouds, or tinged with brilliant ultramarine or purple.[1]

(*b*) *Littoral Squatters.*—In the mud at the mouths of rivulets and streams, and in the lagoons, the common Eel (*Anguilla vulgaris*) is common, its long, slimy body beautifully clouded with purplish brown and salmon-pink.

Of the Amphibious Carnivoræ, the common Seal (*Phoca vitulina*),[2] the Sea-Wolf of most Mediterranean people, ranging from the northern latitudes, is said to enter the Adriatic, and occasionally to be caught at Ragusa, but not further north. They are believed to go ashore in the Ombla valley in quest of grapes during the vintage season.

The Adriatic seal "The Monk" (*Pelagus, Phoca,* or *Leptonyx monachus*) also belongs to the littoral forms, but makes its appearance only on the eastern shores of the Quarnero. It is reported not to be uncommon in the bay of Carin, but only when the Bora blows across the channel of Morlacca; and it is abundant about the islands of the Dalmatian Archipelago.[3]

The tortoise (*Chelonia caretta*) must also be included amongst the littoral forms; but it is rarely caught so far north as the Quarnero.

---

[1] See Forbes and Godwin-Austen.

[2] Consult Petter's "Dalmatia," also Cornalia, "Fauna d'Italia," part i. p. 62; the identity of this species as applied to these waters is, however, doubted by many authorities; E. H. Giglioli says that the assertion as to the presence of this species in these waters "è basato su erronea identificazione specifica"; and it is not altogether impossible that the above species may have been confused with "the Monk."

[3] This species is said to commit great havoc in the vineyards of Sardinia and Sicily at the time of the vintage.

2. *Forms of the declivity and shallows* in depths of 15 to 20 fathoms.

(*a.*) *Rovers.*—The ragged steps and prongs of the rocky declivity, overgrown with tangles, also the rocky shallows, which here and there crown the deeper loam-beds, swarm with Sea-perches, several species of Scorpions, Gurnards, Wrasses, and Sea-breams, which form a characteristic *facies* of this locality, vulgarly termed *Pesci di Grotta.*

The most common are *Box salpa*, *Box boops* (the Bogue of British waters), *Sargus annularis* and *Oblata melanura*, which rove in large shoals. In smaller shoals are *Sargus Rondeletii, Pagellus mormyrus, P. erythrinus* (the red, or Spanish Sea-bream of British waters), *Cantharus orbicularis*, and *Charax puntazzo.*

Solitary mature specimens of *Dentex vulgaris* (the British Dentex, or Toothed Gilt-head, the much-valued *Dentale* of these climes), and *Chrysophris aurata* (the Gilt-head, or *Dorada* of these shores) roam about amongst the rest.

The Sea-breams are often joined by the Umbrina of British waters (*Umbrina cirrhosa*), less frequently by *Corvina nigra*, also by Bloch's Gurnard (*Trigla cuculus* Bl.), the Piper, or Lyra (*Tr. lyra*). The streaked Gurnard (*Trigla lineata*) only frequents the deep loam-bed. In their company also appear *Serranus scriba, S. cabrilla*, also the smooth Serranus (never *S. hepatus*), *Scorpæna porcus, S. scrofa, Labrus festivus, L. trimaculatus* (the Three-spotted Wrasse) ; a British species.

On the lower declivity and over deep crags range the Stone-basse (*Polyprion cernium*), the John Dory (*Zeus Faber*), sometimes also the Boarfish (*Capros aper*), all belonging to the British fauna.

Several varieties of Sea-horses (*Hippocampus*) are found over the whole declivity down to 30 fathoms : these belong, however, rather to the pelagic class.

Most Cephalopods frequent the overgrown rocky ground in average depths : the Squid (*Loligo vulg.*), the Cuttle-fish (*Sepia officinalis*), which often rise to the littoral zones. *Sepiola Rondeletii, Octopus vulgaris* (the Poulp, or common Octopus), and *Eledone moschata* prefer the open sea, on loam-beds.

Other forms frequent the sand-banks and zostera fields, such as *Smaris vulgaris, Sm. gracilis, Mæna vulgaris, Trachinus draco* (the Great Weever) and *Belone acus* (the Gar-Pike), more rarely the Spet (*Sphyræna vulgaris*), the Scald-fish (*Arnoglossus laterna*), and several species of the Pipe, or Needle-fishes (*Syngnathus*).

Some *migratory* forms, especially the *Clupeidæ*, represented chiefly by the Anchovy and Pilchard (the Sardine of commerce), and a species peculiar to the Mediterranean fauna, *Cl. papalina*, periodically appear on these grounds.

(*b.*) *Squatters.*—The Conger-eel (*Conger vulgaris*) lurks in holes and crevices of the lower declivity. Where the declivity changes at no great depth into flat loam-beds, or narrow channels, is the dwelling-place of the flat-fish tribe, such as the Turbot (*Rhombus maximus*), the Italian Flounder (*Pleuronectes italicus*), the Common Sole (*Solea vulgaris*), *S. monochir, S. lascaris, S. lutea*, and the British species, Bloch's Topknot (*Phrynorhombus unimaculatus*).

3. *Forms of the deep-bed.*—These are all *squatters;* the principal group amongst which is that of the *Gadidæ*, or Cod tribe, a specifically northern family, only few of the less valuable species of which appear in these waters, such as the Poor, or Capelan (*G. minutus*), the Whiting (*G. merlangus*), the Bib, or Whiting Pout (*G. luscus*), the Hake (*Merlucius vulgaris*), the three-bearded Rockling (*Motella vulgaris*), all British species, which, with the exception of the last-named rare species, form the chief produce of the ground fisheries.

Amongst these live shoals of the red Band-fish (*Cepola rubescens*), Star-gazers (*Uranoscopus scaber*), and *Serranus hepatus*, mostly imbedded in the mud, whereas the *Gadidæ* hover one or two feet above the bed.

The Rays come next in order of importance. These are the Thornback (*Raja clavata*), *R. punctata*, the Burton Skate (*R. oxyrhynchus*), *R. miraletus*, the Bordered Ray (*R. marginata*), the Eagle Ray (*Myliobatis aquila*[1]), the Sting Ray (*Trygon pastinaca*), *Tr. brucco;* the Electric Ray (*Torpedo*

---

[1] This is rather one of the pelagic forms.

Galvanii), and another species *T. narce*. They inhabit exclusively the soft loam-beds in 20–60 fathoms water.

They are often joined by the Angler, or Fishing Frog (*Lophius piscatorius*), which, however, also frequents shallow waters.

The young and immature Sharks also inhabit these regions,—probably also the mature ones, although these are rather to be classed amongst the migratory class of fishes. Amongst them the Angel-fish (*Rhina squatina*), the Spiny Dog-fish (*Acanthias sp.*), the Spotted Dog-fish (*Scyllium sp.*), are the most prevalent; the Blue Shark (*Carcharias glaucus*) is rare; and *Centrina Salviani* is very rare.

Class II.—Migratory Forms.

The *migratory* or *pelagic* forms comprise fishes, Cephalopods, Medusæ, also some species of Tunicates, and Gasteropods, which plough the deep without fixed abode, and without reference to coast and bed. Their movements are determined entirely by the properties of their element, *i.e.* by the temperature, composition, and depth of water, as also by the amount and quality of the nourishment it affords. They come mostly in dense shoals, and this is the season most propitious for their capture; others, again, follow these shoals in pursuit of prey.

They appear near land only during certain months. At other times they are supposed to be in deep water, and perhaps far away. But absolutely nothing is known on the subject, nor is a satisfactory reason given why they approach the land: the idea of their coming for spawning, if not altogether a fallacy, is at all events questionable as regards the majority, whose ova and young are found at a great distance from the shore.

In the upper strata of water, down to 10 fathoms' depth, *Rhizostoma Cuvieri* are common, often as much as one mètre long, and 40 lb. weight, $99\frac{1}{2}$ per cent. of which, however, is water, $\frac{1}{4}$ lb. being the actual weight of animal substance when exposed to the air. Less frequently met with are species of *Pelagia, Oceana ampullacea* (a kind of medusa), *Beroë cucumis*,[1]

---

[1] The members of the Medusa tribe which appear to abound most in the Arctic Seas

the "Fountain-fish" of the early voyagers to Spitzbergen; *Salpa maxima* often appears, of which sometimes a hundred or more individuals are united together, forming long chains, known as "*Serpents de mer*," several of which often swim in company, producing the most intense phosphorescence; from these chains each individual detaches itself, in its turn, for purposes of reproducing its species. The progeny is a single individual which, totally dissimilar from its parent, carries on its solitary existence until it, in its turn, produces a whole chain, consisting of hundreds linked together, but each like the grandmother.

Tethys fimbria is less frequent; it is one of the most beautiful, as it is the largest, naked sea-snail in the Mediterranean; it is furnished with lateral protuberances, extending on either side of the back, which it moves backwards and forwards to serve as oars, besides a sail which, in a specimen 5 inches in length, measured as much as $4\frac{1}{2}$ inches across, the foremost lateral extensions measuring 2 inches; it is particularly remarkable for the phosphorescence it produces.[1]

The Nautilus, or Paper sailor (*Argonauta papiracea*), is not uncommon in the waters of the islands of Lissa and Lésina, and occasionally, but quite accidentally, it finds its way as far north as the Gulf of Trieste.

Some minute species of Pteropods, probably belonging to the genus of

---

are Ciliograda, creatures which are, for the most part, more or less spherical in shape, or else simulate strips of riband, transparent as the purest crystal, and moving through the water by means of variously-arranged bands of thread-like hyaline fins, which, as they flap, all keeping exact time, in each long row, decompose the rays of light, and glitter with the hues of the rainbow. More exquisitely beautiful creatures than these *Beroidæ* (for so the tribe is called) do not exist among all the wondrous beings that people the seas. The elegance of their shape is equalled by the grace of their movements; and when the prismatic lustre of their bands of cilia marks the course of their crystal bodies, as they swim with gentle motion through the water, they seem as if they were diamonds endowed with life. Some, such as the *Beroë cucumis*, one of the most characteristic of the northern forms, yet having a wide range to the south, although in fewer numbers, are tinged with a charming amethystine blush. This is the "*Fountain-fish*" of the early voyagers to Spitzbergen, who, mistaking the cause of the eight bands of iridescence, gleaming along the sides of its body, fancied they were so many rivulets of lustrous water.—Forbes and Godwin-Austen, "Natural History of the European Seas."

[1] See Dr. Grube's work, "Ein Ausflug," &c., p. 29, and illustration 12. Taf. i.

Cleodora, also appear sometimes with the outward semblance of so many minute icicles.

The representative forms of *migratory*[1] fish are the Basse (*Labrax lupus*), one of the most voracious, as it is also one of the best fishes frequenting these waters; the Grey Mullet species, *Mugil auratus*, the Sea-lamprey (*Petromyzon marinus*), mostly to be found in 12 fathom waters.

Mugil auratus often seeks the shallows in hungry shoals; *Labrax lupus* approach the shore mostly after rain, when the effect of the swollen streams and torrents is to cloud the sea; *Petromyzon marinus* is fond of the brackish waters.

The Herring tribe : *Clupea sardina*, the Pilchard of British waters, comes in tremendous shoals, less frequently the Anchovy (*Engraulis encrasicholus*), and in isolated forms the Shad, (*Alosa vulgaris*); they hover about half way between the surface and zostera and cystoseira banks, which lie in 15 to 25 fathoms, on which they settle for pasture. They are, however, chased by Dolphins down to the bed in 30 to 40 fathoms, and also by the Mackerel (*Scomber scombrus*), which attacks them from below, thus driving them to the surface.

The Pilchards seek for given temperatures of water more than any other fish, and, in the Quarnero, they seem to prefer the medium depths, where a temperature of 55° F. is to be met with. This temperature occurs twice a year,—in April to May, and in September to November, and these are the seasons in which they visit us; during the rest of the year they are absolute strangers to these shores.

The Pilchard is followed in spring by the family of Mackerels; the common Mackerel (*Scomber scombrus*) at their head. There is no fish of the migratory class that approaches nearer to the shore at certain seasons, but there is no doubt about its spawning in the open sea, and it approaches

---

[1] I.e. *migratory* in the sense that they migrate from the sea into fresh and brackish waters, and *vice versâ*, but not *migratory* as are the Mackerel and Tunny, which are representative species of the true *pelagic* class of fishes. Basse is, in fact, a shore-rover, Grey-mullet and Lampreys are fishes of the brackish waters.

PROMONTORE LIGHTHOUSE.

the shore only after the spawning is over; it frequents these waters in dense shoals from April to October, and is the most lucrative object of the summer fisheries. The Spanish Mackerel (*Sc. colias*), the Horse Mackerel (*Caranx trachurus*), appear in their company; also the Flying-fish (*Exocœtus volitans*), besides smaller shoals of the common Tunny (*Thynnus vulgaris*), and, more rarely, the Pelamid (*Scomber pelamys*).

Lichia amia and *L. glauca* (the Derbio) are rarely met with; and the Sword-fish (*Xyphias gladius*) and the Pilot-fish (*Naucrates ductor*), thus called from its sometimes preceding vessels into harbour, as if to show them the way, belong rather to the exception.

The Remora, or Sucking-fish (*Echeneis remora*), is found adhering close to the bronchial aperture of Sharks, the Sword-fish, the Tunny, but it is very rarely met with.

Seriola Dumerilii (Yellow-tails), *Centrolophus* (Black-fish), *Coryphœna hyppurus* and *pelagica* (known by misapplication as Dolphins), and *Brama Raii* (Ray's Sea-bream) occasionally make their appearance in the Gulf of Trieste. The flying Gurnard does not appear to proceed north of Lissa.

Mullidœ,[1] or Red Mullet family, abound hovering about the shores in medium depths in summer, and retreating to the deep waters on the approach of cold weather: the striped Surmullet (*Mullus surmuletus*) is the most prevalent kind, the Red Mullet (*M. barbatus*) is found in lesser quantities.

Delphinus delphis (the common Dolphin), and *D. phocœna*, the former being the most prevalent, plough the deep in chase of the dense shoals of Mackerel, and Pilchards; although causing great havoc amongst the shoals of fish, and doing, often, great damage to the nets, they are seldom destroyed by the fishermen, by whom they are considered a favourable augury of a plenteous catch.

The huge Sharks,—such as the Fox Shark (*Alopias vulpes*), the Blue Shark (*Carcharias*), the Hammer-headed Shark (*Zygœna malleus*), so called on account of its peculiar hammer-shaped head, scud about in search of prey.

The Tope (*Galeus canis*) is often common towards the end of autumn;

---

[1] See note, page 32. Mullidæ belong to the class of shore fishes.

the Smooth Hound (*Mustelus vulgaris*) generally so;[1] the Grey Notidanus (*Notidanus griseus*), known as the *Pesce Manzo*, or "Ox-fish," from the resemblance of its eye to that of an ox, specimens of which weighing as much as 900 lb. have been caught, is, on the contrary, rare; and also another species (*Notidanus barbarus*, Nardo), a specimen of which was fished in the Quarnero in the year 1770. The other Sharks are all more or less rare; thirty species are enumerated as belonging to the Adriatic fauna, of which fourteen extend to British waters.

The Molebut, or Sun-fish (*Orthagoriscus mola*), is often found quite near the surface of the sea, and *Orthagoriscus planci* occasionally so. The *Hippocampus* is common.

RECAPITULATION.

Dr. Lorenz has found and enumerated 460 Invertebrates, Articulates, and Radiates; Dr. Grube, 412. Combining the two lists, we arrive at the following results: viz.—Mollusks, 220; Arthropods, 117; Vermes, 100; Radiata, 56; Sponges, 17; total, 510 species.[2]

The following number of the different types are especially characteristic of the various zones described by Dr. Lorenz.

Characteristic Species of the various Zones.

Zones of Dr. Lorenz.	Crustaceans.	Mollusks.	Annelides.	Polyps.	Echinoderms.	Sponges.	Total.
I.	1	...	...	...	...	...	1
II.	3	8	1	1	...	...	13
III.	10	40	6	4	4	3	67
IV.	4	10	1	1	2	1	19
V.	8	22	4	2	8	2	46
VI.	3	14	2	3	3	4	29
VII.	...	3	...	1	...	...	4
Total ...	29	97	14	12	17	10	179

[1] *Galeus, Mustelus,* belong to the class of shore fishes.
[2] These numbers refer to the Quarnero; Professor Stossich enumerates 13 cephalopods, 371

The third, or submerged littoral zone is the richest in animal, as it is also in vegetable, life, two-fifths of the above species being common to, one-fifth being exclusively found in, and one-seventh being characteristic of, this zone.

The relative figures are :—

Zones.	Species common to the various Zones.	Species found exclusively in the various Zones.
I.	1	1
II.	30	8
III.	206	104
IV.	139	16
V.	187	32
VI.	92	15
VII.	6	3

Of those which have an "*extended*" vertical distribution in the Quarnero, there are 36 whose horizontal distribution are known; of these 8 have a "*limited*" extension (only Mediterranean), whereas 28 are known to have an "*extended*" horizontal distribution; of those which are limited to one zone, 59 are known to have a "*limited*," and 71 to have an "*extended*" horizontal distribution.

If, however, the Celtic-Lusitanian region[1] be comprised within the denomination "*limited distribution*," thus drawing into one region the Mediterranean, the Celtic-Mediterranean, the Celtic-Lusitanian and the Canary-Lusitanian regions combined, as against the Lusitanian, Celtic and Boreal regions, as representing the "*extended*" *distribution*, we find :—

	horizontal distribution,	
In the first instance (as above stated),—	*limited*	*extended*
extended vertical distribution in the Quarnero	8	28
limited to one zone..	59	71

---

univalves, 191 bivalves, 369 crustaceans, and 311 vermes as belonging to the Adriatic fauna. See Appendix No. 5.

[1] The regions are according to the map in the "Nat. Hist. of the European Seas."

In the second instance,—   *horizontal distribution,*
                                                   limited   extended
extended vertical distribution in the Quarnero 27 9
limited to one zone... 103 27
both of which results (we quote Dr. Lorenz) would speak against the theory of Professor Forbes (a theory which in the case of Algæ is fully borne out), viz.,—that an "*extended*" *vertical distribution speaks, at the same time, for an* "*extended*" *horizontal distribution, and vice versâ.*

At any rate, the greater number of species, which, according to this theory, should have an "*extended*" distribution, belong, on the contrary, to the "*limited*" distribution in whichever sense we chose to comprehend the term "*limited*"; on the other hand, however, it is fully borne out in the instance of some species, such as, — *Ophiotrix fragilis, Asteracanthion glacialis, Echinus microtuberculatus, Xantho rivulosus,* and *Portunus Rondeletii,* which are distributed throughout most of the zones, and have, likewise, a wide horizontal distribution, even as far as the Indian Ocean and the Arctic regions.

The lower we proceed the higher becomes the percentage of Northern forms.

The following table shows the horizontal distribution of those species whose general distribution is known :—

Description.	Number of Species found in the Quarnero, whose general distribution is known.	Regions to which they are known to extend, and number of Species belonging to each region.		
		Lus.; Lus. Can.; Med.	C.; C. Med.; C. Lus.	Lus. C. Bor.
Polyps	7	1	6	—
Echinoderms	24	14	1	9 [1]
Annellides	27	10	13	4 [2]
Crustaceans	49	19	28	2
Bivalves	66	22	25	19 [3]
Univalves	76	48	12	16
Total	249	114	85	50

[1] Of which 4 are almost exclusively Boreal.
[2] Of which 3   ditto   ditto.
[3] Of which 3 extend to the Arctic regions.

The following is an enumeration of those species which extend to the L. C. Bor. region; those marked with an asterisk being those which are almost exclusively Northern species, or, in the case of three bivalves, extend to the Arctic regions; and showing, likewise, the zones to which they extend in the Quarnero :—

9 Echinoderms : *Ophiolepis ciliata*, V. VI. ; *O. Sundevalli*, V. ; *Ophiotrix fragilis*, III.—VII. ; *Astropecten aurantiacus*, IV. V. ; *Asteriscus palmipes*, V. VI. ; *Asteracanthion glacialis*, II.—V. ; *Echinus lividus*, III. ; *Echinocyamus tarentinus* (?) ; *Cladodactyla pentactes*, V. VI.

3 Annellides : *Pomatocerus tricuspis*, V. ; *Eulalia viridis*, III. ; *Polynoë cirrata*, IV. V. VI.

2 Crustaceans : *Nephrops norvegicus*, V. ; *Stenorhyncus phalangium*, V. VI.

19 Bivalves : *Pecten opercularis*, V. VI. ; *P. pusio*, V. VI. ; *P. varius*, V. VI. ; *Modiola discrepans*, V. ; *Pectunculus pilosus*, V. VI. ; *Nucula margaritacea*, III.—V. ; *Cardium echinatum*, V. ; *C. edule*, IV. ; *C. lævigatum*, V. VI. ; *Venus fasciata*, VI. VII. ; *V. gallina*, III. IV. ; *V. læta*, III. ; *V. ovata*, VI. ; *Venerupis Irus*, III. ; *Saxicava arctica*, III. ; *Donax trunculus*, V. VI. ; *Tellina donacina*, V. ; *Corbula nucleus*, V. ; *Teredo sp.* (?) V. VI.

16 Univalves: *Aplysia depilans*, IV.—VI. ; *Bullæa aperta*, III.—V. ; *Bulla hydatis*, V. ; *Chiton fascicularis*, III.—V. ; *C. lævis*, VI. ; *Dentalium entalis*, V. ; *Fissurella græca*, IV. V. ; *Capulus hungaricus*, V. VI. ; *Scalaria communis*, III. ; *Trochus magus*, V. VI. ; *Littorina littorea*, II. III. ; *Phasianella pulla*, III. ; *Turritella ungulina*, V. VI. ; *Cerithium lima*, III.—V. ; *Aporrhais pes pelicani*, V. VI. ; *Buccinum reticulatum*, III.

Turning to the *pisces*, we find 316 species of sea-fishes, belonging to 137 genera, 51 families; and 66 species of fresh-water fishes, belonging to 27 genera, and 14 families, which are found in the watershed of the Adriatic. This gives a total of 382 species belonging to 161 genera, 57 families, 10 orders, and 4 sub-classes.

Of the fresh-water fishes, 21 species (belonging to 9 families) are also common to the sea ; they either prefer the brackish waters, such as the Pike, the Sticklebacks and *Cyprinodon calaritanus*, also 2 Gobies (*G. panizzæ*,

G. punctatissimus); or descend the rivers and enter the sea at regular intervals —such as the Eels, also *Salmo carpio* and *Salmo trutta*; or ascend the rivers at certain seasons, chiefly for the purpose of spawning, such as the Shad, which only ascend the rivers in spring, the Sturgeon, and the Lamprey. The fresh-water Perch is also occasionally met with in brackish water.

Amongst the sea-fishes, the Italian Flounder (*Pleuronectes italicus*) frequents brackish waters, and even sometimes enters the rivers; some frequent and prosper in the Lagoons—such as the Atherines, two Blennies (*Bl. gattorugine, Bl. galerita*), Sea-horses, and the Greater Pipe-fish; others only occasionally frequent the lagoons and brackish waters—such as the Three-bearded Rockling, the Turbot, Brill, common Sole, Basse, several species of the Grey Mullet tribe, the Gilt-head, the Black-fish (*Centrolophus pompilus*), *Mæna vulg.* and *Sargus vulg.*; whilst others only frequent the deeper channels in the vicinity of the lagoons, such as—the Black Bream, the *Umbrina*, the Red Mullet, the Sapphirine Gurnard, also *Gobius paganellus*, *Lichia amia*, *Scomber pneumatophorus*, the Horse Mackerel, and the Gar-Pike.

The Bogue, the Flying-fish, the Pilot-fish, the File-fish, the Molebut, also *Carcharias Milberti* and *Falx Venetorum*, are only accidentally met with in the lagoons and brackish waters.

The Eel, Flounder, Turbot, Sole, Gilt-head, Basse, Sand-smelt, five grey and two red Mullets, and three Gobies are reared in the lagoons, the Mullet species, Turbot, Sole, and Gilt-head being introduced as young fry.

Only 126 species belonging to 86 genera of the sea-fishes, and 24 species belonging to 18 genera of the fresh-water fishes extend to British waters.

Of the sea-fishes, 125 species are more or less common all over the Adriatic; 70 species are more or less rare; 90 species are so rare as to be of no importance; whilst 31 species are only quite accidentally met with; 14 species belong more especially to the Venetian fauna, 77 species to the Dalmatian fauna, and 29 species are exclusively and only occasionally caught on the southern shores of Dalmatia; 5 species belong specifically to the Adriatic fauna. Only 100 species have a recognised commercial value,

40 coming under the denomination of *prime*, whereas 60 are only consumed by the poor; the rest are absolutely worthless, excepting as manure, although many are of surprising beauty in form and colour.

Amongst the fresh-water fishes, only the Trout, Pike, Shad, Eel, Sturgeon, and Lamprey have any value, commercially speaking, and, of the invertebrates, 10 crustaceans and 30 mollusks.

NOTE.—The Italian fauna of both seas (Mediterranean and Adriatic) comprises about 570 species of fishes, of which 74 species are fresh-water fishes.

CHAPTER II.

HISTORICAL.—LEGISLATION.—THE CHIOGGIOTTI.

Historical.—State of the coast, political and economic.—Inland markets; fluctuations of the trade.—Trawlers.—Statistics.—Ice.—Salt.—Italian fishermen.—Legislation.—Privileges of the Italian fishermen.—Titles from which the fishing rights were derived under the Republic of Venice.—Treaty between Austria and Italy.—The Chioggiotti; their craft engaged in the Austrian fisheries; proceeds of their share in the fisheries.—Count Marazzi.—Professor Ninni.—Individual profit of the Chioggiotti.—Consul Revest.—Distribution of the Italian fishing fleet on the Austrian coast; value of craft and gear employed.—Total value of craft and gear at Chioggia and Pelestrina.—The Italian fisheries.—Italian fishing craft; ditto engaged in the Austrian fisheries; ditto engaged in the foreign fisheries.—Value of the Chioggia fisheries.—Imports and exports of fish at Venice.—Venetian fisheries.—Craft and crew.

HE Austrian fisheries partake of the character of our coast fisheries and the *petite pêche* of the French, and they are carried on in the manner and with the appliances in use many centuries ago. The political condition of affairs on the Adriatic shores has necessarily cast its shadow on the state of the fisheries. The constant change of rulers up to within the last sixty-five years impeded the organisation and consolidation of the country, and no thought was given, under such circumstances, to the regulation of fisheries, or to other economical measures of still greater importance. Even the long period of peace which followed the Treaty of Vienna, by which the Dalmatian coast, increased by Ragusa, once more reverted to Austria, proved of small avail to the newly-acquired provinces; there was a total want of union and consciousness of identity of interests with the rest of the Empire.

On account of its poverty, the country was looked upon in the light

BRAGOZZI AT ANCHOR.

of a burden,[1] as in the days of Charlemagne, when the conquest of Istria, Liburnia, and Dalmatia is described by Gibbon as an easy though unprofitable acquisition. A civil or military appointment to any post in Dalmatia was considered a banishment, as it is indeed even now. Thus, all interest in these provinces was nipped in the bud, and the brilliant history of Venice and Ragusa was entirely ignored..

It is not until very recently, and under the present reign, that the impulse has been given to deal with the existing order of things. Politically speaking, progress has been urged by the occupation of Bosnia and Herzegovina, the acquisition of which had become almost a question of political existence to Dalmatia. This shore-land, although in the possession of the finest natural harbours in the Mediterranean, and thus pre-eminently adapted as an outlet of commerce, was precluded from securing the advantages to which its natural position entitled it, as long as it remained a mere strip of coast without any back-country.[2] Economically speaking, the country has gained by the creation of a marine section of the Ministry of Commerce, and the execution of the more important harbour works, foremost amongst which may be mentioned those of Trieste,[3] the great emporium of Austrian commerce; Fiume,[4] which is fast becoming the great outlet of Hungarian produce, and the rival port of Trieste; and Spalato, which is the "coming" port of Dalmatia.

Lastly, an attempt is being made to organise and develope the fisheries, which have always proved a most important branch of industry to every country which has the good fortune to be in the possession of a seaboard, not only on account of the immediate profits it brings to those personally

---

[1] The remark of Emperor Joseph is characteristic; when told that all the roads, piers, forts, &c., had been constructed by the French during their occupation of Dalmatia, he said that he thought it was a pity they had been driven out of the country so soon.

[2] The greatest breadth of Dalmatia is only thirty-seven Italian miles; near Ragusa it is only one mile, and at Cattaro still less.

[3] See "The Port of Trieste, Ancient and Modern," by Capt. R. F. Burton, H.B.M. Consul at Trieste (*Journal of the Society of Arts*, Oct. 29 and Nov. 5, 1875).

[4] See "Fiume and her New Port," by G. L. Faber, Esq., H.B.M. Consul at Fiume (*Journal of the Society of Arts*, Nov. 9 and 16, 1877).

engaged in its exercise, but for the highest State reasons, as it is the best school for training seamen,—a fact which nowadays is generally recognised.[1]

Hitherto, the poverty of the inhabitants, and the want of markets other than their own, where they could dispose of the superfluous produce of the fisheries, were the chief causes which acted in unison to damp all enterprise, and to restrict it to the most immediate wants of the communities themselves, and thus check a regular development.

But, by degrees, other markets are being opened up by the construction of railways, and, instead of the complaints formerly heard as to the want of sale, we now hear complaints of shortness of supply, and dearness of the prices. This is natural and easily explained. The same change has occurred in England, only in a much more acute form; the railways have brought about an entire revolution in the trade, which is now concentrated in the metropolis, and to such an extent that seaport towns draw their supply thence. This is by no means the case here; the railways have enlarged the market to some inland towns, it is true, but only, as yet, to a very limited extent. Yet the difference is such that hitherto the fishermen were dependent on the local demand; whereas, now, the consumer is mainly dependent upon the fisherman, and the difference is felt.

The increase of the demand and the opening-up of new markets should lead, by a very natural inference, to a proportionate increase in the enterprise of the fishermen. But this is only the case in a much less degree than it could be thought possible; the people require goading on to enterprise, and there is an entire want of that free impulse to which one is accustomed in England, which works on ahead, regardless of all obstacles instead of only

---

[1] Thus for instance, by France, under Napoleon III., and by Germany since 1870, who have done everything in their power to foster and encourage their national fisheries. This was particularly the case in Germany, whose fisheries had, since 1847, been on the decrease. The "Deutsche Fischerei Verein," several establishments of pisciculture, foremost amongst which the I. Centralanstalt zu Hünnigen have since been founded, besides a joint-stock company for Herring-fisheries started at Emden in 1872, with six boats, realising 87,000 florins gross profits on a capital of 105,000 florins. The exhibition of fisheries at Berlin is another instance of the importance attached to her fisheries by Germany.

following in the wake of the most needful requirements. It will thus take years before the much-desired development is brought about, owing chiefly to the difficulty which prevails in attracting the necessary capital. It is, however, ridiculous to hear the complaints which burst forth at times, and which, for want of a better reason, assume the form of an indictment against the Italian trawlers and the bad effects of trawling.

As a class, fishermen are always given to grumbling. The fluctuations in the yield of their industry are necessarily subject to greater movement than most other trades—fluctuations which are, no doubt, due, in a great measure, to the habits of the migratory class of fish, and the influences, climatory and others, which direct their movements, rather than the direct action of man; but until more is known on the subject it is impossible to supply a satisfactory explanation for their recurrence. The fishermen often fish by instinct, rather than upon any regulated principles: their success is, to a great extent, due to their luck; and the assumption is, therefore, permissible, that the rules which guide their efforts may often be at fault.

The consumers, on their part, set down everything to a decrease in the yield, and purposely ignore all other considerations which bear on the subject, such as the effect of the railways, which has been the principal cause in bringing about an increase of 50 per cent. and more in the prices.

The usual charges against the trawlers are that they destroy the young fry, frightening away the shoals, preventing their passage to the inner parts of creeks and bays; but the real objection is, obviously, that the larger hauls by the trawls tend to lower the market price of fish and the profits of the other fishermen.

Similar disputes have been common elsewhere, and restrictions brought to bear on the use of the trawl, as it has generally turned out, with little or no reason. The subject has been fully gone into by successive Royal Commissions in England, and the result has been an entire condemnation of all restrictions on trawling, as it was distinctly proved that the fluctuations in the yield of the several fisheries had been fully as great after the restrictions had been put in force as before, and, consequently, trawling was again permitted as before, and has increased with wonderful success and rapidity.

The disinclination of migratory fish to enter, in certain seasons, water which they otherwise frequent has been shown to extend to waters where trawling is unknown; and this amply proves that the periodical scarcity of fish which is noticed in other places has nothing to do with trawling.

The disappearance of fish from waters where trawling was carried on has repeatedly led to the usual outcry against trawlers, but the dispute invariably ends in the reappearance of the fish the next season, notwithstanding the trawlers.

It must be remarked that most of the charges against trawlers are due to the idea that the spawn of fish is destroyed by their action. But the notion is now exploded, since it has been proved that the spawn of most deep-sea fish is not deposited at the bottom, but floats freely in the water, and there is not the least evidence of spawn being destroyed by the action of the trawl.[1]

One of more important innovations, the importance of which cannot be over-estimated, is the regular publication of detailed statistics on everything appertaining to the fisheries; by this means, an opportunity is given of finding out what is wanting, and where a screw may be loose. The issue of such statistics rests with the Marine Section; their great difficulty, however, is to overcome the suspicions of the fishermen, who are always inclined to think that information of the kind is required with a view to an increase of taxation: hence we may conclude that, as a rule, they are understated. Thus, their reliance is doubtful on the face of them, yet, by their regular recurrence, a standard is obtained by means of which inferences may be drawn, and this is their principal value. By such means we have the opportunity of ascertaining to some extent the quantities of fish annually brought to market, which, hitherto, we have only been able to judge approximately: there is no reason to doubt its increase, but it is only by the aid of figures that comparisons can be made and conclusions drawn, and elsewhere it has become an accepted fact, that where railway communication exists the more important a place as a fishing-station, the more difficult it is for the local inhabitants to procure fish.

---

[1] See "Sea Fisheries." By E. W. H. Holdsworth, F.L.S., F.Z.S., &c. London: 1877.

This coast is not likely to prove an exception to the rule, and, although the trade is yet in its infancy, it is no doubt capable of great development, if the value of ice were fully understood and recognised.

Ice becomes a necessary item in order successfully to carry on the trade; and as there is a superfluity of it in Carinthia and Carniola, to be procured for the mere cost of transport, there would be no difficulty in introducing it as a necessary element of the trade.

One of the great drawbacks to development is also the State monopoly of salt. The fishermen are, it is true, allowed a certain quantity of salt at reduced prices, but not sufficient, and very often they fall short of their supply. Thus, when large hauls of mackerel, pilchard, &c., are made, so that they cannot be consumed in their fresh state, or the fishing craft are becalmed, the fish has often to be thrown away from want of a sufficient quantity of salt; this ought to be remedied, and the fishermen allowed as much salt as they please, returning what is not consumed.

We are now brought to consider the position of the Italian fishermen on these shores.

They chiefly hail from Chioggia, in the province of Venice, a town composed almost exclusively of fishermen, and which up to 1866 was under Austrian dominion; they go by the name of *Chioggiotti*, and are expert fishermen and mariners. Their boats, called *bragozzi*, and described elsewhere, are constructed at Chioggia; they are good sea-boats and above the average size of the Austrian fishing-boats; they are used exclusively for trawling (*cocchia*); the sails are, as a rule, of a dusky brick colour, and ornamented with various designs more or less fantastic, in order the better to recognise one another in the exercise of their vocation, especially at night-time, as they always fish in pairs.

These boats are to be seen all along the Austrian-Hungarian seaboard, where they are engaged for months far away from their homes. Their concourse in these waters dates from the most remote times, and they have always been able to sustain a reputation of being hardy seamen, skilled in their profession, sober and frugal in their habits, and daring, when it became a question of risking their lives either in the pursuit of their own trade, or in saving the lives of their fellow-creatures from the fury of the deep.

The difference in the conformation of the Eastern and Western shores, the iron-bound character of the Western coast, the want of safe harbours and secure anchorage-grounds, as compared with the advantages which the Eastern coast affords, alike to the development of animal life and the industry of man,—these causes, combined with the proximity of the two shores, have necessarily led to the encroachment of the Italians on the rights of the Austrian-Hungarian fishermen, and to everlasting quarrels which descend from the most remote times, recurring on identical grounds.

Vice-Consul Count Antonio Marazzi has written a very interesting report[1] on the subject of the fishermen of Chioggia, and the laws regulating the fisheries in the Adriatic: from it much of the foregoing and following remarks are gleaned.

It appears that the privilege of the Italian fishermen to exercise their industry on the Eastern shores is based on usage rather than on right; yet the privilege seems to have been recognised under the Venetian Republic, as may be seen by their ordinances, and the custom is so fully established that Austria-Hungary has thought fit to recognise—or may be to tolerate—the continuation of the practice under the commercial treaty with Italy, subject, however, to the rights of the local fishermen and the municipal laws. This concession, or privilege, granted to the Italians by Austria, has become a matter of such importance to the Italians, that it was one of the main levers by which the renewal of the commercial treaty with Italy was brought about by Austria in 1878, it may be said, at the twelfth hour.

The regulations, decrees, and ordinances bearing upon the fisheries on the Austrian coast have retained an exclusively local character, and have not been embodied in a general law.

The exclusive rights originate from three titles, viz:—

1. *Privata proprietà* (private property);
2. *Baronia* (seigneurie);
3. *Comune* (communal);

---

[1] "Bollettino Consolare" of July, 1873.

the rights having been absolute in the first instance, whereas, in the second and third instances, they were confined to the usufruct of the produce, as an attribute of jurisdiction conceded by the reigning lord.

In the case of the *Communes*, this right extended only to those in possession of land (*dominio*), called *capo comuni* in contradistinction to the *comuni, vassali, soggeti*, or *tributari*.

As a rule, the possession of estates brought with them, as a natural consequence, the fishing rights over the adjacent waters; but there were exceptions in the case of waters held independently of the territory they washed, and which were transferable as any other property.

This theory was adopted by the Venetians, who, in emancipating the littoral communes (*comuni litorani*), drew the difference between *comuni di terra* and *comuni di mare*.

Those were held *di mare*, or *marittimi*, whose chief town (*capoluogo*) was situate either on the shore, or was in communication by water with the seas; whereas, those whose chief town was situate inland were considered *di terra*, though they might be in possession of seaboard.

The fishing-rights were conferred on the *comuni di mare*, to the exclusion of the *comuni di terra*. Hence arose the anomaly of some *Communes* holding fishing rights over tracts of water the shores of which belonged to other communities, which were thus excluded from the rights of fishing on their own shores.

The Republic, nevertheless, retained her supreme rights over the seas, and required, in each case, the payment of a nominal sum of one gold coin each year in acknowledgment of these rights.

The *comuni* and *baroni*, however, generally transferred their rights of fishing to the inhabitants of the bordering coast.

The *baroni* generally claimed a fixed rent, whereas the *comuni* saddled the fishermen with the engagement to supply the adjoining markets with fish at fixed moderate prices.

The Republic defended the privileges and rights of her subjects with the utmost rigour, and nobody dared encroach on them.

The law established by these ancient and traditional customs, and handed down from generation to generation, had thus become so engrafted in the minds of the inhabitants of the coast, that when Austria first came into possession of the coast it was thought impolitic to meddle with it.

Even the Regolamento of Dandolo, the Provveditore of Dalmatia under the French in 1808, did not attempt to interfere with rights based upon usage, but only regulated the exercise of those rights, and thus we find these feudal principles retained, until a law of 1835 attempted to deal with them.

By virtue of this law the deep-sea fisheries were declared free, the rights of fishing within the territorial boundary—*i.e.*, within one mile of the coast—being reserved to the inhabitants of seaboard, and the ancient rights pertaining to the barons and the *Communes* were thus virtually abolished.

But the new law gave rise to so much litigation, that an explanatory notification had to be issued two years later, to the effect that fishing rights based upon private civil contracts, or derived from ancient conventional customs, were not infringed thereby.

Nevertheless, such rights were upheld only in exceptional cases, in order to prevent needless litigation, and the rule was only intended to ease the transition from the old to the new state of things introduced by the law of 1835, and, later on, more fully borne out by the general law of 1848, which abolished all feudal holding of landed property.

It must, therefore, be inferred that the possession of fishing rights based upon feudal principles have no longer any legal *locus standi;* moreover, the law does not exclude the right of transferring the fisheries to others by those not choosing to exercise the rights themselves; it is thus that many *Communes* have let their fisheries to the Italian fishermen within the territorial waters, thus giving rise to the protests and jealousy of the neighbouring local fishermen.[1]

Beyond the general laws above cited, no special law concerning the fisheries in Austria-Hungary has been passed, owing, probably, to the difficulty that exists in reconciling the different interests, and at present it

---

[1] The *treaty* rights of the Italian fishermen are limited to the waters *outside* the territorial boundary.

BRAGOZZI LEAVING PORT.

must be said that the fisheries are guided entirely by municipal regulations, and, to a great extent, by custom and usage.

The necessity of passing a special and general law is, however, generally acknowledged, and, may be, it is being worked out at the present moment. In this the Italians have gained a march on the Austrians; their law regulating the fisheries was passed on March 4, 1877, and came into force December 31, 1879. They do not, however, definitely deal with the private fisheries, but merely regulate their exercise.

It has thus been shown how the Chioggiotti have been able to maintain their position in these waters, notwithstanding the opposition they often meet with, caused by the enmity and jealousy of the local fishermen.

In Istria, their share of the fishing exceeds that of the native fishermen, and they still retain an important share of the Dalmatian fisheries.

The produce of the trawls is chiefly composed of the ordinary class of fish (*pesce populo*), in contradistinction to the "prime" (*pesce fino*). This, as it constitutes almost exclusively the animal food of the poorer inhabitants of the greater part of the coast, is always of ready sale at low prices; and as the indolence of the inhabitants, and their non-use of the trawl, preclude them from competing with the Italians in the sufficient supply of this important article of consumption, the consequence is that their presence is, as a rule, welcomed by all classes, and often sought by the *Communes*. In their absence fish becomes a luxury, and is only within reach of the purses of the richer classes.

In some places, and particularly in the south of Dalmatia, at Ragusa, and in the Bocche di Cattaro, also at Barcola, near Grado, opposite Trieste, they meet with so much opposition from the local fishermen, that they have had to give up exercising their profession there in favour of more genial and hospitable waters. But in such cases the consuming population are the sufferers, the local fishermen drive a grinding monopoly, and in some places only go out fishing on the eve of fast-days, when they are sure of selling their small catch at exorbitant prices to the over-confiding public, that can ill afford to pay for it, but are obliged to do so from religious motives.

There are also many kinds of "prime" fish, the supply of which is entirely dependent on the Italian trawlers, such as the flat-fish tribe, the Norway lobster, and other kinds inhabiting the deep sea-bed.

The complaints that are made against the Chioggiotti are based chiefly upon the small-meshed nets in use by them; that they fish the greater part of the year, and closer in-shore than their treaty-right admits, owing to which facts, it is contended, they disturb the spawning grounds (which has been shown to be a popular fallacy), and that they either catch or destroy a quantity of worthless fry.

The fact is, they offer great competition to the local fishermen, in as far as by their greater industry and laboriousness they are to a large extent enabled to regulate the market prices, whereas the local fishermen would prefer a monopoly in their favour, do as little work, and make as high prices as possible.

The question as to the spawn having been disproved, there remains the complaint as to the young fry, in respect of which is to be said that, undoubtedly, the local fishermen do infinitely more damage themselves by the use of the ground or foot-seine, worked off-shore, or in shallow creeks and bays,—a mode of fishing most commonly in use all the year round, and very pernicious to the development of the fry.

On the other hand, there is no doubt that the Italians do often fish closer in shore than they have the right to do, and this they should avoid in their own interest; moreover, they are subject to the municipal laws wherever they happen to be, and the municipalities are able to enforce the rules as to the season of their fishing, and the limits which they should not overstep, by withdrawing their licences in cases of contravention.

In any case, the privilege derived by the treaty to the Italian fishermen of the Venetian estuary is the source of sustenance to a great number of the Italian population of that coast, and its withdrawal would cause great misery; and it would be difficult for them to find a new field of action which would compensate them for their loss.

The average number of Italian boats fishing in the Austrian-Hungarian waters is about 600, of 6,000 tons burden, and a crew of 2,500 men: of these, 580—590 hail from Chioggia, the remaining 10—20 being Romagnoli.

According to statistics of 1869, the Chioggia boats engaged in the fisheries on the Austrian coast were thus divided:—

	Boats.	Tonnage.	Crew.
Istria	437	4,321	1,787
Croatia	64	547	278
Dalmatia	85	853	351
	586	5,721	2,416

This gives an average of ten tons and four men for each boat.

On the other hand, the Austrian fishing-craft is three times the number, but their tonnage is less than that of the Italian craft.

The crews of the Italian boats are one man for 2·4 tons, as against one man for 0·78 tons in the Austrian boats. Count Marazzi values the share of the Italian boats in the Austrian fisheries at—

Kilos.	
995,000	Gorizia, Istria and the Quarnero.
7,000	Croatian coast.
760,000	Dalmatian coast and islands.

Together, 1,762,000 kilos, of which—

			Francs.
460,000	prime	value	650,000
1,302,000	ordinary	,,	976,500
1,762,000	kilos	,,	1,626,500[1]

The greater part of this is sold on the coast, say, for about 1,000,000 francs; the sale is effected by middle men, the local dealers, who resell to the

---

[1] Assuming the quantity to be right, I should be inclined to put the value at, say, 400,000 florins (= 870,000 francs). Count Marazzi has, I consider, set down too high prices; but, on the other hand, he has understated the yield: hence it may be assumed that the value given may not be far out.

consumers at a large profit, and the balance is transported in their own boats to Venice, Chioggia, and other Italian ports.[1]

According to the statistics of 1870, the value of imports of fish into Italy from Austria-Hungary was 1,486,606 francs; and the value of exports from Italy into Austria-Hungary 356,085 francs.

Comparing the two sets of figures, we find:—

	Francs.
Average value of fish caught by the Italian boats on the Austrian-Hungarian coast	1,626,500
Exports to Austria-Hungary	356,085
	1,982,585
Imports from Austria-Hungary	1,486,606
Value of fish caught by Austrian boats in Italian waters, not above, say	20,000
	1,506,606

Or a balance of 475,979 francs in favour of Italy.

The individual profit to the fishermen may be stated thus,[2] viz.—

	Francs.
Value of fish caught	1,626,500
From which deduct for expenses, wear and tear of nets, &c., taxes, &c.	276,500
Leaving a net profit of	1,350,000

---

[1] Professor Dr. A. P. Ninni gives the following results of the Chioggia fishing-boats fishing in foreign waters (*i.e.* Austrian-Hungarian seaboard):—374 boats, manned by 1,147 men, produce 2,900,000 kilos, value 2,270,000 lire; of which 1,700,000 kilos, value 1,770,000 lire, is sold abroad; and 1,200,000 kilos, value 500,000 lire, is brought to Italy for sale. But the value of the fish sold on the spot is here again set down at too high a figure, as in the case of Count Marazzi's estimate. I should reduce the amount by one-half.

[2] I am still quoting Count Marazzi.

to be divided amongst 600 boats and 2,500 men; = 2,250 francs per boat and 540 francs, or 248 florins, per man; or about 1¼ franc per day for the fisherman and his family. This is not over-flourishing, considering the constant life of toil and danger these men have to lead.[1]

Consul Revest, formerly Italian Consul at Fiume, in his report of 1878, estimates the proceeds of thirty pair of boats fishing in the Quarnero at a still lower figure, viz. :—

	Florins.
One pair at 6 florins a day—30 pair at 6 florins a day = 180 florins—for six months	32,300
Less expenses, 10 florins a week	7,800
	24,500

Two-thirds to the fishermen	16,333

divided amongst 240 men = 69 florins per man, for 7 months.

---

[1] I should be inclined to alter the above calculation as follows:—

	Francs.
Value of fish caught	1,626,500
Deduct one-third, which goes to the owners of the boats as their share of the yield	542,167
Leaving	1,084,333

as the share of the crew, or, taking an average crew of 4 men per boat = 452 francs, or 203 florins per man.

If we deduct expenses, say 500 francs per boat for the season, including wear and tear, taxes, &c., we obtain the following result :—

	Francs.
Gross amount	1,626,500
Less expenses 500 francs per boat	300,000
	1,326,500

One-third share of owners of craft	442,167
Two-thirds share of crew ...	884,333

Or 369 francs = 166 florins per man.

But the yield of the year 1877 was exceptionally low; according to the official statistics it was only 198,187 kilos, against 272,402 kilos in 1878, and 319,978 kilos in 1879.

	Florins.
Taking the lowest average value of the yield at 22½ soldi per kilo, it represents a sum of ...	45,583
From which amount deduct expenses at the rate of 500 francs per boat for the season, say ...	12,900 [1]
Leaving	32,683

of which two-thirds, say 21,789 florins, divided amongst 240 men, = 91 florins per man, for the season of 7 months.

In like manner, the yield of 1878 represents a value of 62,652 florins, and a net value of 56,202 florins; of which two-thirds, or 37,468 florins, divided amongst only 30 bragozzi and 120 men, = 312 florins per man.

In the year 1878 the Italian fishing fleet was distributed as follows:—

Trieste	Winter season	60	Summer season	95
Rovigno ...	,, ,,	30	,, ,,	27
Pola ...	,, ,,	42	,, ,,	26
Lussinpiccolo	,, ,,	12	,, ,,	12
H. Croatian littoral	,,	38	,, ,,	38
Zara ...	,, ,,	12	,, ,,	14
Spalato ...	,, ,,	27	,, ,,	8
		221		220

representing a value of about 300,000 florins; and the gear in use, a value of about 75,000 florins.

The following is an extract of a report made to the Austrian Ministry of Commerce on the subject of the Chioggia fisheries in 1862, for the preceding ten years, showing the number of fishermen, boats and tonnage thereof,

---

[1] M. Revest puts it at 7,800 florins only.

engaged, capital invested, and other details. These include the two fishing places Chioggia and Pelestrina.

41 *Tartani.*

Each craft has 5 shares of the gain	=	5 shares.
Crew of 6 men, each 1 share ...	=	6 ,,
41 × 11 × 130 florins ...	=	florins 58,630

399 *Bragozzi.*

Each craft has 2 shares...	=	2 shares.
Crew of 3 men, each 1 share ...	=	3 ,,
399 × 5 × 130 florins ...	=	florins 259,350

133 *Bragozzetti.*

Each craft has $1\frac{1}{2}$ share...	=	$1\frac{1}{4}$ share.
Crew of 3 men, each 1 share ...	=	3 ,,
133 × $4\frac{1}{2}$ × 130 florins ...	=	florins 77,805

626 *Battelli.*

Each craft has 1 share ...	=	1 share.
Crew of 3 men, each 1 share ...	=	3 shares.
626 × 4 × 130 florins ...	=	florins 325,520

300 *Battelli* and *Sandoli* engaged in the lagoon and *valli*-fisheries, of which

100 *Boats, with a total crew of* 150, *are estimated to gain*—

37 soldi for the crew.
20 ,, for the boat.
19 ,, for the owners of the *valli* in which they are allowed to fish.

76 soldi per day for 1 boat, or

76 florins per day for 100 boats, or, per annum, = florins 27,740

Carried forward florins 749,045

Brought forward florins 749,045

200 *Boats, with a total crew of* 300—

  30 soldi for the crew.
  20 ,, for the boat.
  ―――
  50 soldi for 1 boat, or
  ―――
100 florins per day for 200 boats, or, per annum, = florins 36,500

	Total florins	785,545
Profit on wholesale sale of fish, 5 per cent.		41,344
Ditto on retail sale of fish, 15 per cent.		145,921
Fish consumed by fishermen on board, say 5,000 @ 5 cents for 300 days		75,000
Gratuities		2,190
	Total florins	1,050,000

Tonnage of Craft.

		Tonnage.
41	Tartani	1,106
532	Bragozzi and Bragozzetti	3,764
626	Battelli ...	1,743
300	Battelletti ...	600
Total 1,499		7,213

5,000 *Fishermen.*

Capital invested.

41	Tartane	@ fl. 4,500		
	Gear ...	@ ,, 1,000		Florins.
		fl. 5,500	=	225,500

۳

BRAGOZZI RUNNING BEFORE THE WIND.

			Florins.
	Brought forward	=	225,500
532 Bragozzi	@ fl. 1,200		
Gear ...	@ ,, 120		
	fl. 1,320	=	702,240
626 Battelli	@ fl. 400		
Gear ...	@ ,, 350		
	fl. 750	=	469,500
300 Battelletti	@ fl. 100		
Gear ...	@ ,, 17½		
	fl. 117½	=	35,250
	Total florins		1,432,490

Thus, we obtain a maximum of 203, and a minimum of 69 florins per man for the season, both of which estimates I am led to consider understated for reasons given elsewhere.

In any case the official estimate, which puts the share at 130 florins, must be considered the lowest possible figure; exceptionally bad seasons may account for lower estimates, but, on an average, I should be inclined to put it at double that amount, and, in some instances, it will be seen that it reaches a still higher figure.[1]

On comparing, for instance, the official statistics for the last five years, we find that the shares of 18 Italian boats fishing in the Zara waters realised 10,136 florins per boat, and 1,382 florins for each man of the crew.

The season in which the Italian boats are allowed to fish on the Austrian coast commences in September and ends with April, which, deducting the festivities and holidays, would leave six months, or 180 days, clear.

The boats return home at given seasons, *i.e.*, at Christmas, Easter, All

---

[1] See Statistics. Dr. C. de Marchesetti estimates it at 300 florins

Saints' Day, the patron saint of the town in June, and for the fair in August. The scenes of festivity at these seasons are very gay and lively.

The return of the father, the brother, the son, the husband, and the sweetheart, is celebrated with a sincerity and good-will, tempered with sobriety, which is the result of the fisherman's humble and laborious calling, producing alike the simplicity of his habits and the morality of his life. His only ambition consists in becoming one day the owner of his own craft, in which he may continue and probably end the rest of his frugal, uniform and always perilous existence.

The number of fishing craft engaged in the fisheries of the Venetian estuary may be given at 3,000, of which 1,000 belong to the deep-sea fisheries and 2,000 to the lagoon fisheries. The deep-sea fishing craft (*barche da mare*) employ the whole population of Chioggia. In the year 1784, 164 *tartane* and 150 *bragozzi* were engaged in the deep-sea fisheries, and employed about 3,500 men.

At present, they are carried on mostly by the smaller *bragozzi*, which have increased to about 800, whereas the *tartane* have decreased to only about 50, about 6,000 fishermen being engaged.

The number of *pieleghi* has not perceptibly increased, the fisheries being carried on mostly by the *bragozzi*.[1]

Italian Fishing Boats.

	Number.	Tonnage.	Crew.	Average tonnage.
1st class	430	3,867	?	9—
2nd ,,	11,222	39,620	?	3.53
In 1871	11,652	43,487	?	3.73
1st class	483	3,884	6,920	8—
2nd ,,	13,543	44,901	30,788	3.32
In 1876	13,926	48,785	37,708	3.50
In 1878	15,441	52,339	?	3.39

[1] *The Italian Fisheries.*—The Italian coast, including the islands, has an extent of 6,341 kilomètres, and the aggregate value of its territorial and deep-sea fisheries is variously estimated

showing an increase of 20 per cent. in the number of craft, and 12 per cent. in the tonnage, from 1871 to 1876, and an increase of 11 per cent. craft, and 7½ per cent. tonnage from 1876 to 1878. There is, however, a decrease throughout in the mean tonnage.

Italian Boats engaged in the Fisheries on the Austrian-Hungarian Coast. 1876.

	Number.	Tonnage.	Crew.
Fiume	88	757	401
Lussinpiccolo	5	53	24
Spalato	26	206	113
Zara	19	235	85
1876	138[1]	1,251	623
1875	132[1]	1,240	595

Numbers of Italian Boats employed in Foreign Fisheries for 1876.

	Common Fisheries.			Coral.			Sponge.		
	Boats.	Tonnage.	Crew.	Boats.	Tonnage.	Crew.	Boats.	Tonnage.	Crew.
Austria	138	1,251	623						
France	59	319	318	25	48	181			
Corsica	17	60	80	71	488	523			
Greece	75	1,084	699						
Monaco	2	2	7	1	2	12			
European Turkey	23	394	208						
Algeria	176	1,720	1,188	54	569	646			
Egypt	15	226	142						
Tunis	68	457	381				9	203	165
Asiatic Turkey	14	263	123						
Total	587	5,776	3,769	151	1,107	1,362	9	203	165

at 35—40 millions of francs. Italy is, nevertheless, a large importer of fish, and consumption exceeds production to the extent of 20 millions of francs: this is the more surprising considering her natural position and length of coast-line, which, one would think, would pre-eminently dispose her to take a foremost rank in this important industry. Thus, the export of salt pilchards from St. Ives is entirely to the Mediterranean, chiefly to Genoa, Leghorn, Civita Vecchia, Naples, and Adriatic ports, and reaches as much as 45,000 hogsheads in particularly good years.

[1] Besides some 4 or 500 boats fishing in extra-territorial waters on the coast of Istria, which do not appear in the official statistics.

Italian Fishing Craft engaged in Foreign Fisheries, from 1864–1876.

Years.	Common Fishery.		Coral.		Sponge.	
	Number.	Tonnage.	Number.	Tonnage.	Number.	Tonnage.
1876	587	5,776	151	1,107	9	203
1875	695	6,115	243	1,972	17	261
1868	451	4,360	71	760	—	—
1867	407	3,951	74	833	16	278
1866	342 [1]	2,689	162	1,621	—	—
1865	288 [1]	1,965	137	1,344	—	—
1864	238 [1]	1,771	127	1,267	—	—

The common fisheries are carried on by Italian craft in France, Corsica, Greece, Monaco, Turkey, Algeria, Egypt, Tunis, Syria and Asiatic Turkey, besides Austria. The coral fisheries in France, Corsica, Monaco, Turkey, Algeria, Asiatic Turkey. Finally the sponge fisheries in Tunis.

CHIOGGIA FISHERIES.

	Kilos.	Lire.
Deep-sea fisheries	6,000,000	... value 2,100,000
Lagoon fisheries ...	700,000	,, 280,000
Total	6,700,000	,, 2,380,000

Imports and Exports of Fish at Venice.

	Lire.
Imported by sea and land ...	value 980,550
Exported ...	,, 1,018,890

---

[1] Exclusive of the Chioggia boats, now included in the returns since Venetia reverted to the Italian kingdom.

VENETIAN FISHERIES.

1872.

Craft employed in the coast fisheries, 117; tonnage, 396.
Craft employed in the deep-sea and foreign fisheries, 681; tonnage, 5069.

FISHERMEN.

Deep-sea Fisheries.

Masters (*direttori*)	822
Fishermen	2,982

Coast Fisheries.

Fishermen	1,229

Lagoon Fisheries.

Fishermen	2,850
Total	7,883

CHAPTER III.

FISHING DISTRICTS.—SEASON OF FISHING.—PRODUCE.

Fishing Districts.—Austria: Gorizia, Gradisca, Trieste.—Istria: Isola, Pirano, Salvore, Umago, Daila, Parenzo, Pola, Lussinpiccolo, Preluca.—Hungarian-Croatian littoral: Fiume, Buccari, Portoré, Segna.—Dalmatia; Zara, Sebenico, Spalato, Ragusa, Cattaro.—Dalmatian Archipelago. —Season of Fishing.—Descriptive part.—Produce.—Pisces.—Sharks, Rays, Sturgeons, Perch tribe, Sea-perches, Red Mullet, Sea-breams, Scorpions, Meagres, Sword-fish, Scabbard-fish, Hair-tail, Horse Mackerel, John Dory, Black-fish, Dolphins, Mackerel, Tunny, Star-gazers, Weevers, Anglers, Gurnards, Flying-Gurnards, Gobies, Dragonets, Band-fishes, Blennies, Spets, Atherines, Mullets, Sticklebacks, Trumpet-fish, Suck-fishes, Lophotes cepedianus, Ribbon-fishes, Coral-fishes, Wrasses, Cod tribe, Ophidium, Fierasfer, Sand-eels, Macrurus, Flat-fish tribe, Scopelidæ, Cyprinodon, Gar-pikes, Flying-fish, Salmon tribe, Herring tribe, Eel tribe, Pipe-fishes, Sea-horses, File-fishes, Sun-fishes, Lampreys, Lancelot.—Mollusks.— Cephalopods, Bivalves, Univalves, Tunicates.—Crustaceans.—Echinoderms.—Actiniæ.— Sponges.—Red Coral.

HE Austrian-Hungarian fisheries may be divided into three principal sections, viz.:—
1. Trieste and the coast of Istria.
2. Fiume and the Hungarian-Croatian littoral.
3. Dalmatian coast and Archipelago.

These are subdivided into the following harbour-masters' districts, given in the order of their importance:—
1. Trieste, Rovigno, Pola and Lussinpiccolo.
2. Fiume, Portoré and Segna.
3. Zara, Spalato, Ragusa and Megline.

These include the minor fishing places, such as Grado, Monfalcone, Muggia, Isola, Capo d'Istria, Umago, Parenzo, Orsero, Sansego, Lésina, Lissa, Lagosta, Macarsca, Trappano and Gravosa; also Buccari, Selce, Segna, &c.

The sponge fisheries are carried on almost exclusively in the vicinity of the island of Crapano, and the coral fisheries near the island of Zlarin, both in the neighbourhood of Sebenico.

The waters washing the counties of GORIZIA (Görz) and GRADISCA, to the north-west of Trieste, are very rich in fish, especially Grado and the neighbouring islands: pilchard and mackerel are prevalent in summer. According to a convention of 1869 with the Italian Government, the fishermen of Grado, on the Austrian side of the frontier, were accorded the right to fish within a mile of the shore, along the Italian coast, within the jurisdiction of the *Commune* of Marano.

The TRIESTE district comprises the Vallone di Muggia and Capo d'Istria. These waters are at all times well supplied with grey mullet, basse, gobies, and in summer with mackerel, pilchard, anchovy, and species of *Mœna* (chiefly *M. vulgaris;* Ital., *Menole*).[1] One-sixth of the local demand is supplied by the Italian trawlers.

The market is daily supplied with large quantities of fish from the Istrian coast, Fiume, and the Quarnero.

ISOLA, PIRANO.—The waters lying between these two places team with pilchard, anchovy, and *Mendole*, these being the most profitable fisheries.

The communal fishermen supply large quantities of grey mullet and basse, most of which are sent fresh to the Trieste market.

The pilchards (sardines of commerce) are sent to the curing establishments of Capo d'Istria, Duino, and Grado : about half of these are supplied by the Italian fishermen (Chioggiotti), and there is little variation in the yield from one season to another.

From Pirano to SALVORE *Mendole* predominates ; also large quantities of mussels, chiefly the arch-mussels, are caught, and, in the open sea, the sole.

The same species occur between UMAGO and DAÏLA, but less anchovies, besides the red mullet and the famous gilt-head.

CITTANUOVA and the mouths of the Quieto river is an important fishing

---

[1] *Mœna vulgaris* has been caught on the British coast ; Couch calls it by its French name "Mendole"; see Couch's "British Fishes," vol. i. page 206.

ground for red and grey mullet, basse, mackerel, pilchard, the gilt-head, and the red or Spanish sea-bream.

PARENZO.—The best fishing waters are off Punta del Dente. Red and grey mullet, basse, gilt-head, red sea-bream, pilchard, soles, both caught in large quantities, and crabs abound; the pilchards are salted and sent to Venice; the common fish, and half the "prime," are consumed on the spot. Excess of "prime" is sent to Trieste.

The channel of LEME furnishes large quantities of grey mullet and basse.

ROVIGNO.—Same character as Parenzo. The Chioggiotti contribute one-fourth of the local consumption.

FASANA.—Similar in character, but more red mullet and scorpions.

POLA is the best district in Istria for the tunny; otherwise, the character is similar to the foregoing. The waters lying between the Brioni Islands and Cape Promontore are favourable for the pilchard fisheries, which are carried on mostly by Italian fishermen; by the Chioggiotti with their trawling-nets (*cocchia*), and *Romagnuoli* (people of Romagna) with their seine-nets (*tratte*). The greater part of the yield is consumed of late years at Pola, where prices range high. The excess of pilchard is salted and exported, sometimes as much as half of the total catch; the excess of fresh tunny is also sent to Trieste and the Italian coast. The Italian fishermen furnish two-fifths of the market supply.

The number of fishermen has much increased of late years, and their profits do not seem to have decreased in the aggregate, owing to the large demand at Pola, and consequent high range of prices.[1]

In addition to the species of fishes hitherto mentioned, the Istrian fisheries yield the conger-eel, gar-pike, the *Oblata melanura*, the black bream, the *Box salpa*, the pelamid, the angel-fish, &c., besides lobsters, sea-spiders, a few oysters, mussels, and the *Squilla mantis*, &c., &c.

LUSSINPICCOLO, including the islands of the Quarnero, is much frequented by the Chioggiotti; the prevalent fishes are *Mendole, Maride* (species

---

[1] Pola is now a town of 20,000 inhabitants, having risen to being what it is since 1856, when it was a fishing village of 600 inhabitants.

TONNÁRA DI PRELUCA.

of *Smaris*), which belong to the "offal" class of fish, being only consumed by the poor. In May, June, July, they engage in the pilchard fisheries off Sansego, which are often very important.

The local fishermen compete in fishing the "prime" fishes, the excess of which is sent to Pola and Trieste. The Italian boats contribute one-eighth of the supply of fish which is sold on the spot.

Tunny fisheries (*Tonnare*) at Preluca[1] (district Volosca, Istria), at the northernmost head of the Gulf of Fiume, and at Castelmuschio, on the island of Veglia (the former communal, the latter private).

FIUME AND THE HUNGARIAN-CROATIAN LITTORAL.—The principal summer fisheries comprise the tunny, mackerel, pelamid, pilchard, and whiting, and are carried on chiefly by the native fishermen (called *Kirzi* or *Ghirzi*), who are of the poorest, their stock-in-trade being of the most primitive kind.

The chief produce of the trawling-nets, which are worked by the Chioggiotti all over the Gulf of Quarnero from September till May, is the hake, whiting, poor (or capelan), most of the flat fish—chiefly the sole—several rays and small sharks, the angler or fishing-frog, and last, not least, the famous *Scampo*, or Norway lobster; red and grey mullets, the basse, and the cephalopods, such as the cuttle-fish, poulp, and squid, are common, more or less, all the year round. The pilchard fisheries of Selce in the Canale della Morlacca yield on an average 75 tons.

Plate I. shows the situation of the fifteen *Tonnare* on the coast, the number of nets belonging to each, their value, and the number of fishermen employed. The principal ones are those of Buccari, Buccarica, San Giacomo, Voz, and Peschera, each of which has two or three nets; the remaining ten have only one net. The value of each net is 600 florins. They are all farmed out for a period of five years to the same farmer for 25,000 florins, say, 5,000 florins per annum, and he has to supply the fish to the various *Communes* at a fixed rate, say, 25 soldi (fivepence) per kilo. The season lasts from the middle of April to the end of September, and is best in April and May, and in August and September. The weight of tunny-

---

[1] See Plate XII.

fish varies from 3 to 300 kilos a head, and the average may be 6 to 8 kilos: fishes of 150 to 200 kilos are not uncommon, beyond 200 kilos they are rare.

The fish is sent on at once to Fiume, and what is in excess of the demand goes by rail to Trieste, and by water to Venice, in which traffic five Italian boats are constantly employed. Fresh tunny-fish is not consumed inland, but it is preserved in oil for the inland markets, and also for export. The tunny fisheries would be much more productive if salt were used for preserving the catch. The fish which is sent to Trieste and Venice, when there is an excess, generally arrives in a state unfit for food, and has to be destroyed; thus, the excess beyond the local demand cannot be reckoned upon with any certainty as a profit to the farmers. The annual catch averages 125 tons, of which 40 tons are exported. The Italian fishermen have no share in the tunny fisheries, but the deep-sea fisheries are, so to say, a monopoly of theirs. They supply one-third of the local demand.

COAST AND ISLANDS NEAR ZARA.—These waters abound in pilchard, mackerel, and grey mullet; the Chioggiotti contribute a quarter of the market supply. About a quarter of the catch is exported, chiefly tunny, pelamid, pilchard, and crustaceans. Oysters are caught along the coast of San Cassano and on the *Scogli* Ostia and Galisniac. The average annual yield is: Tunny 140 tons, pelamid 45 tons, mackerel and Spanish mackerel 75 tons, dentex 44 tons, *Mendole* 200 tons, and oysters 30 mille.

SEBENICO.—The best fishing grounds are the channel and harbour, which team with tunny, pelamid, the famous dentex (known here by the name of *Dentale della corona*), and pilchard off the island of Zuri. The annual average yield of the tunny fisheries is 43 tons.

Fresh tunny and salted pilchard are exported hence to Trieste, Venice, Chioggia, Ancona, &c. The Italian fishermen are not met with here, not being allowed to trawl. The *Teredo navalis* is the curse of these waters.

SPALATO.—This district is the most favourable of all on this coast, owing to its special configuration being rocky, and cut up by innumerable channels and bays. Unfortunately, the fisheries suffer from the want of proper organisation and supervision, and an utter want of economy tends to diminish the large profits which otherwise could not fail to accrue. The

Diagram *of the* Tonnare *in the* Quarnero, *showing their situation, the number and value of nets & the number of fishermen employed.*

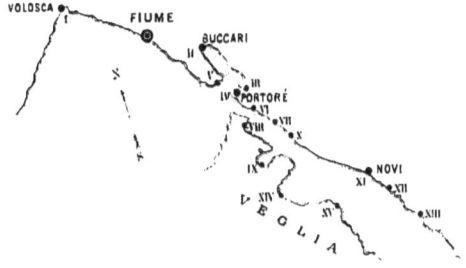

	Place	Number of Nets.	Value	Number of fishermen employed.
I	PRELUCA	1	fl. 600	8
II	BUCCARI	2	1100	16
III	BUCCARICA	3 (+1)	1900	34
IV	PORTORÉ	1	600	8
V	SERSTICE	1	600	8
VI	DUBNO	1	600	8
VII	S. GIACOMO	2	1100	16
VIII	VOZ	2	1300	16
IX	PESCHERA	3	2000	24
X	KACIAK	1	500	8
XI	NOVI	1	600	8
XII	SELCE	1	600	9
XIII	ZRNOVNICE	1	600	8
XIV	SILO	1	600	8
XV	VRBENICO	1	600	8
			Total 13000 *florins*	186 *fishermen*

pilchard fishery is the only one which is carried on with some degree of energy by the inhabitants of the coast, owing to the large gains it often brings. The waters off Lissa, Lésina, and Scoglio Sant' Andrea, furnish the best hauls; next in importance are the channels of Traü, Spalato, and off the islands of Brazza and Macarsca.

Grey mullet is caught in masses at the mouths of the river Narenta, and tunny in the channel of the same name. Besides these, mackerel, the Spanish mackerel, anchovy, *Lichia*, pelamid, basse, turbot, and *Smaris*—the latter species being most prevalent at the mouths of the rivers Narenta, Zermagna, Kerka, Cetina, Giadro, and Ombla. Ostriculture might be cultivated here to advantage, as also sponge fisheries, but both are unknown.

One-third of the produce of the fisheries, consisting principally of salted pilchards and fresh tunny, is exported to Trieste, Venice, Ancona, Bari, and even to Greece.

The produce of the sardine fisheries varies from year to year. More than half is caught by the Chioggiotti, but they only supply five per cent. of the local demand.

COAST AND ISLANDS OFF RAGUSA.—These waters team with fish; those species which frequent rocky ground and calm waters abound in the channels of Calamotta, Meleda, and Stagno. In Meleda there is a salt lake containing an abundance of fish, but it is little fished, owing to its distance from Ragusa. Oysters and other mollusks are reared in the Bay of Stagno, where sweet springs temper the salt water; sardines are here the produce of the chief fisheries, *Smaris* come next in order; the first are shoals in passage, the second are indigenous. Sardines are fished all along the coast from Budua to the extremity of the island of Curzola; the best fishing grounds are the channel of Cattaro, Ragusavecchia, le Bocche False, and between Curzola and Pelagosa.

The larger sardine (pilchard) is fished in the open sea, whereas the smaller kinds frequent the channels and sheltered waters: the smallest species (*Clupea papalina* or *sardelline*) is caught chiefly near Stagno and the Narenta. When the yield is good, the sardine fisheries are the chief source of livelihood to the inhabitants of Ragusavecchia (old "Epidaurus"), Calamotta, Mezzo, Giuppana, and Trappano. Smaris is taken in large quantities at Curzola;

the fish next in order of importance are mackerel, Spanish mackerel, pelamid, tunny, rays, &c. Tunny is caught in the channel of Cattaro, off Ragusa-vecchia, in the Valle di Brenno, and above all in the Bocche False; these fisheries belong to Government, who farm them out. The oyster fisheries at Stagno belong to the *Commune* of that place, and are farmed out for twenty years at a time, in order that they may be worked on principles of economy.

The Italian fishermen are not tolerated on this coast by the native fishermen. The consequence is that the fish markets of Ragusa, Cattaro, and other places are badly stocked with *prime* fish, as the native fishermen enjoy a kind of monopoly, and do not find it worth their while to engage in any other than the principal fisheries above cited: moreover, the deep-sea fish, caught by the Italian trawling-nets, are, as a rule, quite wanting, and fish often fetch fancy prices in consequence. It is surprising how a whole population can allow itself to be so treated by a greedy *camora*, particularly as the remedy is in their own hands.

Three-quarters of the yield are exported in the shape of salt fish, comprising tunny, pilchard, and other fishes; two-thirds of which is sent to Greece and one-third to Italy. The average export of salt sardines amounts to about 10,000 barrels of 1 cwt. a piece, representing a value of about £10,000.

The principal fisheries of Dalmatia are carried on by the inhabitants of the islands of Zuri, Lissa, Brazza, Lésina, Lagosta, and more especially by those of Lissa and Lésina. The fishermen of Lésina, alone of their class in the whole Empire, extend their operations beyond the limits of their native waters. They carry on the pilchard fisheries with drift-nets on the coast of Africa; thirty-four boats are at present engaged in these fisheries, and each boat carries twenty-four pieces (*spedoni*) of drift-net, each measuring eight fathoms in depth, and ten fathoms in length. The catch averages about 10,000 barrels, which find a market in Italy and the Levant.

SEASON OF FISHING.

Fishing is carried on, more or less, all the year round, with the exception of the height of summer, when the catch is small, and is chiefly limited to line-fishing for mackerel and whiting.

The Italian boats make their appearance on the eastern shores at about the end of August, and begin to take their departure in April, and it is only during their presence (where they are tolerated) that the markets are well stocked; in other seasons the produce of the trawl-nets is entirely wanting.

When the North-Easter (*Bora*), or the South-Easter (*Scirocco*), is blowing a gale, or during calms in the height of summer, and after Sundays and holidays, the markets are mostly empty, and the time thus lost may be set down at four months in the year.

The fishing is carried on chiefly in the day-time, by preference at dawn or at sun-set, and also by night, either with or without the aid of artificial lights. The Italians get through a great deal of fishing on moonlight nights, which are more favourable for catching the *Scampi* than dark nights, the proportion being, it is said, as 5 to 2.

PRODUCE.—PISCES.

The SHARK tribe has become much more numerous in the Adriatic of late years, probably owing to the opening of the Suez Canal, some say in consequence of the naval battle of Lissa in 1866, having been attracted by the smell of the decomposing bodies.

The smaller ground Sharks are numerous and common all along the shores of the Adriatic, and constantly furnish the markets with food for the lower classes, the spiny Dog-fish (*Acanthias*) being the most valued, then the Smooth-hound (*Mustelus*), the spotted Dog-fish (*Scyllium*), the Angel-fish (*Rhinidæ*), and lastly the Tope (*Galeus*).

The larger Sharks of the Pelagic order, which are caught occasionally, such as the Blue Shark (*Carcharias*), the hammer-headed Shark (*Zygæna*), the Porbeagle (*Lamna*), the Fox (*Alopias*), the Notidanus, and other still larger Sharks, which occur quite accidentally in these waters, are eaten only by the poorest classes; they are too uncommon to be of any use for the extraction of the oil on a large scale, or for the sale of their fins, as in India and

China. The skins of the Tope, the Spotted Dog-fishes, and Angel-fishes are dried and preserved and used as elsewhere, for polishing purposes in domestic households and by cabinet-makers. The Tope and spiny Dog-fish are very troublesome to the fishermen; they bite through the nets and steal the fishes, or watch for hooked fish, biting through the lines. The Fox follows the shoals of pilchards, the Blue Shark is found in chase of tunny.

The RAYS are mostly the inhabitants of the loam-beds, or the muddy bottom near the mouths of rivers. They are mostly caught by means of the Italian trawling-nets (*cocchia*). They are all more or less eaten by the poor. The Thornback (*Rasa spinosa*) and Raja miraletus (*Quattrocchi*) are the best of the kind and belong to Class No. 2; the rest must be classed as No. 3, although the flesh of some—such as the Sting-rays and Devil-fishes—is so indifferent as to be eaten only by the poorest classes. The Electric-rays are sometimes caught in large quantities, dried, and shipped to the Levant. The Sting-rays (*Trigonidæ*) and Devil-fishes (*Myliobatidæ*) attain to great size and weight; some are mentioned of 1,250 lb. weight and 20 feet length. The tail of the Sting-ray is furnished with a weapon, whose wound is much feared by the fishermen, and the tail is generally cut off when the fish is brought to market.

The STURGEONS are represented in the Adriatic by seven species, four of which are absolutely distinct, whereas the other three are held by many to be mere varieties of one or more of the other species, without being able to lay claim to a distinct identity. They frequent the western head of the Gulfs of Venice and Trieste, near the estuaries of the principal rivers, such as the Po, Tagliamento, Livenza, Piave, Brenta, Adige and Bacchiglione, which they ascend in spring to spawn. They are seldom found on the eastern shores of the gulf, where there are no important rivers.

The common Sturgeon (*Acipenser sturio*) does not attain to the high state of development met with elsewhere, and seldom exceeds 5 or 6 feet in length. Its flesh is far superior to that of the other species and, being much esteemed in the markets of Venice and Trieste, it is one of the dearest fishes on the Dalmatian coast. It is occasionally, but rarely, caught in the Quarnero. The Adriatic Sturgeon (*A. naccarii*, Bp.) is smaller in size, the average length being 3 feet, although sometimes attaining to as much as 5 feet in length; the flesh is far inferior to the foregoing.

A. nardoi (*Heck.*), *A. nasus* (*Heck.*), and *A. Heckelii* (*Fitz.*), are held by many authorities to be mere varieties of the foregoing species: they are caught under similar circumstances, either in the Venetian lagoons or in the rivers, and are brought to market as one and the same kind under the name of *Côpese* at Venice and *Sporzella* at Trieste. The Huso (*Ladano* at Venice) is but occasionally caught at Venice, and in the river Po; it attains to a length of 7 feet and a weight of 100 lb. *Acipenser stellatus* (*Pall.*) is reported as having been caught in one instance in Zara waters.

Of the PERCH tribe the most important, as regards its prevalence and the excellence of its flesh as food, is the Basse (*Labrax lupus*)[1]; it is common, more or less, at all seasons, and attains to a size of as much as 3 feet in length and 20 lb. in weight. It is generally found close to the shore and in brackish waters, and is caught by net, line, and prong; and it never enters fresh water. The adult is best in April, the young in November; it is reared in the fish-ponds (*valli*) of the lagoons.

The Sea-perches (*Serranina*) are represented by seven species, of which four belong to the genus *Serranus* (Sea-perches proper); none are of importance, the more prevalent kinds having little value as food. The two common are *S. hepatus*, which is sold amongst the *Minutaja* (mixed fish), with other small fish of little value, and the *S. scriba*, which belongs to class No. 2; the latter frequents shallow rocks on sheltered shores.

Anthias sacer is a very rare species, of little or no value as food, which has been caught on the Dalmatian coast south of Lissa; Dr. Günther mentions that, according to Aristotle, the fishers of sponges called this fish sacred, because no voracious fishes came to the places which it frequented, and the diver might descend with safety.

---

[1] Termed "Lupus" by the Romans, on account of its voracity; by the Greeks it was so highly esteemed that Archestratus called it "Offspring of the Gods"; they attributed to it a tender regard for its own safety; and Aristotle says that it is the most cunning of fishes, and that, when surrounded by the net, it digs for itself a channel of escape through the sand.—GÜNTHER.

The smooth Serranus (*S. cabrilla*), a British species, is also found on the Dalmatian coast, where it goes by the name of *Pirka;* it frequents the high seas, and approaches the shore only in spring to spawn: its flesh is inferior to that of the *S. scriba*.

The dusky Serranus (*S. gigas*) is an Atlantic species, rarely met with in the Adriatic, and is evidently accustomed to colder climes. It is occasionally met with in deep water, in small shoals, where it eagerly seeks the shade alongside any craft, and is so unwilling to quit its quarters that it is easily caught with a hand-net. It is known in the Adriatic by the name of *Cherna*, or *Chierna* (pronounced *Kerna*, *Kierna*), a word probably borrowed from the Stone-basse (*Polyprion cernium*), which is known as *Cherne* by the Portuguese (pronounced *Shareny*); *Chernotte* at Madeira,[1] and *Cernio* at Nice; thus, at Naples, both are called *Cernia*, the former *Cernia di scoglio*, the latter *Cernia de funnale;* and, indeed, the confusion of the two is easily explained by the close resemblance of their habits, if not so much of their form, as the *Polyprion cernium*, or Stone-basse, has the same attributes, accompanying floating wood, whence it has been called the wreck-fish. The latter is known here and at Trieste, under the name of *Scarpena salvatica*, in Venice *Scarpena de sasso*, owing to the resemblance of its dorsals with those of the common Scorpions, with which it is generally sold as one and the same species. At Spalato it appears to be common in deep water and over rocky bottoms. The flesh of both the dusky Serranus and the Stone-basse is much prized, and, next to the common Basse, is the best of their kind.

Apogon imberbis (L.) is a species not unfrequently met with in Dalmatia, especially in winter; in other waters it is rare.

The group *Pristipomatidæ* furnishes the Dentex, or toothed Gilt-head (*Dentex vulgaris*), which holds the first rank amongst the "prime" class of edible fishes of these seas. It attains to great size and development, specimens of 2–2½ feet in length and 15–20 lb. in weight not being uncommon. It abounds more or less all the year round, more especially in autumn. An

---

[1] See Yarrell's "British Fishes," 3rd ed., vol. ii. p. 127.

VOLOSCA HARBOUR

abnormity of this species (*Dentex gibbosus*, Cocco) is common at Sebenico, where it is known by the name of *Dentale della Corona*, and is held in particular esteem all along the coast. Two other species of *Dentex* have been fished in Dalmatian waters, but they have only a scientific interest.

Three species of *Mæna* and four species of *Smaris* belong to the same group, and their flesh is so inferior in quality as food, that it is a common mode of derision at Venice to accuse a person of eating this class of fish (*Magna menole!—i.e.*, he eats *Menole!*). They are sometimes caught in large quantities by the Italian trawling-nets, and furnish cheap food for the poorest class of the population of the coast; the surplus is salted, and forms an article of export to Greece and the Levant. One species (*Smaris vulgaris*) is reared in the fish-ponds (*valli*) of the lagoons.

RED MULLET is common in most seasons, and the yield of the fisheries is worth £12,000 a year; the larger species (*M. surmuletus*) attains to a weight of from 2 to 3 lb., and is known by the name of *Triglia*, because, according to the ancients, it was reputed to spawn three times a year. The specific difference of the two kinds is not established, and Dr. Günther holds, with Gronovius, that they form only one species, *M. surmuletus* being probably the female. The Romans prized it above any other fish, and paid its weight in silver. Even to this day it ranks amongst the most delicate of the edible fishes.

The genus is commonly known as *Pesce rosso*, and is caught with the trammel; and both species are reared in the artificial ponds in the lagoons of Venice. At Naples three species are distinguished; they are known by the names of *Triglia saponara*, of a pale reddish hue, frequenting sandy bottoms, far from rocks; *Triglia di fango*, of a pale, fleshy colour, only the head being bright red, and frequenting, as the name implies, muddy bottoms; and *Triglia di aurito*, of a brown colour, frequenting the beds overgrown with *algæ* (see Canestrini, " Fauna d'Italia," parte terza, p. 80). At Spalato, a variety is distinguished by the name of *Sgrïcnice*, which is applied to them for the reason that they rise to the surface, twisting and wriggling their bodies in the shape of a semicircle, thus remaining for a certain time, then straightening themselves up again, and then recommencing the contortion of their bodies; the fishermen consider them a distinct species (see "Kolombatović"). These are, however, apparently mere varieties of colouring, due to the conditions of the beds they frequent, as fishes are known to assimilate themselves in colour and otherwise to the surrounding circumstances (see Günther, "On the Variation of Colour—an Introduction to the Study of Fishes," page 183).

The family of SEA-BREAMS (*Sparidæ*) furnishes twenty different species, three of which are much valued for the excellence of their flesh. These are the Gilt-head (*Chrysophrys aurata*[1]), the red or Spanish Sea-bream (*Pagellus erythrinus*), and the Braize, or Becker (*Pagrus vulgaris*), which, together with the basse, dentex, and red mullet, are the fishes which hold the foremost rank amongst the class of "prime," or *Pesce nobile*, a term whose signification varies considerably according to locality, and is to a great extent arbitrary as regards a number of fishes which are often included in the denomination. The group *Cantharina* comprises three specimens of *Cantharus*, amongst which are the Black Sea-bream, a British species, which is not uncommon in winter, and *C. orbicularis*, the best of the genus. *Box vulgaris* is the better of the two Bogues, although neither are much valued as food; *Oblata melanura* is a better class of fish, as are also the three more common species of *Sargina*. *Charax puntazzo*, known as *Pesce morti*, on account of its stripes, is little valued.

Of the group *Pagrina*, the Gilt-head is the most important. These fish are caught with a line in summer, and in winter they are encircled by a net at night-time and then pronged individually, artificial illumination being used to keep them from effecting their escape underneath the net, as they are wont

---

[1] *Aurata* was the Latin name; and the Greeks called it *Chrysophrys* (*i.e.*, "golden eyebrow"), in allusion to the brilliant spot of gold which it bears between its eyes. According to Columella, the *Aurata* was among the number of fishes brought up by the Romans in their *vivaria*; and the inventor of those *vivaria*, one Sergius Orata, is supposed to have derived his name from this fish. It is said to grow extremely fat in artificial ponds. Duhamel states that it stirs up the sand with its tail, so as to discover the shell-fish concealed in it. It is extremely fond of mussels, and its near presence is sometimes ascertained by the noise it makes in breaking their shells with its teeth (see Günther, "Introduction to the Study of Fishes," p. 409).

to do. By this means, many hundred are sometimes caught at a time, and not a single one attempts to escape. The Gilt-head is one of the fish which is reared in the artificial ponds (*valli chiuse*) of the Venetian lagoons, and attains to a size of 2½ feet in length and 20 lb. in weight.

The genus *Pagrus* is too scarce to be of much importance; but the red, or Spanish Sea-bream (*Pagellus erythrinus*) is both common and much valued as food. *P. mormyrus* is not uncommon, but inferior in quality to the foregoing species.

The SCORPION family is represented by three species. One is the *Sebastes imperialis*, a rare kind inhabiting deep waters; and the other two belong to the genus *Scorpæna*, of which *S. scrofa* is the larger, attaining to as much as 4 lb. in weight, whereas *S. porcus* seldom exceeds 2 lb. They are shore-fishes inhabiting the beds, and the latter generally appear in shoals; their name is due to the prickly nature of their dorsal fins, with which they are apt to inflict painful stings, causing inflammation, if one is not careful in handling them when alive. The gall of this fish is used as a remedy for its sting; they are generally caught by means of the trammel-net or shore-seine, and belong to the second class of fish.

Of the MEAGRE family, the Umbrina holds the first rank; it frequents brackish waters, and is reared in the ponds (*valli*) of the Venetian lagoons; it attains to 3 feet in length and 20 lb. in weight, as does also the Meagre proper (*Sciæna aquila*), a species which is, however, by no means common in these waters; the latter also frequents the mouths of rivers and brackish waters, and makes a noise, or grunts, when taken out of the water, similar to the gurnards. *Corvina nigra* is the third species of this tribe; it frequents the stony beds, where it deposits its spawn; hence it is called *di sasso*, or *di scoglio*. The flesh of all three kinds is much esteemed.

SWORD-FISHES belong rather to the exception in the Adriatic, although common in Sicilian waters, where the fisheries constitute an important industry,[1] their flesh selling as well as that of the tunny; they are some-

---

[1] See "La pesca del Pesce-Spada nello Stretto di Messina." Messina: 1880.

times caught in the tunny-nets. *Histiophorus belone* is not uncommon at Spalato.

The SCABBARD-FISH is quite exceptional; a species in the Trieste Museum was caught off Zaole after a hurricane; it is a deep-sea fish, and its flesh is said to be excellent. The Hair-tail is likewise accidental; a species in the Trieste Museum was caught on the Dalmatian coast. *Thyrsites pretiosus* was found in one instance on the beach of the island of Solta (Dalmatia).

The family *Carangidæ* comprises nine species, of which the common HORSE MACKEREL and *Lichia amia* are the two most important; they are all much esteemed as food, with the exception of the Boar-fish, which is not eaten. Three species of *Lichia*, the Pilot-fish, and *Caranx dentex* are more especially prized, whereas the Horse Mackerel belongs to the second class, being inferior to the common mackerel. The Horse Mackerel is common in summer, when it migrates to these shores in company of the *Scombridæ*, or mackerel tribe; they are caught by net and line, and owe their local denomination (*Cantarini*, *Musicanti*) to the sound they emit when drawn from the water. *Caranx dentex* has been caught on the Dalmatian coast, and *Seriola Dumerilii* has been fished at Venice, Trieste, and Ragusa. The Pilot-fish is general, and, at times, not uncommon; as many as twenty have been caught at a time in the harbour of Fiume, having arrived in the company of a vessel: Prof. Kolombatović mentions an instance of one hundred having been caught at Spalato in November, 1880, under similar circumstances. From this habit of accompanying vessels and large fish, such as sharks, it has derived its name; it is the *Pompilus*[1] of the ancients, who held it sacred. *Lichia amia*[2] is not uncommon in summer; it attains to a length of upwards of 3 feet, and its flesh is much esteemed, being fully on a par with that of the tunny. The other two species of this genus, amongst which is the Derbio, a British species, are both rare: the Skipjack has been caught in Dalmatia; and the Boar-fish is very rare, and of no value.

---

[1] See "An Introduction to the Study of Fishes," by Günther, p. 444; also, Yarrell's "British Fishes," vol. ii. p. 227.

[2] It is reared in the lagoons.

JOHN DORYS are common at all seasons, and belong to the second class of fishes. Their Latin name was *Janitor*, the door-keeper, in allusion to Saint Peter; hence they have probably derived their vulgar name (*Pesce San Pietro*); the popular legend points to this fish as being the one out of whose mouth the Apostle took the tribute-money, the marks on either side of its body being supposed to be the impressions of his thumb and finger.

The family of BLACK-FISHES is of little or no value; it is represented by two species of *Stromateus*, which are common, but have little value as food, and two species of *Centrolophus*, which are rare. *Centrolophus pompilus* frequents brackish waters, the mouths of rivers, and the lagoons of Venice; it has also been caught at Trieste and in Dalmatia.

The DOLPHINS, a name which is misapplied to the genus *Coryphæna*, are rare in the gulf; two species are known, and single specimens are sometimes fished in the course of the summer; *C. pelagica* has been caught at Trieste; their flesh is not bad. Ray's Sea-bream belongs to the same family; its flesh is good, but it is too rare to be of any value in the fisheries. *Ausonia Cuvieri* is occasionally met with, but is very rare; it attains to great size, and in December, 1879, a specimen of 50 kilos weight was caught at Miramare, near Trieste. Twenty years ago one was caught at Muggia, also near Trieste; its flesh is said to be excellent. *Schedophilus Botteri* has been found in one instance off Lésina. The *Coryphænidæ* are all pelagic forms.

The MACKEREL family furnishes the chief produce of the summer fisheries, but the take is subject to great fluctuations, and it almost seems that the stream of the migrations of this tribe does not always reach the head of the Adriatic Gulf. The fishing lasts from May to September, and angling for mackerel constitutes a favourite summer sport. The Spanish mackerel is not uncommon at Spalato, but is inferior in quality to the common mackerel. *Scomber pneumatophorus* is a southern species, with an air-bladder, only occasionally met with.

The common Tunny[1] and the *Thynnus thunnina* are the chief repre-

---

[1] Its salted preparation was esteemed by the Romans under the name of *Saltamentum Sardicum*.—GÜNTHER.

sentatives of this genus in these waters, whereas the Bonito and the Germon, although occasionally met with, can hardly be taken into consideration; they are both Atlantic species, which seldom enter the Mediterranean, and the latter frequents the high seas, rarely approaching the shores. The common tunny attains to great size and weight: specimens are mentioned of 10 feet in length, and 1,000 lb. in weight, and those of 5 to 6 feet are by no means uncommon in these waters. *T. thunnina* is smaller in size, but equally good eating: the Pelamid (*Pelamis sarda*) is common on the Dalmatian coast, but is inferior to both the tunny and the mackerel as food.

The tunny fisheries of the Adriatic are much behind those of the Mediterranean in their development, and the preserving of the fish is not understood here as it is, for instance, at Genoa, Marseilles, and other places. In the Quarnero, however, large hauls are sometimes made; thus, in 1872, 40 tons were taken at one spot in the course of three days. The surplus of the Quarnero fisheries is exported in a fresh state to Trieste and Venice. The average annual value of the tunny fisheries is £15,000.

The Remora must be mentioned here, but it has no value.

The Star-gazers, thus called on account of the position of the eyes being on the upper surface of the head, are common shore-fishes, which frequent the beds in small depths amongst the stones and belong to the second class of fishes. They class under the family of WEEVERS (*Trachinidæ*), which comprises also four species of *Trachinus*, three of which are common and esteemed as food. *T. araneus*, the best of its kind, attains to as much as 4 lb. in weight, the other species being much smaller.

This genus has the same properties as the scorpions to inflict most painful wounds with its dorsal and opercular spines, which create intense inflammation and fever; and, indeed, amputation of the wounded limb has had, it is said, to be resorted to in some cases. The sting of the lesser Weever (*T. vipera*), also called the Sting-fish, or Adder-pike, is the most redoubted; hence its name. According to Dr. Günther, "no special poison-organ has been found in these fishes, but there is no doubt that the mucous secretion in the vicinity of the spines has poisonous properties. The dorsal spines, as well as the opercular spine, have a deep double groove, in which the poisonous fluid is lodged, and by which it is inoculated into the punctured wound." The white gall of the cuttle-fish is used for wounds inflicted by these fishes and the sting-ray, and, according to Costa, the fishermen of Gaëta apply the juice of the *Euphorbia titimalus* as a remedy for the sting of the Adder-pike. The spine of the operculum is generally cut off before exposure for sale.

There are two species of FISHING-FROGS, or ANGLERS, the British species *Lophius piscatorius*, and a second species *L. budegassa*, which is the smaller but the preferable of the two, and is sometimes very common at Fiume; these are amongst the most common of fishes, and are to be found in our markets all the year round, furnishing cheap food for the lower classes. They owe their name to a filament placed in the middle of the head, which terminates in a lappet, and is movable in every direction, and is used by the fish to play just in front of its wide mouth as a bait to allure fishes, which are thus caught; they inhabit the beds, and hide in the sand or amongst sea-weed.

The GURNARDS (*Triglidæ*) are little valued as food, and belong to the third class. The Sapphirine Gurnard (*Lucerna venetorum*) is the best of the genus, and owes its name (*Lucerna*) to the great phosphorescence it produces. This species, besides the streaked Gurnard, and the Piper, are the commonest of the tribe; they are not caught in sufficient quantities to be of any importance. Dr. Günther informs us that the grunting noise made by gurnards when taken out of the water is caused by the escape of gas from the air-bladder through the open pneumatic duct. There are altogether seven species of this tribe.

The *Cataphracti* furnish two species, both rare in the Adriatic, viz., the mailed Gurnard, or "Fork-fish" (*Forcato*), a name derived from its prolonged præorbitals, which project beyond the snout in the shape of a fork, and which are often broken off against the rocks: it inhabits deep water, and has been caught in the Dalmatian archipelago. The second species is the Flying Gurnard (*Dactylopterus volitans*), a species which belongs to the class generally known as Flying-fishes, which comprises the Flying-herrings (*Exocœtus*), these being the only two fishes which are enabled by their long pectoral fins to take flying leaps out of the water (Günther). They are much heavier and larger than the *Exocœti*, and have not been caught, as far as I am aware, north of Lissa (Dalmatia).

Of the family of *Discoboli*, the Lump-sucker (*Cyclopterus lumpus*) is mentioned by Nardo, amongst other fishes, as having been observed in the Dalmatian archipelago, on the authority of Botteri, Heckel, Stalio, and Belotti. This fish also appears in Perugia's list of the Trieste Museum. Dr. de Marchesetti, however, pronounces Perugia's citation altogether a mistake, and I hardly think I should be justified in including the species in the Adriatic fauna.

The family of *Gobidæ*, or GOBIES, comprises thirty species, of which six belong to the genus *Callionymus*, or Dragonets; they are all small fishes and belong to the class of *minutaja* (mixed fish), with the exception of *G. capito*, the largest of its kind. They are found, more or less, everywhere, and at all seasons, and furnish food to a great portion of the poorer classes; they are shore-fishes, frequenting, as a rule, rocky coasts. Three species frequent brackish waters, and are reared in the *valli* of the lagoons, viz., *G. jozo, elongatus* and *paganellus*, whilst three others are fresh-water fishes.

The RED BAND-FISH (*Cepola rubescens*) is common, but of little or no value.

The BLENNIES rank with the Gobies in many respects; they are shore-fishes, and some of them enter brackish waters and have become fresh-water fishes; they belong, as a rule, to the class of *minutaja* (mixed fish); the only exceptions are two species, viz., *B. gattorugine*, which attains to a length of twelve inches, and *B. ocellaris*, both British species. Two are fresh-water fishes.

The SPET (*Sphyræna vulgaris*) is one of the rare class, and has no importance in the fisheries.

The ATHERINES, to which the name of Smelt is misapplied from their resemblance to the real smelt, have little value as food; they are common in summer all over the gulf, and the young fry is sold in many sea-ports fried or baked in milk under the name of *Nonnati* (*Nonnat*[1] of the French,

---

[1] The young, for some time after they are hatched, cling together in dense masses, and in

ZOPPOLI AT BUCCARI.

Aphyes of the Ancients); they are also preserved in oil (*Anguèla marinata*). They are, however, only consumed by the poor. Being one of the few kinds of fish which spawn in the lagoons and brackish waters, their chief value is as food for the more valuable kinds of fishes which are reared in the *valli* of the lagoons. There they come under the denomination of *Pesce da strame* (*strame* = fodder). Sometimes they are caught in such quantities in the lagoons of Commacchio that whole cargoes are shipped to serve as manure. They are shore-fishes, living in large shoals, and the fry collects and ascends the rivers in shoals. Three species are known here, all are common.

The GREY MULLETS (*Mugilidæ*), known in these parts by the general term of *Cievolame*, are of great importance; there are five common species, all of which are numerous, prolific, and develope rapidly. They endure more than other kinds of fishes the rapid changes of temperature; they prefer brackish waters, and the small fry enters in multitudes the mouths of rivers, the lagoons, and the *valli chiuse;* they are, therefore, of prime importance in the fisheries of the *valli;* their roe is smoked in Dalmatia, and is known by the name of *Botarga;* it is considered a delicacy, and the produce of Tunis and Carthagena is the most renowned in the Mediterranean. In the *valli*, they come under the class of fish known as *Pesce bianco;* three species extend to British waters, and *M. chelo* is known to ascend the rivers and to live in lakes, returning to the sea for spawning. *M. labeo* is a new species for these seas which has been caught at Ragusa.

The STICKLEBACKS frequent the Venetian lagoons, and the TRUMPET-FISH (*Centriscus scolopax*) is occasionally caught, but neither of them have any value.

There are seven species of SUCK-FISHES (*Gobiesocidæ*), all small fishes exhibiting brilliant colours and not exceeding four inches in length: two are common, and belong to the class of *minutaja;* the remainder are only occasionally met with.

Lophotes cepedianus is a deep-sea fish, which only occurs quite accidentally.

---

numbers almost incredible. The inhabitants of the Mediterranean coast of France called these newly-hatched Atherines *nonnat* (unborn).—GÜNTHER.

The RIBBON-FISHES (*Trachypteridæ*) are likewise deep-sea fishes, but it has not been ascertained at what maximum depth they live: their occurrence is general in these waters, though rare; they are common in the south, for instance, at Naples, where their flesh is considered a delicacy.

Only one species of the genus *Heliastes* is known here; it is common, but little valued as food.

The WRASSES (*Labridæ*) constitute one-seventh of the Mediterranean fauna, and are, therefore, one of its chief characteristics. Twenty-one species are, more or less common to these seas: some show the most brilliant colouring, hence they derive such names as Peacock, Rainbow, Parrot, Butterfly, Damsel, &c. They do not seem to exceed a length of 12–15 inches. and are almost valueless as food, the smaller ones being thrown in amongst the *minutaja* (mixed fish). The Ballan Wrasse and the striped Wrasse, the Cork-wing and the Rainbow Wrasse, are species which extend to British waters.

The COD TRIBE (*Gadidæ*) is poorly represented in these seas; its most valuable representatives, viz., the Cod, Haddock, Coal-fish, Pollack, and the Ling, are altogether wanting. Three kinds, however, are of some importance in the fisheries on these coasts, *i.e.*, the Hake (*Merluccius vulgaris*), the Poor, or Capelan (*Gadus minutus*) and the Whiting (*Gadus merlangus*). They constitute a considerable share of the produce of the trawlers; they are also caught by means of the ground-line, and these are infinitely superior in quality to the produce of the trawls. *Gadus euxinus* and *Gadus luscus* (Bib, Pout, or Whiting-Pout) do not come into consideration, from the fact of their rarity.[1] Hake is caught all the year round, and is best eating in winter, the Poor in October. Ground-line fishing for Whiting is a favourite summer sport. The Hake attains to a length of 28 to 32 inches, and the Poor to a weight of 2 lb.; Poor and Whiting are common only in the north. Next in importance is the three-bearded Rock-ling (*Motella tricirrata*) which attains to a length of 8–12 inches, and is pretty common in summer. The two kindred species,

---

[1] *Gadus euxinus* is not rare at Spalato, where, in summer, it is more common than *G. minutus.*—KOLOMBATOVIĆ.

M. maculata and *M. mustela*, are exceptional; two species of *Phycis*, or Forked-Hake, are occasionally found in the north; they frequent deep water, and attain to a length of from 16 to 20 inches. *Lota argentea* has been met with at Trieste. The *Gadidæ* belong to the class of *Pesce bianco*, and to the better kinds of fish consumed by the lower orders known as *Pesce populo* (people's fish).

The family *Ophidiidæ* furnishes *Pteridium atrum*, four species of *Ophidium*, one of which is not uncommon; two species of *Fierasfer*, and the Sand-eel, or Launce (*Ammodytes siculus*),[1] both of which are rare. None of the species of this family have any value in the fisheries.

Macrurus cælorhyncus is a deep-sea fish, which occurs in the south of Dalmatia.

The FLAT-FISH TRIBE is represented by twenty-two species, amongst which the Turbot, Brill, and common Sole hold the first rank, the next in importance being the Italian Flounder (*Pleuronectes italicus*); the remainder are all of minor importance. They live on the bottoms, and are caught in considerable quantities by the Italian trawlers, chiefly over the sandy beds off the coast of Grado.

The Turbot seems to attain to greater size in the Adriatic than in the Mediterranean; specimens of 8–10 lb. are common, and it is said to attain to as much as 3 feet in length and 30 lb. in weight. It is best in September, and from December to February: at other seasons it is apt, when cooked, to become a mere mass of jelly. The Brill seldom exceeds 18 inches in length, 10 inches in breadth, and 2 lb. in weight: it sometimes ascends the rivers for a great distance; hence it is called "Strombutte" in North Germany. The common Sole occurs, more or less, all the year round, and is best in winter. The Italian Flounder, an Adriatic (not Mediterranean) species, likewise ascends the rivers, and is common in the brackish waters of the Venetian lagoons and the Narenta: it seldom exceeds 12 inches in length, 6 inches in breadth, and $\frac{3}{4}$ lb. in weight. The four foregoing species are all reared in the *valli*, or fish-ponds, of the lagoons. Other kinds of minor importance are common

---

[1] It is very similar to the British species *A. tobianus*, with which it is often confused.

in the Venetian lagoons, but are not reared in the *valli*, such as the Scaldfish (*Arnoglossus laterna*) and *Arnoglossus Grohmanni:* they evidently prefer brackish waters, and belong, together with the small Soles, to the class of *minutaja*. *Citharus linguátula* is common, but inferior as food. Two species of *Rhomboidichtys* are rare, and occur only on the coast of Dalmatia.

Only two specimens of the Plaice (*Pleuronectes platessa*) have been found by Professor Trois in the fish-market at Venice, said to have been caught in the Quarnero. The Soles, with the exception of the common Sole, are either rare, or have little value as food. Generally speaking, it may be said that the flat-fish caught in these seas are inferior to their brethren in more northern climes: the flesh is flaccid and less firm.

Two specimens of the family of *Scopelidæ*, which have been met with on the southern coast of Dalmatia, have no interest but from an ichthyological point of view. *Cyprinodon calaritanus* is half a fresh-water fish, for it ascends the rivers for a considerable distance : it occurs in the brackish Venetian lagoons, and in places where the sea is collected for evaporation (*saline*) and where the degree of saltness is much greater than the ordinary sea-water. Like most fish which lie imbedded in mud or frequent the muddy beds, it has no value as food.

The GAR-PIKE, caught in considerable quantities at Sansego and Lussin, is one of the fish which is reared in the *valli*. The Saury-pike occurs, quite exceptionally, on the Dalmatian coast only, and is a pelagic species, as is also the closely-allied genus of *Exocœtus*, or Flying-fishes. The latter seldom come so far north, and that only in the height of summer. The common Pike (*Esox*) has been observed in the brackish waters of the Venetian lagoons.

Of the SALMON family, five species of Trout belong to this fauna, two of which are non-migratory species of Dalmatia : *Salmo fario ausonii* is the one common on the northern shores (at Trieste and Fiume), and *Salmo carpio* occurs in the Venetian watershed. The Grayling is found in the northern and western watershed, but not on the eastern coast : the Argentine has a southern extension, and being, moreover, a deep-sea fish, it is seldom met with in the north. A specimen of *Salmo trotta* (L.) is mentioned by

Giglioli as having been caught near Spalato; this appears to be the first notice of this species in Mediterranean waters.

Of the HERRING tribe (*Clupeidæ*) the more important northern forms, such as the Herring, Sprat, and Whitebait (fry of the Herring), are not met with in these waters; but the kindred species, Pilchard, or Sardine, and *Clupea papalina*, commonly called *Papalina*, a Mediterranean species, and the Anchovy (*Engraulis encrasicholus*) are the representative species of this tribe, and form the chief staples of these fisheries.

The Anchovy is common all over the Adriatic, from May to September, and seldom occurs further north; *Clupea aurita* has occasionally been observed on the coast of Dalmatia, and is generally mistaken for the common Sardine, though its flesh is far inferior: the *Papalina* occurs under the same conditions, and is as much esteemed as the common Sardine. It attains a length of 4 inches. This species is not described by the learned ichthyologist Dr. Günther, his nearest description as applying to it being that of *C. aurita*, as synonymous with *C. phalerica* (Risso), which latter Canestrini, on his part, renders as synonymous with *C. papalina* (Bp.). Dr. de Marchesetti has been good enough to point out the difference between the illustration of Valencienne and the description of Günther, on the one hand, and the *C. papalina*, as known here, on the other hand (see SYSTEMATIC LIST OF FISHES, No. 322).

The Sardine is common all over the Adriatic from May to October, and is eaten fresh, salted, smoked, and preserved in oil, like the "Sardines de Nantes." Risso made the observation at Nice that only every fifth year was a good year for the Sardine fisheries on those coasts. Here, the fishermen consider themselves lucky if every fourth or fifth year prove a good one, but in some places a really good season is not known for seven, twelve, or fourteen years, the same being the case in respect of mackerel. The salting is carried on chiefly on the west coast of Istria, on the coast of Dalmatia (Ragusa), and the Dalmatian islands, the produce of Rovigno (Istria) and the island of Lissa being especially renowned.[1]

---

[1] See methods of curing and cooking fish.

The Sardine fisheries hold the first rank amongst the sea-fisheries of the Austrian-Hungarian coast. Their average annual value is computed at £40,000, and the value of the Anchovy fisheries at £4,000. The total value of the produce of the Sardine and Anchovy fisheries in the Mediterranean does not probably exceed £400,000; this is trifling in comparison to the Herring fisheries in the north, whose value is estimated at at least £3,000,000. In the south, the Sardine is fished sometimes in considerable quantities, even in the winter, and Professor Kolombatović mentions that in the winter of 1880 eighty barrels were cured at Spalato, besides those consumed fresh. This may also be said of the *Papalina*, which, however, appears by no means to be so common in the south.

The Allice-Shad (*C. alosa*) is said to ascend the rivers of northern Italy and to enter the lakes of Garda and Como for spawning. It appears doubtful whether this species occurs on the eastern coast, and whether it is not the inferior Twaite-Shad (*C. finta*), which is common there, and with which the former has been confused. The specimens in the Trieste Museum are all *C. finta*, and the resemblance of the two species accounts for the uncertainty on the point; in fact, many authors, amongst whom Canestrini, Valencienne, Heckel, and Kner, consider them identical.

The COMMON EEL is of prime importance in the fisheries of the lagoons on the Venetian coast and near Grado,[1] and it is pickled (*marinato*) and preserved in oil to a large extent.

Two kinds of Conger-eels are caught, the common species being much esteemed as food; they are also dried and smoked. Three species of *Ophichthys* and two species of *Muræna* (the Murry) occur occasionally, but they all have a southern extension, and seldom find their way very far north.

Some of the PIPE-FISHES are common in summer, but they have no value

---

[1] There are 173 *valli*, or breeding-ponds, on the Venetian coast, of which 63 are in the lagoons of Venice alone; they employ upwards of 1,000 fishermen, and produce upwards of 2,600 tons of fish a year; one alone—that of Comacchio—yields 1,200 tons of fish, 800 tons of which are Eels. Such results would not be possible were it not for the quantities of atherines and *Crangon vulgaris*, which serve as food for other fishes (see NETS, *Valli*).

in the fisheries; they frequent the Venetian lagoons and other brackish waters, as do also the SEA-HORSES. FILE-FISHES and SUN-FISHES are rare on these shores; they are more common in the south, and are occasionally met with in the lagoons of Venice: they have no culinary value. LAMPREYS belong rather to the exception on the eastern coast; they are more common on the western coast, and in the lagoons and watershed of Venice.

The LANCELET has been caught off the island of Lésina (Dalmatia).

MOLLUSKS.

The Mollusks, generally speaking, are much more numerous in variety than in northern waters. Some 600 species are common to the Mediterranean fauna (exclusively of nudibranchs and tunicates), whereas this number decreases to 400 in British, and to 300 in Scandinavian waters. On the other hand, the prevalence of certain of the more useful kinds, such as Oysters, *Pectinæ, Cardium, Mytilus*, &c., is not to be compared with what is found in northern waters.

CEPHALOPODS are much consumed, throughout the Adriatic and Mediterranean, by all classes of the population, although despised in the north of Europe. When caught in large quantities, they are dried and exported to the Levant, where they are in great demand by the Greek population. They are mostly caught by means of the *fiocina* (prongs), exceptionally so in nets, and sometimes in the basket-traps (*nasse*) set for fish, which they enter in pursuit of Lobsters, Conger-eels, &c.

The Squid (*Loligo vulgaris*) is the most valued of the kind, *Sepiola Rondeletii* is next best in quality. The average annual catch of the various kinds of Cephalopods is 600 tons, valued at £12,000.

OYSTERS are found mostly on rocky shores in 2–5 fathoms; on a bank to the south-west of Grado, near the estuary of the river Isonzo; on a smaller bank west of Isola, near Capo d'Istria; near Pola and Novegradi, east of Zara; along the coast of San Cassano, and on the *Scogli* Ostia and Galisniae. They occur also near Sebenico, Stagno, &c.; on the Italian coast, near Brindisi, Ancona, Punto di Maestra and Chioggia, and near the mouths of the rivers Pô, Adige, and Brenta. They are caught in the open by means of the *ostrighera;* in the lagoons with the *cassa*, or by hand; in harbours with the *fiocina a branche curve*, and on piles, dams, and rocks by the *rasparetta*, or *mezzaluna*. Three-year old oysters are the best. The annual consumption at Trieste is 10,000, @ 5 to 10 soldi a piece. The inland import is inconsiderable, as Vienna is supplied from Hamburg and Ostende. The annual yield is estimated at 70 to 80 mille, valued at £600.

Ostreoculture[1] is carried on in a most primitive manner by the fishermen of Monfalcone, Duino, Zaole, Muggia, &c. It consists in driving piles, or rather oak branches (*pali*), into the bed of the sea, in 1½-2 fathoms water. This is done in spring; and in autumn, when the spat has settled on them, they are transferred into deeper waters, there to await their development after the third season. In Dalmatia, the branches of oak are merely thrown into the water, and there allowed to remain until the oysters mature and fall off.

At Grado, the French system known as *Claires* was tried, but it proved a failure, and had to be abandoned, chiefly on account of the small tides prevalent in these waters, which accounts for the high mortality of the oysters, which perished of cold in winter and of heat in summer.

A great deal more might, no doubt, be done in the way of ostreoculture, and the Hungarian Government is anxious to promote something of the kind in the bay of Buccari. Capt. R. F. Burton, H.B.M. Consul for Trieste, has also interested himself in the matter, and has proposed a company for the purpose: Val d'Arsa, in Istria, would be a most suitable ground for carrying out the project, the more so as it is connected by rail with Vienna.

There are five different kinds of oysters common to the Adria, viz., *O. adriatica* (Lam.), (*Ostrica di palo, Ostrica dell' Adriatico*), found generally on the limestone-beds of the Adriatic, but neither in the lagoons nor in the oyster-ponds; *O. lamellosa* (Brocchi), (*Ostrica à lamelle*), a species which is reared in ponds on a large scale, attains to large dimensions, and is the most savoury of the Adriatic species; three varieties of *O. edulis* (L.), viz., *var. depressa* (Phillipi), (*Ostrica commune depressa*, vulgo *Ostrichino*), a small species

---

[1] Consult "Die Bewirthschaftung der Meeres," &c., von Anton Gareis.

SCOGLIO SAN MARCO, FROM THE ISLAND OF VEGLIA.

common to the lagoons and at Zaole, found attached to wood, and the mussels Pinna and Mytilus, and much liked on account of its savoury taste; *var. cristata* (Auct. (?) Born. (?)) (*Ostrica commune crestata*), and *var. falcata* (Chiereghin) (*Ostrica commune falcata*), both found in the lagoons, ponds, harbours, on limestone and muddy beds. The former is the only kind which occurs in the Quarnero.

The COMMON MUSSEL (*Mytilus edulis*), *Moule* of the French (*Pedocchio*, "sea-louse"),[1] is found in large quantities on piles in the Trieste Harbour; on stones near Novegradi; at Stagno, and between Grado and the mouths of the Tagliamento, in a depth of 80 feet and about nine miles from the shore; also on the rocks on the coast of Istria. This is the most valuable species after the oyster;[2] it is both well-flavoured and prolific, and well deserves to be reared as in France, viz., by collecting the spawn in artificial ponds. Mussels are caught by means of the *cassa*, or an iron hook. The annual yield is about four millions, valued at £400.

The next most important species are: *Pectinæ* (*Capa santa* and *Canestrello*), of which there are some ten different species, all more or less prized; *Cardium edule* and *rusticum* (*Capa tonda*), the latter being the most important of its genus, forming large banks in the mud of the lagoons; *Venus* (*Biberazzi, Caparoni, Caparozzoli*); *Solen* (*Capa longa*); *Pinna* (*Stura*); *Arca* (*Cofano, Mussolo*); *Pectunculus* (*Piè d'asino*); *Mactra* (*Biberon*); *Spondylus gæderopus Gaidero, Jardon*); *Modiola barbata* (*Pedocchio peloso*); *Lithodomus lithophagus* (*Dattolo di pietra*, "stone-date"); *Pholas dactylus* (*Dattolo di mar*, "sea-(date"); *Lutraria compressa* (*Loca*); *Lima inflata* (*Sorbolo di mar*), and other species of more or less value, either from a culinary point of view or as bait. Most of these are caught by the *cassa* or *ostreghera*, or by hand; the *cape longhe* by means of an iron rod with a conical knob at the end; this is passed between the shells which close upon it, and are thus drawn up. *Solen siliqua* is also called *Capa tabacchina*, on account of its taste resembling that of tobacco. The *dattoli* are especially prized in some places, but are

---

[1] So the Arabs call shrimps and prawns: *Barghût el-bahr*—sea-fleas.
[2] See "Die Bewirthschaftung des Meeres," &c., von Anton Gareis.

not consumed everywhere as food, for instance, at Ancona, although caught there in large quantities; in France they are eaten and are also used for bait. The shells of the *Cytherea chione*, L. (*Issolone*), and the *Unio pictorum* (*Unione*, or *Sbadiglia dei pittori*, vulgo *Caparone d' acqua dolce, Cucchiarella*), are used as painters' pallets; those of the *Pecten jacobæus* (L.), as ornaments by the pilgrims to S. Iago di Compostella and other places, whence the name of *Capa santa*.[1]

The UNIVALVES are very numerous on the eastern shores of the Adriatic, but are much inferior in quality to the bivalves, and are, as a rule, eaten only by the poorer classes.

Those which most deserve notice are: species of *Trochus* (*Caragolo, Neridola*); *Turbo rugosus* (*Occhio di Santa Lucia*); *Cassidaria tyrrhena* (*Porcelletta*); *Cerithium vulgatum* (*Caragolo longo, Campanari*); *Murex brandaris* (*Garusoli*), attached to the shells of which is generally found an *Actinia effœta*; *Murex trunculus* (*Garusoli*), the species which is supposed to have supplied the purple of the Romans; *Aporrhais pes pelicani* (*Zama-rugolo*); *Haliotis tuberculata* (*Orecchio di San Pietro*, "St. Peter's ear"); species of *Fissurella* and *Patella* (*Pantalena*). The shells of *Turbo rugosus* and *Trochus adriaticus* are made use of as women's ornaments (*Caragoletti da galanterie*). The NUDIBRANCHS are not eaten.

Of the TUNICATES may be mentioned *Cynthia microcosmus*, called *Sponga mangiabile* by misapplication. They are found on hard beds in open, shallow waters, generally in company of the arch shells, together with which they are usually caught from November to March by means of the *Mussolera*. After removing the outside coating, or mantle, the inside, resembling the yellow of an egg, but tasting somewhat bitter, is eaten either raw by the

---

[1] See Capt. Burton's account of the Legend of St. James, in "Camoens: his Life and his Lusiads," vol. i. p. 207. ". . . . and during the height of his (the Saint's) fame, a hundred thousand 'Saint Jaquè's pilgrims,' many of them English, who preferred it even to Canterbury and her 'holy blisful martir,' made pious visitations to 'Sanctus Jacobus Apostola' (Compostella). The cockle-shell was the badge of this tribe, as the palm was of the 'palmer,' or Jerusalem pilgrim. Our 'remember the grotto' is connected with St. James. . . . ."

fishermen themselves, or otherwise is sprinkled with flour and fried in oil. The liver is also eaten, but the outside coating, hard and indigestible, resembles the fibres of wood.

CRUSTACEANS.

Ligia italica (*Salizzoni delle rive*) does great damage in the fishing-ponds (*valli*), gnawing the fishing-nets. *Squilla mantis* (*Canocchie*) is found on muddy beds between the Istrian and Italian shores, as far as Ancona, in 4–10 fathoms water; in lesser quantities on the eastern coast of Istria, near the islands of Ulbo and Selve; otherwise it is rare. It is in season from September till March, and is caught by the Italian trawling-nets; it is much consumed in Italy, and the females, before they are in egg, are highly esteemed. The annual consumption at Trieste is 3,000 kilos @ 12–40 soldi per kilo.

The PRAWN, *Palæmon squilla* (*Gambaro*), *Salicoques* of the French, is found near the shore, in bays and creeks, on sandy and overgrown beds, in spring and autumn, and in deeper water in summer and winter, chiefly near Grado and on the Istrian coast; also near Ulbo, Selve, Novegrad, Sebenico, Spalato, Curzola, &c. It is in season all the year round, particularly in spring and autumn, and is caught with the hand-nets known as the *Cogòlo, Guatto*, and the trawls; it is also reared in the lagoons and used as bait for the basse; it is generally sprinkled with flour and fried in oil, and is also used as bait. The annual consumption at Trieste is 200 kilos @ 12–50 soldi per kilo.

The SHRIMP, *Crangon vulgaris* (*Schilla*) is caught and sold together with the *Gambari;* it is used as bait for the basse, and is fished in autumn. Those reared in the *valli* are the most prized, and fetch higher prices.

Gebia litoralis (*Corbola* or *Scardobola*) is, when alive, used as bait for the basse, the gilt-head, and the *Sargus vulgaris*, and is plentiful in the Bay of Noghera.

Calianassa subterranea (*Scardobola falsa*) is similar to the foregoing species, and is found imbedded in the sand; it is used chiefly as bait.

The celebrated NORWAY LOBSTER (*Scampo*) is limited to certain parts of the Gulf of Quarnero, about the islands of Veglia and Cherso, where the temperature of the water on the bed is low. It is in season all the year round, but is caught exclusively by the Italian trawls from September to March. Thirty thousand kilos are brought to market at Fiume, and sell at 60–250 soldi per kilo; it is exported to Trieste and the interior, also to Venice and Chioggia. At Venice the tails fetch, in times of scarcity, as much as 8 lire a kilo. The annual value of the fisheries may be given at £2,000.[1]

LOBSTERS (*Astice*) are found chiefly on the west coast of Istria, less commonly in Dalmatia, on rocky shores in 7–15 fathoms; they are caught with a trammel-net, or with a number of willow-basket traps (*Nasse, Verse*) baited with sea-spiders or sardines, &c., or by night with the prong by artificial illumination. The annual consumption at Trieste is 1,700 @ 1–5 florins each; a considerable number is also sent inland. The average catch is about 30 thousand a year, valued at £2,000; these figures include the ROCK-LOBSTER, *Palinurus vulgaris* (*Languste*), which is caught in Dalmatia from May to August, especially off the islands of Lésina, and Lissa; near Rogosnica, Sebenico, &c., as far as San Pietro, just south of the island of Lussin. It is not caught further north. As food it is inferior to the lobster. The annual consumption at Trieste is 2,000 at from 1–5 florins each, the latter price when very fine.

Dromia vulgaris (*Fachino*), of no importance and not abundant, is caught near the shore.

The SEA-SPIDER, *Maja squinado* (*Granzo* or *Granzon*, male, *Granzéola*, female), is found on rocky beds along the whole coast of Istria, especially on the west coast, near the islands of Ulbo and Selve, and as far south as the islands of Incoronata; it is less abundant further south to Ragusa. In April and May it is often met with in shoals in 2½–10 fathoms; it is in season from March to June. It is caught by the *Squænera*, *Popovnica* or *Volega* attached to a long pole, *Grampa*, *Fiocina*, and *Ganzo*. It has a good flavour, and is much used as bait for sardines, and, in some waters, for catching the

---

[1] For illustrations of the Norway Lobster and the Rock Lobster (*Palinurus vulgaris*) consult Prof. T. H. Huxley's monograph, "The Crayfish, an introduction to the study of Zoology." London: Kegan Paul, 1880.

young fry of fish destined for the fishing-ponds. The annual consumption at Trieste is 3,000 kilos @ 20-50 soldi per kilo. The fisheries yield on an average 400 thousand a year, valued at £2,200.

Maja verrucosa (*Pea*) is smaller and less frequent than the foregoing species; it is found near the shore.

Eriphia spinifrons (*Granzipóro*, male, *Poressa*, female) is found near the shore, chiefly on the west coast of Istria, on rocky beds, where crevices and fissures abound, often on breakwaters: it is in season from February till April, and is caught by the *Togna*, *Nassa*, *Ganzetto*, and *Prongs*. The annual consumption at Trieste is 500 @ 3-5 soldi a piece.

The COMMON SHORE or HARRY CRAB, *Carcinus mœnas* (*Granzo*, *Gambero*, *Spiantano* (male), *Masanetta* (female), in egg, and *Molecca*, pl. *Molecche*, with the soft shell). The *Molecche* form an important article of commerce, this being the term applied to the crab after the shedding of the skin, or cuticular layer, a process of moulting technically termed *ecdysis*, or exuviation. They are found in warm weather in shallow, brackish waters, on muddy beds, in creeks and lagoons, and often, at ebb-tide, on the damp shore; in winter they seek greater depths. They are most abundant near Grado and Venice; they are rare on the rocky shores of Istria, and still more so in the Quarnero and in Dalmatia. They are in season from April to September, *i.e.*, during the sardine fisheries. They are caught by means of a small bag and also by the hand; and in winter by the Italian trawls (*Cocchia*). Sprinkled with flour and fried in oil, the *Molecche* are considered a savoury dish; 150,000 to 200,000 sacks, each averaging 40 kilos at 80 soldi a sack, are sent from Venice to Istria for bait; further, 40,000 sacks of *Masanette*, *i.e.*, females whilst in egg, at 70 soldi a sack; whilst 80,000 to 100,000 sacks of *Molecche* are consumed inland. This is one of the most important fisheries of the lagoons, and those of Grado alone net 100,000 florins per annum.

The following kinds of crabs are rare and not eaten:—*Scyllarus latus*, *S. arctos*, both of which species appear only in Dalmatia; *Galathea strigosa*, *Numida rugosa*; species of *Pagurus* (Hermit Crabs) in the shells of *Murex* (*Bulli col granzo*); *Pagurus striatus*, in the shells of *Dolium galea*, and *Cassidaria tyrrhena*; *Pagurus varians*, in the shells of *Trochus Biasoletti*;

Calappa granulata; Cancer pagurus (Granziporo); Xantho rivolosus (Forfetula); Portunus depurator (Gambero dell' ala), found in small quantities on rocky shores ; *P. arcuatus* and *P. corrugator*, both rare, the latter found chiefly on the Dalmatian coast ; *Grapsus marmoratus (Granzo piatto)*, sometimes found on rocky beds.

Pinnotherus veterum, "the watchman of the Pinnæ" (*Granzetto dell' Ostrega*), is found in the shells of living bivalves, such as *Pinna, Mytilus, Modiola, Ostrea*, &c., in which it seeks refuge, living on the small *animalculæ* contained in the constant stream of water which flows in and out of these mollusks.

The fancy of our forefathers has attributed the status thus existing between the two species as arising from a friendly alliance based upon mutual benefits rendered, viz., protection and board afforded, on the one hand, by the mollusk, whilst the duties of the "watchman" consist, on the other hand, in giving due warning of the approach of an enemy, such as a star-fish or crab, thus enabling the host to ensure protection by closing its doors on the intruder. And these observations descend from so early a date, that we find the *pinna* and the crab amongst the early Egyptian hieroglyphs, bearing the interpretation of the duty incumbent on the "pater-familias" of duly providing for his offspring. According to Grube, the crab is also found in the respiratory cavity of *Phallusia mamillata*.

Pinnotheres pisum, a smaller species than the foregoing, lives in *Modiola* shells, sometimes as many as a whole family, consisting of one male, several females, and their offspring, all in one shell.

These kinds are generally eaten together with the mollusks.

Species of *Porcellana* are also found in the shells of mollusks.

RADIATES.

The ECHINODERMS play a very unimportant part as nourishment to man, although some species are consumed, and even regarded as delicacies, in some countries, for instance, in China, where the Sea-Slug, *Holothuria edulis*, or *Trepang*, which attains to a length of 12 inches, forms an important article of commerce. *H. tubulosa* is eaten at Naples, but only by the lowest classes; it is not eaten at all in the Adriatic.

SEA-URCHINS (*Rizzi di mare*) and STAR-FISHES (*Stelle marine*) are sometimes caught in large quantities by the trawls and seines, and the latter are generally reconsigned to the deep. This is a mistake, as they might be used as manure; besides which, they commit great ravages on the oyster-banks. The Urchins, when in egg, are eaten raw, and, on account of their greater development than in northern waters, become rather important articles of food for the lower classes in winter and spring; this is especially the case with *Echinus melo*.

In Sicily they are in season about the full moon of March, where *E. esculentus* still goes by the name of "King of Urchins," whilst the larger "Melon" Urchin (*Melon di mare*) is popularly considered to be its mother; hence its name, *Echinometra*, among the ancient naturalists. The size and abundance of these edible species is a striking peculiarity of all Mediterranean and Adriatic fish-markets.

At Trieste and Fiume the consumption is small, but they are eaten more or less along the whole coast, and the consumption increases in the south, especially on the coasts of Greece, and generally by Greek sailors, when in season. In Dalmatia they are pounded and used as bait in the basket-traps (*Nasse*), and also as a cure for diarrhœa.

E. brevispinosus and *E. lividus* are eaten at Trieste and in Istria under the name of *Rizzi di mare*; *E. melo* in Dalmatia, under the name of *Melone di mare*.

All Sea-anemones (*Actiniæ*) are edible, and are to be met with in large quantities in most French fish-markets, such as Marseilles, Cette, Bordeaux, Bayonne, &c., under the name of *cul de mulet*.

Here the green Actinia (*Actinia viridis*), *Madrona*, occasionally appears in the markets of Trieste and on the coast of Istria, where it is caught near the shore, on stony and sandy beds; it is sprinkled with flour and fried in oil.

SPONGES.[1]

According to Dr. Syrski many more than 100 different kinds are found in the Adriatic, none of which, however, have any value, commercially speaking, excepting the one species *Spongia adriatica* (*Sponga*). It appears on the coast between Budua on the one hand, and Trieste and Duino on the other, on rocky or otherwise hard beds, in 3 to 10 fathoms. The fisheries are carried on almost exclusively by the inhabitants of the island of Crapano (west of Sebenico), during calm weather, from March to October. The sponges are torn off or raised by means of prongs, or tongs; they are well pressed and washed, sometimes bleached, and exposed in bags in the sea, and once more soaked. There are 80 to 100 boats engaged in these fisheries, each manned with two men, and each boat fishes, on an average, 300 to 400 lb. a year, or together about 320 cwt., fetching from 15 to 100 florins, or an aggregate of 20,000 florins.

Three qualities are prepared for the trade; the first (*Spugne da bagno, o levantine*) comes from the islands of Incoronata and Zara vecchia, and is worth 10 florins a kilo; the second (*Spugne da cavallo, od equine*) is worth 5 florins; and the third (*Spugne Zimocca*) is worth 3 florins, and is fished on the coast of Istria. The greater part of the take is forwarded to Trieste, whereas little is sold on the Dalmatian coast.

Little or no economy is observed in the sponge fisheries. The fishermen go over the same grounds year after year, instead of taking the various grounds by rotation of four or five years, as ought to be the case, in order to allow the sponges time for their development. This want of economy is in a great part due to the customary method of fishing, which is of the most primitive character, and wasteful in the highest degree. Divers and divers' apparatus are unknown; the sponges are torn off indiscriminately, whether mature or not; a number are lost in drawing up the prongs, or tongs, and most of what is brought to the surface is more or less damaged;

---

[1] A collection of about 100 species was arranged and exhibited by MM. G. R. von Eckel at the Berlin Exhibition of Fisheries, 1880.

BRAGOZZI FISHING.

in fact, everything is left to chance, as the fishermen have little or no idea of the state of the ground they are working over; and it is, therefore, hardly surprising that the fisheries do not assume more importance.[1]

RED CORAL.

Red Coral (*Corallium rubrum*), *Corallo rosso*, is found on the Dalmatian coast from Budua as far as the island of Grossa, to the west of Zara; thence, in a lesser degree, to the islands of Unie and Cherso, in the Gulf of Quarnero, on rocky beds, in depths of 10 to 150 fathoms.[1]

The season of fishing lasts from May to September, and is carried on only in calm weather. The fishing gear is described elsewhere (see NETS).

The proceeds of the fisheries are variously estimated at 6,000 florins and 14,000 florins : exports to Genoa for about 10,000 florins, where it is valued on account of its consistence and pale red colour. Up to 1868 the coral fisheries were crown property, and were farmed out for about 1,000 florins; since 1868 they are free, but only to Austrian subjects. They are exclusively carried on by the inhabitants of the island of Zlarin, near Sebenico, by means of eight boats, each manned with a crew of five men; each boat requires in the course of the season 3 to 6 cwt. of hemp, and, in order to supply this and the necessary stores of provisions, each boat requires about 500 florins to fit out; in order to provide this, the fishermen are generally forced to sell the produce of their labour beforehand, at prices ranging from 6 to 9 florins per pound.[2] The yield of each boat varies from 80 to 100 lb. in the course of the season, say from 600 to 800 florins in value, which is very small in comparison to that in the Mediterranean.[3] The fisheries are on the decrease; only three boats were engaged in the fisheries in 1881, and the total catch was under 150 kilogrammes.

---

[1] See "Die Bewirthschaftung des Meeres," &c., von Anton Gareis.
[2] The price of coral in the market varies from 40 frs. to 70 frs. per kilo, and choice thick and pale red coral (*peau d'ange*) is worth 400 to 500 frs., and even more.
[3] The average yield of a boat on the coast of Algiers is 200 kilos.

The remarks concerning the sponge fisheries apply equally in this case; the fishing gear is primitive, and improvements introduced elsewhere have not been applied here; divers are not employed, no close time is observed, and no system prevails in respect of fishing over the same grounds only after a given rotation of years,[1]—in one word, there is a total want of economy in their practice.[2]

NOTE.—The number of distinct genera of fish and invertebrates, caught on the Austro-Hungarian coast, attained to 123 in the year 1877–1878. The different districts yielded each the following numbers, viz.: Trieste, 86; Rovigno, 70; Pola, 73; Lussinpiccolo, 66; Hungarian-Croatian littoral, 62; Zara, 66; Spalato, 101; Ragusa, 56; Megline, 38. These numbers represent only those which have a marketable value, and similar species of one and the same genus figure as one.

---

[1] For instance, in the Straits of Messina the waters are divided into ten allotments, only one of which is allowed to be fished over each year. Consult on this subject "L'Industria del Corallo in Torre del Greco," per Giov. Mazzei-Megale. Napoli: 1880.

[2] The Austrian coral fisheries are of little or no importance as compared with the fisheries of the Mediterranean. Thus the French fisheries employed, in 1855, 226 boats and 2,000 men, and yielded 2,700,000 frs. The Italian fisheries are still more important; thus, Torre del Greco, renowned for its tunny fisheries, has always carried on important coral fisheries, in which, 100 years ago, 300 boats were engaged (in 1858, 330 boats). Elba and Leghorn have likewise over 50 boats engaged in the fisheries; altogether some 900 to 1,000 boats, and 7,000 to 8,000 men are employed, and the produce amounts to at least 12 million francs.

TOPPO.

ZOPPOLO.

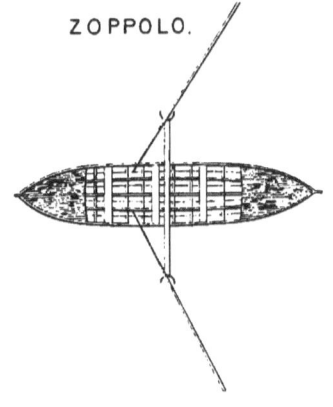

1c

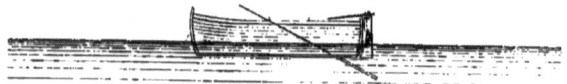

BATELLO DI MUGGIA.

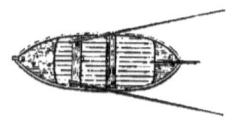

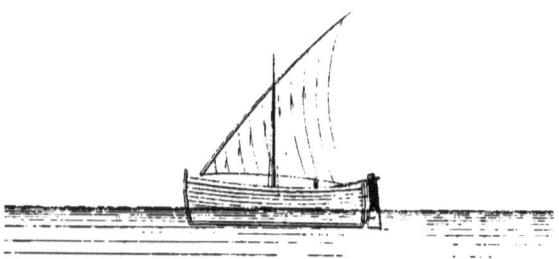

BARCA DI MUGGIA.

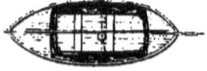

CHAPTER IV.

THE FISHING CRAFT.

Description of craft.—Value of the same.

HESE are constructed chiefly at Grado, Rovigno, Bescanova (Veglia), Traù, Milnà, and Curzola; the framework is of oak and the planking of pine.

The *Sandolo*, or *Cio*, is a small flat boat (½ to 1 ton burden), used in the lagoon fisheries and brackish waters near Grado; 6 to 8 m. in length. Crew, two to three men.

The *Zoppolo* (Croat. *Ladva, Kirska ladja*, Ital. *Nazádra*) is a rather larger boat, used by the fishermen of Monfalcone, S. Bortolo, and on the Croatian coast; it is hewn out of a single trunk, and the sides are raised by planking. In order to obviate the tendency to capsize of so narrow a craft, a broad plank (Croat. *Jaram, Igo*) 3 m. long is nailed across the boat, extending about 1 m. on either side. It serves at the same time as an outrigger, the row-locks being fixed on to the ends. Length, 4 m.[1]; breadth, 1 m.; cost, 50 fl. to 60 fl.[2] (see Plate II.).

The *Toppo* is a flat boat, 7–8 m. long, 3–4 inches draught, 1–4 tons burden, used at Venice in the lagoon fisheries, and latterly also at Zaole, near Trieste, and Muggia, for fishing with the trawl-net called *Grippo;* with a shifting mast, lug sail, and small jib sail. Crew, one to five men; cost, 100 fl. to 150 fl. (see Plate II.).

The *Guzzo* is a small rowing boat used in the Quarnero for line-fishing.

The *Batello* is a decked boat of different sizes in use on the west coast of Istria, chiefly at Rovigno, for casting the Sardine and Anchovy nets, for

---

[1] m. denotes mètres. [2] fl. denotes Austrian florins; 12 fl. = £1.

fishing with prong or line; it often has two masts and two sails; length, 5–8 m.; tonnage (*tonellata*), 1–8 tons; for three to five oars. This name is also applied to an undecked boat, from 18–36 feet long, with pointed bow and circular poop, used in the lagoon fisheries, in which two sails can be hoisted.

The *Barca, Barca di Muggia*, is a flat-bottomed, fore-decked boat, about the size of the foregoing, with one mast and lateen sail; used on the west coast of Istria, chiefly at Rovigno and Muggia, near Trieste (see Plate III.).

The *Bragagna*, or *Bragagnello*, is a deep undecked boat, 30–40 feet long, with two masts and two *spunteri*, or spars, common to the *Tartana*, to the ends of which are attached the ropes (*resta*) of the trawling-net *Tartana*; used in the lagoons, and worked by two or more men. In calm weather the boat is worked by means of a windlass (*argano*). Burden, 1–2 tons; crew, two to four men (see Plate IV.).

The *Brazzera di Capo d'Istria* is a large broad open boat now little in use, but still used at Capo d'Istria for casting the large seine-nets; with one mast and lateen sail and a flying jib. Burden, 2–3 tons; cost, 200 fl. to 400 fl. (see Plate V.).

The *Gaëta* is a partly decked boat used chiefly in Dalmatia; one mast and lateen sail, three oars; crew, three to five men; tonnage, 2–4 tons; length, 5–6 m.; breadth, 4 feet; price, 70 to 100 fl. Used for casting the Sardine drift and other nets; furnished with an iron basket (*Graticola*), for the purpose of holding fuel, which is required for artificial illumination for night fishing. The *Illuminatore* (Croat *Svićarica*) is used in the Sardine fisheries with the large seine-nets on dark, calm nights by the light of resinous pine-wood. One of the fishermen has a weighted line (*Scandaglio*), by means of which he finds out the position of the shoals, or schools, which, attracted by the light, are slowly and quietly led into a creek, encircled in the net, and drawn ashore. It is surprising how clever the men are in feeling their way about with the line, and thus divining, with a great amount of certainty, not only the exact position of the shoal, but also the class of fish, on their mere contact with the line (see Plate V.).

The *Leuto* is a decked boat, with an opening in the middle, which can be closed; one-masted, with a large lateen sail and flying jib (*flocco*); four or

BRAGAGNA.

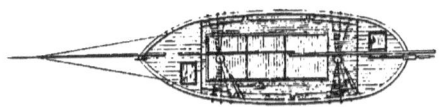

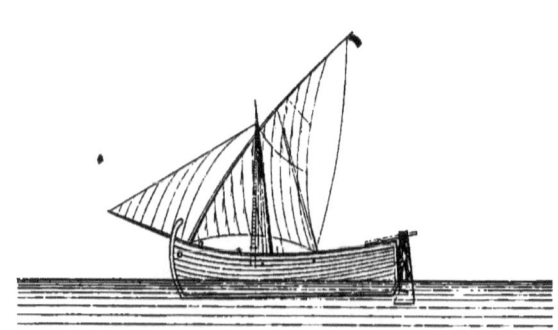

BRAZZERA DI CAPO D'ISTRIA

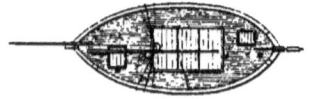

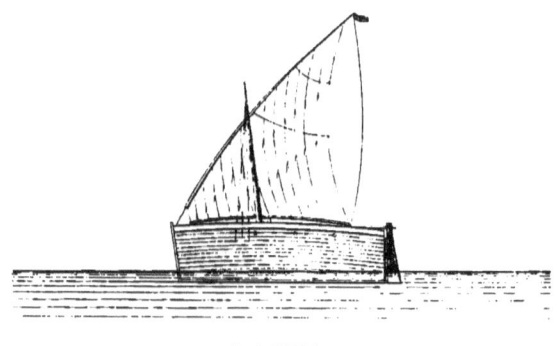

GAETA

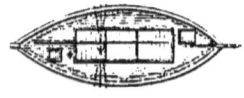

more oars ; crew, five to seven men ; 3–5 tons ; 6–8 m. long ; price, 100 fl. to 350 fl. Used in Dalmatia for the trawl and seine-nets (see Plate VI.).

The *Bragozzo*, or *Schiletto*, as it is called at Ancona, is a fore and aft decked boat, constructed at Chioggia, and used exclusively by the fishermen of that place. The undecked part is called *boccaporta*. Two masts, with *trabaccolo* sails ; foremast and sail much smaller than the main, and foremast raking considerably forward ; fore stem ornamented with polished iron stem and hawser-holes (*occhi della catena*); flat-bottomed, and rudder extending considerably beyond the bottom, to obtain stiffness. Length, 30–40 feet ; 6–10 tons burden ; crew, four to five men ; price, 350–1,000 fl. To be met with all over the Adriatic, fishing in couples, and running parallel to each other before the wind, each having one end of the trawling-net known as *cocchia* in tow ; they have great beam, and sail in the strongest *bora* which many larger vessels are afraid to face, with lowered fore-sail and treble-reefed main-sail luffing up to the wind as each successive gust strikes them. The deep rudder contributes materially to the stability of the craft, and on this, in fact, it mainly depends, as is the case with the American centre-boards ; it is so fixed to the stern-post, that, when passing in shallow water, it can be hoisted by a block fixed on the mainmast, so that it does not touch the ground (see Plate VII.).

The device carried by these boats on the top of their masts in fine weather, or when in port, is most elaborate ; it is known by the name of *Cimarol*,[1] and is fixed into the mast-head, acting as a weather-cock. It is carved out of a single piece of wood, and is divided into three fields, containing an allegorical design of some religious subject. In the specimen represented (Plate VIII.), the centre piece represents the Passion of Christ ; there is the cross, the crown, the ladder, the vinegar-vessel, &c. ; above is S. George and the dragon, and below are represented the patron saints of Chioggia (S. Felice and S. Fortunato).

The woodwork, being perforated, presents in itself no hold for the wind, and for this reason the outer edge is bordered with a piece of canvas, on

---

[1] *Cimarol*, derived from *Cima* — mast-head.

which the wind acts as on a sail; above are two turtle-doves, the messengers of peace and the emblems of constancy, with extended wings, each supporting a wind-rose; above each turtle-dove are real palm-branches, which are fixed there on Palm Sunday and renewed each year, emblematic of success; at the top is the Italian flag, held by a mariner, bearing on one side the initials of the name of the boat, and on the other side the initials of the name of the owner; the flag-staff is crowned by the cross, and the whole device is ornamented by a number of small banners, placed there as records, and probably in consequence of vows made at the time of escapes from danger. The whole device is extremely elegant, and is a novel and tasteful decoration wherever it may be seen; it gives a fair idea of the simplicity of thought, the piety and at once the ingenuity of these laborious, nerved, and frugal seamen, in their dangerous calling. The whole is balanced to a nicety, and moves easily when fanned by the slightest breeze. The foremast carries a similar, though smaller and less elaborate, device; the design varies in shape and details amongst the different craft, but the emblems are more or less common to all. They are so coloured, that they appear as of bright metal when the sun shines on them.

The *Tartane* are somewhat out of use, their number having decreased to about fifty. They likewise hail from Chioggia, but they originate from the south, and are very much more common in Sicilian waters and in the Gulf of Naples: the Spaniards have very large ones, exceeding 100 tons. They work the trawl singly (not in couples, as is the case with the *Bragozzi*), and the drag-ropes (*alzane*) are attached to two long spars (*spuntieri*, or *spouteri*), extending fore and aft, the vessel drifting broadside on. The trawling-net is also known by the same name of *Tartana*. This craft varies from 60–100 feet in length, is decked throughout, with circular bows and poop, and more beam than the *Bragozzo;* it is of 10–15 tons burden, and is worked by a crew of eight men. It has not so much spring aforehead as the *Trabaccolo*, and the helm does not extend beyond the after-steven. The rig consists of one mast raking a little forward, a very large lateen sail, a driver and jib like the *Brazzera;* it is seldom met with on the eastern coast (see Plate VI.).

The *Tartanella* is a decked shore-boat used in Dalmatia, particularly

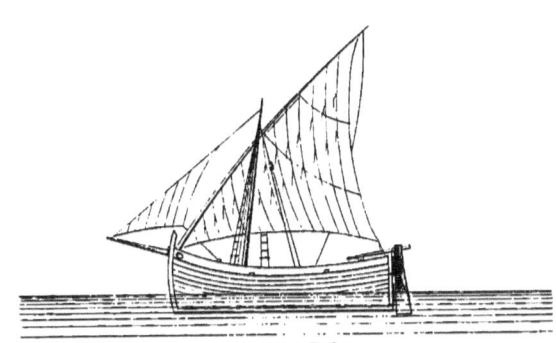

LEUTO.

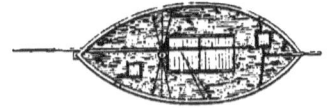

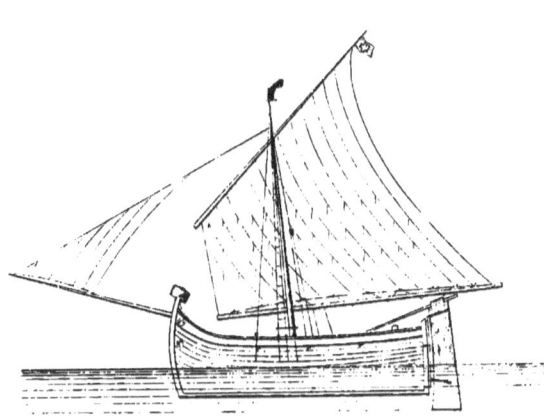

at Sebenico and the neighbouring islands; one lateen sail and jib; 2-4 tons.

The *Portellata* is similar to the *Bragozzo*, but smaller, and is generally used for carrying on the service between the trawlers, when these are actively employed, and the shore ; it is also used occasionally instead of the *Bragozzi* or *Tartane* for trawling.

The *Batelli, Tartane, Bragozzi,* and *Portellate* are all Italian boats, the first used in the lagoon fisheries and on the west coast of Istria, whereas the remainder are used in the deep-sea trawling fisheries.

Other boats peculiar to the lagoon fisheries are the *Batellazzo*, or *Sardellera*,[1] *Burchiella, Caorlina*,[2] &c.

The value of the fishing craft belonging to the Austrian-Hungarian coast represents an amount of 600,000 fl.

---

[1] Length, 9-12 m.; tonnage, 1-3 tons; crew, three to four men.
[2] Length, 9-11 m.; tonnage, 1-2 tons; crew, two to eight men.

CHAPTER V.

THE NETS.

Process of making, tanning, and mounting.—Drift-nets; Trammel-nets; Circle-nets; Seine-nets; Trawling-nets; Hand-nets.—Fish-weirs and ponds.—Snares.—Basket-traps.—Store-pots, &c.—Value of the fishing gear.

LL nets and fishing gear go by the name of *Arti*, or *Arte*. The fine nets are made of flax (*Lino*) and the coarser ones of hemp (*Canapin*, or *Grisiolo*), whilst the strongest fixed nets, such as the *Tonnare*, are made of *Canapa*, or *Trada*, and are imported from Italy. *Canapa* is the hemp in its raw state; *Trada* consists of the longest, strongest, and whitest fibres of hemp, collected after the process of combing has taken place; *Canapin* is the second quality, the fibres of which are shorter; and *Grisiolo* is the third quality, or refuse, consisting only of short fibres. The strongest twine (*tregina*) made for nets consists exclusively of *trada*, three threads or strands being twisted together; this twine is also used for fishing-lines. The smaller nets are made by the fishermen themselves and their wives, who also spin the hemp or flax for the purpose; the tanning process of home and machine-made nets is also done by them. Nets are made at Grado, Isola, Loyrana, Rovigno, Spalato, and Ragusa, or imported from Venice, Chioggia, Ancona, and more especially from Apulia.

The tanning process (*intenzer la rè*) is effected by a solution of the bark of the *Pinus maritima* (*scorza de pin mazenà*), which is ground fine and boiled in sea-water; the solution is either repeatedly poured over the net, or the net is boiled in it and then dried in the sun. The finer nets are tanned either with the branches and leaves of the *Pistacia lentiscus*, the leaves of the Shumac (*Rhus cotinus*), the myrtle (*Myrtus italica*), and the *Erica*

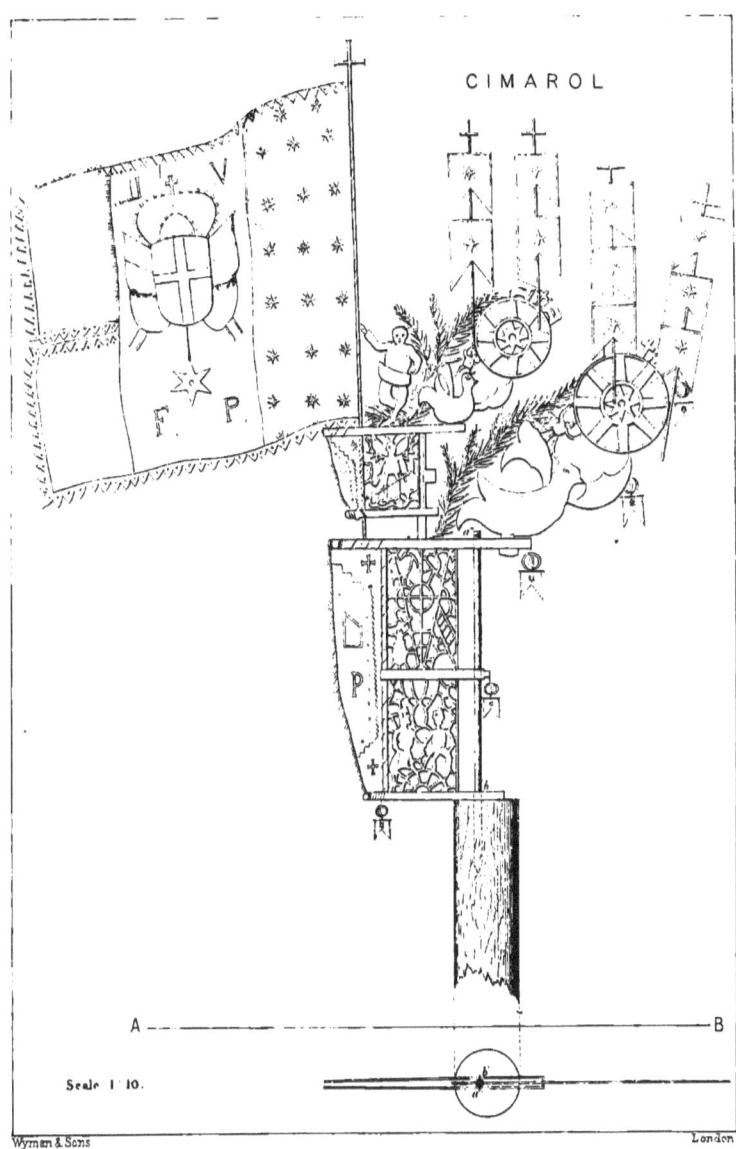

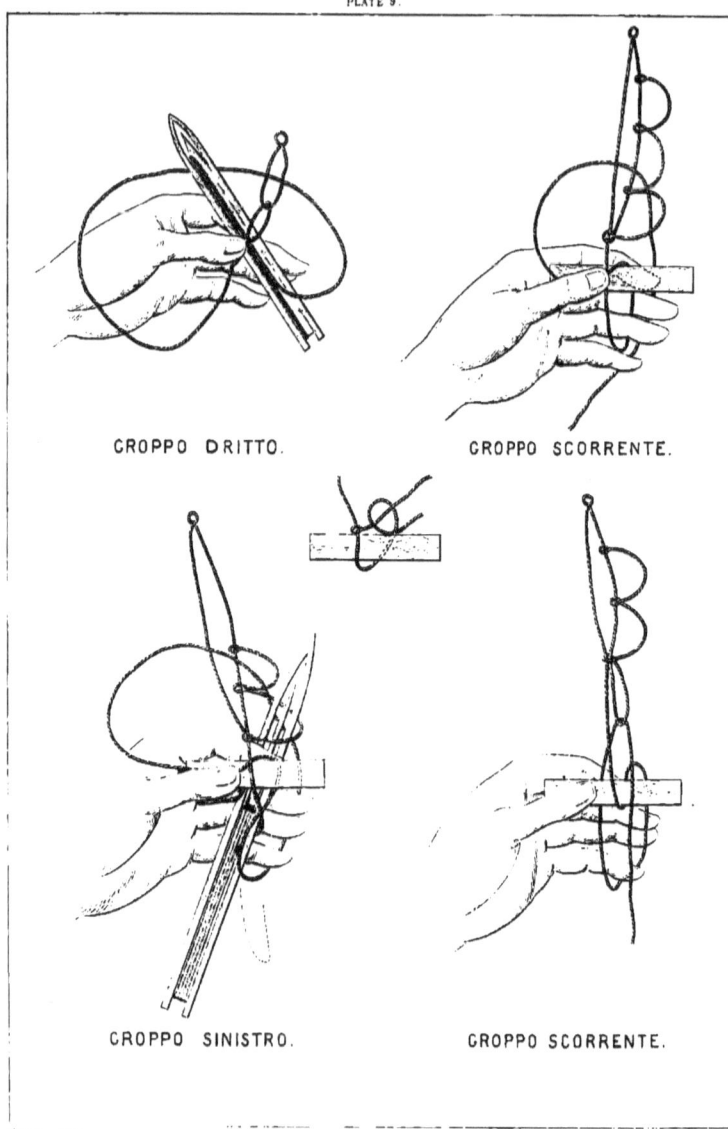

vulgaris, a species of heath, of which a solution is prepared and used in a similar manner to that described above. Nets in constant use are tanned, as a rule, once every one to three months, and last one to three years; if only occasionally used, and dried after use, the fine thread-nets last six to ten years, with the aid of trifling repairs; untanned nets are naturally less durable, but are preferable, as being less conspicuous in the water. The coarser twine nets which are tanned, and still more so those which are tarred, as is the case in the north of Dalmatia, last eight years and more.

When tanned, the nets are "mounted," *i.e.*, cut to their proper shape and size; the lower edge, "foot," or "sole" (*ima*), is then weighted with lead (*piombi*), and the "back," or uppermost part, is edged with rope, as also the "heads," or ends of the net; the back is further provided with the necessary cork floats (*corteghe*, or *sugheri*), and ropes for hauling in.

The common knots (*groppi*) in use are illustrated on Plate IX. They consist of the *groppo dritto* (right-hand knot), the *groppo sinistro* (left-hand knot), and the *groppo scorrente* (sliding-knot). The prevalent classes of meshes (*maglia*) are illustrated on Plate X.

The different kinds of nets in use may be classed as follows:—

1. DRIFT-NETS

(*Standnetze, Poste*), or *Reti da posta, d' imbrocco, da incetto*, generic terms used to designate the class of nets into which the fish enter of their own accord, or are allured by bait, or are driven in by fright, and, once embroiled in the meshes, are there held by their gills,—terms which comprise the trammel-nets. They are called also *reti semplici*, or *nude*, *i.e.* "simple," or "naked," in contradistinction to the trammel-nets, which are known as *trimagliate*, or *vestite*, *i.e.* "dressed" (see Plate X.). Foremost amongst these is the *Sardellera* (called *Voiga*, or *Budello* in Dalmatia, and *Manaida* or *Signorella* in Italy), a hanging-net consisting of one large or eight to sixteen smaller pieces (*Spedoni* or *Budelli*), joined together so as to form a long straight wall, several hundred yards long and several yards deep, the "head" being supported by floats at or near the surface, and the "foot" weighted so that the net hangs perpendicularly in the water; the "head" is mounted on a shorter length of line, so as to hang slack in the water, and to give way when the fish strike it. Four *Spedoni* joined together form what is called a *giogo*.

The net is attached at one end by a rope to a stone, and at the other end to a float, consisting either of an empty cask or of cork; it is then allowed to drift at the mercy of winds or currents.

The net is "cast," or "shot," by first casting anchor, from which spot the boat is then withdrawn to a certain distance, where the stone is sunk to which one end of the net is attached; the boat is then hauled in by the anchor-rope, whilst the net is being paid out by two men. If bait is used, as on the west coast of Istria, it is scattered about before paying out the net, and subsequently, also, in a circle round the position of the net.

If mackerel, or horse mackerel, make their appearance, they are looked upon as the forerunners of sardines; which is, however, not always the case.

The nets act as barriers for intercepting moving shoals, and the fish become meshed in their efforts to pass through, forcing their heads into the meshes, the size of mesh varying according to whether mackerel, or other fish, are to be caught, and being made so as to allow the head and gill-covers to pass through, but not so the body of the fish. When the fish has passed through beyond the gills, it is effectually caught, and there is little chance of escape, the opening of the gill-covers which enable the fish to breathe, and the act of breathing itself, causing the mesh to slip forward and catch in the gill-opening, by which action the fish is prevented from withdrawing the head.[1]

If the net is moved, and scales appear at the surface, it is a sure sign that the net has been "struck," and the net is then drawn in, commencing at one end, and by degrees, as it is drawn in, the fish are extracted and put in casks, or tubs, being at the same time sprinkled with salt.

The catch is effected most profitably just before sunrise, or just after sunset, when the net escapes the notice of the fish.

The sardine rises to the surface only in fine and moderately warm weather;

---

[1] E. W. H. Holdsworth.

RETI DA IMBROCCO SEMPLICI.

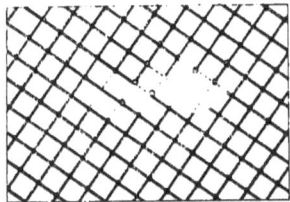
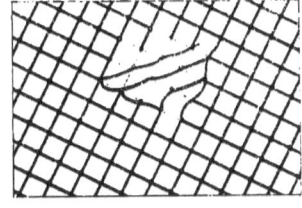

TONNARA.
PALANDARA.

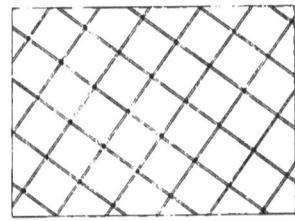
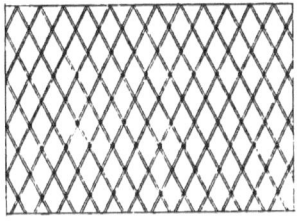

SALTARELLO.
TRIMAGLIATA.

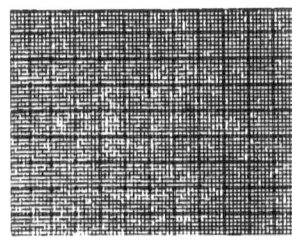

whereas the cold or heat, the wind or rain, are so many inducements for it to seek the greater depths; thus, fishing at the surface is carried on chiefly in the months of June to September. The most profitable fisheries are in June; in the cooler months of April and May, and October and November, the fishing is carried on with the same nets in deeper waters, the nets being extra weighted by means of stones.

These nets are used for mackerel, sardines, and anchovies.

On the west coast of Istria, the harry crab (*Carcinas mœnas*), brought almost exclusively from Venice and Grado, and the sea-spider (*Maia squinado*), caught on the coast, are used as bait; and, in the season of the Sardine fisheries, as many as 1,000 sacks of this bait are used a day. They are kept alive until used, then pounded in a stone mortar, and mixed with sea-water; the liquid bait (*tritura, pacciugo, pastello, pesto di granzetti*) is thrown into the sea round about where the net is cast; the sardines are very greedy, dart after it and dash against the net, where they become embroiled. In Dalmatia, the seine-net and the *Illuminatore*, which will be presently described, take the place of this mode of fishing.

A bait made of salt herrings has also been used with success.

Length of one piece (*spedone*), 30 m.; depth of ditto, 8 m.; size of mesh for sardines, $1\frac{1}{2}$ to 2 c.[1] diagonally; price, 30 fl.

The *Rete di Sardelletti* is a smaller-meshed net of the same description, for catching the small sardines (*Clupea papalina*). Length, 40 m.; depth, 8 m.; price, 35 fl.

The *Sardonera* is a still smaller-meshed net, of coarser twine than the *Sardellera*, for catching anchovies (*Sardoni*), used chiefly in the month of July. Mesh, 1 c. in the diagonal. Length, 40-60 m.; depth, 5 m.; price, 35-60 fl.

The *Anguellera* (*Rete d'angudella*) is a ground-net for catching the fry of atherines (*Anguelle*), the smallest-meshed net of all (8 mm. diagonally); eight to ten lengths of which are generally joined together. One length, 30 m.; depth, 3 m.; price, 20-35 fl.

---

[1] C denotes centimètre, m. mètre, and mm. millimètre.

The *Zerer* is a similar net to the foregoing one, made of very fine twine, and used at Rovigno. Mesh, 1 c. in the diagonal. Length, 25 m.; depth, 2 m.

The *Agonera* (*Gavonera* in Dalmatia) is a ground-net for full-grown atherines (*Agoni, Gavoni, Gerai*). Mesh, 1 c. in the diagonal. Length, 40 m.; depth, 3 m.; price, 25 fl.

The *Senello* is a ground-net of fine twine, for *Menole* (*Mæna vulgaris*), and young grey mullet (*Cievoli*). Mesh, 38 mm. in the diagonal. Length, 20–30 m.; depth, 1¼ m.; price, 15 fl.

The *Spirone di Verzelate* is a ground-net for grey mullet (*Verzelate* = *Mugil saliens*), which is cast in a circle. Mesh, 5 c. in the diagonal. Length, 25 m.; depth, 8 m.; price, 30 fl.

The *Spirone da Lotregani*, or *Cievolera*, is a similar net of finer twine for grey mullet (*Lotregan* = *Mugil auratus*, and *Cievolo* = *Mugil cephalus*). Mesh, 4 c. diagonally.

The *Prostica* is a ground-net used in Dalmatia for catching red mullet, bogue, *Oblata melanura*, and *Mænidæ*, generally cast in the evening and drawn up the following morning. Mesh, 26 mm. in the diagonal; length, 100 m.; depth, 4 m.; price, 50 fl.

The *Bobera* (*Posta di bobe*, Croat. *Bukvare*) is a ground-net for the bogue, mackerel, horse mackerel, and mendole. Mesh, 35 mm. in the diagonal; length, 20–100 m.; depth, 6–7 m.; price, 20–80 fl. In many places this net is used for the kind of fishing known as *pesca da ludro*.

The *Scombrera* is a smaller ground-net for mackerel (*Scombri*). Length, 50 m.; depth, 5 m.; price, 30 fl.

The *Caguera* (*Rete di can*) is a ground-net weighted with stones for small sharks (*pesce can*), and rays, in the open sea; used at Zara, and in the Quarnero. Length, 40 m.; depth, 2 m.; price, 25 fl.

The *Squaënera* is a ground-net of coarse twine for angel sharks (*Squaëne*), and rays, also for sea-spiders, and lobsters. Mesh, 20 c. in the diagonal. Length, 20 m.; depth, 1½ m.; price, 15 fl.

The *Poklopnica* is a net similar to the *Prostica*, with the difference that the "head" is weighted instead of being sustained by floats. It is held

PLATE II

SALTARELLO.

stretched by means of wooden laths, and its position in the water is horizontal. It is used at Lésina for fishing mendole, and the net is cast just over the shoals, or schools, of fish. Although made of fine twine, the net is heavily weighted.

2. TRAMMEL, OR SET-NETS,

Reti tramacchiate, or *tramagliate*, or *vestite*, *i.e.* dressed, derived from the Latin *tres maculæ*, *i.e.*, three meshes ; it is known in France by the name of *tremail*, or *tramail* (from *trois mailles*), and in low Latin by the name of *tramallum*, or *tramela* (see Plate X.).

They consist of three long nets, placed side by side, and fastened together at the back, foot, and ends. The middle net is small-meshed (*nappa sottile*), 2–3 c. in the diagonal, and is made both longer and wider than the two outside nets, the excess being gathered in at short intervals along the edges, where the three nets are fastened together. The consequence is that the middle net hangs slack between the two outer nets. The two outer nets (*Chiaroni*) are made of coarse twine, the mesh called (*Cerbere*) measuring 15–34 c. in the diagonal ; they are mounted so that the meshes are exactly opposite one another, the inner net hanging loosely between them, and, being fully extended, the meshes are wide open, thus allowing a free passage for the fish. When a fish passes through the first outer net, it meets the inner small, meshed net, and carries a portion of it through the other outer net, thus producing a bag or pocket beyond it, whence is derived the term of *Reti d'insacco*, by which these nets are also known. The more the fish struggles to escape, the more hopelessly it becomes entangled.

The trammel is cast so that its length is in the direction of the tide, being anchored and buoyed or sustained by means of dry pumpkins at both ends ; the back, or upper side, being well corked, and the foot weighted, to keep the whole net in its proper position. It is generally left down over night, sometimes longer, and the fish either enter by chance, or are driven towards it by striking on the water.

The *Saltarello* (at Naples called *Vollari*) is a combination of a simple ground-net composed of several *Spedoni* hanging perpendicularly in the water, by means of which the fish, chiefly grey mullet and basse, are encircled, together with a trammel-net, which is made to float on the surface of the water outside the ground-net, but attached to it, and entirely surrounding it. In practice it acts so that the fish, finding themselves closed in by the ground-net, and finding exit impossible, are given to jump (*saltare*) out of water in their endeavours to clear the obstruction of the ground-net, and thus fall on to the trammel (*il salto*), in which they entangle themselves.

On the Istrian coast the trammel is kept afloat by means of cork floats, and the ground-net is secured by piles driven into the bed of the sea; in Dalmatia, it is supported by reeds, which are tied to it at intervals of 1½ to 2 feet, and act as floats. It is generally set close to the shore, the outside forming a semicircle, whereas the shore-side is cast in a straight line, and consists merely of the ground-net without the floating trammel. Length of ground-net, 200–300 m.; depth, 8 m.; length of trammel, 60 m.; breadth, 2 m.; price of the whole, 300–500 fl.

In use at all seasons (see Plates X. and XI.).

The *Cerberao*, or *Rete tramezzata*, is a ground-trammel cast in a straight line or semicircle, into which basse and gilt-head are driven by shouts, or by striking the water; used chiefly in spring. Length, 20–30 m.; depth, inner net, 6–8 m.; outer net, 4–6 m.; price, 18 fl. Mesh, inner net, 5 c.; outer net, 21 c.

The *Baicolera* is a similar but smaller-meshed trammel, for catching the fry of the basse (*Baicoli*) at the commencement of the winter.

The *Bombina*, or *Gombina* (Croat. *Popovnica*), is a trammel generally used for grey mullet, toothed gilt-head, *Occhiada*, *Spizzo*, *Sargo*, *Sparo*, scorpions, &c., into which they are driven. Length, 20–25 m.; depth, 2–4 m.; price, 10–30 fl. Mesh, inner net, 4 c.; outer net, 30 c.

The *Tarabara* is a similar net in use in the Quarnero.

The *Passelera* is a ground-net for flounders (*Passera*), rays, soles, scorpions, &c. Length, 8–12 m.; depth, 70–90 c.; price, 15 fl. Mesh, inner net, 6–8 c.; outer net, 30 c. This net is generally cast over night, and drawn up in the morning. At Grado they distinguish two kinds, viz., *Passarella da palude, i.e.*, for the marshes or lagoons, and *Passarella da fondo, i.e.*, for deep-

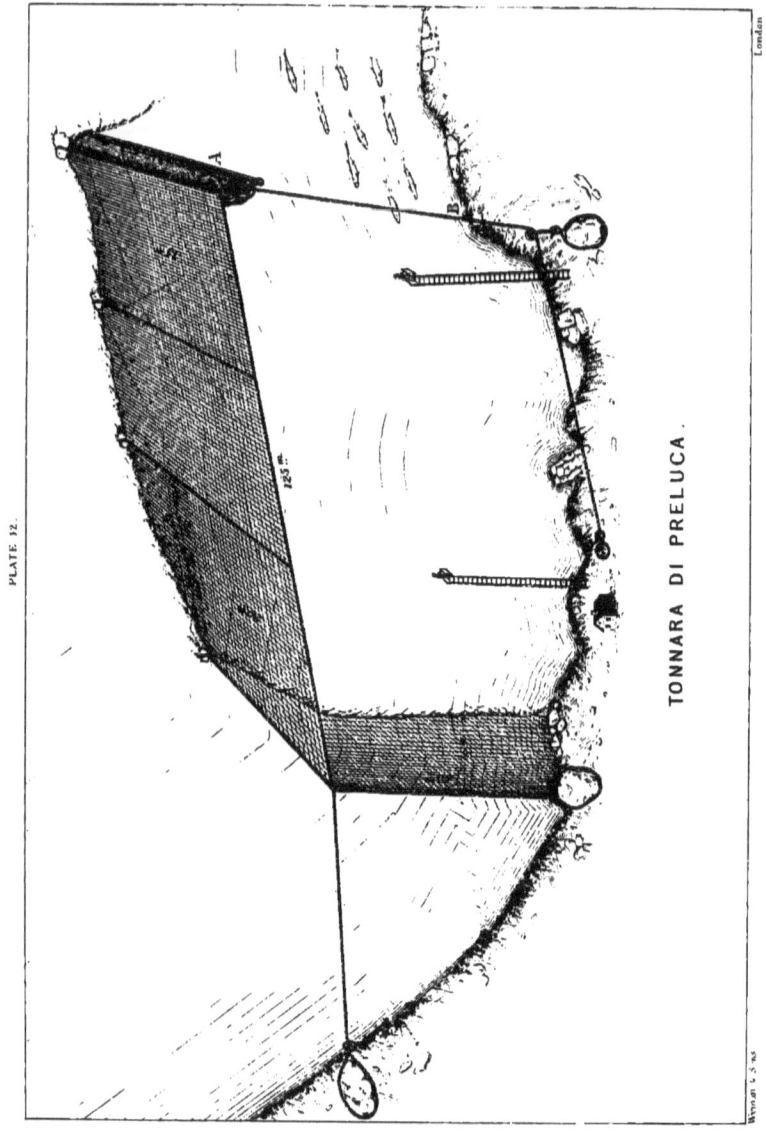

PLATE 12.

TONNARA DI PRELUCA.

sea fishing. The latter is known at Rovigno as *Passarella da pelago*. The former is used only in shallow waters and is less substantial in make than the other kinds: the drag-ropes are of bulrushes, the twine is slender, and the net is not heavily weighted.

The *Sfogliante*, or *Rete di Sfoglie*, is a ground-net for soles (*Sfoglic*). Length, 20 m.; depth, 1½ m.; price, 15 fl.

The *Rete di Barboni, Barbonera* (or *Tarantella* in the Quarnero), is a ground-net for red mullet (*Barboni*), small scorpions, &c. Length, 20–35 m.; depth, 2 m.; price, 20 fl. Mesh, inner net, 2½ c.; outer net, 26 c.

The *Rete di Guatti di sasso* is a ground-net for gobies (*Guatti*). Length, 10 m.; depth, 1–2 m.; price, 8–10 fl. Mesh, inner net, 2½ c.; outer net, 22 c.

3. SET, OR CIRCLE-NETS (*Reti a fermo* or *da chiusa*).

These are fixed nets, used for the capture of tunny, made of thick cord, with floats but without leads, and sometimes as much as 250 fathoms long and 15 fathoms deep (see Plate X.).

The *Tonnare* (*Madrague* of France), or *Poste di Ton*, are found all along the coast, but mostly on the Croatian seaboard, and they are much on the increase in Dalmatia. The distribution of the net is, as a rule, semicircular, one end being anchored close in shore; the net is then drawn out seawards, the outer part being parallel with the land, thus forming an enclosure, with one side left open for the passage of the fish. The locality is chosen according to the formation of the shore and bed, the chief condition being deep water, especially at the entrance. This favours the passage of the tunny, which is in the habit of approaching the shore in shoals, either in pursuit of mackerel, or, as is generally believed to be the case, to scratch itself against the rocks in order to rid itself of a parasite which irritates it. Thus, a deep creek, or bay, is favourable for fixing the net, particularly where the channel forming the opening is narrow and deep: in this case a net is simply drawn across, leaving the channel free.

Special regard has to be paid, in fixing the locality of these nets, to the course frequented by this eminently migratory genus in its annual passage from the Atlantic to the Black Sea and Sea of Azov, a distance of 2,800 miles, and back again. Its course is always the same, from one year to the other, and, as it would seem, age after age,—an ever-living stream of undiminished fulness, furnishing food to thousands of the Mediterranean populations.[1]

The fishermen must be continually on the watch for the shoals of fish; and for this purpose a watchman is constantly posted, during the season of passage, at the top of an inclined ladder, at an angle of about 75°, forming a kind of observatory, or crow's nest, whence the entrance of the fish can be seen. These are the *Thynnoscopi*, or *Ichthyoscopi* of the Greeks. When the shoal has entered the enclosure, the entrance is at once closed by drawing ashore a sufficient quantity of slack netting, which is left hanging for this purpose at the outer end of the net, by means of a rope, the end of which is kept on shore (see Plate XII., *Tonnara di Preluca*). The alarm is then sounded by throwing stones near the inlet through which the fish have just passed, and by raising a hue and cry, in which all join, in order to drive the shoal towards the closed end of the enclosure. The scene is now one of intense excitement and bustle, the nets are hauled in, and the fish are killed by means of spikes and oars, thrown ashore, disembowelled, and sent to market.

The *Tonnara di Buccarica* (see Plate XIII.) is constructed in a more complicated style, forming a series of three nets similar to that of Preluca. The shoals of Tunny generally hug the land and enter the smaller net close to the shore; but, owing to the irregular conformation of the coast, they are apt sometimes to pass outside the first or second net, in which case the second and third larger nets are ready for their reception. Owing, again, to the sea-bed not being properly levelled, the shoals sometimes escape under the nets, in which cases the outer nets serve to prevent their further escape, unless they find another exit below the next nets. As a last resource, a net is drawn across the entrance of the bay in which the three nets are fixed, by means of a boat, from the points, A B, shown in Plate XIII. The value of a Tonnara varies in price from 600 florins (Preluca) to 2,000 florins (Peschera):

---

[1] Godwin-Austen.

PLATE 13.

Croazia.

Net for closing the Bay in case the Shoals of Fish escape beneath the inner nets.

a Portore

TONNÁRA DI BUCCARICA.

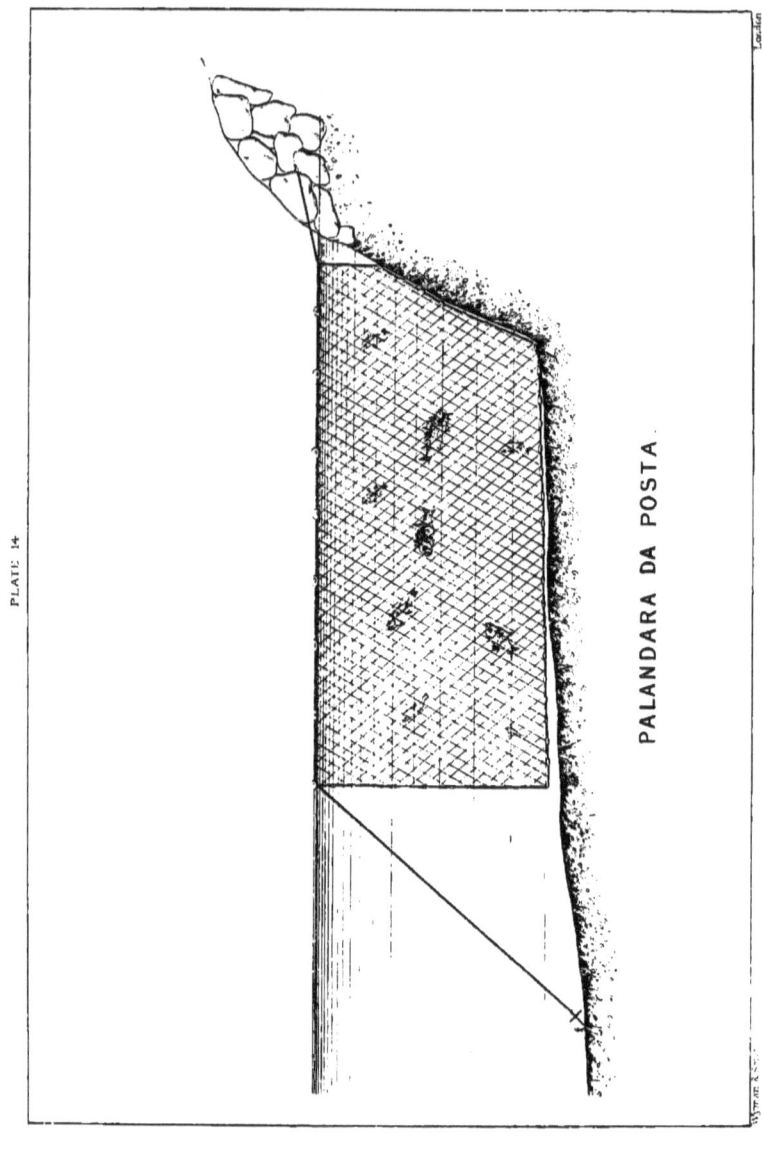

PLATE 14

PALANDARA DA POSTA

that of Buccarica costs 1,900 florins. The fishermen employed vary from eight men (Preluca) to thirty-four (Buccarica).

The *Palandara da posta* is a net fixed at right-angles to the shore, in which the fish are caught on whichever side they strike the net. It is used for bonito (Croat. *Palanda*). Length, 100 m.; depth, 20 m.; mesh, 11 c.; price, 150 fl. (see Plate XIV.).

4. Seine, Draw, or Circle Nets (*Tratte*).

This is the most common, as it is the most antiquated mode of fishing. The Phœnicians are known to have used the net; and it remains to this day the mode of fishing most generally adopted by the fishermen of these shores. It corresponds to the English seine fishing, and its special character —subject to variations according to the object for which it is used—is to enclose or surround the fish, which are drawn ashore and thus captured. It consists of a long piece of netting, varying in its dimensions according to circumstances, sometimes as much as 300 fathoms long, and 25 fathoms deep in the centre; but the middle, or "bunt," as it is called in England, is always deeper than the "wings" or "sleeves" (*ali* or *pareti*), as the ends are called, forming a kind of bag (*Panza, Sacco*), thus preventing the escape of the fish underneath when the net is being hauled in.

It is used for catching fish which are found near the surface of the water: the "back" (*ima da cortici*) is well supported by corks, and the "foot" (*ima da piombo*) sufficiently weighted to maintain the perpendicular position in the water. If worked from the shore, it is cast in a semicircle, and in a circle if worked from the boats; in either case the ends are, sooner or later, brought together, thus enclosing the fish. The net does not touch the bed when cast, but when drawn ashore by both ends simultaneously the whole "foot," or lower edge of the net, as a rule, touches the shore-incline at the same time, by reason of the greater depth of the middle than the wings; as the net is drawn in, the fish congregate in the bag and are hauled ashore. The net is so made that when suspended in the water the meshes are opened by the intrinsic weight of the net, but when in the act of being hauled in the meshes close, the tension being horizontal instead of vertical; and the fish, finding no issue at the sides, which form an impervious barrier, rush to the bag, whence there is no escape for them.

Foremost amongst these is,—

The *Tratta di Sardelle* (*Tratta grande d'estate*). The employment of this net is subject to certain provisoes—instituted by a *Regolamento*, or enactment, of *Dandolo*, the French *Provveditore* of Dalmatia in 1808, and subsequently revised by an enactment of 1861,—according to which the proprietors of nets, wishing to fish during the ensuing seasons, have to register their application before the municipal authorities, and later on to appear in person. Their nets and boats are subject to inspection, and those that are in proper condition are divided into groups, called *Broschetti*, to each of which suitable fishing tracts, *i.e.*, small creeks and bays with flat beds, called *Poste*, are allotted, which they subdivide amongst themselves by drawing lots. The object of this supervision is to insure the due and proper exercise of the fisheries, upon the yield of which so large a part of the community depends either directly or indirectly.

The fishing is carried on only during dark nights of the months of May, June, July, August, and September, *i.e.*, more or less during 21 nights of each month, or 105 nights in all.

The *Regolamento* requires three boats for each net; one of these is the *Gaëta*, which carries the fire-basket and a supply of fire-wood for one night, and is termed the *Luminiero*. An experienced fisherman proceeds in this boat about a mile from the shore in search of the Sardines (*Sardelle*), which he leads into the bay,[1] where, at a distance of 300 to 500 m. from the shore, they are enclosed in the net, the manipulation of which is carried on on board a second boat called *Leuto*. The net is then hauled ashore, and the depth of the bag (*Panza, Sacco*) is regulated, *i.e.*, drawn up, or lowered, according to the position of the fish in the water, and the depth of the water itself, by a line which is worked on board a third small boat which follows in the wake of the net. The net is 120-200 m. in length, sometimes longer; depth of bag, 20-40 m.; mesh, 2 c.; cost, 600-800 fl. and upwards.

---

[1] See description given under the heading Boats (*Gaëta*).

PALANDARA DA TIRO.

PLATE 16

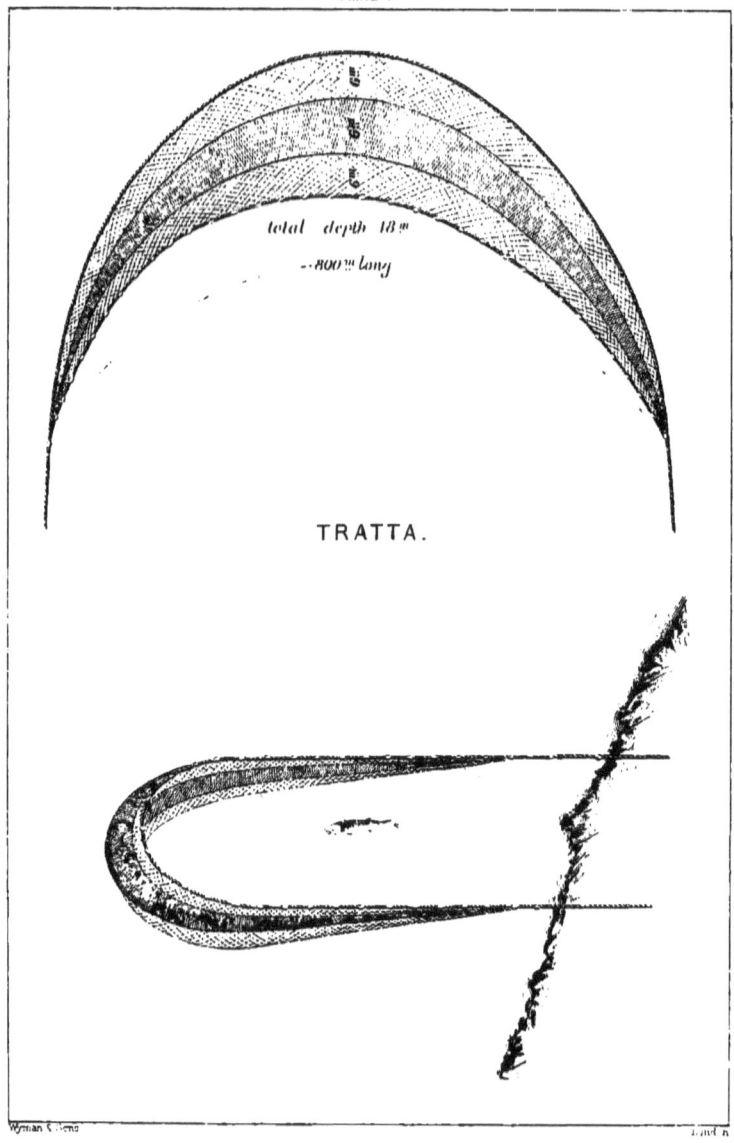

TRATTA.

The crew of the three boats consists of fifteen men; the cost of the net and the boats is 1,500 fl., and of the wood burnt in one season by each group of three boats 375 fl. The proprietors of the nets are often well-to-do people, who have the fishermen in their employ, supplying them with cash and provisions on usurious terms, besides drawing one half-share of the yield as the share of the net (see Chapter VII., DIVISION OF PROFITS).

The question of the seine fisheries *versus* the drift-net fisheries is often a very vexatious one, and great rivalry exists between the fishermen exercising the one mode as against those exercising the other. A great deal is to be said for both, and there are no reasons for favouring the one to the detriment of the other; yet the drift-nets have sometimes been banished in favour of the seine, although there is no satisfactory reason why they should not be placed on a footing of equality, and suitable tracts allotted to each, to the exclusion of the other.

The drift-net fisheries are carried on entirely by the poorer class, and the fishermen themselves are, as a rule, the owners of the craft and nets; hence greater consideration is due to them, if any difference is to be made, than to the seine fisheries, the greater part of whose yield is absorbed by people who have nothing to do with their immediate exercise and the labour and dangers consequent thereon. Besides this, the fish caught in the bag of the *Tratta* is often more or less damaged, and the produce of drift-nets is, for this reason, infinitely preferred by the curing establishments.

The *Tratta d'Angusigole*, or *Agugliara*, Croat. *Iaglitara*, is a seine for gar-pike (*Angusigole*, Croat. *Iaglica*) carried on the deck of one boat, the end being drawn by another smaller boat, by which the net is cast in a circle, the end being brought back to the first boat, on which the net is then hauled in. The net is well corked and remains at the surface; this mode of fishing being known as *pesca a volo*. Length, 100 m.; depth of centre bunt, 20–24 m.; depth of wings, 2 m.; mesh, 2 c.; price, 300 fl.

The *Tratta da Sardoni* is used for anchovies (*Sardoni*). Length, 150–300 m.; depth, 20–25 m.; mesh 1½ c.; price, 600–1,000 fl.

The *Tratta da Scombri* is for mackerel (*Scombri*), Spanish mackerel, bogue, &c., in use in the Quarnero and on the coast of Dalmatia. Length, 200 m.; depth, 24 m.; mesh, 1½ c.; price, 500 fl.

The *Tratta da Cicvoli* is made of coarse twine and is used in the Gulf of Trieste, in autumn, for grey mullet (*Cicvoli*). Length, 600–1,000 m.; depth, 20 m.; price, 2,000–8,000 fl.; mesh, 4 c.

The *Tratta da Orate* is a smaller-meshed net (mesh, 2 c.) for gilt-head (*Orate*). Length, 300 m.; depth, 12–16 m.

The *Palandara da Tiro* is for tunny and bonito (Croat., *Palanda*), and is drawn by a boat under sail or oars, or by hand from shore. Length, 80–100 m.; depth, 30–50 m.; price, 100–120 fl. (see Plate XV.).

The *Tratta di Ton* (called *Sabakone* or *žabakun* in Dalmatia), likewise for tunny and bonito. Length, 400 m.; depth, 50 m.; price, 800 fl.

The common *Tratta*, also called *Sciabica* (*žabica*) and *Rezzola* (*Rezzuola*), which corresponds with what is called in England the ground or foot-seine, or seringe-net, is much used all along the coast by the native fishermen, as it gives comparatively little trouble. It is worked from the shore; each wing is attached to a long drag-rope, and when the net is shot one end is left on shore, and made fast. The whole of the net is then put in a boat, which is rowed out from the shore and proceeds in a semicircle, casting the net on its course, and landing the drag-rope of the other end on the beach at some distance from the starting-point. The two ropes are, after a while, hauled in, the men working the drag-ropes approaching one another as the net comes to land, until at last they meet, and then the bunt of the net, in which the fish are collected, is drawn ashore. This net is familiar to everybody who has visited the shores of the Mediterranean.

Like all *tratte*, they are netted on the same principle, viz., that the meshes open out by the vertical strain in the water, and close by the longitudinal strain when being hauled in. It is the one most in use in the Quarnero, made of coarse string; depth of bunt as much as 20 to 25 fathoms; size of mesh diagonally,—bunt 1 cent., wings 4 cent.; they are sometimes 400 to 500 mètres in length (see Plates XVI., XVII., XVIII).

PLATE 17

TRATTA.

PLATE 74.

SCIABICA.

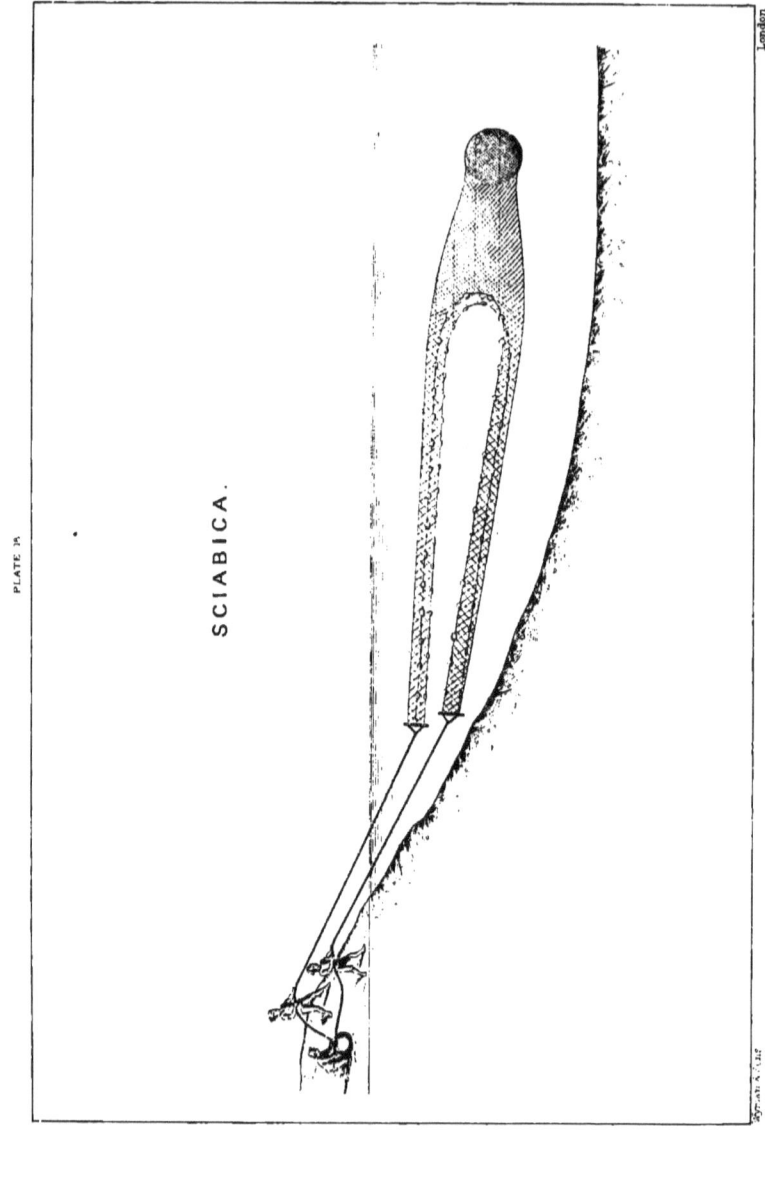

5. TRAWLING-NETS,

Reti a strascino (strascico), *Reti raschianti*, a term which is applied not only to the trawl proper, as we understand it in England, but also to a variety of seine-nets which are shot in a semicircle and both ends drawn towards some place, either on shore or to a boat at anchor, where the net is gathered in. Among the latter may be mentioned the *Tratta di fondo* and *Grippo*, a mode of fishing which is infinitely more pernicious to the fisheries in general than any properly-worked trawl, as it is carried on in shallow waters, and often close in shore, thus destroying a quantity of young, and, at the time of catching, worthless fry.

The systems adopted by the Italian fishermen (*Chioggiotti*), which are known as the *Cocchia* and *Tartana*, are the only ones which at all come up to our ideas of trawling, the principal difference being that no beam is used as in England.

The *Cocchia*, or *coccia* (see Plate XIX.), is used exclusively by the *Chioggiotti*, and drawn by two boats (*bragozzi*) under sail, each boat running parallel to the other and drawing one end of the net, which is held by means of drag-ropes (*alzana*) 40 to 50 fathoms in length. It is worked, by preference, against the current, over muddy grounds by day,—the mud raised by the passage of the net clouding the water and shutting out the light, which renders the fish confused and motionless, whereby they become an easy prey. By night-time it is worked over rocky beds. The depth varies from 20 to 50 fathoms.

The structure of this net differs from that of the seine (*tratta*) in the shape of the bag (*sacco* or *panza*), which, in this case, is conical, measuring 5 to 6 fathoms across at the opening, and narrowing by degrees to 8 to 10 feet diameter. Here commences a kind of funnel, which is kept open by means of hoops, and ends in a purse, the opening of which measures 5 feet across, and the ends of which are gathered together and secured by a rope. This has simply to be undone when the net is hauled on deck, and the fish fall out at the end. The funnel and purse is known as the *Cogòlo*, and forms about one-half of the total depth of the bag, which is 6 fathoms;

the *Cogòlo* is generally enclosed in a second net of coarse string in order to protect it against the friction with the bed and the depredations of the dolphins, which are apt, at times, to injure the net. The length of the wings, or arms, is sometimes as much as 30 fathoms each, the depth being 10 feet at the ends, and 20 feet towards the middle, where the bag commences. The bag is small-meshed ($1\frac{1}{2}$–2 c.), and well corked at the head, to keep it well open whilst in motion. It is also extra weighted at the foot, so that it falls quickly to the bottom, and is thus trawled along the ground, the boats being under full sail, the faster the better, the Italian fishermen fishing in almost all kinds of weather. Two pieces of wood are fastened longitudinally to the under side of the bag to protect it from friction with the ground and to enable it to slide along with greater facility. The value of the *Cocchia* is about 100 fl. This mode of fishing was prohibited by the Venetian Republic in former times, and by the Austrian Government by the enactment of 1835; but the want of organised inspection rendered it impossible to enforce the prohibition, and it was once more recognised under the Austro-Hungarian and Italian treaties of commerce of 1867 and 1878.

As to the destruction of spawn, Professor G. O. Sars has proved that the ova of the best-known and most valuable fish are found floating at the surface during the whole period of their development. This is the case with cod and haddock, and probably also with whiting, coal-fish, pollack, hake, and tusk. The spawning of mackerel at the surface has been repeatedly seen, and the ova identified. The common plaice has also the habit of spawning near the surface, and its ova float during the whole of their development. This being the typical representative of the flat-fish, it is probable that the turbot, brill, and sole do not differ in this respect. Several other kinds have been identified, such as the gar-fish, gurnard, &c. Hitherto the only fish whose spawn has been found on the ground is the herring. It is, therefore, a mistake to assume that trawling is more liable to destroy the spawn than any other modes of fishing.[1]

The *Cogòlo* is a hempen net made in the shape of a long conical bag, nar-

---

[1] See Holdsworth's "Sea Fisheries."

COCCHIA.

rowing by degrees to the tail end, and held open by successive hoops (*cerchietti*). It is composed of different parts: the first, called *chiara*, is large-meshed; the second is the *busto*, and is made of smaller meshes; the third is the *mezzana*, made of still smaller meshes; last comes the *pillela*, or *picla*, the purse, made of very coarse and strong twine, and very small-meshed, into which the fish enter through a kind of very narrow funnel called *cuca*. Once inside, they become packed, and are unable to turn back. It is also used for catching eels in the fishing-ponds (*valli chiuse*).

The *Bragagna*, worked by a boat called *Bragagna*, or *Bragagnella*, is a seine combined with the *Cogòlo*. The boat having previously cast anchor, at a short distance off, hauls in the anchor chain on a roller (*molinello*), thus drawing the net in its wake. The net has no floats to keep up the head, but it is held stretched in the water by a series of sticks fixed vertically along the two wings and around the mouth of the bag. At the end of each of the wings there is a small *Cogòlo* with three hoops with the opening in an opposite direction to that of the middle bag.

It is well weighted at the foot (*ima*) to keep it down, and the drag-rope ends are attached to the bows and the poop, the boat moving broadside on (*in fianco*), the net grazing the ground; worked by day or night, on muddy beds, in shallow water, in creeks and lagoons, chiefly for gobies and small shore-fish. Length, 20 m.; depth, 4 m.; mesh, $2\frac{1}{2}$ c.; price, 60 florins.

The *Grippo* is similar to the foregoing almost in every respect. It is smaller-meshed ($1\frac{1}{4}$ c.), and, instead of the two *Cogòli* at the ends of the wings, it has two small bags without hoops. It is less heavily weighted at the foot; it is sustained in the water by corks at the head; and has fewer sticks to keep it extended.

The *Tartana* is composed of the *Sacco* and *Cogòlo*, somewhat similar to the *Grippo*, and is used by the *Chioggiotti* for catching ground-fish in 15-fathoms water; it is drawn by a single boat of the same name under sail, the drag-ropes being attached to two spars (*spuntieri* or *spouteri*), one fore and the other aft, in order to keep the net better extended in the water, the boat drifting broadside on (*in fianco*). Total length, 12 m. This method is falling gradually into disuse, in favour of the *Cocchia*.

The *Tartana* is still met with in the Gulf of Trieste, and on the west coast of Istria, but it is hardly known on the rest of the Austrian-Hungarian seaboard (see Plate XX.).

The *Tratta da Menole* (*Giravica*, *Oližnica*, or *Tratta piccola d'inverno* in Dalmatia) is similar to the sardine seine-net, only smaller and of coarse twine; used for *Mænidæ* (*Menole*), and *Smaridæ* (*Gira*, or *Girica*, Croat.). Length, 120 m.; depth, 8–10 m.; mesh at the wings 3 c., at the bunt 1½ c.; price, 100–150 florins.

The *Tratta da fondo* (*Migavica*,[1] or *Sabaka*, or *žabaka*, in Dalmatia) consists of a small-meshed bag in the middle, without the hoops used in the *Cogòlo*; it has longer wings, of larger meshes, than the *Grippo*; it is used for catching all kinds of shore-fish. Length, 180 m.; depth of bunt, 30–35 m.; mesh at the ends of the wings 11 c., decreasing to 4½ c. towards the bunt; bunt 2 c.; price, 120–300 florins. The net of this name used on the coast of Istria is smaller and has no bag. Length, 50 m.; depth, 8 m. The *Tratta per novellame* is a very small trawl used for catching fry for the fish-ponds (*valli*). Length, 4 m.; depth, 65 c.; mesh 1 c. at the sides, ½ c. in the middle.

The *Trattisella* is a small trawling-net.

6. HAND-NETS.

The *Ostreghera*, *Ostricara*, or *Cassa* (Ital., *Cucchiaia*, or ladle), is a coarse and strong large-meshed (6 c.) hempen net, fixed to a heavy semi-circular iron-rod frame, after the fashion of a weeding-hook; turbots and flounders, and other ground-fish are caught with this. Iron spikes are, sometimes, fixed to the under side for the purpose of raking the ground, and thus forcing up certain species, which would otherwise remain buried in the mud or sand. The net is bag-shaped, and is held extended lengthways by a thick pole 2 m. long, and vertically by a cross-bar fixed to the middle of the pole. Inside the net there is sometimes a small net-bag, so constructed that

---

[1] The meaning of this word is to "wink" (with the eye). This term is in allusion to the closing of the meshes by the horizontal tension of the net.

PLATE 20

TARTANA.

the fish can enter but cannot get out, being unable to turn round. The *Ostreghera da palude*, *i.e.*, for marshes, is used at Grado; it has no inner net, and the mesh only measures 5 c.; price, 8-10 fl.

The *Ostreghera a piombo*, or *Mussolera*, is the same description of net, well weighted, so as to scrape the ground when drawn in the wake of a rowing boat; it is used for scraping together oysters (*Ostreghe*) and mussels (*Mussoli*). Length of bag, 2 m.; breadth of opening, 2 m.; price, 10 florins.

The *Rete da Capparozzoli* is fixed to a triangular frame, the foot of which is furnished with prongs, forming a rake 3½ feet long; the angle opposite the rake is fixed to a handle by which the net is worked; used for catching *Venus decussata*, *V. gallina*, *V. verrucosa* (*Capparozzoli*), by raking it through the sand. Length of net, 4 feet; price, 6 florins.

The *Guatta* is a bag-net fixed on a semicircular frame, the upper side of which is straight, and is fixed to a handle several feet long; it is worked by a man wading in shallow water, who shoves the net in front of him, so that the semicircular foot of the frame passes through the mud; used for catching gobies (*Guatti*). Length of bag, 6 feet; width of opening, 4½ feet; price, 4 florins.

The *Saccoleva*, literally "bag-lift" (called *Bragotto*, or *Bragottin di mar* in the lagoons of Venice), is a square, very small-meshed net fixed on a frame, for catching young fry (*pesce novello*) in spring for the fish-ponds (*valli*). *Ordega* is the name more commonly applied to this net on these shores; it is called *Zel* at Rovigno. It is fixed to a circular wire frame 2 m. in diameter, the bag having a mesh of 1½ c. The frame is tied by a number of short strings to a single rope, by means of which the net is submerged and drawn up. The fish are attracted to it by bait.

The *Tela* is similar in form, for similar purposes; made of cotton cloth.

The *Ordegno*, or *Ingegno di pesca del Corallo*, is an apparatus for fishing Coral. This is of the most antiquated kind. Two wooden beams, 3 to 4 feet long, are fixed transversely in the shape of a cross, and weighted with a stone at the point of intersection. Two branch spars (*coscioni*), 2-3 m. long, are fastened at right-angles to the cross-beams, and loose hempen nets (*radazze*), 1½ m. long, hang suspended from the ends of the spars. Besides these,

R

four other nets are tied to as many cords, 1½–2 m. long, and disposed at the point of intersection of the spars and the beams. The stone, which weighs 60 kilogr., is fixed to the cross-beams by what is called the *gassa;* to this are attached double ropes (*fregana*), 20 m. long, which,, in their turn, are tied to the drag-ropes (*alzane*), 120–200 m. long. The apparatus is drawn by a rowing boat at full speed over the coral beds, and is constantly raised and lowered so as to suit the depth of water and only to graze the bed. By this means, where coral is met with, and particularly on the projecting points (*secche*), the branches are broken off, and get entangled in the loose netting; but everything is left to chance, and, doubtless, much of the coral is lost. For working under projections of rocks a single beam is used, to which a ring is attached for hanging a net. As a great deal of netting is destroyed by the constant friction with the rocks, as much as 300 to 600 lb. of hemp are required each season by each apparatus.

Rizzajo (*Rizzagio, Rizzagno, Rizzer*, also *Gaccio*, or *Giacchio*) has somewhat the form of an open umbrella, which is thrown over a swarm of fish, such as grey mullet, salpa, &c. The lower part is well weighted, so that it sinks rapidly, and is, at the same time, fixed by a number of strings, which pass inside the net through an aperture in the centre of the top, and which are held in the hand of the fisherman. When the net is thrown over the fish, the lower sides are almost instantaneously drawn together at the centre aperture, by which means a greater or lesser number of fish is captured. Sometimes 5–10 kilogr. of fish are caught at a time. Price, 8–10 fl. (see Plate XXIV.).

The *Volega*, or *Oprara* (in Venice *Vuoega*, Germ., *Koeseher*, Croat., *Špurtilo*), is a kind of butterfly-net, for taking fish out of the seine-nets. *Cerchio* and *Cerchiello* are similar nets, used for similar purposes in the lagoons.

7. Fish-Weirs and Ponds.

These are peculiar to the Venetian lagoons, but they are also found on the coast near Grado and Capo d'Istria; and, although they pertain rather to the Italian than to the Austrian fisheries, they deserve mention here, as they form an important item in the fisheries of the northern head of the

Adriatic, and were, moreover, for a succession of years comprised in the Austrian fisheries.

Fish-weirs (*Fischwehren, Fischzäune*) *Serragli*, or *Serragie*, constructed either of nets (*S. di reti*), or of reed-screens (*S. di grigiuoli*)[1] fixed to piles driven into the bed; the latter mode is adopted near Grado, Capo d'Istria, &c. The thickness of the screens varies according to the use they are put to, in some places double or treble screens being used. From point to point the screen sides are made to converge towards one another, forming a funnel-shaped enclosure called *lavoriero;* at the narrowest point are fixed the *Cogòlo*-nets, which allow of the entrance of the fish, but from which the exit is impossible. As the tide recedes, the fish find their way into the *Cogòli*, which are drawn up by means of a float to which they are attached, and emptied of their contents. The *Cogòli* are made of three different sizes, as regards the size of mesh and of the entrance, according to the species of fish for which they are intended, viz., for eels, grey mullet, and gobies.

The foundation of the *serragli* is commonly called *zocco*, and by the *valligiani, i.e.*, the people who have charge of the ponds, *sciassa;* the broken and useless reed-screens, which have to be cleared away before new ones are set, are called *scattaroni*, and the act of clearing them away, which is done once or twice a year, *scattaronare*.

Fish-ponds (*valli*), chiefly on the coast of Venice,[2] also on the coast near

---

[1] *Grigiuoli, Griziole*, and *Canne* are screens, or mats, made of marsh reeds by fastenings or ties, called *drezze:* when the reeds are fastened together singly, the screen is called *pesson*, and when in bunches *griziole*. Their height is regulated according to the number of *drezze* they contain; the higher ones have eighteen, the lowest four or five; the *drezze* should be a foot apart: 100 *drezze* form a *cusidura*—a term used in contracts.

[2] The Venetian lagoons comprise that of Marano, or Friuli, with an area of 55 square miles (60 to 1°); that of Caorle (area 160 square miles), and that of Venice proper (200 square miles): to these may be added the lagoon of Chioggia, lying to the south (33 square miles), and the lagoon of Comacchio with an extent of 49,000 hectares. (See "Industrie de la Lagune de Comacchio," by Coste; also Friedländer, "La pesca nelle Lagune di Comacchio," 1872; also the "Fisheries of Comacchio and Ferrara," by Mr. Consul Colnaghi, September, 1876, in the Consular Reports, 1877, and Journal S. A., vol. xxv., No. 1,304). North-East of Comacchio are the minor lagoons of Messola (23,000 hectares), Codigoro (2,374 hectares), and Massa Fiscaglia (1,000 hectares).

Grado, consisting of a space of water partitioned off from the rest of lagoons, in which they are situated, by reed-screens (*valle a griginoli* or *grisiole*), or by dams and sluices (*valle chiusa arginata*); there are also *valli semi-arginate*.

La valle chiusa ad argine is so constructed that the sea-water can flow in at different points, the in-flow being regulated by means of sluices (*chiaviche*), so that the water does not become stagnant. The bed must vary in its quality and depth of water, so as to suit the requirements of the different kinds of fish as to food and temperature. In winter a stream of sweet water is let in, in order to facilitate the freezing of the surface, and thus afford greater protection to the fish from the cold.

The *valli a griginoli*, and *semi-arginate*, are built on the same principle, but they are liable to destruction by storms or floods, and require more expense for keeping in repair. The people in charge are called *vallicultori*, or *valligiani*, and the head man *Paron* (*padron*) *da valle*. The pond proper is termed *Lago*, or *Campo della valle*, where the young fish (*pesce novello*) is allowed three years to mature. The *cogolera* is a labyrinth of reed-screens and *Cogòli*, similar to the *serragli*, into which fresh water is at times let, thus alluring the fish into the nets; the mature fish are taken out in the autumn and winter. In the pond there are deeper basins and channels (*Gorghi*), to enable the fish to seek refuge from the great heats and colds; otherwise they die off.

The pond proper is separated from the *cogolera* by a dam (*traghetto*) with an opening furnished with a sluice. The approach to the *cogolera* is called *Vegnua*, or *Venuta;* an obstruction to the passage of grey mullet and gilt-head is the *fermativa di cievoli e orade*, by means of which they are isolated; further on is a similar obstruction for eels, the *fermativa di bisatti*, and another called *chila*, for catching the eels that escape from the former.

On either side of the *cogolera* are ditches (*depositi*), partly roofed over, affording protection to the young fry in hot or cold weather; a trellis-work separating the *depositi* from the rest of the *cogolera*, in order to afford protection to the fry from the pursuit of the mature fish.

The *valli* are opened in spring, allowing the free passage of the fish, which accordingly enter of their own accord; this is called the "*montata*,"

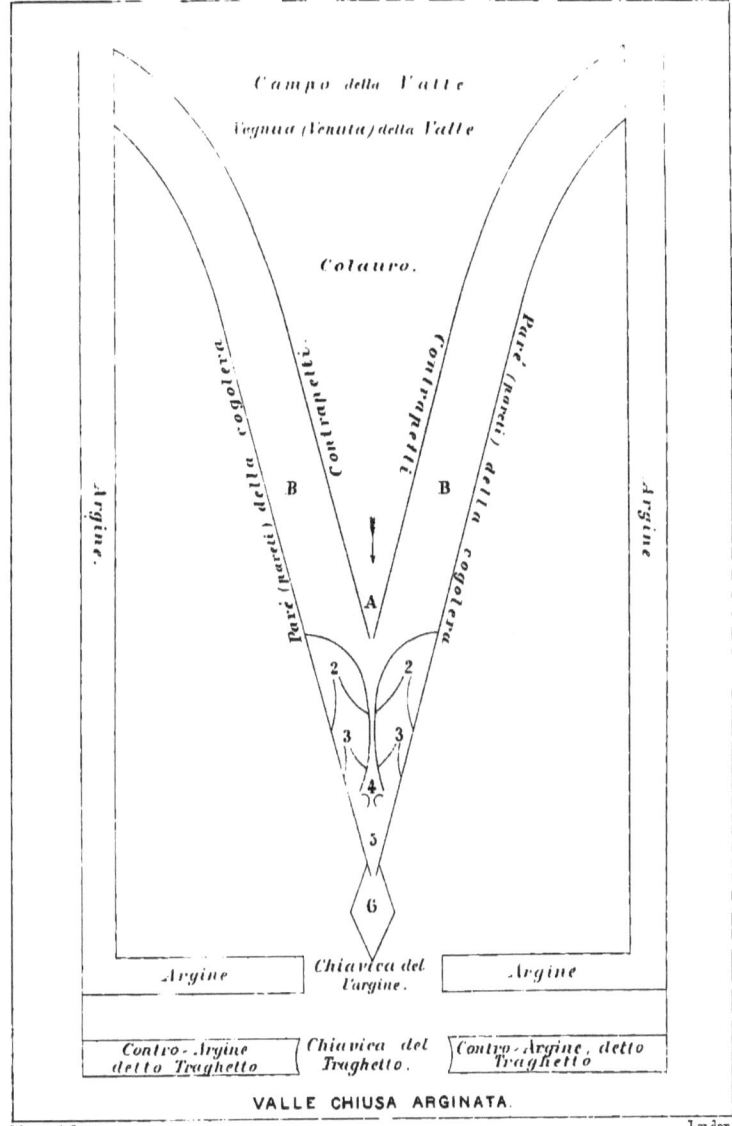

and occurs chiefly in the months of March and April, and the *valli* are closed when the heat of the sun becomes scorching, as, otherwise, the fish would escape into deeper and cooler waters.

The diked ponds are again opened in the months of August and September, at which season the grey mullet species (*Mugil saliens*) ascends, the reed-ponds remaining closed, as the young fry, even if it were admitted at this season, would escape through the reed-screens on the first approach of the cold weather. In the case of the diked ponds, the dikes and sluices prevent the escape of all fish.

The descent of those species of mature fish which enter the sea at regular seasons, for spawning or other purposes, is known as the *calata;* this is the time which is looked forward to with the greatest impatience by all concerned. It is the season when the catch of eels, and the so-called *pesce bianco*, is at its height, *i.e.*, at the commencement of November; it is also known as the *fraima*, or *frimas*, *i.e.*, the hoar-frost (*infra hyemem*). The scene on a night of *fraima* is indescribably lively and exciting; nobody, who has not witnessed it, can have any idea of the feelings of wonder and astonishment it produces in the spectator, and it requires the pen of an artist properly to describe it.

A *valle* gives a profitable yield, so to say, all the year round; thus, a pound of eel-fry (*Elvers*) (known as *capillari*) will yield from 3,000 to 4,000 kilogrammes, at the age of five or six years; and a pound of grey mullet-fry will yield 170 kilos of flesh in the course of a year. A second catch of eels takes place during Lent; this is known as the *pesca quaresimale*. As most of the *valli* are able to sustain a greater quantity of fish than enters of its own accord, this being particularly the case in respect of the diked ponds, to which the passage is limited to the apertures in the dikes known as *bove*, recourse is had to what is called *seminagione*, *i.e.*, the replenishment of the ponds with *pesce novello*, which is caught by the *pescenovellanti*, as described elsewhere. Fry of the gilt-head is worth 10 florins per mille; grey mullet 1 florin per mille.

Great care is requisite for rearing the fish which has entered the *valli;* the different species are carefully separated according to the state of their maturity, and are restrained from returning to the sea during the great heats or colds.

The eels change their name from *Capillari* (Elvers, or fry) to *Pasciuti* in the course of their development, and to *Anguille* or *Bisatti* when mature; these, again, are distinguished by the names of *Anguille comuni*, *Anguillazzi*, *Rocche*, *Miglioramenti*, and *Capitoni*.

DESCRIPTION TO PLATE No. XXI.—The fish enter from the *Campo della Valle*, through the *Vegnua* or *Venula*, into the *Colauro* or *Colaura* (*dove cola il pesce*), which is formed of screens, called *contrapetti;* thence through the aperture, A, called *boccarin* or *boccariolo*, into the space, B, called *anticamera*, whence they are distributed in the various *fermative*, *camarelle*, or *Otelle* (*Ostelli*), after passing through the *lavoriero*, 4, also called the *cappello a tre venti*, into 5, the *pizzo*. 2, are the *Otelle* (*Ostelli*); 3, the *camarelle* or *fermative*, forming so many obstructions to the passage of different kinds of fish which are to be separated from the rest; 6 is the *chila* or *chilla*, for catching the eels which escape from 3.

A fresh-water supply is kept up through the double sluices (*chiaviche*), first, of the *Traghetto* or outer dam; and, second, of the *Argine* or dam proper.

DESCRIPTION TO PLATE No. XXII.—Instead of dikes or dams, the sides or partitions consist of reed-screens fixed to piles driven into the bed 1½ foot apart, and the rampart is somewhat higher than the high-water mark at spring-tides.

1. *Lavoriero* or *Cappello a tre venti*.
2. *Pizzo*, or *gomio*.
3. *Boccariol dell' otella* (or *fermativa*) *da cievoli* (grey mullet), through which mouth (*bocca*) or entrance the fish pass into
4. *Camarella* ⎫
5. *Otella* ⎬ *da cievoli* (grey mullet).
6. *Camarella* ⎫
7. *Otella* ⎬ *da strame*, or *pesce moro*.
8. *Camarella del pizzo*.

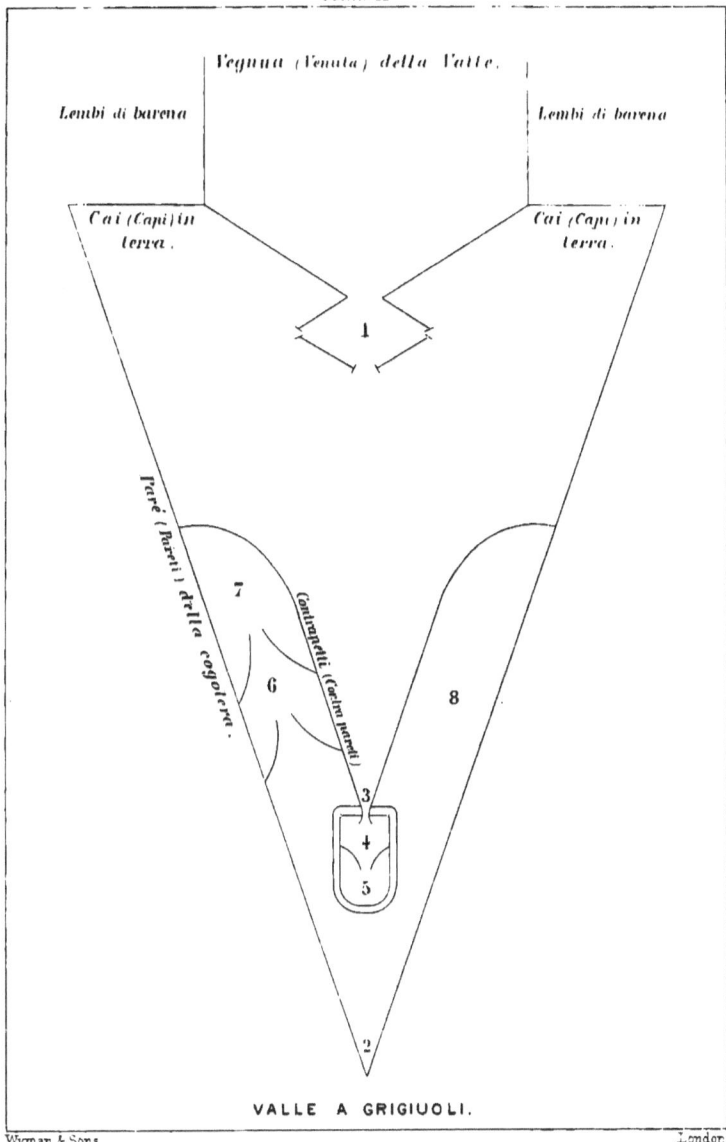

VALLE A GRIGIUOLI.

Pesce da strame designates the fish of minor value serving as food to the more valuable kinds, in contradistinction to the *pesce bianco* (grey mullet and eels), *strame* meaning litterally straw or fodder. The fish included in this term are gobies, flounders, and smelts (atherines).

The space marked 8, not partitioned off by *Cogòli*, or forming special *Camarelle* or *Fermative* (such as 6 and 7), is occupied by the eels, which require more room in which to circulate freely.

Cogolere, furnished with the *camarelle*, or *otelle*, are called *Cogolera maestra;* and those which have not these are called *Cogolera da bisatti* and *da strame*.

In the Venetian lagoons, there are as many as 135 *cogolere* in a single *valle;* their number depends, as a matter of course, on the size and position of the *valle*, and other less important circumstances.[1]

FISH WHICH ARE REARED IN THE VALLI.

Angusigola, the Gar-fish.
Anguèla, the Smelt (Atherine).
Barbon (*Mullus barbatus*, L.), Red Mullet.
Bisatto, the Eel.

---

[1] *Produce of the valli from the Po to Grado, according to the investigations of the Sub-Commission of Fisheries at Chioggia.*

	Kilogr.	Lire.
Eels,	800,000	640,000
Grey Mullet, Gilt-head, Basse	1,200,000	840,000
Sole, Goby, Carcinus mænas, and other Crustaceæ	600,000	150,000
Total	2,600,000	1,630,000

Fishermen employed in the *valli*, 1,000.
Produce of the Campi (*valli*) of Comacchio from 1,000,000 to 1,500,000 kilogr. per annum.

Bosega (*Mugil chelo*), a Grey Mullet species.
Branzin, the Basse.
Corbetto, the Umbrina.
Caustelo (*Mugil capito*, Cuv.), a Grey Mullet species.
Gò, Goby species (*G. jozo*, L.).
Dotregan (*Mugil auratus*), a Grey Mullet species.
Lizza (*Lichia amia*, Cuv.).
Lucerna, the Sapphirine Gurnard.
Marsion, a Goby (*G. elongatus*, Can.).
Menola bianca (*Smaris vulgaris*).
Orada, the Gilt-head.
Paganello, a Goby (*G. paganellus*, L.).
Passarin, the Italian Flounder.
Rombo, the Turbot.
Sfoglio, the Sole.
Soazo, the Brill.
Triglia, the Striped Surmullet.
Volpina, the common Grey Mullet (*M. cephalus*).
Verzelata (*Mugil saliens*), a Grey Mullet species.

8. Snares.

Nasse, or *Verse*, are basket-traps, made of willow withes in the shape of casks, with funnel-shaped entrances at either end, through which fish, cephalopods, and crabs enter, allured by means of bait. Once inside, the prey is prevented from escaping by the pointed ends of the willow switches. These traps are provided with an aperture closed by a lid, by which the captives are secured. Their size varies from $1\frac{1}{2}$ to 6 feet in length and 8 to 30 inches in breadth; the width of the entrances varies according to the description of fish they are set to catch. Several of them, as many as a dozen, are generally laid together in 6 fathoms of water, well baited with produce of the sea, either living or dead, pieces of grilled or smoked fish, crabs and sea-spiders, pieces of cephalopods, small fish and sometimes a paste made of bread or flour and cheese, mixed with the refuse water of salted sardines.

They are used chiefly for wrasses, gobies, red mullets, gilt-heads, scorpions, conger-eels, cephalopods, lobsters, &c., in spring, summer, and autumn, and are drawn up for examination once in twenty-four or forty-eight hours (see Plate XXIV.).

The *Vivajo*, or *Viera*, derived from the Latin *vivarium*, is a paunch-bellied willow basket, with a narrow mouth and cover, for keeping fish alive in the sea until sold; used as store-pots for eels, turbots, crabs, &c. They are much used in the lagoons, where they are sunk in sheltered waters, and secured by cross-piles (*barriaghi*). The common shore-crabs are kept in them to await the process of *ecdysis* or moulting (shedding of the skin), when they are sold as *molecche* ("soft crabs" of the United States). These baskets are both wider and deeper than the common.

The *Marotta*, or *Burchio*, is a boat for keeping fish alive in, also *Burchio da bisatti* for eels; length, 2 to 12 m.; price, 10 to 25 fl., and above. The holes in them are, however, generally too small, and the fish are apt to die from this cause: perhaps, also, from the fact of the water getting foul, or not being exactly what is required, either as regards its temperature or its saltness, these boats being, as a rule, moored in harbours, and in the proximity of the shore and of sweet-water springs or courses.

The *Burchiello* is a smaller boat of the same description, used by the *tognaroli* in line-fishing.

The value of the fishing gear on the Austro-Hungarian coast, belonging to native fishermen, represents an amount of 1,150,000 fl. For further particulars on this subject, see STATISTICS.

CHAPTER VI.

LINE-FISHING.

Lines.—Hooks.—Implements of various kinds.—Prongs, &c.—Scares.—Bait.

INE-FISHING is not of great importance in these waters, and is not carried on on a scale to render it of much consideration. There is, consequently, little to be said on this head. Suffice it to enumerate the different kinds of lines in use. These consist, as elsewhere, of the hand-lines which the fishermen hold, and of the long lines which are shot or trailed in the wake of a boat and then hauled in.

The *Canna* is a simple hand-line, to which two or three hooks (*ami*) are fixed, baited with worms or smelts, and used from the shore with or without a rod, for gobies, the smooth serranus, *Sargo*, *Sparo*, *Spizzo*, *Occhiada*, &c.

The *Pannola* is a line 15 to 40 fathoms long, weighted with lead at intervals of 10 to 15 feet. At its end there is a copper wire 10 feet long, to which one, two, or more hooks are attached; it is sometimes made of horsehair and wound on a large piece of cork. The hooks are baited with small fishes, or pieces of dried sardines, which shine in the water, and the line is towed by a boat close in shore, and hauled in from time to time. It is used for catching mackerel, basse, *Occhiada*, gar-fish, gobies, &c. (see Plate XXIV.). The *pannola da scombri* (for mackerel) is rather complicated. It consists of the principal line (*maistra*), 15 m. long. At the end of this are four snoods; two (*i volanti*) are of the ordinary kind ending in catgut, and two hooks; the other two (*le piombere*) are heavily weighted with shot (60–70, at intervals of 1–2 inches), and end, likewise, in catgut and two hooks. The *pannola da dentale* (for dentex) is 30 m. long, with copper wire at the end

PARANGALA DISTESA.

PARANGALA GALLEGIANTE.

and two hooks; the line is well weighted at intervals of 6 inches. Besides these, there are the *pannola da occhiate* (for *Oblata melanura*) and the *pannola da branzin* (for basse); the former ends in wire, the latter in catgut.

The *Lenza* is a similar line to the foregoing, made of three or four horse-hairs twined together, but with larger hooks, for catching gilt-head.

The *Traèna*, or *Trajna*, is similar in form, made of coarse twine; length, 50 fathoms and above. At the end there is a copper wire 10 feet long, with two large hooks; it is drawn by a sailing or rowing boat at a fair speed, and is used in the south of Dalmatia for gilt-head, dentex, *Lizza* (see Plate XXIV.).

The *Togna* is a hand-line without lead, with 3 to 10 or more small hooks, used from a stationary boat for gobies, mendole, and *Maride*, &c. (see Plate XXIV.). There are various kinds, viz., the *Togna da menole*, the *Togna da spari*, and the *Togna da orate*, &c., according to the variety of fish they are used for.

The *Squadrale* is a hand-line for dentex. It is made of coarse twine 80 m. in length, and 20 m. are kept in hand by the fisherman to ease the line (*filare lo squadrale*) in case a large fish makes a bite. It is well weighted at intervals of 2 m., and ends in a copper wire 8–10 m. long and two hooks fixed in opposite directions to one another. It is drawn by a sailing or rowing boat at full speed.

The *Parangale* is a line, 50 to 250 fathoms long, which carries 100 to 300 hooks on snoods two or three feet long and about a yard or two yards apart. According to the fish to be caught, the cord is either kept up by floats near the surface, the hooks hanging down, as in the case of gar-fish (*Parangale galleggiante*); or it is sunk at the bottom of the sea, being weighted by stones at the one end, and buoyed to a floating signal (*segnale*) at the other, from which it is hauled in, as is the case with the conger-eel, sharks, rays, &c. (*Parangale distesa*). The hooks are baited with small mendole or pieces of cephalopods, and the line is drawn up for examination every two or three hours, or left down over night (see Plate XXIII.).

The *Dentalà* is a similar long line for the dentex (*Dentale*).

The *Parangale a vela a angusigole* is a similar line for gar-fish (*angusigole*).

used near Pola, fixed by one end to the shore, the other being attached to a floating plank (*barchetta*), on which is hoisted a sail, when the wind is blowing off shore. The snoods are of horsehair, so as not to become entangled.

The *Canavaca* is a deep-sea line, 30 to 40 fathoms long, with four or six snoods at the end, baited with sardine and well weighted to keep the baited hooks near the sea-bed. It is for catching poor, whiting, hake, &c., in summer, at Fiume (see Plate XXIV.).

The *Brancarella* is an 8-inch staff attached to a line, the under end of which forms a crown of 16 to 25 hooks bent upwards. The bait (*esca*) consists of a bogue, or other fish, through which the staff is passed, the head of the fish being at the upper end. It is used for catching the cuttle-fish, which darts at the bait and is caught by the upturned hooks.

The *Puschia* is similar in form, but smaller.

The *Sustavica* is similar to the foregoing, the only difference being that the staff is covered with white rabbit-skin. It is used for catching the squid (*Calamaro*), near the islands of Selve and Arbe (see Plate XXIV.).

The *Sepparola* is a dummy cuttle-fish made of wood, painted and weighted, with glass eyes, attached to a line and drawn by a boat. It is used as a snare for the cuttle-fish, which follows and encircles it, both being drawn up together (see Plate XXIV.).

Various Implements.

Implements of different kinds for raising sponges, mussels, &c., or for spiking fish and cephalopods in clear water not above 5 fathoms in depth.

Great practice and skill are required for using with effect the prongs for spiking fish and cephalophods. This mode of fishing is carried on chiefly at night by the light of torches, which attracts the fish (chiefly the dentex and the basse), the fishermen of the channel of Novigrad being especially expert.

Quicklime is often used to burn the octopus out of the holes or interstices of rocks in which it has sought refuge after an unlucky attempt to prong it. By this means it is often forced out of the place of retreat on finding no

PLATE 24

other exit; but these animals are so wary that they often elude all pursuit after an unsuccessful attack, and, in this way, it is often a game of hide-and-seek for hours together between the fisherman and his prey. Sometimes they are only brought out piecemeal, so firmly do they adhere to whatever they catch hold of, if not successfully drawn up on the first attack.

The *Tanaglia* is a kind of tongs, one side of which is fixed to a long pole, the other being worked by a cord; it is used for laying hold of sponges, &c. (see Plate XXIV.).

Prongs.

The *Asturera* is a double-toothed prong, the teeth being bent inwards at right-angles; it is for raising the *Stura* (*Pinna rudis, P. squamosa*) off sandy or muddy beds.

The *Grampa* is a trident with bent prongs, used at Zara for catching sea-spiders, *Mytilus edulis*, and *Modiola barbata* (see Plate XXIV.).

The *Grampon*, similar to the *Asturera*, is used on the coast near Rovigno, in Istria, for raising oysters, sponges, &c.

The *Fiocina*, or *Foscina* (Lat., *Fuscina*), is a straight prong with five to eleven teeth, with barbed heads, fixed at the end of a pole, which is often as much as 25 feet long. It is handled by a man stationed at the bows of a boat, sculled slowly and with as little noise and motion as possible, by day or more frequently at night by torchlight, for spiking grey mullet, dentex, basse, gilt-head, cephalopods, sea-spiders, crabs, lobsters, &c. It is also used for spiking large fish caught in the seine; and, attached to a cord, it is sometimes cast at the fish at some distance off (see Plate XXIV.).

The *Fossenin*, or *Fossenigolo*, is a small *Foscina* with two or three prongs for smaller fish.

The *Delfinera* is a harpoon for casting at dolphins, tunny-fish, and the like (see Plate XXIV.).

Scares.

For driving or scaring the fish into the nets (*Pesca a spavento, a ludro*). The *Piston*, or *Pobug*, also called in some districts *Stumigio*, and *Stambul*, is a hollow cone at the end of a pole, for striking the surface of the water; at Trieste, a square board is substituted for the cone.

The *Tramata* is a cord for the same purpose.

The *Fraschiata* is a similar cord, to which are tied bundles of brushwood, at intervals from one another.

BAIT (*Esca, Esche*).

Besides the bait commonly used elsewhere, poisonous bait is used in some places, for instance, the sap of the *Euphorbia cyparisias* is used near Rogosnica, Milna, and at the mouth of the Narenta, to stupefy the basse; also the fruit of the South Asiatic plant, *Menispermum cuculus*, which is sold in retail at about a penny for five grains in the form of a powder, and is made into paste with flour. The latter is often used near Meligne.

SEGNALE (BARREL BUOY).

CHAPTER VII.

NAMES APPLIED TO FISHERMEN AND VARIOUS MODES OF FISHING. SARDINE FISHERIES. DIVISION OF PROFITS.

HE names of the fishing classes are derived either from their mode of fishing or from the names of the boats they use. For instance, *Bragozzanti* are those that work on board the *bragozzo*. *Pieleganti, Tartananti, Bragagnanti*, &c., are used in the same sense.

Trattarioi are those who fish with the seine (*tratta*); *Foscinanti* use the *foscina;* *Tognaroli* the *togna*, &c.

Sometimes also the names of the fish designate the fishermen; for instance, *Pescenovellanti, Sardellanti, Cievolanti, Baicolanti, Passerinanti, Rombarioi, Capparioi, Mazaneteri,* &c., &c.

The union of two or more boats which fish in company, as is the case with the *bragozzi*, is called *compagnia*, each of which has its *capo*, or head. They are managed according to established customs and rules; the temporary chief is called *capo de mare* at sea, and on shore *vendatore*. The latter receives the fish caught by the union in the boat called *portellata*, and is charged with the sale; he keeps the accounts, supplies the provisions for the boats, in fact, he looks after the business on shore, and receives five per cent. commission on the sale.

The wholesale dealer is called *basegaro;* the retail dealer, *compravendi, pescivendolo, pesciaiuolo*.

The commonest kind of fish is called *pesce populo, pesce misto,* or *minutaja* (*menuagia*), *minutaglia, pesce minuto;* the medium class, *pesce ordinario, pesce salvatico;* the prime, *pesce nobile, pesce fino*.

NAMES APPLIED TO THE DIFFERENT MODES OF FISHING.

The different modes of fishing are designated, as a rule, by the names of the fishing gear; for instance, *pesca a cocchia, a cassa, a cerberai, a bragagna, colle bombine, a foscina, a togna, a tratta, a tartana,* &c., &c.

Other modes of fishing, again, are designated by special terms; for, instance, the opening of the *valli chiuse*, in order to allow the fish to enter the fish-ponds, is called *pesca a montada*, or *pesca a valle; pesca a saltarello* is with a rowing boat, at night, with a light in the bows, the rowers pulling hard but with muffled oars, and the fish, following in the wake of the boat, jump (*saltare*) out of the water and into the boat. The fish thus caught are grey mullet (*volpine* and *cievoli*).

Pesca a zattera is similar in principle, but differs in one respect, that no light is used, the fish, also grey mullet, being scared in a given direction by striking the surface of the water; they meet with an obstruction, which they jump over, and are caught in a net, on the principle of the *Saltarello*, described amongst the trammel-nets.

The boat called *Pielego* drags in its wake a heavily-weighted line, to which are attached a number of baited hooks on snoods at equal distances apart, the end of the line grazing the bed. This is called *pesca a pielego*.

Pesca a parangala is carried on with a similar line, which remains motionless in the water (described under LINE-FISHERIES).

Pesca a spavento, or *a ludro*, is when the fish are driven or scared into nets by artificial means, such as by striking the surface of the water, &c.

Pesca a comagna is carried on with a very fine net called *fiorese* in the lagoons, for catching grey mullet (*cievoli*) when feeding: hence the term *comagna*, a distortion of *quando mangia* (*i.e.*, when it eats).

Pescar' a braccio, a fiappar, a palpar, is also a method of fishing in use in the lagoons, and consists in wading in the shallows, and extracting by hand the gobies which are immersed in the mud. This mode is also employed, in mild autumns and winters, for catching flounders and turbots at the heads of channels.

Pescar colle peche, or *orme*, or *pedate* (footsteps), consists in leaving imprints of the foot on soft mud or sand, which retain the water at ebb-tide, and thus attract crabs (*granchi*), which are thus caught by hand. This is also known by the term of *facendo le zappeghe*.

The fisheries are also designated by the names of fish; for instance, *pesca a pesce novello*, which is carried on by means of the *tela*, or *bragotto*; *pesca a scombri* is the line-fishing for mackerel (*scombri*) with the *togna*; *pesca a sardella* is the sardine fishery with the boats known as *Sardellere*, &c., &c.

When fishing is carried on without defined aim, it is called *pesca vagantiva*; *pesca al menuo*, or *pesca minuta*, is when the fishing is limited to small fish of little or no value (*minutaja*).

Deep-sea fishing is called *pesca da mar*, such as is exercised by the Chioggiotti; *pesca da marina* is fishing from the shore; *pesca da valle*, such as is practised by the *valesani* in the *valli* (fish-ponds), especially in the season of the *fraima*. Those that fish at random in the lagoons are called *mestieretti*, or *pescaoreti*.

SARDINE FISHERIES.

It is necessary to supplement the description given at pages 100 and 114 by a few remarks. The single hauls made by the drift-nets are much smaller than those of the seine-nets. They seldom exceed 40-50 casks in the first instance, whereas hauls of 500 and even 700 casks are occasionally made by the seine-nets. In Dalmatia the fisheries are carried on only on the dark nights (*scuri*). In Istria the fishing goes on also by moonlight. The *scuri* from May to September are known as the *scuri principali*. Then the fishing is carried on promiscuously off the islands of Lissa, Lésina, Brazza, and Curzola. The *scuri* before May and after September are called *venturini*. In this season the fishermen are only allowed to exercise their calling in their own fishing districts.

The fishermen of Comisa (western Lissa) are chiefly engaged in these fisheries, and they export 10-12,000 casks of salted sardines a year. After a mild winter the first shoals of sardines put in an appearance in the South Adriatic at the beginning of March, and at this season the fishermen of

Comisa are already on the watch for fish at the more distant *poste* off the island of Pelagosa.

The groups (*Broschetti*) consist of four nets. The nets vary from 40–100 fathoms in length, 12–18 fathoms depth of bag, the wings measuring 4 fathoms in depth. The Croat names used in Dalmatia are as follow :— the seine-net is called *Mrježa srdeljna;* the bag, *Gaja;* the mouth of the bag, *Goše;* the wings, *Krilo.* One of the drag-ropes is called *usa prva;* the other, *usa zalega;* they are kept at the surface of the water by means of small casks.

The iron basket, carried by the boat, *Gaëta* (see page 100), for fuel, is called *Svitalo;* the fuel itself, *Luč*. The third boat, which is used for landing the fish, is called *Ciglarica.* While the fishing is going on, a fire is kept burning on the shore to serve as a landmark: this fire is called *palak.* The weighted line (*škandaj*), used on board the *Gaëta* (see page 100), has a hollow pumpkin (*tikva*) to sustain it in the water.

The fuel required is a considerable item of expense. Fifteen cubic m. are used for each net during the twenty *scuri* of each month, thus making 75 m., or 375 florins for the season, at 5 florins per mètre. Thirty *tratte* from Lissa consume 2,250 cubic m. in the course of the season at a cost of 10,000 florins; and eighty *tratte*, hailing from Lésina, 6,000 cubic m. at an expense of 27,000 florins. The devastation of the forests caused by these requirements accounts for the rise in prices from 1⅓ fl. to 5 fl. per cubic m. On the island of Lésina alone 50,000 trees are felled every year for the purpose of these fisheries. Supplies are also drawn from Curzola (*Corcyra nigra* of old, thus called on account of its dense forests), Lagosta, Lissa, Brazza, Meleda, &c. The wood used is the *Pinus maritima* (Croat. *morski bor*), *Juniperus oxycedrus* (Croat. *smrč*), *Juniperus phœnicea* (Croat. *gluhač*), and *Juniperus macrocarpa* (Croat. *puk*). Common fir-wood (*zappino*) is also imported from Apulia, the demand exceeding the local supply.

Division of Profits.

The division of the yield of the seine-fisheries amongst the fishermen is deserving of notice. It varies according to locality and season. During the *venturini*, *i.e.*, out of the regular season, half of the proceeds goes to the master (*padrone*), and half to the crew, each supplying his own victuals, and the *padrone* the wood for lighting. During the regular season, from May to September (*scuri principali*), the partition is of a more complicated description. The *padrone* provides bread and wine for the crew for the twenty nights (*scuri*), and the firewood for lighting. After each day's haul, ten per cent. is equally divided on the spot amongst the crew, and three and one-third per cent. between the *direttore della tratta* and the *vogatore* (rower). The former is the master of the seine, and the latter the master of the Gaëta, with whom rests the responsibility of finding out the shoals, and leading the craft to a convenient place for making the haul, by means of the artificial light he carries on board.

This first division is known as the *porzione piccola* (small share).

At the end of the twenty nights' fishing in each month of the *scuri principali* the accounts are made up, and the net proceeds are divided into twenty-six shares. Of these four go to the owners of the net, one share to the owners of each of the three boats engaged in the fisheries, and one share to the Church for the privilege of being allowed to fish on Sundays and feast-days, in virtue of a Bull of Pope Alexander III. The remaining eighteen are equally divided amongst the crew, including the master (*direttore*). Thus, if, as is sometimes the case, the *direttore* happens to be at the same time the *padrone*, or owner of craft and gear, he receives altogether eight shares.

The cost of outfit, *i.e.*, bread, wine, and firewood, is deducted from the proceeds before the final distribution takes place, so that, in fact, everybody bears his share. But, if no catch is made during the month, the *padrone*, who provides for the outlay in the first instance, has to bear the whole loss, as the expense cannot be carried over to the next month's account. On the other hand, the *padrone* has the advantage, that the crew is obliged to sell him its share of the catch at about ten shillings a barrel, or half the market value, the difference being supposed to defray the cost of curing and packing. The crew retains for its own use only one barrel for every ten barrels thus sold to the *padrone*. If the *direttore* is not at the same time *padrone*, he receives from the latter a gratuity.

This is the mode of partition in vogue off the islands of Lissa, Lésina, Brazza, and Curzola, where the principal sardine fisheries are carried on.

At Trieste, Cattaro, Giuppana, Calamotta, and Sebenico, the *padrone* generally receives half, the other half being equally divided amongst the crew.

At Pola one-sixth falls to the share of the owner of the craft, one-sixth to the owner of the seine, one-sixth to the master (*direttore*), and one-half is equally divided amongst the crew.

At Spalato the *padrone* is in the habit of receiving seven shares; the crew of three men each two shares; the boat which carries the fresh fish to market two shares, and the master (*direttore*) two shares; together, seventeen shares. The *direttore* likewise receives a weekly pay of fifty soldi (ten pence).

At Gravosa two-thirds fall to the share of the owners of craft and gear, and one-third to the crew.

At Curzola five shares go to the owner of the net, one share to the boat, and one share to each man of the crew, including the master (*direttore*).

At Zara and along the Hungarian-Croatian littoral the crew, as a rule, is paid fixed daily wages and finds its own victuals: the wages vary from one shilling to two shillings and sixpence a day according to the season.

In the case of the drift-net fisheries (*voigari*), carried on chiefly off the coast of Istria, the accounts are made up at the end of the season, the value of the fish being calculated at export prices current at the time. After deducting the cost of victuals supplied to the crew by the *padrone* and the cost of salt and barrels for curing purposes, the balance is divided into sixteen shares, of which the *padrone* receives three, the master (*direttore*) three, and each of the five men two shares.

FIUME FROM THE EAST.

CHAPTER VIII.

THE FISH-MARKETS.

Description.

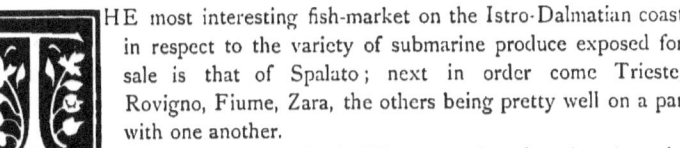HE most interesting fish-market on the Istro-Dalmatian coast in respect to the variety of submarine produce exposed for sale is that of Spalato; next in order come Trieste, Rovigno, Fiume, Zara, the others being pretty well on a par with one another.

Out of a total of 118 different species of produce brought to market in 1878, the respective official figures were:— Spalato, 95; Trieste, 78; Rovigno, 70; Pola, 56; Zara, 55; Lussinpiccolo and Ragusa, 54; Megline, 38. Of Fiume there are no data.[1]

Each market has its *spécialité* at certain seasons; for instance, Fiume, the *Scampi* (Norway Lobster); Zara, a great variety of Crustaceans, amongst which is the Rock Lobster (*Palinurus vulgaris*); Sebenico, the *Dentale della corona* (*Dentex gibbosus*), whilst at Spalato the Pelamid and Lichia (*Lizza*) are very abundant. Trieste being the best market, most of the *spécialités* of other markets are sent there for sale, for instance, the *Scampo* of Fiume, the Tunny of Croatia, and the Rock Lobster from Dalmatia, &c.

As a rule, the most valued of the Adriatic fishes are the Basse (*Branzin*), the Dentex (*Dentale*), the Surmullets (*Barbone* and *Triglia*), the Red, or Spanish Sea-bream (*Ribone*), the Gilt-head (*Orada*); these are always more or less common, especially in autumn and spring. The summer fisheries

---

[1] The well-defined, prevalent species which, according to the official statistics, appear in the Adriatic fish-markets, may be given at ten crustaceans, thirty mollusks, and about ninety fishes, excluding the larger sharks, and uniting under one name various species of the same genus.

yield the Mackerel (*Scombro*) and its relatives the Tunny (*Ton*), the Pelamid (*Palamida*), and the plain Bonito (*Tombarello*), the latter being only occasionally met with. To these must be added the *Lizza* (*Lichia amia*). Of the flat-fish tribe, occur the Turbot (*Rombo*), the Brill (*Suazo*), and the Sole (*Sfoglia*), which are most prevalent and best for eating in the autumn and winter months. Of the Herring family, are the Pilchard (*Sardella*), the Anchovy (*Sardon*), and the *Papalina* or *Sardellina* (*Clupea papalina*), which belong to the yield of the summer fisheries. Pilchard comes early and late in summer; Anchovy in autumn. These are all, more or less, to be classed among the prime fish, *Pesce nobile* or *fino*.

Amongst the second class of fish, known as *Pesce ordinario*, or *salvatico*, are included the five species of *Mugilidæ*, or Grey Mullet tribe (*Volpina, Cievolo*, &c.): they are almost always in the market, and in Fiume they are distinguished by the vulgar names of *metja, divi, pravi, bon*. Besides these are the two Scorpions (*Scarpena*), two Gurnards (*Lucerna, Anzoletto*), four Weevers (*Ragno*), the Star-gazer (*Bocca in cao*), some of the better of the Serranus tribe, the *Cantharus orbicularis*, the Bogue (*Bobba*), the *Oblata melanura* (*Occhiada*), the *Sargus Rondeletii* (*Sargo*), the *S. annularis* (*Sparo*), the Meagres and Umbrina (*Corbo*), the John Dory (*Pesce San Pietro*), the Horse Mackerel (*Suro, Saron*), some of the better class of Gobies not included amongst the class of *Minutaja* (mixed fishes), most of the Cod tribe (*Gadidæ*), the Whiting (*Molo da parangolo*), the Poor, or Capelan (*Pesce molo, Busbana*), the Hake (*Asinello, Merluzzo*) and the Rock Ling (*Mare dei gronghi*). Of the flat-fish tribe is the *Citharus linguatula* (*Pataraccia*) besides the Gar-pike (*Angosigola*); and the Conger-eel (*Grongo*). The Shark tribe supplies the Spiny Dogs (*Assià*), which are not despised even by the better class; and the Ray, the Thornbacks (*Razza spinosa*) and *Raja miraletus* (*Quattr' occhi*).

The third class of fish, known as *Pesce populo*, comprises the *minutaja*, or *misto* (mixed fish), the Mendole (*Menole, Maride, Garizzo*), the *Cantharus vulgaris* (*Cantaro*), the Box Salpa (*Salpa*), the *Charax puntazzo* (*Spizzo, Pesce morti*), the common kinds of Gurnards (*Anzoletti*), the genus *Stromateus* (*Pesce figo*), the common kinds of Gobies (*Guatti*), and Blennies

(*Gattorusole*), the Anglers (*Rospi*), the Atherines (*Auguèle*), the Red Band-fish (*Pesce cordéla*), the *Heliastes chromis* (*Pesce fabbro*), the Wrasses (*Liba, donzella*), and, generally speaking, the Sharks and Rays, amongst the latter the Electric Ray (*Tremolo*).

The smell of the Sharks is anything but agreeable; they are at once gutted, and the bowels thrown away; the body is cut open lengthways and the larger fish divided in their breadth; this is also the case with the Rays, Tunny, and Pelamid. The entrails of some fish, such as the Grey Mullet, are a delicacy (like the Woodcock's), and are not extracted.

The Spiny Dogs (*Assià*) are the most esteemed amongst the Sharks, and both the Smooth Hound (*Cagnetto*) and the Spotted Dogs (*Gatte*) are often sold in their stead, although much inferior. The better to deceive purchasers, they are skinned previous to exposure for sale, only a strip of the dorsal fin being retained in order to simulate the spine peculiar to the former species. The oil extracted from the liver of *Centrina Salviani* (*Pesce Porco*) is much valued for healing burns and wounds, and that of the *Notidanus* is light and good.

Small Sharks and Rays, Anglers, the Hake and Rock Ling, the Star-gazers, and John Dorys are common features in almost all markets during the greater part of the year; they are most prevalent and best for eating in winter, when they are brought to market, sometimes in large quantities, by the Italian trawlers. They find a ready sale among the poorer classes.

Hake caught by the line (*Asinello d'amo*) is much superior in quality to that caught in the trawling-nets, and is held a delicacy and preferred by many people to the Basse. This circumstance, or else the prevalence of this fish on the Croatian shores, has given rise to the vulgar name by which it is known at Fiume, *Branzin croato*, which is applied in a contumelious sense against the Croats. Specimens are sometimes caught 3 feet in length. A favourite way of preparing them for the table is to "lard" them with salted sardines and to broil them in cream. Hake is a *spécialité* of the Fiume and Croatian markets: 125 tons are bought and sold in the course of the year. The supply of the Austrian markets is only 10 tons. The chief take of Poor and Whiting extends likewise along the eastern coast as far as Zara. The relative figures are: Fiume and Croatian ports, 80 tons; Zara, 140 tons; and the remaining ports together, 60 tons.

The huge Sharks make their appearance only during the summer heats. Gurnards are most prevalent in winter and early spring; Weevers, Scorpions, and the Poor in spring and autumn; Meagres in spring and summer; Gar-pike, Whiting, Horse Mackerel, and *Lizza* in summer; Mendole and Conger-eels in summer and autumn. The Cephalopods are never missing in the markets, and, especially the young ones, are much esteemed as food in winter. The Cuttle-fish (*Seppa*), the Octopus (*Folpo*), and *Eledone moschata* are the cheapest produce of the sea, and are favourites with the lower classes. The flesh of the Squid (*Calamaro*) is sweetish, and hard as leather; it is indigestible, even in the best of seasons, yet it is a favourite with the better classes, to judge by the price it sometimes fetches. *Sepiola Rondeletii* (*Sepiola*) is often served on the tables of the rich, and is not to be despised.

Among the Crustaceans the Norway Lobster (*Scampo*) undoubtedly holds the first rank in the Fiume market; it is found throughout the winter, from September to April, when the Italian trawling-boats ply, and it sells, as a rule, at 1s. to 1s. 6d. per kilo, and at 3s. to 4s., exceptionally, for instance, at Christmas and Easter. In Trieste and Venice it is considered a great delicacy. The heads are removed for transit, and only the tails are offered for sale, fetching as much as 10s. a kilo. The common Lobster (*Astice*) is common on the west coast of Istria and Trieste, and the Rock Lobster (*Languste*) on the Dalmatian coast; they are often very abundant in summer, selling at Fiume and Trieste at 1s. to 1s. 6d. a piece. At other seasons they sometimes fetch as much as 10s. for the inland markets.

Crabs are not much cared for: the larger kinds, such as the Sea-spider (*Granzeole*), and the Harry Crab (*Granzi*), when plentiful, sell at 1d. or 2d. each. The Fiume market is very poor in this respect, the variety in other fish-markets being much greater. Shrimps and Prawns (*Skilla, Gambaretto*) are caught in large quantities on the sand-beds near Grado and in the lagoons of Venice, whence they are brought to market at Trieste.

The rest of the submarine animal produce goes by the name of *Frutti di*

SHIP-BUILDING, SCOGLIO SAN MARCO.

mar; this term includes all mollusks, such as Oysters (*Ostriche*), the *Solen siliqua* (*Cape lunghe*), the Rock-borers (*Pholas dactylus*) and the Date Shell (*Dattoli*), the latter being considered a great delicacy; likewise the Mussels, *Mytilus edulis* (*Pedocchio*) and *Modiola barbata* (*Mussoli*). The poorer classes of Trieste and Venice consume a quantity of *Pectines*, chiefly *Pecten jacobæus* (*Cape sante*), also *Arca Noæ* (*Cofani di grotta*), *Cardium rusticum* (*Cape tonde*), *Venus gallina* (*Peverazze*), *V. decussata*, *Scrobicularia piperita* (*Caparozzoli*). *Pinna rudis*, *P. squamosa*, *P. muricata* (*Asture*, or *Palóstriche*), are also eaten.

Some Sea-snails are regularly sold at Trieste and other markets, such as *Helix sp.* (*Buovoli*) and *Murex brandaris* (*Garusoli*), the latter often in large quantities, overgrown by *Actinia effœta*. The *Murex trunculus* is covered with a kind of slime of the brightest violet colour, from which the purple of the Roman Cæsars was made.

The stranger will be struck in many markets by the appearance of *Ascidia microcosmus*, which looks anything but appetising; in like manner the Sea Urchins (*Rizzi di mar*), *Echinus lividus* and *E. melo*, which show signs of life by the fact of their prickles being constantly in motion. They are eaten, but only when they are in egg, and in this state they form an important article of food in all southern waters. They are in season in winter. Nardo says that they are not consumed at Venice. The most prevalent is *E. lividus*, which is abundant, adhering to the rocks just below the water-mark, and the small *E. microtuberculatus*. The large violet *E. brevispinosus*, Risso, is not so common. It is armed with short white-tipped prickles, and was formerly considered identical with the northern species, *E. esculentus*. An Actinia (*A. cereus*) is also consumed by the poor classes at Trieste and at Nice, whence Risso has called it *A. edulis*.

Besides the foregoing produce, which is common to most fish-markets, and is more or less prevalent according to the seasons in which each particular species occurs, there are other species, which form the exception. The latter are looked upon as curiosities, and find their way into the hands of the ichthyologist, if he be lucky, or, as is more frequently the case, they are sold together with the other commoner kinds of fish without any special distinction. Amongst these may be mentioned the dusky Serranus (*Cherne*), the Stone Basse, the *Sebastes imperialis*, the Flying Gurnard (*Rondinella*), the Spet (*Pesche schermo*), and the Scabbard-fish (*Spada argentina*), which has been caught after a hurricane off Zaole; also the Hair-tail, the Atlantic Bonito, the Germon and the Pilot-fish (*Fanfano*), which occasionally enters the ports in the company of vessels; the Remora, attached to the bronchial aperture of sharks, tunny, and sword-fish; the Black-fish (*Centrolophus* sp.), Dolphins (*Coryphæna* sp.), Ray's Sea-bream and *Ausonia Cuvieri* (*Pesce gallo*), a specimen of which was caught near Trieste in December, 1879, weighing 50 kilos, the first time since twenty years ago, when one was caught at Muggia; also the *Caranx dentex*, the *Seriola Dumerilii*, the Derbio (*Lizza bastarda*), the *Lichia vadigo*, the Boar-fish, the Sword-fish (*Pesce spada*), the Ribbon-fish (*Pesce falce*), the *Histiophorus belone*, the Trumpet-fish (*Pesce trombetta*), besides various of the rarer species of the Goby, Blenny, Wrasse, Cod, and Flat-fish tribes; the larger kinds of Sharks, which only occur sporadically in these waters; the File and Sunfishes, the Needle-fishes, &c., &c. A specimen of *Orthagoriscus Planci*, the truncated Sun-fish (*Girasol*) was caught not long since in the Quarnero, likewise a specimen of the Flying-fish (*Exocœtus*). To these may be added the following species, viz., the Hammer-headed Shark, the *Notidanus barbarus*, the *Sargus Salviani*, the mailed Gurnard, the *Coris Giofredi*, the *Phycis blennioides*, the *Phycis mediterraneus*, the *Pleuronectes platessa*, the *Myrus vulgaris*. The Sturgeon is but rarely met with on the eastern coast, but a specimen has been caught in a trawling-net in the Quarnero in the month of October.

The Sea-spider (*Grazèole*) is seldom to be found in the Fiume market though common at Trieste. Other kinds of crabs, as for instance, *Stenorrhynchus phalangium*, *Xantho floridus*, *Pagurus* sp., *Galathea* sp., are occasionally met with. *Dromia Rumphii* and *Pinnotherus veterum* are less prevalent. Amongst the shell-fish, *Spondylus aculcatus*, *Haliotis tuberculata*, *Dentalium entalis*, *Cerithium vulgatum*, *Turritella communis*, *Aporrhais pes pelecani*, and *Dolium galea*, are occasionally to be found, especially so at Trieste.

Specimens of the Echinoderms *Alecto europaea*, *Ophiotrix fragilis*, *Astropecten bispinosus* and *aurantiacus*, *Asteracanthion gelatinosum*, and *Schizaster canaliferus*, likewise occur.

The large Sea-tortoise, *Chelonia atra*, is sometimes brought to market in Dalmatia, specimens of which weigh as much as 80 lb. Small fresh-water Turtles are sometimes brought by the ship-load from Greece and Albania, and are much consumed in Fiume and all over Istria, selling at 2d. to 3d. a piece. They are considered a delicacy.

CHAPTER IX.

METHODS OF CURING AND COOKING FISH.

Curing Pilchards, Anchovies, &c.—Preserving Pilchards, Tunny, Norway-lobster, &c. in oil.—Fishes which are smoked, or dried for exportation.—Ways of preparing various fishes and other produce of the sea for the table.

ALT FISH is prepared chiefly on the west coast of Istria, at Isola, Capo d'Istria, Pirano, Rovigno, &c., and on the islands Lésina, Lissa, Lagosta, &c. The curing of Pilchards and Anchovies is the most extensive; next in importance are Mackerel, Horse Mackerel, Gar-fish, *Smaris vulgaris*. The Pilchards are, as a rule, slightly salted, and packed in casks or tubs on board the fishing craft. On landing they are sorted and washed in sea-water. Those in good condition are then packed tightly in small pine casks 18 by 12 inches, about 1 lb. of clean white salt being spread between each alternate layer of fish. When the cask is full, a circular piece of wood (*fracca*), rather smaller than the head of the cask, is placed on the top of the fish, weighted with a stone of about 2 cwt., so as gradually to press out the brine and oil, and by compressing to exclude the air. The hoops of the cask being loose, the brine and oil drain through the sides and bottom of the cask. This is called the *primo stivaggio*. After twenty-five or thirty days the stone is removed; the brine (*Salamoja*) is allowed to run off, the cask is filled up with fish and salt as before, and re-weighted. This process, called the *secondo stivaggio*, or *dare il colmo* (*colmo* = superfluity), is repeated until the fish is sufficiently compressed (*saldo*); the cask is then closed and brine is poured on the cover until sold, in order to keep the contents fresh and moist.

This operation is carried on on a stone, or, generally speaking, on a hard and waterproof ground-floor, built on a slant so as to allow the brine to run off by gutters made for this purpose in the floor, into a well or cistern, for further use in moistening the fish. The liquid fat or oil which floats on the water is put in casks and sold to leather-dressers. The due degree of saltness of the brine is ascertained by means of a raw hen's egg; if it sinks, more salt must be added.

The number of fish contained in each cask is marked on the outside; thus: ✚ = 1,000; ✚ = 1,500; ✚ = 1,700; ✚ = 1,750; ✚ = 2,000. A cask contains from 1,200–2,200 Sardines, or 400 Mackerel.

Three to five months after salting, the fish is in proper condition for consumption; well-cured fish keeps for two or three years; the colour becomes dark-red, the smell aromatic, and the flavour spicy. In commerce a pointed stick, or skewer, is stuck into the midst of the fish in order to see whether the fish is in good condition, which is ascertained by the smell; this is called *speronare il pesce*.

The fish caught by the seine-nets (*Tratte*) do not cure as well as those caught in the drift-nets (*Reti d' imbrocco*), being more or less damaged by pressure and devoid of scales; hence the latter are preferred for curing purposes.

Anchovies (*Sardoni*) and *Smaris sp.* (*Menole*) are preserved in like manner, chiefly in small tubs, but not so durably, on account of the easier access of the air.

The pine wood of which the casks are made comes from Croatia and Bosnia; a cask costs 80 soldi, = 1s. 4d.; a tub, 30 soldi, = 6d. The salt used for a cask, say about 40 lb., is supplied by the Government monopoly at half the usual price charged, say 4 fl. to 4·65 fl. per 100 kilogr., = 6s. 8d. to 7s. 6d.

The curer and packer is, as a rule, also the fisherman. When this is not the case, he pays the fisherman 9–12 fl. (15s.–20s.) for the fresh fish requisite for one cask, say 1,500 larger, or 1,600 smaller fish. The cask of cured fish sells at 15–22 fl. (25s. to 36s. 8d.). The retail price is one soldo a piece, or 5–6 for a penny. A tub of salt fish contains 22 kilos, for which 8 kilos of salt are required. The packer pays 3–5 fl. for the fish (5s. to

8s. 4d.), and sells the cured fish at 6–7 fl. (10s.–11s. 8d.), the retail price being 2–5 fish a penny (1–2 soldi a piece).

The labour of salting and packing is carried on chiefly by women, for which service they receive, as a rule, 5 soldi (1d.) per mille pilchards, and one-half of the damaged fish and of the pressed fat gained from the process of curing. Some are paid as much as 12 soldi per mille; the foreman receives 25 fl. per month during the curing season, and 10 fl. per month up to the time of sale. Rovigno, in Istria, is the principal place of this industry, which is, on the whole, flourishing, though the export to Italy has decreased since 1866. The produce was 3,600 casks in 1872; that of Pirano was 1,400 casks *Sardelle*, and 600 tubs *Menole*, in 1870. This industry seems to have declined since the former century. The Venetian Senate assigned to the *Commune* of Rovigno an annual allowance of 580 tons of salt in 1753. This is sufficient for curing 30,000 casks after deducting a third for domestic purposes. Dalmatia exports from 30,000–50,000 casks of salt fish a year; Lissa, 10,000 casks.

Meanwhile a new industry has sprung up at Barcola, Duino, and Grado, consisting in curing the Pilchards in oil, after the fashion of the *Sardines de Nantes*, in small tins and casks. Lissa exports 500 small casks of Sardines in oil, and 3,000–4,000 tins, of which 2,500 are Sardines, 1,000 Anchovies, and 500 Mackerel. The fish is bought at 3–4 florins (5s. to 6s. 8d.) per 1,000, the drift-net fish being preferred to the seine-net fish. The heads are cut off and the fish gutted. They are next washed, put in baskets and strewed with salt. After a lapse of eight hours, they are washed in sea-water and exposed to the sun to dry on small gridirons. If the weather is damp, they are put in a drying-room. They are then put into large kettles and cooked in oil heated by means of steam. During the latter process they remain on the gridirons, by means of which they are put into and extracted from the kettles. They are then brought on to large tables, covered with zinc plates, and there packed into tins of 6, 7, 8, 12, 20, 30, and 50 fish. The open tins are put into a large tank which is filled with oil, and in which they remain twenty-four hours, so as to allow the oil time to soak the fish. The surplus oil is then drained off by means of a tap, and the tins are taken out and soldered.

The closed tins are then boiled for a few hours, in large kettles, at a temperature of 212° F. The tins are then examined for leakage, and the sound ones are packed in cases. The tins are made on the establishment, the tin-plates being imported from England. The manufacturers receive a drawback on the tins exported equal to the amount of duty paid on the tin-plates. They also buy the salt from Government on the same terms as the common curers. The oil is imported from Italy or France, paying a duty of 5s. per 100 kilogr., the inland oil from Istria and Dalmatia not being sufficiently clean for the purpose; a process for filtering the oil is also adopted. The empty tins cost from 8–20 soldi ($1\frac{3}{5}$d.–4d.) a piece, according to size. The Sardines in tins are sold at Trieste, the small ones at 30 soldi (6d.); those containing 12, at 45 soldi (9d.); 20, at 60 soldi (1s.); and 30, at 1 fl. (1s. 8d.).[1]

The success of this new industry, which is daily assuming larger proportions, and bids fair to supplant the common method of curing, is due to Mr. Carl Warhanek, who first tried this process at Fiume in 1861, and then removed to Gelsa, on the island of Lésina. The high import duties on the oil and tins in Dalmatia forced him to renounce Gelsa, whence he removed to Barcola (S. Bortolo), near Trieste, where, at length, his venture met with well-earned success. In 1872 he extended his establishment to Grado. The establishment at San Bortolo has since been abandoned, and new factories have been started at Duino, Isola, and Rovigno. A similar establishment, started at Fiume about the year 1870, proved unsuccessful, for what reason it is difficult to say. Besides the Sardine, the Norway Lobster (*Scampo*) and the Tunny (*Ton*) are preserved in oil at Duino.

On the islands of the Quarnero and in South Dalmatia many kinds of submarine animals,—chiefly Cephalopods, Conger-eels, Sharks, Rays, sometimes also the Basse and Gilt-head,—are split up along the belly, the soft parts extracted, and the flesh either simply dried in the sun, or slightly salted and smoked and kept for winter food. The Cephalopods are also exported

---

[1] As the florin is subject to constant fluctuations, the value in sterling can only be given approximately; throughout, the florin, Austrian currency, has been taken at 1*s.* 8*d.*

to Greece, but this article is of a very inferior quality. Conger-eels, Gilt-head, Mackerel, Red Mullet, Dentex, and Grey Mullet are smoked in Dalmatia and Istria.

The roe of the Grey Mullet is extracted, smoked separately, and sold under the name of *Bottarga*, the *botargo* of our Elizabethan writers. This is the chief occupation of the fishermen of Trappano and Makarska, who are engaged in the Grey Mullet fisheries at the mouths of the Narenta in the months of October and November. The catch at Trappano is 15 tons of fish, producing 300 kilogr. of roe; the fish is eaten on the spot.

In some parts, especially in the *piccolo mare* of Taranto, the Red Mullet (*Barbon*) is sometimes so fat, especially at the time of the new moon, that it falls to pieces when cooked, and has, therefore, to be cooked wrapped up in a piece of paper.

Sea Urchins are eaten raw; Anemones are fried in oil; Crabs are either simply boiled and the flesh eaten with finely-cut garlic and parsley, or else the water, in which they have been partly boiled, is poured off, and the flesh stewed in vinegar and oil, and seasoned with garlic, parsley, pepper, &c.; or, after being well washed and sprinkled with salt, they are fried in oil. Mussels are generally stewed in their own water in addition to salt and oil, or else fried with bread-crumbs, parsley, oil, and pepper, lemon-juice being added. A soup is also made by boiling them in their own water, water and bread being added, or else olive oil with as much rice as may be needed, with a seasoning of garlic, parsley, and pepper. Periwinkles are first boiled, extracted from the shell by the aid of a pin, and eaten either with salt alone, or dipped in a broth of oil, pepper, and salt.

Cephalopods, when large, are boiled and eaten in a broth of vinegar and oil well seasoned with pepper and salt; the Octopus has first to be well beaten, on account of its toughness; the smaller ones are generally fried in oil and are a favourite dish, especially in winter. The favourite way of eating all kinds of fish is in a broth made of the water in which they have been boiled, to which oil is added and a seasoning of garlic, parsley, and pepper. This mode of cooking is called *brodetto*, and, as a rule, it is eaten with a great deal of rice. The Stock-fish (*baccalà*) is eaten in this way, and is a

GULF OF BUCCARI, PORTO RÈ.

C.

favourite dish on fast-days. Otherwise, fishes are boiled, dipped in oil and grilled, or fried in oil with bread-crumbs, much the same as in other countries, the only difference being that oil is substituted for butter. Some fishes (Hake, for instance) are "larded" with salt sardines and broiled in cream. The livers of large Sharks are boiled down, as in Iceland, for oil, mostly "Cod-liver oil."

CHAPTER X.

STATISTICS.[1]

Proceeds of the fisheries.—The Austrian fishing fleet; its distribution on the coast.—Yield of the Istrian, Hungarian-Croatian, and Dalmatian fisheries.—Recapitulation.—Share of the Italian boats.—Statistics of the Austrian sea-fisheries; ditto of the Hungarian sea-fisheries.—Total yield.—Craft belonging to the Hungarian-Croatian seaboard.—Imports and exports of fish.—Fish sold in the Fiume fish-market.

 HAVE mentioned how difficult it is to collect reliable statistical data on the subject of the fisheries, wherefore they can at best be given approximately, and, as a rule, it must be assumed that they are under-stated. Professor Schmarda estimates the value of the Austrian fisheries at three and a half million florins, including the *valli chiuse*, or fishing ponds of the lagoons. This comprises, however, the fisheries of the coast of Venice, which at the time belonged to Austria, consisting of about 1,000 boats of 6,000 tons burden and a crew of 5,000 men, but which now belong to Italy. In 1864, before the cession of Venice by Austria, the Austrian fishing fleet comprised 2,340 boats of about 10,000

---

[1] The statistics of the Austrian sea-fisheries are compiled with commendable exactitude and completeness, and, what is more, they are regularly published in the "Austria," a statistical periodical of the Austrian Ministry of Commerce. Strange to say, this state of things bears a favourable comparison to England, where it is a matter of great difficulty, not to say of impossibility, to attain anything like exhaustive data on the subject of the British sea-fisheries; and this is the more remarkable, considering their great national importance, representing, as they do, a value of something like twelve millions sterling, and probably more. Even Ireland has her Inspectors of fisheries and Scotland her Fishery Board, both of which publish statistics in their reports to Parliament, but these relate almost entirely to the salmon fisheries. As to the sea-fisheries of Great Britain, it appears that the Board of Trade has no official statistics on the

tons, and a crew of 8,000 men. On the cession of Venice, in 1867, it fell to 1,296 boats, of 3,892 tons and 2,571 crew.

The following table shows to what extent the Austro-Hungarian fishing fleet has increased during the ten years 1868–1877:—

Year.	Number of Boats.	Tonnage.	Crew.
1868	1,269	3,799	4,049
1869	1,859	4,967	5,228
1870	1,880	4,992	5,322
1871	1,349	3,802	4,303
1872	1,894	5,533	7,117
1873	1,952	5,670	7,196
1874	1,959	5,688	7,264
1875	1,966	5,787	7,341
1876	1,990	6,056	7,400
1877	2,004	5,877	7,489
1878	2,184	6,397	8,544

In 1872 the distribution of the fleet was as follows:—

	Boats.	Tonnage.	Crew.
Gorizia, Gradisca	65	292	254
Istria, Islands of the Quarnero	508	1,678	1,953
Hungarian-Croatian littoral	73	187	248
Dalmatia and islands	1,248	3,376	4,662
Total	1,894	5,533	7,117

subject. It is to be hoped that the International Fisheries Exhibition of 1883 may serve to do something to remedy this deficiency. The Hungarian statistics fall short in completeness and clearness of those of the sister country, and they are not published; but, then, her fisheries are of small significance, and people here are only beginning to awaken to the fact of the importance of the sea-fisheries if properly carried on, and of the vast amount of capital swimming in the seas, which they only have to stretch forth their hands to secure. Improved railway communication may contribute in a main degree to improve this state of things, for hitherto the great drawback has been the want of market for the sale of the yield in excess of the local consumption.

or an average of rather less than three tons and a crew of four men per craft, which has since remained unchanged.

1. The average yield of the *Istrian* fisheries, including Trieste, Gorizia, and the islands of the Quarnero, Veglia, Cherso, and Lussin, may be given at between three and three and a half million kilogr., valued at about 600 to 650 thousand florins, of which about one-half is consumed on the spot, three-fifths of the prime and two-fifths of the ordinary being exported. The proportion of prime and ordinary varies according to the yield of the Sardine fisheries, the proportion of prime being larger when the Sardine fisheries are favourable; in average years it may be taken at two-fifths prime and three-fifths ordinary. The neighbourhood of Trieste and Venice facilitates the sale, and the market is extending rapidly in consequence of the railway communication, the value of which will only in course of time be fully appreciated by those engaged in the fishing trade. At present it is looked upon as a luxury to send fish by rail inland, but the time will come when the inland markets will look for their supply of sea fish with the same regularity as of meat. This is the case in other countries, and it will be the case here sooner or later; indeed, signs are not wanting even now that the local supply suffers under the innovation; and, as the supply of fresh fish in Austria is largely supplemented by the importation of salt fish, there is no doubt that fresh sea fish will, in course of time, find its way to those inland markets best able to pay the higher prices. Even nowadays sea fish from Trieste is sometimes to be had at Vienna at lower prices than at Trieste. About two-thirds of the take is consumed or exported in a fresh state, whilst one-third, and sometimes more, is salted; this depends on the catch of Mackerel (*Scombri*), Spanish Mackerel (*Lanzardo*), *Menole*, and *Maride*, which are salted in seasons of large takes.

In normal years it may be assumed that the fish cured by salting consists of two-thirds of Sardines, one-sixth of Anchovies, one-twelfth of *Menole*, and one-twelfth of Mackerel, Spanish Mackerel (*Lanzardo*), *Maride*, and Tunny-fish.

2. On the *Hungarian-Croatian* littoral Tunny predominates, hence also

the proportion of prime fish; the yield of the Tunny fisheries is liable to great fluctuations, thus:—

in 1877	68,140 kilogr.;	value,	26,271	florins;
in 1878	157,113 „	„	79,462	„
in 1879	87,068 „	„	34,828	„

The average yield for eight years was 122,000 kilogr.; value, 60,000 florins. The total yield of the fisheries in the said years amounted to:—

in 1877	744,374 kilogr.;	value,	144,217	florins;
in 1878	927,474 „	„	228,874	„
in 1879	529,508 „	„	143,197	„

The average yield for eight years was 778,000 kilogr. of fish and 31,000 crabs; value, 152,000 florins. The share of the Italian fishermen was between one-fourth and three-fifths of the total catch:—

1877	198,187	kilogr.
1878	272,402	„
1879	319,978	„

The ordinary fish is consumed on the coast; whereas the prime, and more especially the tunny-fish, is much exported to the neighbouring markets and to Italy, in a fresh state. The proportion of salted fish was formerly higher than in Istria on account of the want of railway communication, but this has since changed in favour of this coast.

3. *Dalmatian Coast and Archipelago.*—Average total, 5,500,000 to 6,000,000 kilogr.; value, 1,400,000 florins. The value suffers from want of markets and railway communication; and this tells most on the value of the prime, which elsewhere is exported in a fresh state. Two-fifths consist of prime and three-fifths of ordinary. The local consumption is large, owing to the long extension of coast and the poverty of the inhabitants, whose

nourishment consists in a great degree of fish; hence it may be taken that the ordinary fish is consumed entirely on the coast, and that the total local consumption amounts to two-thirds of the whole take. The greater part of the prime (including sardines) is salted for export to Trieste, Italy, and Genoa.

Exportation of salt fish from Dalmatia.

	Casks of 50 kilogr.	Value in Florins.
1869	24,649	394,384
1870	33,269	532,304
1871	37,452	599,232
1875	50,476	807,616
1876	54,594	873,504
1877	33,276	532,416
1878	32,730	523,680

If we recapitulate, we arrive at the following figures :—

total catch, say, 10,000,000 kilogr. ;
value .... 2,100,000 florins;

or an average price of 21 soldi per kilo. This is, however, probably a minimum estimate. I should be inclined to put it at 2,500,000 florins, if not more.[1]

The share of the Italian fishermen in the Austrian-Hungarian fisheries, according to the official statistics for the year 1878 to 1879, is as follows :—

---

[1] Part of the foregoing information is taken from Count Marazzi's report, but I have been obliged to demur to his concluding figures; Count M. puts the total yield at 5,750,000 kilogr., which is too low; and the value at 5,690,000 francs, which, proportionately to the quantity given, is much too high; but it must not be forgotten that Count M. had not to hand the official statistics that are now published.

Statistics of the Austrian Sea-Fisheries.
(Published by the Statistical Department of the Austrian Ministry of Commerce.)

Harbour Master's Districts.	Catch.			Material used.				Fishermen engaged.	Local Consumption.	
				Craft.		Gear.				
	Number.	Kilogr.	Value in florins.	Number.	Value, fl.	Number.	Value, fl.		Number.	Kilogr.
From 23 April to 22 October, 1877.										
Trieste	1,745	1,435,147	160,766	482	196,492	19,030	225,946	2,131	1,745	327,380
Rovigno	82,198	382,944	90,443	204	63,360	8,741	143,856	979	31,454	150,263
Pola	472,079	143,676	47,375	147	143,309	1,600	44,494	705	132,779	132,656
Lussinpiccolo	24,868	304,426	62,308	232	43,300	1,802	69,987	926	22,797	181,011
Zara	1,577,691	1,769,348	391,900	362	66,683	1,531	150,825	1,700	1,551,368	1,608,678
Spalato	129,258	2,069,608	421,394	739	169,322	2,819	212,942	3,587	124,150	315,484
Ragusa	1,398	273,573	55,619	306	65,640	1,297	106,027	904	1,880	123,274
Megline	?	38,600	14,901	23	5,450	33	6,778	130	?	38,600
Total	2,289,237	6,417,552	1,244,906	2,495	753,554	36,943	963,857	11,062[1]	1,865,173	2,877,346
From 23 October, 1877, to 22 April, 1878.										
Trieste	11,530	524,394	103,913	673	195,336	24,023	214,662	2,115	11,530	191,870
Rovigno	48,892	214,360	66,885	165	96,240	7,201	64,415	746	7,792	134,334
Pola	270,420	252,804	58,820	147	143,870	7,987	117,577	615	78,770	126,394
Lussinpiccolo	4,901	95,800	19,977	217	50,440	1,681	48,763	847	4,901	78,070
Zara	3,363,588	1,019,171	479,443	363	76,667	1,614	153,706	1,200	3,150,473	1,737,958
Spalato	309,316	737,183	113,502	580	153,137	2,467	107,478	2,519	308,316	617,604
Ragusa	758	282,212	44,779	309	69,262	1,561	88,667	1,076	506	142,876
Megline	2,000	18,530	8,059	12	2,000	233	6,980	110	2,000	18,530
Total	4,017,405	4,044,634[14]	895,978[14]	2,466[1]	775,152[1]	46,857[10]	802,253[11]	9,228[2]	3,594,378	3,067,636
From 23 April to 22 October, 1878.										
Trieste	7,550	772,787	165,548	716	244,240	31,388	400,435	2,459	6,840	594,131
Rovigno	42,946	475,856	104,132	148	81,710	7,067	69,522	981	18,728	90,389
Pola	1,239,729	116,550	41,854	146	100,690	4,363	71,433	550	1,090,029	83,498
Lussinpiccolo	5,030	355,484	77,153	210	50,540	1,680	63,545	883	5,030	133,792
Zara	1,845,139	1,505,658	404,408	357	78,703	1,416	152,079	1,380	1,787,579	1,450,014
Spalato	90,118	1,825,810	341,563	720	162,604	3,092	208,418	3,556	89,898	574,578
Ragusa	1,461	328,945	66,505	314	68,540	1,470	103,525	1,084	1,447	132,130
Megline	2,400	42,460	15,601	15	3,000	19	6,750	86	2,400	42,400
Total	3,234,373	5,483,559[15]	1,216,966[16]	2,636[1]	790,087[5]	50,495[6]	1,075,707[7]	10,979[2]	3,007,951	3,101,292

Notes to the Statistics on the Austrian Fisheries.

The numbers of the different kinds of produce caught are *not* given in every instance, so that the sum total is not exact.

[1] Comprising 865 Italians.
[2] Comprising 880 Italians.
[3] Comprising 1,180 Italians.
[4] Comprising 181 Italian craft.
[5] Comprising 257,750 florins, value of the Italian craft.
[6] Comprising 970 Italian gear.
[7] Comprising 60,150 florins, value of the Italian gear.
[8] Comprising 183 Italian craft.
[9] Comprising 271,900 florins, value of the Italian craft.
[10] Comprising 981 Italian fishing gear.
[11] Comprising 48,510 florins, value of the Italian fishing gear.
[12] Comprising 902,513 kilos caught by Italian craft.
[13] Comprising 193,090 florins as the share of Italian craft.
[14] Comprising 716,709 kilos caught by Italian craft.
[15] Comprising 149,934 florins as the share of Italian craft.

Total amount of Capital Invested from 23 April to 22 October, 1878.

Native Capital, florins 1,547,914
Italian   ,,   ,, ... 317,880

Total florins 1,865,794

Total amount of Native Capital invested, irrespective of its actual employment, 1,731,991 florins.

	Summer.	Winter.
Trieste	24,158	14,682
Rovigno	10,038	25,143
Pola	9,601	20,368
Lussinpiccolo	3,650	4,640
Hungarian-Croatian littoral	14,453	67,586
Zara	88,247	117,517
Spalato	13,180	10,740
Florins	163,327	260,676
		163,327
	Total florins...	424,003[1]

but this represents only the fish actually sold on the coast, which Count Marazzi puts at about the same figure (one million francs[2]), the excess, valued at 250,000 florins, being sent *direct* to Italy. The total value Count M. puts at 1,626,500 frcs. (600,000 florins), and, making due allowance for differences of yield and value, I should be inclined to consider this a minimum figure; 750,000 florins would probably be nearer the mark.

---

[1] The average for five years is 400,000 florins. [2] See Chapter II., "Chioggiotti."

[*Hung.-Cr. Littoral.*

Statistics of the Hungarian-Croatian Littoral.

1876, 1877.

Districts.	Caught by Native Fishermen. Kilogr.	Caught by Italian Fishermen. Kilogr.	Value in Florins.	Tunny Fisheries. Kilogr.	Value in Florins.
Fiume	325,753	198,187	91,806		
Buccari	10,516	...	2,268	25,500	9,900
Portoré	15,260	...	1,453	42,000	16,300
Selce	29,361	...	3,194	450	50
Segna	64,486	...	17,483		
Carlopago	32,671	...	1,742	190	21
	478,047	198,187	117,946	68,140	26,271
Italian Fishermen	198,187				
Tunny Fisheries	68,140		26,271		
Total	744,374	...	144,217[1]		

1877, 1878.

Districts.	Caught by Native Fishermen. Kilogr.	Caught by Italian Fishermen. Kilogr.	Value in Florins.	Tunny Fisheries. Kilogr.	Value in Florins.
Fiume	423,821	272,402	132,548		
Buccari	17,850	...	2,764	50,000	16,600
Portoré	17,766	...	1,784	101,000	60,600
Segna	23,050	...	9,372	6,113	2,262
Selce	15,472	...	2,944		
Carlopago					
	497,959	272,402	149,412	157,113	79,462
Italian Fishermen	272,402				
Tunny Fisheries	157,113		79,462		
Total	927,474		228,874[1]		

[1] The average for eight years is officially stated at 152,000 florins.

Statistics of the Hungarian Fisheries.

Species.	Total Catch in kilogrammes.		Share of the Italian boats in kilogrammes.		Total Value in florins.	
	Summer season.	Winter season.	Summer season.	Winter season.	Summer season.	Winter season.
Palæmon rectirostris and Crangon vulgaris	...	22,400	...	22,400	...	6,720
Nephrops norvegicus	5,545	26,630	5,545	26,630	2,772	10,652
Homarus vulgaris	...	100	...	...	...	45
Maja squinado	...	6,063	...	6,063	...	1,819
Carcinus mænas	1,700	...	1,700	...	680	...
Lithodomus lithophagus	...	800	...	...	...	80
Pectunculus glycimeris	...	30	...	...	...	13
Sepia officinalis	4,475	19,930	2,815	18,125	895	3,986
Loligo vulgaris	3,547	2,070	...	970	1,064	621
Eledone moschata	9,610	13,617	3,285	11,017	1,922	1,361
Galeus canis	...	4,040	...	4,040	...	808
Mustelus vulgaris	200	280	...	...	...	...
Carcarodon Rondeletii	880[1]	15[2]	...	...	...	...
[1] Two specimens. [2] One specimen.						
Scyllium canicula	...	4,090	...	3,840	...	818
Acanthias vulgaris	1,070	...	...	...	428	...
Raja clavata	4,440	23,952	3,115	23,352	1,332	7,186
Myliobatis aquila	500	50	...	...	60	5
Alosa finta	290	300	...	...	58	60
Alosa major (?)	...	585	...	585	...	146
Clupea sardina	8,896	3,980	...	1,175	1,779	796
Clupea papalina	1,700	34,570	...	33,870	340	6,914
Engraulis encrasicholus	2,485	2,785	...	2,585	297	357
Anguilla vulgaris	150	21,645	...	21,425	25	4,329
Conger vulgaris	450	990	...	570	180	198
Merlucius vulgaris	15,505	1,200	13,685	...	3,101	360
Gadus sp.	11,805	21,431	10,465	19,831	3,545	4,286
Solea vulgaris	255	370	...	245	102	148
Platessa passer	...	20	...	...	...	2
Rhombus maximus	1,653	1,900	400	1,220	496	760
Belone acus	2,685	...	...	...	805	...
Labrax lupus	1,131	1,040	...	470	452	312
Exocœtus exiliens	...	20	...	...	...	2
Trachinus draco	50	60	...	...	5	6
Uranoscopus scaber	2,680	100	2,660	...	268	10
Mullus surmuletus	3,789	8,900	3,165	7,375	1,515	2,670
Trigla lyra	260	...	260	...	26	...
Scorpæna porcus	1,165	606	...	305	466	60
Serranus cabrilla	390	...	...	...	98	...
Sargus annularis	65	14,185	...	14,085	26	4,255
Sargus vulgaris	25	9,935	...	9,895	10	1,987
Chrysophrys auratus	1,927	1,100	...	200	578	330
Cantharus vulgaris	470	450	...	350	188	75
Charax puntazzo	...	60	...	...	...	12
Box boops	1,275	300	...	...	510	120
Box salpa	2,705	...	...	...	682	...
Oblata melanura	1,995	100	...	...	798	40
Dentex vulgaris	2,642	2,190	...	1,740	660	547
Smaris vulgaris	15,322	9,500	...	5,890	4,597	2,850
Mugil cephalus	350	2,125	...	1,870	175	638
Scomber scombrus	16,193	5,170	...	...	3,239	1,034
Scomber colias	6,570	900	...	...	1,314	180
Thynnus vulgaris	71,898	3,300	...	...	28,760	1,320
Thynnus pelamys	11,870	...	...	...	4,748	...
Zeus faber	1,658	1,330	1,630	1,330	663	532
Caranx trachurus	650	...	...	...	195	...
Lichia amia	835	...	...	...	167	...
Gobius jozo	1,613	...	1,455	...	242	...
Gobius paganellus	120	15	...	...	20	1
Gobius ophiocephalus	100	...	...	...	20	20
Lophius piscatorius	3,790	24,570	3,775	24,570	948	2,457
Delphinus delphis[3]	230	...	...	...	28	...
[3] Three sp.						
Total	229,009	299,899	53,955	266,023	71,279	71,918

[To face page 161.

The foregoing table gives the yield of the fisheries on the Hungarian-Croatian littoral from 25 April, 1878, to 24 April, 1879, showing the total catch of each principal class of produce, the share of the Italian boats, and the total market value. The summer season is from 25 April, 1878, to 24 October, 1878; and the winter season from 25 October, 1878, to 24 April, 1879.

The principal produce of the fisheries at Fiume in the order of their importance are :—

Summer fisheries.—Tunny, Mackerel, Hake, Poor and Whiting, *Smaris vulgaris*, Pilchard, Cephalopods, &c.

Winter fisheries.—Cephalopods, Pilchard, Norway Lobsters, Anglers, Rays, Crabs, Eels, Poor and Whiting, *Sargus annularis*, *Sargus vulgaris*, *Smaris vulgaris*, Red Mullet, &c.

Italian fishing craft.—Cephalopods, Pilchard, Norway Lobsters, Poor, Whiting, Anglers, Rays, Crabs, Eels, *Sargus annularis* and *vulgaris*, Hake, Red Mullet, &c.

The value of the shares taken by the Italian boats is
        14,453 florins during the summer season ;
        67,586 florins during the winter season ;

   total ...... 82,039 florins, divided amongst 38 boats.

If we deduct 500 frcs. per boat for expenses, say 8,170 florins, there remain 73,869 florins, of which one-third share, or 24,623 florins, goes to the owners of the boats, leaving 49,246 florins to be divided amongst the crews of 152 men. This would give each man a share of 324 florins, an amount which exceeds all former estimates given.[1]

An average of three years is, however, more likely to lead us to a due appreciation of the results of the fisheries carried on by the Italian fishermen.

---

[1] The Italian boats fishing in Zara waters yielded a much higher average (see page 57).

The value of the produce of the Italian bragozzi in the Quarnero was
45,583 florins in 1877;
62,652 florins in 1878;
82,039 florins in 1879;

total ...... 190,274 florins for three years,[1]

to be divided amongst 130 bragozzi and 520 men. Expenses deducted (26,000 florins), there remain 109,516 florins as the two-thirds share of the crew, or 210 florins per man. The yield of 182 bragozzi in the Austrian fisheries in the year 1877–8 (see STATISTICS) was 342,324 florins;[2] deducting expenses (36,400 florins), there remain 203,948 florins as the two-thirds share of a crew of 728 men, or 280 florins. Reviewing the figures given here and elsewhere (see pages 53–57), we may fairly come to the conclusion that the average share of the Italian fishermen in the Austrian-Hungarian fisheries amounts to from 200 to 300 florins per man. The average value of the Italian fishing craft and gear engaged in the Austro-Hungarian fisheries is 400,000 fl.

In order to arrive at an approximate estimate of the individual share of the native fishermen, we will take the official statistics to hand, viz.:—

Austrian Fisheries.

	Florins.
Summer fisheries...	1,216,966
Winter fisheries ...	895,978
	2,112,944
Deduct shares of Italian craft ...	342,324
	1,770,620[3]

---

[1] Taking the official average figures for eight years, this would be only 146,000 fl.
[2] The official average values for five years are as nearly as possible the same figure.
[3] If we take the average yield for five years, this sum would be 1,604,000 fl.

Hungarian Fisheries.

		Florins.
1876—77 ...	...	117,946
1877—78 ...	...	149,412
1878—79 ...	...	108,369
excluding the produce of the tunny fisheries ...	...	375,727
Deduct share of Italian craft for the said three years ...	...	190,274
Total for three years ...	...	185,453

Average per annum, 61,818 florins.[1]

We thus arrive at a total yield of 1,832,438[2] florins, excluding the share of the Italian craft and the produce of the tunny fisheries on the Hungarian-Croatian littoral, which are worked by contractors (see page 65). Some of the fisheries are worked on the system of shares, such as the sardine seine-fisheries (see page 139) and the tunny fisheries (see page 165); in other cases the fishermen are paid fixed wages at the rate of 70 soldi to 150 soldi a day. It is, therefore, difficult to arrive at a fixed valuation of the individual gain derived from the yield of the fisheries.

The value of the material used, the property of native fishermen, represents an amount of 1,650,000 florins; one-third of this amount, say 550,000 fl., would represent the interest on capital, wear and tear of material, &c. This would leave a net yield of, say roughly, 1,280,000 fl., or, according to the lower estimate, 1,130,000 fl., to be divided amongst, say on an average, 10,000 men, more or less, engaged in the fisheries, or 113–128 fl. per man. The gross yield would be from 168–183 fl. per man. This is, probably, the lowest figure that can be taken. Considering, however, that many of the fishermen do not devote the whole of their time to fishing but have other occupations besides, it is easily explained how the average gain of each

---

[1] If we take the average for eight years, this sum would be 78,700 fl.
[2] Or, according to the official averages for five and eight years, 1,683,700 fl.

individual native fisherman falls short of the gain of the Italian fishermen, who devote the whole of their time to fishing and exercise their calling on a much more extensive scale, considering the number of men employed and the capital invested in their craft and gear. The gross profit of the fisheries, compared with the capital invested, is as nearly as possible 100 % in both instances.

The yield of the tunny fisheries on the Hungarian-Croatian coast was:—

	Florins.	Tons.
1876—77	26,271 ...	68
1877—78	79,462 ...	157
1878—79	34,828 ...	87
total for three years ...	140,561 ...	312

Average per annum, 46,854 florins; 104 tons.[1]

The fishermen engaged in the Tunny fisheries on the Hungarian-Croatian littoral receive from 28 florins to 72 florins per ton, according to circumstances, say, an average of 50 florins, or 5,200 florins on 104 tons. If we, further, deduct rent, 5,000 florins; interest on capital invested, 1,200 florins; wear and tear and maintenance, 3,000 florins; sundries, 2,000 florins, there remains a profit of 30,000 florins to the farmer,—a profit which might be greatly increased if a system of properly salting the fish caught in excess of the local demand were introduced.

NOTE.—This calculation is based on the supposition that all the fish caught is sold; but it appears that a great quantity of fish caught in excess of the local demand is spoiled in transit to other markets, owing to the want of a proper system of salting; and, whereas the local demand is probably not more than one-half the quantity which serves as the basis of this calculation, it is safer not to put the net profit to the farmer at above from 15,000 to 20,000 florins.

---

[1] The average for eight years is 122 tons.

The individual gain of the fishermen employed in the tunny fisheries is very small; their share varies from 28 to 72 florins per ton of fish, say, an average of 50 florins; 186 men are employed in the various *Tonnare* on this coast, and their share varies from 20 to 42 florins a season, the average being 30 florins, or from 5 to 6 florins a month, if we take the highest figure, 8 florins a month. During the seven months of the year when the fisheries are at a stand-still, these men have to seek other occupations, for the fisheries afford them but a bare existence during the time they are actually employed in them.

TABLE *showing the various Craft and Fishing Gear used in Fishing on the Hungarian-Croatian Littoral during the period from April 25, 1878, to April 24, 1879, and their relative Value (according to Official Statistics).*

Boats.	Number.	Value per Boat. Florins.	Total Value. Florins.	Nets.	Number.	Value per Net. Florins.	Total Value. Florins.
(a.) *Fiume.*				Cocchia	22	850	18,700
Bragozzi	38	1,000	38,000	Tratte	9	250	2,250
(b.) *Segna.*							
Gaëte	6	300	1,800	Reti	10	100	1,000
(c.) *Buccari.*				Reti fiochini	10	3	30
Barche	6	200	1,200				
Zoppoli	2	60	120	Tonnare	7	1,200	8,400
(d.) *Selce.*				Grippe	20	110	2,200
Gaëte and Zoppoli	32	80	2,560	Majo di ferro	3	3	9
(e.) *Portorè.*							
Guzzi	7	60	420		81		32,589
Zoppoli	4	60	240				
(f.) *Carlopago.*							
Guzzi	10	60	600	Fishermen engaged in fishing	386		
Total	105		44,940				

Fish brought to market at Fiume during the winter season of 1879–1880.
Weight in kilogrammes; value in florins.

Description. Local terms and equivalents.	October. Weight.	October. Value.	November. Weight.	November. Value.	December. Weight.	December. Value.
16. Agoni (*Smaris gracilis*, Bp.)	...	...	...	...	40	20
41. Angosigole (*Gar-pike*)	...	...	...	...	...	...
11. Anguille (*Eels*)	...	...	100	60	1,335	483
25. Arbori (*Red, or Spanish Sea-bream*)	...	...	...	...	...	...
9. Barboni (*Red Mullet*)	633	284	622	221	355	186
30. Barracole (*Thornback*)	...	...	95	17	...	...
35. Bobe (*Bogue*)	...	...	...	...	50	30
23. Branzini (*Basse*)	20	16	20	16	40	72
20. Calamari (*Squid*)	...	...	20	10	115	75
14. Cani (*Sharks*)	250	43	210	35	80	32
40. Cantre (*Sea-bream*)	...	...	15	2	...	...
15. Cievoli (*Grey Mullet*)	30	18	100	36	350	210
38. Colombi (*Whip, or Eagle Ray*)	...	...	...	...	...	...
37. Dentali (*Toothed Gilt-head*)	...	...	...	...	...	...
7. Folpi (*Poulp, Octopus*)	1,715	216	1,610	246	810	182
17. Gatti (*Spotted Dog-fish*)	...	...	40	6	...	...
28. Girai (*Sand Smelts*)	...	...	...	...	45	27
19. Grancevole (*Sea-spiders*)	...	...	...	...	...	...
26. Granzi (*Harry Crabs*)	...	...	40	6	180	16
29. Gronghi (*Conger-eel*)	10	6	45	27	...	...
13. Menole (*Maena vulg., Smaris vulg.*)	...	...	321	64	255	81
1. Merluzzi (*Hake*)	11,370	2,436	8,405	1,565	4,080	1,312
5. Misti (*mixed*)	1,950	148	1,385	210	723	186
2. Molli (*Poor and Whiting*)	4,040	1,140	3,278	811	1,140	414
27. Occhiade (*Oblata melanura*)	...	...	...	...	...	...
12. Orade (*Gilt-head*)	50	31	10	8	95	72
6. Rase (*Rays*)	1,240	196	1,420	210	450	108
4. Rospi (*Angler, Frog-fish*)	2,075	192	2,200	265	735	167
36. Salpe (*Box salpa*)	20	6	...	...	40	19
24. Sardelle (*Pilchard*)	265	81	10	4	...	...
3. Sardellini (*Clupea papalina*)	9,930	823	1,155	115	280	38
18. Sardoni (*Anchovies*)	70	17	470	83	...	...
31. Sarghi (*Sargus Rondeletii*)	...	...	...	...	...	...
33. San Pietro (*John Dory*)	...	...	...	...	10	4
10. Scampi (*Norway lobster*)	1,520	641	839	370	147	146
39. Scarpene (*Scorpions*)	...	...	...	...	...	...
34. Scombri (*Mackerel*)	50	32	25	16	...	...
8. Seppie (*Cuttle-fish*)	1,511	495	1,086	371	349	156
32. Sfoglie (*Soles*)	40	29	20	16	20	36
42. Spizzi (*Sargus vulgaris*)	...	...	...	...	...	...
21. Tombarelli (*Plain Bonito*)	385	73	20	5	...	...
22. Tonno (*Tunny*)	253	150	77	39	15	12
Total	37,427	7,073	23,638	4,834	11,739	4,084

N.B.—The numbers prefixed to the names indicate the order of importance according to the quantity.

Fish brought to market at Fiume during the winter season of 1879–1880.
Weight in kilogrammes; value in florins.

Description. Local terms.	January. Weight.	January. Value.	February. Weight.	February. Value.	March. Weight.	March. Value.	Total. Weight.	Total. Value.
16. Agoni	155	63	210	109	371	192	776	384
41. Angosigole	...	...	...	...	10	5	10	5
11. Anguille	...	...	380	202	655	200	2,470	945
25. Arbori	185	45	80	18	...	...	265	63
9. Barboni	973	455	910	442	947	553	4,440	2,141
30. Barracole	...	...	...	...	...	...	95	17
35. Bobe	...	...	...	...	20	10	70	40
23. Branzini	67	73	93	64	61	56	301	297
20. Calamari	50	30	83	17	164	104	432	236
14. Cani	140	39	150	43	90	26	920	218
40. Cantre	...	...	...	...	...	...	15	2
15. Cievoli	205	105	10	6	151	95	846	470
38. Colombi	30	6	...	...	...	...	30	6
37. Dentali	20	16	16	12	...	...	36	28
7. Folpi	105	210	711	140	660	177	5,611	1,171
17. Gatti	225	50	80	19	240	58	585	133
28. Girai	20	5	10	6	90	51	165	89
19. Grancevole	...	...	190	38	278	56	468	94
26. Granzi	...	...	...	...	...	...	220	22
29. Gronghi	...	...	15	10	46	27	116	70
13. Menole	1,000	164	360	70	60	14	1,996	393
1. Merluzzi	6,300	1,762	8,210	868	5,234	1,617	43,599	9,560
5. Misti	1,590	333	2,290	631	1,351	393	9,289	1,901
2. Molli	2,162	662	2,375	658	4,969	824	17,964	4,509
27. Occhiade	37	14	21	6	115	39	173	59
12. Orade	925	520	675	402	336	234	2,091	1,267
6. Rase	1,520	311	1,313	270	1,970	448	7,913	1,543
4. Rospi	1,485	200	1,820	380	1,621	287	9,936	1,491
36. Salpe	...	...	...	...	...	...	60	25
24. Sardelle	...	...	...	...	...	...	275	85
3. Sardellini	2,110	242	960	167	3,360	742	17,795	2,127
18. Sardoni	...	...	...	...	...	...	540	100
31. Sarghi	...	...	50	4	38	21	88	25
33. San Pietro	60	29	...	...	12	5	82	38
10. Scampi	215	186	886	460	821	659	4,428	2,462
39. Scarpene	30	14	...	...	...	...	30	14
34. Scombri	...	...	...	...	...	...	75	48
8. Seppie	553	258	865	348	920	488	5,284	2,116
32. Sfoglie	5	5	...	...	...	...	85	86
42. Spizzi	10	6	...	...	...	...	10	6
21. Tombarelli	...	...	...	...	...	...	405	78
22. Tonno	...	...	...	...	...	...	345	201
Total	20,177	5,803	22,763	5,390	24,590	7,381	140,334	34,565

N.B.—The numbers prefixed to the names indicate the order of importance according to the quantity.

Quantity and Value of the Imports and Exports of Fish in the Austrian-Hungarian Empire during the Year 1878.

	IMPORTS.			EXPORTS.		
	Quantity in 100 kilogr.	Of which Hungary.	As compared with 1877.	Quantity in 100 kilogr.	Of which Hungary.	As compared with 1877.
(a.) Fish and Shell-fish, living and dead............	5,484	318	+ 472	8,628	132	+ 1,571
(b.) Herrings, salt and smoked...	62,759	2,659	+ 14,989			
(c.) Stock-fish, &c.	4,943	275	− 77			
(d.) Undefined, prepared and preserved Caviar, Sardines salted and in oil......	23,879	5,265	+ 2,004	642	248	− 962
Total	97,065	8,517	+ 17,388	9.270	380	+ 609
Value florins ...... 2,726,036.				Florins ...... 552,406.		
Excess of Imports over Exports...... { Quantity...... 87,795 8,137 + 16,779 Value florins ...... 2,173,540.						
DALMATIA, 1878.						
					100 kilogr.	Value in florins.
Exports					14,534	460,066
Imports					5,677	113,840
Excess of Exports					8,857	346,226

In the above returns the fish caught by the Italian fishermen and taken by them direct to Italy is not included amongst the exports: this may be taken, as has been shown elsewhere, at at least 600,000 francs, or 250,000 florins, or 1¼ million kilogrammes at an average price of 20 soldi per kilogr. The excess of imports over exports is 7,894 tons; value, 1,827,404 fl.; as against a yield of the sea-fisheries of 10,000 tons; value, 2,100,000 fl. The consumption is, therefore, nearly double the yield of the sea-fisheries. The conclusion may be drawn that the yield of the sea-fisheries may be easily doubled without affecting prices.

Austrian Sea-Fisheries.

Annual average for the last five years (1877–1882), from Official Statistics.

Description.	Average Annual Produce of Fisheries.					Average Annual Local Consumption.		Average Annual Exports.	
	1,000 kilogrammes.	Value in 1,000 florins.	Average price per kilogramme in soldi.	Share of Native Fishermen in 1,000 florins.	Share of Italian Fishermen in 1,000 florins.	1,000 kilogrammes.	Value in 1,000 florins.	1,000 kilogrammes.	Value in 1,000 florins.
Fishes	7,642	1,740	22½	...		4,740		2,902	...
Mollusks	955	154	16	...		661		294	...
Crustaceans	58	58	100	...		32		26	...
Total	8,655	1,952		1,604	348	5,433	1,233	3,222[1]	720[1]

[1] Not including direct exports to Italy effected by Italian fishing-boats engaged in the fisheries off the Austrian coast.

Austrian Sea-Fisheries.

Annual average for the last five years (1877–1882), from Official Statistics.

District.	Extent of Sea Coast in nautical miles.	Absolute Proceeds of the fisheries per nautical mile of coast extent in florins.	Order of importance according to Proceeds per nautical mile of coast extent.	Total Annual Value of Fisheries in 1,000 florins.	Boats. Number.	Boats. Value in 1,000 florins.	Gear. Number in 100.	Gear. Value in 1,000 florins.	Total. Value in 1,000 florins.	Native Fishermen actually engaged in the fisheries.	Italian Fishermen actually engaged in the fisheries.	Number of Native Fishermen registered 22nd April, 1882.	Number of Native Fishermen per mile of coast extent.
Trieste	75	4,056	1	304	894	189	393	399	588	2,022	383	2,636	35
Rovigno	79	1,676	2	132	150	43	91	78	121	688	318	599	8
Pola	131	882	4	115	150	15	17	37	52	496	178	477	4
Lussinpiccolo	329	214	8	70	143	27	12	48	75	665	58	517	2
Zara	986	726	5	716	427	85	23	215	300	1,288	86	1,652	2
Spalato	505	955	3	482	793	195	31	216	411	3,489	138	3,588	7
Ragusa	380	273	6	104	316	68	28	109	177	1,060	...	1,246	4
Meglinc	119	235	7	28	39	5	1	13	18	153	...	158	1
Total	2,604	750	...	1,952	2,912	627	595	1,116	1,743	9,861	1,161	10,873	4

GOVERNMENT pays for the capture of the shark of the species *Carcharodon* a reward varying from 20 florins for specimens under 1 mètre in length to 100 florins for specimens over 4 m. in length, if casually caught; but, if special chase is made after a particular Shark, its capture is rewarded with 100 florins for specimens from 1 m. to 4 m. in length, and with 500 florins if above 4 m. in length. Of 53 Sharks sent to the Trieste Museum, from 1872 to 1882, for identification, there were :—

    21 Carcharodon Rondeletii.   2 Odontaspis taurus.
    23 Lamna Spallanzanii.   2 Notidanus griseus.
    2 Odontaspis ferox.   2 Carcharias lamia.
                         1 Carcharias glyphis.

These varied in length from 1·46 m. to 5·30 m., 7 were above 4 m. in length, and the largest Lamna measured 3·50 m.

SPECIFICATION *of the average annual quantity and value of* FISHING CRAFT AND GEAR, *native and Italian, actually engaged in the Austrian fisheries (the Hungarian-Croatian littoral excluded) during the last five years (from Official Statistics).*

FISHING DISTRICTS.	FISHING CRAFT.				FISHING GEAR.			
	Native.		Italian.		Native.		Italian.	
	Number.	Value in 1,000 Fls.	Number.	Value in 1,000 Fls.	Number in 100.	Value in 1,000 Fls.	Number.	Value in 1,000 Fls.
Trieste	665	161	89	77	292	336	131	34
Rovigno	155	44	42	59	81	79	965	9
Pola	154	28	43	81	122	91	200	11
Lussin	182	30	11	14	15	56	30	3
Zara	315	69	18	11	16	171	37	4
Spalato	723	164	32	34	31	205	16	3
Ragusa	305	67	—	...	18	104	...	...
Megline	32	5	—	...	2	11	...	...
TOTAL	2,531	568	235	276	577	1,053	1,379	64

SPECIFICATION of native FISHING GEAR registered on April 22, 1882, on the Austrian Littoral (Hungarian-Croatian Littoral excluded).

Description.	Number.	Value 1,000 Florins.
A—DRIFT-NETS.		
1. Sardellere	13,006	429
2. Sardonere	635	26
3. Agonere	252	16
4. Zereri	4	—
5. Spironi da verzellate	240	8
6. Prostice	234	8
7. Bobere	260	4
8. Reti da ludro	209	8
9. Scombrere	141	12
10. Cagnere	55	2
11. Squænere	11,016	24
B—TRAMMEL-NETS.		
12. Gombine	7,150	83
13. Cerberai	431	6
14. Passelere	3,468	92
15. Barbonere	23	1
16. Saltarelli	12	1
C—SET-NETS.		
17. Pallandare	120	90
18. Tonnare	24	24
D—SEINE, DRAG, AND TRAWLING-NETS, &c.		
19. Tratte	1,082	213
20. Bragagne	5	1
21. Cocchie	14	3
22. Tartane	144	5
23. Grippi	70	3
24. Sciabacche	125	10
25. Mussolere	16	} 1
26. Ostregheri	1,011	
27. Guatte a mano	56	
E—SUNDRIES.		
28. Various implements, lines, &c.	19,797	46
Total	59,500	1,116

SPECIFICATION *of the* QUANTITY AND VALUE *of the various kinds of* FISHES *caught on the Austrian-Littoral (Hungarian-Croatian Littoral excluded), viz., the average annual yield for the last five years from Official Statistics.*

Description	Number per thousand	Weight 1000 Kilogrs.	Value 1,000 Florins.	Description	Number per thousand	Weight 1000 Kilogrs.	Value 1,000 Florins.
Pilchard	...	2,077	432[1]	Eels	...	42	15
Red Mullet	...	386	131[2]	Black Sea-bream	...	62	13
Tunny	...	354	122[3]	Horse Mackerel	...	80	12
Mænidæ, Smaridæ	...	1,089	176[4]	Italian Flounder	...	39	12
Coly Mackerel	...	404	77[5]	Gobius jozo	...	82	11
Grey Mullet	...	227	68[6]	Smooth Hound	...	54	10
Squid	...	162	63[7]	Spanish Sea-bream	...	32	9
Basse	...	102	47[8]	Black Gobies	...	38	9
Whiting, poor	...	198	43[9]	Clupea papalina	...	60	9
Anchovy	...	318	40[10]	Oysters	71	...	8
Conger Eel	...	110	38[11]	Eagle Rays	...	42	7
Gilt-head	...	98	37[12]	John Dorys	...	30	6
Sargus annularis	...	226	35[13]	Sargus Rondeletii	...	19	5
Dentex	...	91	35[14]	Modiola barbata	3,839	...	5
Pelamid	...	100	35[15]	Turbot	...	11	4
Box Salpa	...	117	34[16]	Picked Dog-fish	...	19	4
Octopus	...	222	31[17]	Mussels	569	...	4
Mackerel	...	106	29[18]	Atherines	...	20	4
Oblata melanura	...	101	29[19]	Hake	...	10	3
Bogue	...	140	29[20]	Norway Lobster	...	9	3
Scorpions	...	106	29[21]	Rays (R. marginata			
Cuttle-fish	...	170	27[22]	„ R. macrorhynchus	...	15	3
Sea-spiders	407	...	26[23]	„ R. oxyrhynchus	...		
Rays (the Thornback)	...	145	24[24]	Spotted Dog-fish	...	14	2
Lobsters	28	...	22[25]	Sting Rays	...	11	2
Soles	...	...	38	19[26]	Gobius paganellus	...	5	1
Gar-pike	...	...	59	15				

[1] Spalato, 227 fls.; Trieste, 81 fls.; Rovigno, 42 fls.; Zara, 33 fls.; Ragusa, 29 fls.; Pola, 14 fls. [2] Zara, 43 fls.; Trieste, 39 fls.; Pola, 25 fls.; Spalato, 12 fls. [3] Zara, 86 fls.; Lussin, 21 fls. [4] Zara, 97 fls.; Spalato, 42 fls.; Ragusa, 23 fls. [5] Spalato, 53 fls.; Zara, 16 fls. [6] Trieste, 34 fls.; Zara, 16 fls. [7] Zara, 46 fls. [8] Trieste, 14 fls.; Zara, 14 fls. [9] Zara, 29 fls. [10] Trieste, 18 fls.; Spalato, 13 fls. [11] Zara, 24 fls. [12] Zara, 18 fls. [13] Zara, 30 fls. [14] Zara, 24 fls. [15] Zara, 23 fls. [16] Zara, 21 fls. [17] Zara, 16 fls. [18] Spalato, 11 fls. [19] Zara, 19 fls. [20] Zara, 12 fls. [21] Zara, 15 fls. [22] Zara, 15 fls. [23] Pola, 11 fls. [24] Zara, 12 fls. [25] Zara, 12 fls. [26] Rovigno, 10 fls.

Values in thousand florins, excluding values under 10 thousand.

TABLE *showing the share taken by Italian boats in the Austro-Hungarian Fisheries during the last five years, 1877-1881, the average annual value of the fish sold on the spot, the average catch per boat, and the individual share of the crew.*

Fishing Districts.	Total number of Craft engaged during five years.	Annual average of Craft engaged.	Annual average of Crews engaged.	Annual average value of Fish sold on the spot, in 1,000 florins.	Average share of each Boat.	Individual share of each Man of the Crews.
Trieste	444	89	383	53	591	64
Rovigno	210	42	318	32	768	47
Pola	213	43	178	46	1,077	135
Lussinpiccolo	57	11	58	9	822	75
Fiume	212	42	180	49	1,167	133
Zara	88	18	86	182	10,136	1,382
Spalato	160	32	138	26	800	90
TOTAL	1,384	277	1,331	397	1,433	166
Besides what is sold on the spot, fish is taken to Italy in their own boats, valued at	...	...	...	240	867	120
TOTAL	1,384	277	1,331	637	2,300	286

Average Annual Catch for Eight Years on the Hungarian-Croatian littoral.

	1,000 KILOGRS.	Comprising—	1,000 KILOGRS.
Fiume and Quarnero	522	Hake	125
Buccari	36	Pilchard *	123
Portoré	71	Tunny †	122
Segna (Zengg)	46	Whiting, Poor	79
Selce	86	Rays	37
Calopago	11	Norway Lobster	30
Jablanaz	4	Octopus	25
Stinizza	2	Mænidæ	20
		Cuttle-fish	18
TOTAL	778	Anglers	18
		Red Mullet	18
		Mackerel	17

* 74 tons were taken at Selce.   † 34 tons at Buccari, 70 tons at Portoré, 9 tons at Segna, 10 tons at Selce.

BUOY.

SPECIFICATION of FISHING CRAFT *belonging to native fishermen on the Austrian Littoral (Hungarian-Croatian Littoral excluded) on 22nd April, 1882, from Official Statistics.*

Description.	Number.	Value in 1,000 Florins.	Average value per craft.
Barche............................	216	103	480
Barchette.......................	34	4	123
Battelle	63	4	60
Battelli...........................	210	37	175
Battellini	75	3	34
Bragozzi	61	51	835
Brazzere	25	14	541
Gaete	1497	324	217
Guzzi	153	14	89
Lancie............................	1	—	80
Leuti	167	56	337
Passere	6	} 1 {	50
Portellate.......................	1		400
Sandoli	318	11	35
Toppi	47	4	75
Zoppoli	38	4	92
TOTAL...............	2912	627	215

FAUNA OF THE ADRIATIC.

PART I.—LIST OF MAMMALIA.

Order—PINNIPEDIA.

Fam. PHOCINA.

Gen. PHOCA, *L.*

1. *PHOCA VITULINA, L.*
   The common Seal.
   Foca (*It.*).
   Croat., Tuljan, nerpa, morsko tele.
   Habit. Only single specimens are occasionally caught at Ragusa, but not further north; identity appears doubtful as regards these waters.

Gen. PELAGIUS, *Cuv.*

2. *PELAGIUS MONACHUS,* L.
   Phoca monachus, *L.*
   The Monk.
   Foca (*It.*).
   Habit. Frequents the reefs (*Scogli*) of the Dalmatian coast, where it is not uncommon; Bay of Carin.

Order—CETACEA.

Fam. DELPHINIDA.

Gen. DELPHINUS, *L.*

3. *DELPHINUS DELPHIS,* L.
   The true Dolphin.
   Delfino comune (*It.*).
   Croat., Pliskavica, piskavica, dupin.
   Habit. The most common sp. of its tribe in the Adriatic, appearing in chase of the shoals of mackerel and pilchards in summer.

4. *DELPHINUS TURSIO,* Fabr.
   Croat., Velika pliskavica.
   Habit. A rare sp. of the Adriatic; Civitanova.

5. *DELPHINUS RISSOANUS,* Laur.
   Grampus griseus, *Cuv.* (?)
   Habit. Only accidentally met with in the Adriatic; Chioggia, Zara.

Gen. PHYSETER, *L.*

6. *PHYSETER MACROCEPHALUS,* L.
   Spermaceti Whale.
   Fisetere (*It.*).
   Croat., Uljesura.
   Habit. Only accidentally met with in the Adriatic; Porto S. Giorgio.

7. *PHYSETER TURSIO,* L.
   Habit. Not unfrequently met with in the Adriatic; sp. from the coasts of Istria and Dalmatia; Umago, Pago.

Part II.—LIST OF REPTILIA.

Order—CHELONIA.

Fam. CHELONIIDÆ—Sea-Turtles or Tortoises—*Schildkröten.*

Gen. CHELONIA, *Brongn.*

1. *CHELONIA MIDAS*, Schweigger.
   Chelonia albiventer, *Nardo (young)*.
   Tartaruga (*It.*).
   Croat., Morska željva.
   Habit.—Only two specimens have hitherto been caught in the Adriatic.

2. *CHELONIA CARETTA*, L.
   Testudo caretta, *Schneider.*
   Tartaruga de mar (*It.*).
   Galana, Gagiandra de mar (*Ven.*).
   Croat., željva glavuša.
   Hab. Pretty general, and not uncommon; has been taken in the port of Trieste.

3. *EMYS LUTARIA*, Mer.
   Vulg., Bissa scudelera, Gagiandra, G lana, Codope (*Venice*).
   Croat., željva muljača.
   Habit. Salt marshes of Venice.

Part III.—GENERAL LIST OF FISHES.

Sub-Class—PALÆICHTHYES.
   Order—CHONDROPTERYGII.
      Sub-Order—PLAGIOSTOMATA.
         A. SELACHOIDEI—Sharks.
            Fam. I. CARCHARIIDÆ.

Gen. I. CARCHARIAS, *Cuv.**

1. *CARCHARIAS GLAUCUS*, Cuv.
The Blue Shark.
Der blaue Hai.
Prionodonte verdesca (*It.*).
Vulg., Cagnizza, a term generally applied to all large sharks, Cagna (*Tr.*).
Cagnizza glauca (*Tr.*).
Can, Pesce Can (*generic terms*).
Can da denti, Can turchin (*Ven.*).
Croat., Pasnica.
Habit. General, but not common; sp. from Dalmatia.
Season. Summer.
Quality. o; flesh tough and inferior.

2. *CARCHARIAS MILBERTI*, Bp.
Prionodonte del Milbert (*It.*).
Vulg., Cagnizza, (*Tr.*).
Cagnea, Caecchia (*Ven.*).
Habit. General, very rare; sp. caught at Trieste and Venice.

Gen. II. GALEUS, *Cuv.*
3. *GALEUS CANIS*, Bp.
The Tope, Toper, Tope Shark, Common Tope, Penny Dog, Miller's Dog.

* *Carcharias lamia* and *C. glyphis*. (*See* Nos. 351, 352.)

Le Milandre.
Der Hundshai, Die Meersau.
Galeo cane (*It.*).
Vulg., Can, Can da denti (*Tr.*, *Fiume*, *Ven.*, *Cattaro*).
Can negro, Moretta (*Ven.*).
Croat., Pas (*generic term*), Pas riba, Pas cèrni, Pas sa zubi, Pas cèrnomanjast (*Croat. littoral*).
Pas crni, Pas butor (*Spalato*).
Habit. Common all the year round, all over the Adriatic; chiefly in autumn; sp. from Trieste and Venice.
Quality. Flesh tough, and little eaten.

Gen. III. ZYGÆNA, *Cuv.*
4. *ZYGÆNA MALLEUS*, Risso.
The Hammer-headed Shark, Balance-fish.
Zygène, Squale marteau.
Der Hammerfisch, Hammerhai.
Sfirna martello (*It.*).
Vulg., Martello, Pesce martello (*Tr.*, *Fiume*, *Ven.*).
Baile, Pesce Baile (*Ven.*).
Croat., Jaram, Joron, Jorona (*Spalato*).
Habit. Very rare; sp. from Dalmatia, Quarnero, Venice.
Season. Summer.

Quality. Flesh tough, and oily taste; only eaten by the very poor.

5. *ZYGÆNA TUDES*, Cuv.
Sfirna tiburo (*It.*).
Vulg., Pesce Pantofola (*Ven.*).
Intermediate sp. between *Z. malleus* and *Z. tiburo* (Heart-headed Shark); Bonap. doubts the validity of this sp.
Habit. Sp. from Venice; very rare.

Gen. IV. MUSTELUS, *Cuv.*
6. *MUSTELUS LÆVIS*, Risso.
Mustelus equestris, *Bp.*
Palombo nocciòlo (*It.*).
Vulg., Can, Cagnetto (*Ven.*).
Habit. More southern sp. than *M. vulgaris*, and rare in the north of the Adriatic; ground fish.
Quality. Flesh fairly good (No. 3).

7. *MUSTELUS VULGARIS*, M. & H.
Mustelus plebejus, *Bp.*
The Smooth Hound, Skate-toothed Shark, Stinkard, Ray-mouthed Dog.
Der Glatthai.
Palombo comune (*It.*).
Vulg., Pesce Can, Can bianco, Cagnetto (*Tr.*, *Fiume*, *Ven.*).
Can macchia, Can pontisà.
Can senza denti (*Ven.*).
Croat., Pas, Pas bulaš (*Spalato*).
Habit. General and common at all seasons; sp. from Trieste, Venice, Quarnero, Spalato.
Quality. Flesh inferior and little valued.

Fam. II. LAMNIDÆ.
Gen. I. LAMNA, *Cuv.*
8. *LAMNA CORNUBICA*, Gm.
Porbeagle, Beaumaris Shark.
Fouille-bœuf, Loutre, Taupe de mer, Squale Nez, Longnez.
Lamna smeriglio (*It.*).
Vulg., Cagnizza (*Tr.*).

Cao da oglio, Cavo d'ojo (*Ven.*, *Fiume*).
Cagnia (*Ven.*).
Habit. Rare; southern sp.

9. *LAMNA SPALLANZANII*, Bonap.
Der Nasenhai, Schnauzenhai.
Ossirino dello Spallanzani (*It.*).
Vulg., Cagnizza nasuta (*Tr.*).
Cagnia (*Ven.*).
Habit. Rare; Dalmatian coast.
Season. In the autumn, 1880, five large sp. were caught in Dalmatia.
Quality. Flesh little or no value.

Gen. II. CARCHARODON, *M. & H.*
10. *CARCHARODON RONDELETII*, M. & H.
The great Blue Shark.
Der Riesenhai, Menschenhai.
Carcarodonte del Rondelezio (*It.*).
Vulg., Cagnissa, Cagnissa vera (*Tr.*), Cagnia (*Ven.*).
Croat., Pasnica, Pas ženska. Kučina (*Spalato*).
Habit. Occasionally, but rarely, met with in the Adriatic; one was caught at Ustrine in September, 1879, measuring 5·30 mètres in length, one of the largest which has been caught in these waters.
Season. Summer.
Quality. Flesh uneatable.

Gen. III. ODONTASPIS, *Ag.**
11. *ODONTASPIS FEROX*, Risso.
Triglochide feroce.
Vulg., Cagnia, Can da denti (*Ven.*).
Habit. Quite accidental in the Adriatic.
Quality. Flesh uneatable.

Gen. IV. ALOPECIAS, *M. & H.*
12. *ALOPIAS VULPES*, Gm.
The Fox Shark, Fox, Sea-Fox, the

---

* *Odontaspis taurus.* (*See* No. 353.)

SYSTEMATIC LIST OF THE FAUNA. 181

Thrasher, or Thresher, Sea-Ape, Long-tailed Shark.
Le renard marin, Singe de mer, Squale renard.
Der Seefuchs, Fuchshai.
Alopia codalunga (*It.*).
Vulg., Volpe, Pesce Volpe, Pesce bandiera, Pesce spada (*Ven., Tr., Fiume*).
Croat., Riba lesica (*Croat. lit.*).
Lisica (*Spalato*).
Pas spadun (*Spalato*).
Habit. General, but rare; sp. from Venice, Rimini, Trieste.
Season. Summer.

Gen. V. SELACHE, *Cuv.*
13. *SELACHE MAXIMA*, Cuv.
The Basking Shark, Sun-fish, Sail-fish, Common Sail-fish.
Le Pèlerin, Squale très-grand.
Selachio gigante (*It.*).
Vulg. Cagnia (*Ven.*).
Habit. Quite accidental in the Adriatic.

Fam. III. NOTIDANIDÆ.
Gen. I. NOTIDANUS, *Cuv.*
14. *NOTIDANUS GRISEUS*, Cuv.
The Grey Notidanus, Six-gilled Shark.
Le griset, Squale griset.
Der Rothbraunehai.
Notidano capo-piatto (*It.*).
Vulg., Pesce manzo (*Ven., Tr., Fiume*).
Gatton bruno (*Tr.*).
Cagnia, Can (*Ven.*).
Croat., Vol (*Croat. littoral*).
Volina (*Spalato*).
Habit. Rare; sp. from Venice, Rimini, Quarnero, Spalato.
Quality. Flesh white, but not good.
Season. Summer; at Spalato two large sp. were caught in the winter of 1880.

15. *NOTIDANUS CINEREUS*, Raf.
Heptanchus cinereus, *Raf.*
Le Perlon.
Der Grauhai.
Eptanco anciolo (*It.*).
Vulg., Gatton grigio (*Tr.*).
Cagnia Can (*Ven.*).
Habit. Rare; sp. from Trieste.
Quality. 3; flesh pretty good.

16. *NOTIDANUS BARBARUS*, Chier.
Notidano del Chiereghin (*It.*).
Vulg., Can barbaro (*Ven.*).
Habit. Very rare; sp. from Venice, Quarnero. Adriatic species.

Fam. IV. SCYLLIIDÆ.
Gen. I. SCYLLIUM, *Cuv.**
17. *SCYLLIUM CANICULA*, L.
The Rough Hound, the Spotted Dog-fish (*female*), Lesser Spotted Dog-fish (*male*), Spotted Shark, Robin Huss, Morgay.
La Squale rousette, Squale rochier.
Der Katzenhai, Seehündchen.
Scillio gattuccio (*It.*).
Vulg., Gatta (*Ven., Tr., Fiume, Cattaro*).
Gatta d'aspreo (*Ven., Tr.*).
Gatta de Quarnero (*Ven.*).
Croat., Mačka, Mačak cërni.
Habit. Common at all seasons all over the Adriatic; on muddy bottom and amongst *algæ* on the hunt after cuttle-fish.
Season. Spring and autumn.
Quality. Flesh has a disagreeable musky smell and oily taste; is tough and stringy; the skin is rough and is much used for polishing cabinet work.

18. *SCYLLIUM STELLARE*, L.
The Spotted Dog-fish, Large Spotted Dog-fish, Rock Dog-fish, Nurse-hound, Bounce, Cat-fish.

---
* *Scyllium acanthonotum*. (*See* No. 354.)

Le Squale Roussette, Chat rochier.
Der Pantherhai.
Scillio gatto-pardo (*It.*).
Vulg., Gatta, Gatta schiava (*Tr.*, *Ven.*, *Fiume*).
Gatta nostrana (*Ven.*).
Croat., Mačak naški, Sužanj mačak, Mačka šargasta (*Spalato*).
Habit. Common in summer; frequents the open sea.
Quality. Flesh less disagreeable than that of the foregoing sp.; skin rougher and tougher, hence more serviceable for the cabinet-maker.

Gen. II. PRISTIURUS, *Bp.*
19. *PRISTIURUS MELANOSTOMUS*, Bp.
The Black-mouthed Dog-fish, Eyed Dog-fish.
Pristiuro boccanera (*It.*).
Habit. Very rare; common in the south of Italy.
Quality. o; flesh uneatable.

Fam. V. SPINACIDÆ.
Gen. I. CENTRINA, *Cuv.*
20. *CENTRINA SALVIANI*, Risso.
Le Squale humantin.
Der Stachelhai.
Centrina porco (*It.*).
Vulg., Pesce porco, Pesce sorcio (*Tr.*, *Ven.*, *Fiume*).
Croat., Prasac, Riba prasac (*Croat. littoral*).
Prasac morski (*Spalato*).
Habit. Not uncommon in the Quarnero in summer; sp. from Venice, Trieste, Fiume, Spalato.
Quality. o; oil used for healing burns; flesh indifferent.

Gen. II. ACANTHIAS, *M. & H.*
21. *ACANTHIAS VULGARIS*, Risso.
The Spiny Dog-fish, the Picked Dog-fish, Common Dog-fish, Hound-fish, Thorn-hound, Bone-dog, Picked Shark.

L'aiguillat.
Der Dornhai, Speerhai, Dornhund.
Spinarolo imperiale (*It.*).
Vulg., Asià, Asiar, Asial (*Tr.*, *Ven.*, *Fiume*, *Cattaro*).
Pesce Can-spinarol (*Fiume*).
Croat., Koščerin. Kostelj (*Spalato*).
Habit. Common at all seasons.
Season. Best for eating in the winter months.
Quality. 3; best of all the sharks.

22. *ACANTHIAS BLAINVILLII*, Risso.
Spiny Dog-fish.
Spinarolo comune (*It.*).
Vulg., same as foregoing sp.
Croat., same as foregoing sp.
Pas, Kostelj vlastelin (*Spalato*).
Habit. Not as common as, and hardly distinct from, the foregoing species.
Season. Autumn, March.
Quality. Inferior to foregoing species, for which it is generally sold.

Gen. III. SPINAX, *M. & H.*
23. *SPINAX NIGER*, Bp.
Le Sagre.
Sagri moretto (*It.*).
Habit. Dalmatian coast in depths of 4—500 fathoms; very rare; does not exceed fourteen inches in length.

Gen. IV. ECHINORHINUS, *Bl.*
24. *ECHINORHINUS SPINOSUS*, L.
The Spinous Shark.
Squale bouclé.
Ronco spinoso (*It.*).
Habit. Quite accidental; Venice.

Fam. VI. RHINIDÆ.
Gen. I. RHINA, *Klein.*
25. *RHINA SQUATINA*, L.
The Angel-fish, Angel Shark, Monk, Monk-fish, Shark Ray.

Squatine, Squale ange.
Der Engelhai, der Meerengel.
Squadrolino pellenera (*It.*).
Vulg., Squaèna (*Ven.*, *Tr.*, *Fiume*).
Squalena, Violin, Pesce Violin (*Ven.*).
Croat., ćuk, sokot, sklat.
Sklat od puriča (*Spalato*).
Habit. Common at all seasons all over the Adriatic; inhabits the deep-beds, and feeds on flat-fish.
Season. January, February, May.
Quality. Flesh somewhat better than that of the Tope; skin used for polishing and as shagreen leather.

26. *SQUATINA OCULATA*, Bp.
Günther cites this fish as synonymous with the foregoing.
The same nomenclature applies to this species.
Vulg., Sagri, Sagrin (*Ven.*).
Croat., Sklat (*Spalato*).
Habit. Venice, Trieste, Spalato.
Season. March.

B. BATOIDEI—Rays.

Fam. I. TORPEDINIDÆ.

Gen. TORPEDO, *Dum.*

27. *TORPEDO HEBETANS*, Lowe.
Torpedo nobiliana, *Bp.*
Electric Ray, New British Torpedo.
Der Zitterrochen.
Torpedine del Nobili (*It.*).
Vulg., Tremolo, Tremola, Pesce Tremolo, (*Ven.*, *Tr.*, *Fiume*, *Cat.*).
Croat., Tèrn, tèrnka, tèrnovka, tararajka, tarnjača, trepljivica, tremavka, tremajuka, trepotnjak; šarena drhtulja (*Spalato*).
Habit. Frequents shallow water on stony bottoms; sp. from Trieste.
Quality. 3; flesh inferior.

28. *TORPEDO NARCE*, Risso.
Der gefleckte Zitterrochen.
Torpedine occhiatella (*It.*).
Vulg., as No. 27, Tremolo occhià, Tremolo a macchie negre (*Ven.*).
Croat., as No. 27.
Drtulja (*Spalato*).
Habit. Very rare in the Adriatic.

29. *TORPEDO MARMORATA*, Risso.
Torpedo galvanii, *L.*
The Electric Ray, or Old British Torpedo, Common Cramp-fish, Numb-fish.
La Torpille.
Der marmorirte Zitterrochen.
Torpedine del Galvani (*It.*).
Vulg., same as No. 27; besides Sgramfo(*Ven.*).
Croat., same as No. 27.
Habit. Found all over the Adriatic; the most common of the genus.
Season. Particularly common in summer months.

Fam. II. RAJIDÆ.

Gen. RAJA, *Cuv.*

30. *RAJA CLAVATA*, L.
Dasybatis clavata, *Blainv.*
The Thornback, Rough Ray.
Raie bouclée.
Der Nagelrochen, Dornrochen, Stachelrochen.
Arzilla chiodata (*It.*).
Vulg., Rasa (*generic*), Barácola (*Ven.*, *Tr.*, *Fiume*, *Cat.*).
Rasa (Razza) spinosa (*Ven.*, *Fiume*).
Croat., Kamenica.
Polig košćati (*Croat. littoral*).
Raža, Barakulà, Ražina dračava (*Spalato*).
Habit. Common at all seasons throughout the Adriatic.
Season. Most common in March, best in January.
Quality. 2; flesh the best of the genus.

31. *RAJA MACULATA*, Mont.
Raja batis, *Bp.*
The Homelyn Ray, Fuller Ray, Spotted or Painted Sand-Ray.
Der gefleckte Rochen.
Dornrochen.
Razza macchiettata (*It.*).
Vulg., Rasa.
Habit. Rare sp. of the Adriatic; sp. from Venice, Trieste.
Note. Identity confused.

32. *RAJA PUNCTATA*, Risso.
Dasybatis asterias, *Bp.*
Der punctirte Rochen, Sternrochen.
Arzilla rossina (*It.*).
Vulg., Rasa (*Tr., Ven., Fiume*).
Rasetta, Baràcola, Baràcola bianca, Baràcola alba (*Ven.*).
Baracoletta (*Fiume*).
Croat., Barakulica, Polig bieli. Ražica (*Spalato*).
Habit. Common at all seasons.
Quality. 3.

33. *RAJA ASTERIAS*, M. & H.
Hardly distinct from the foregoing sp.; Canestrini cites it as synonymous with *R. maculata* Montagu.
Habit. Venice.

34. *RAJA FULLONICA*, L.
The Shagreen Ray.
Arzilla scardasso (*It.*).
Vulg., Rasetta, Baracola (*Ven.*).
Habit. Rare; Venice.
Quality. 3.

35. *RAJA ASPERA*, Bp.
Vulg., Rasa (*Tr.*).
Baracola vera (*Ven.*).
Habit. Venice, Trieste; common in summer.
Quality. 3.

Note. Canestrini doubts the identity of this sp. with the figure described by Bp.; represented in the Trieste Museum.

36. *RAJA MIRALETUS*, L.
Der zweifleckige Rochen.
Das Vierauge.
Razza baraccola (*It.*).
Vulg., Quattro occhi, quattr' occhi (*Tr., Ven., Fiume*), Baosa, Scarparo, (*Ven.*).
Croat., četiri oči. Barakula (*Spalato*).
Habit. Common at all seasons.
Quality. 2.

37. *RAJA RADULA*, Delar.
The Sandy Ray (*Yarrow*).
The Cuckoo Ray (*Yarrow*).
Razza scuffina (*It.*).
Vulg., Rasa.
Habit. Only accidentally met with in the Adriatic; frequents the southern waters; sp. from Trieste.
Quality. 3.
Note. Almost identical with the *R. circularis* of Couch. (*See* Note, No. 41.)

38. *RAJA MARGINATA*, Lac.
The Bordered Ray.
Raie petit museau.
Der Randrochen.
Razza marginata (*It.*).
Vulg., Rasa (*Tr., Fiume*).
Baracoletta (*Ven., Fiume*).
Bavosa, Baosa (*Ven.*).
Croat., Buča. Volinica (*Spalato*).
Habit. More or less throughout the Adriatic; not very common.
Season. Always.
Quality. 3.

39. *RAJA MACRORHYNCHUS*, Bp.
Der dickschnauzige Rochen.
Razza bavosa (*It.*).
Vulg., Rasa, Bavosa (*Tr., Ven., Fiume*).

Moro (*Tr.*).
Rasa di sabbia (*Fiume*).
Croat., Klinka. Volina (*Spalato*).
Habit. Common all the year round.
Quality. 3.

40. *RAJA OXYRHYNCHUS*, L.
    The Burton Skate.
    Der Schlammrochen.
    Der spitzschnauzige Rochen.
    Die Spitzchnauze.
    Razza monaca (*It.*).
    Vulg., Bavosa, Baosa (*Tr.*, *Ven.*, *Fiume*).
    Croat., Volina. Klinka (*Spalato*).
    Habit. More or less common all the year round, throughout the Adriatic.
    Quality. 3.

41. *RAJA QUADRIMACULATA*, Risso.
    Raja circularis, *Couch.*(?)
    Raja miraletus, *Couch.*(?)
    The Sandy Ray, *Couch.*(?)
    The Cuckoo Ray, *Couch.*(?)
    Der vierfleckige Rochen.
    Razza quattrocchi (*It.*).
    Note. Identity hardly confirmed; in any case a very rare species in these waters. Prof. Kolombatović has met with it at Spalato. Couch distinguishes his *R. circularis* or Sandy Ray, from his *R. miraletus* or Cuckoo Ray, whereas Günther cites the two sp. as identical. Nos. 36, 37, and 41 are very similar.

Fam. III. TRYGONIDÆ.
  Gen. I. TRYGON, *Adanson*.
42. *TRYGON THALASSIA*, Column.
    Trigone talassia (*It.*).
    Croat., šiba. Velik sunj (*Spalato*).
    Habit. An Adriatic species, though rare; specimens from Spalato.

43. *TRYGON BRUCCO*, Bp.
    Trygone brucco (*It.*).
    Vulg., Matan (*Tr.*).

Croat., Buča. Sunj (*Spalato*).
Habit. Pretty common at all seasons, frequents muddy bottoms at the mouths of rivers, and in the lagoons.
Quality. 3.

44. *TRYGON PASTINACA*, L.
    The Sting Ray, Fire-Flaire, Fiery-Flaw, Common Trygon.
    La Pastinaque.
    Der Stechrochen.
    Der Pfeilschwanz.
    Trigone pastinaca (*It.*).
    Vulg., Matàn, Matana, also (by misapplication) Pesce Colombo (*Tr.*, *Fiume*, *Ven.*).
    Colombo (*Cattaro*).
    Muccio, Mucchio, Baracola (*Ven.*).
    Croat., as above. Viža, žutulja (*Spalato*).
    Habit. As above, but much more common than the foregoing sp.
    Quality. 3.

  Gen. II. PTEROPLATEA, *M. & H.*
45. *PTEROPLATEA ALTAVELA*, L.
    Pteroplatea altavela (*It.*).
    Altavela (*Naples*), Altavida, Altavila, Tavila (*Sicily*).
    Croat., Pazdrk (*Spalato*).
    Habit. A species of Neapolitan and Sicilian waters, which has been met with in the Gulf of Venice, and seems to be indigenous to a *scoglio* in the Canale delle Castella, Spalato, where two specimens were caught in August, September, 1880. It has also been caught at Zara.
    Season. January, August, September.
    Quality. 3.

Fam. IV. MYLIOBATIDÆ.
  Gen. I. MYLIOBATIS, *Cuv.*
46. *MYLIOBATIS AQUILA*, L.
    The Whip-Ray, Eagle Ray, Devil-fish, Sea-Devil, Toad-fish, Sea-Eagle.

Raie aigle.
Der Adlerrochen.
Miliobate aquila (*It.*).
Vulg., Colombo, Pesce Colombo, also (by misapplication), Matàn (*Tr., Ven., Fiume*), Colombo di Mar (*Fiume*).
Croat., Golub, Golub morski (*Croat. littoral*), Žutulja, Kosir (*Spalato*).
Habit. Common at all seasons, more particularly small ones. The adults are rare.
Quality. 3.

47. *MYLIOBATIS NOCTULA*, Bp.
Der Eulenrochen.
Die Meer Eule.
Miliobate nottola (*It.*).
Vulg., Colombo vescovo (*Tr., Ven., Fiume*).
Vladika (*Cattaro*).

Croat., Golub, Biškup, šiba (*Croat. littoral*), Golub (*Spalato*), Vladika (*Cattaro*).
Habit. As above, but more common.
Quality. 3.

Gen. II. RHINOPTERA, *Kuhl.*
48. *RHINOPTERA MARGINATA*, Cuv.
Habit. Coast of Dalmatia; rarely met with.

Gen. III. DICEROBATIS, *Blainv.*
49. *DICEROBATIS GIORNÆ*, Lac.
Cephaloptera Giorna, *Cuv.*
The Ox Ray, Horned Ray, Devil-fish, Sea-Devil.
Habit. Accidental in the Adriatic; sp. from Trieste.
Quality. o.

Order—GANOIDEI.
Sub-Order—CHONDROSTEI. Sturgeons.
Fam.—ACIPENSERIDÆ.

Gen. ACIPENSER, *Art.*
50. *ACIPENSER NACCARII*, Bp.
The Adriatic Sturgeon.
L'Esturgeon.
Der Adriatische Stör.
Storione cobice (*It.*).
Vulg., Coppèse (*Tr., Fiume*).
Còpese (*Ven.*).
Sporcella (*Tr.*).
Croat., štiriun.
Habit. A species confined to the Adriatic; inhabits the rivers Pô, Isonzo, and other watercourses of the Gulfs of Venice and Trieste;* frequents also the lagoons of Venice in autumn.
Season. March, April, November, December; more or less common at all seasons.

* Has been caught in the rivers Brenta, Adige, Piave, Livenza, Bacchiglione and Tagliamento.

Quality. Flesh inferior to that of the common Sturgeon.

51. *ACIPENSER NARDOI*, Heck.
Described by Heckel as a distinct sp., but Günther cites it as synonymous with the foregoing sp. (*See* Catalogue of Fishes in the British Museum, Vol. VIII. page 336.)
Nomenclature and remarks as above apply equally to this sp.; the two species are generally sold together.

52. *ACIPENSER NASUS*, Heck.
The specimen described by Heckel was 26 in. long (Heck. and Kner, "Süsswasserf.," p. 360). Prof. Brandt rejects this and other sp. established by Heckel (Bull. Ac. Sc. St. Petersburg, 1869, p. 171), and considers this sp. as synonymous with *A. naccarii*. (*See*

Catalogue of Fishes in the British Museum, Vol. VIII. page 517.)
Habit. Pô and the Venetian lagoons. In practice, the three species merge into one.

53. *ACIPENSER HUSO*, L.
The Broad-nosed, or Blunt-nosed Sturgeon.
The Huso.
Le grand Esturgeon.
Der Hausen.
Storione ladano (*It.*).
Vulg., Ladano (*Ven.*).
Croat., Moruna, Morun.
Habit. A rare visitor in the Adriatic; occasionally found at Venice, and ascends the Pô, in which river specimens are sometimes caught weighing 100 lb. and measuring seven feet.

54. *ACIPENSER HECKELII*, Fitz.
Vulg., Còpese (*Ven.*).
Another variety from Venice described by Heck. (Heck. and Kner, "Süsswasserf.," p. 357), but which, according to Günther, does not appear to be a distinct sp.; he considers it identical with *A. güldenstädtii* (*See* Catalogue of Fishes in the British Museum, Vol. VIII. p. 341), whilst Prof. Brandt considers it identical with *A. naccarii*. (*See* Catalogue of Fishes in the British Museum, Vol. VIII. p. 517.)

55. *ACIPENSER STURIO*, L.*
The Sturgeon, Common Sturgeon.
L'Esturgeon, L'Esturgeon ordinaire.
Der Stör, der gemeine Stör.
Storione comune (*It.*).
Vulg., Adilo, Adello, Adano (*Prov.*).
Storion, Sturione, Sporzella (young) (*Tr., Fiume*).
Sturion, Porzella, Porcelletta (young), Speardo (*Ven., Treviso*).
Storione, Porzella (young) (*Verona*).
Croat., štiriun, Jesetra, Jesetre (plur.), (*generic terms*), Pravi jesctar.
Habit. This species is also caught on the eastern shores; it frequents the sea during the greater part of the year, and ascends the Pô and other rivers of the Gulf of Venice in the spring to deposit its spawn; it is not uncommon at Spalato, and is also occasionally caught in the Quarnero. One specimen has also been caught in the River Narenta, but this seems to be quite accidental.
Season. February, May, and more or less all the year round.
Quality. 1; and much superior to the other sp.

Sub-Class—TELEOSTEI.
Order—ACANTHOPTERYGII.
Fam. I. PERCIDÆ—Perch Tribe.

Gen. I. PERCA, *Art.*
56. *PERCA FLUVIATILIS*, L.
Perca italica, *C. & V.*
The Perch, the Fresh-water Perch.
La Perche.
Der Flussbarsch.
Pesce Persico (*It.*).
Vulg., Persego (*Trentino, Verona, Ven.*).
Pesce Perseghin (*Bologna*).

Perso di fiume (*Tuscany*).
Croat., Ostrieš, bulja.
Habit. General; fresh-water courses and lakes; Lake of Garda.
Season. May, July, September, October, and more or less all the year round.
Quality. 2.

---

* *Acipenser stellatus.* (*See* No. 355.)

Gen. II. LABRAX, *C. & V.*

57. *LABRAX LUPUS*, Cuv.

The Basse, Common Basse.
Le Loup, Loubine.
Der Seebarsch, Wolfsbarsch, Gemeiner Wolfsbarsch.
Labrace, Spigula ragno (*It.*).
Vulg., Branzin (*Ven.*, *Tr.*, *Fiume*, *Cattaro*).
Varolo, Variolo (*Ven.*).
Ragno (*Tuscany*).
Baïcolo (*when young*) (*Ven.*, *Tr.*, *Fiume*).
Croat., Luben, Lubin, Lubanj, Ljubljnj, Smudut, Agača.
Habit. General, all over the Adriatic; enters the brackish waters and mouths of rivers.
Season. Common all the year round; best in autumn.
Quality. 1.

Gen. III. LUCIOPERCA, *Cuv.*

58. *LUCIOPERCA SANDRA*, Cuv.

The Pike-perch.
Le Sandre.
Der Sander, Zander, Sandbarsch, Hechtbarsch, Schiel, Schill.
Lucioperca sandra (*It.*).
Hungarian, Fogas (*mature*), Süllö (*young*).
Croat., Smudj, šilj.
Habit. Has a northern extension; its southernmost limits are the rivers Isonzo and Adige.
Quality. 1.

Gen. IV. CENTROPRISTIS, *C. & V.*

59. *CENTROPRISTIS HEPATUS*, Gm.

Serranus hepatus, *C. & V.*
Le Serran.
Der Beutelbarsch.
Schiarrano sacchetto (*It.*).
Vulg., Sacchetto (*Ven.*, *Tr.*, *Fiume*).
Croat., Pinzulić, Sanketice (*Croat. littoral*).
Vučić, čučina (*Spalato*).
Habit. General; throughout the Adriatic.

Season. Always common.
Quality. 3; *Minutaja* (mixed fish).

Gen. V. ANTHIAS, *Schn.*

60. *ANTHIAS SACER*, Bl.

Le Barbier.
Der Röthling.
Canario largo (*It.*).
Croat., Kirnja velika. Kirnja mala (*Spalato*).
Habit. Dalmatia, Lissa, Comisa.
Season. May, September, November. Very rare.
Quality. 3.

Gen. VI. SERRANUS, *Cuv.**
(Sea-Perches proper.)

61. *SERRANUS SCRIBA*, C. & V.

Der Schriftbarsch, Buchstabenbarsch.
Sciarrano scrittura (*It.*).
Vulg., Perga, Sperga, Merlo di mar (*Tr.*).
Sperga, Perga, Merlo di mar, Donzela, Papagà (*Ven.*).
Perha (*Fiume*).
Croat., Lenica, Smokvača, Kanjac. Pirka (*Spalato*).
Habit. General; Venice, Trieste, Quarnero.
Season. Always common.
Quality. 2.

62. *SERRANUS CABRILLA*, C. & V.

The Comber, the Smooth Serranus.
Der Sägebarsch.
Sciarrano cabrilla (*It.*).
Vulg., Perga dalmata, Cánissi, Cánizzi (*Tr.*).
Perha (*Fiume*).
Sperga, Donzella, Cortesan de caorle, Schiavon, Crágnizi (*Ven.*).
Croat., Pirka (*Dalmatia*).
Kanjac (*Spalato*).
Habit. Eastern shores of the Adriatic; frequents the deep on sandy bottoms.
Season. Spring, autumn; common.
Quality. 2.

---

* *Serranus acutirostris.* (*See* No. 356.)

63. *SERRANUS GIGAS*, C. & V.
The Dusky Serranus, or Dusky Perch.
Le Méron.
Der braune Serran, grosser Sägebarsch.
Sciarrano gigante (*It.*).
Vulg., Chierna (*Tr.*, *Cattaro*), Cherne (*Fiume*).
Croat., Kerna, Kirnja prava. Kraja (*Spalato*).
Habit. An Atlantic sp.; Trieste, Fiume, Spalato; frequents deep water on rocky beds.
Season. Winter; occasional; common at Spalato, where it attains to a weight of 18 kilos.
Quality. 1.

Gen. VII. POLYPRION, *C. & V.*
64. *POLYPRION CERNIUM*, Cuv.
The Stone-Basse, Wreck-fish, Couch's Polyprion.
Die gefleckte Vielsäge.
Cerniola (*It.*).
Vulg., Scarpena di sasso (?), Scarpena salvatico (?) (*Ven.*, *Tr.*).
Habit. A northern species, frequenting depths of 500 fathoms; Cherso, Fiume, Spalato.
Season. Very rare; March, May, August.
Quality. 1.

Gen. VIII. APOGON, *Lac.*
65. *APOGON IMBERBIS*, L.
Apogon rex mullorum, *Cuv.*
Apogone (*It.*).
Croat., Kirnja mala. Matulić (*Spalato*).
Habit. South of Dalmatia, Spalato; in deep waters.
Season. Very rare; not uncommon at Spalato in winter.

Gen. IX. DENTEX, *Cuv.**
66. *DENTEX VULGARIS*, C. & V.
The Sparus, Dentex, Toothed Gilthead, Four-toothed Sparus.

Spare dentée.
Der Zahnbrassen.
Dentale comune (*It.*). .
Vulg., Dental (*Ven.*, *Tr.*, *Fiume*).
Croat., Zubac, Zubatac.
Habit. General.
Season. Always; chiefly autumn; common.
Quality. 1.

DENTEX GIBBOSUS, Cocco.
Abnormity of the foregoing sp.
Vulg., Dentale della corona (*Sebenico*).
Croat., Zubatac od krune, Zubatac krunaš.
Habit. Sebenico.
Season. October.
Quality. 1.

Gen. X. MÆNA, *Cuv.*
67. *MÆNA VULGARIS*, C. & V.
Mendole, Cackarel. La spare Mendole.
Der Laxirfisch.
Menola comune (*It.*).
Vulg., Menola schiava (*Tr.*, *Fiume*).
Menola, M. chiava, Pontio (*Ven.*).
Croat., Modrak, Modraš, Trog, Gira.
Gira oblica (*Spalato*).
Habit. General.
Season. Common in summer and autumn.
Quality. 3.

68. *MÆNA JUSCULUM*, C. & V.
Menola schiava (*It.*).
Habit. Venice.
Season. Rare; autumn.
Quality. 3.

69. *MÆNA ZEBRA*, Brünn.
Mæna Osbeckii, *C. & V.*
Menola zebra (*It.*).
Vulg., Menola schiava, Bufalo de aspreo, Sparo bastardo (*Ven.*).
Habit. General; chiefly in southern waters.
Season. May, September; common.
Quality. 3.

---
* *Dentex filosus* and *Dentex macrophthalmus*. (See Nos. 357, 358.)

Gen. XI. SMARIS, *Cuv.*

70. *SMARIS VULGARIS,* C. & V.
Der weisse 'Schauzenbrassen, gemeiner Picarel.
Menola zerolo (*It.*).
Vulg., Menola, Marida, Maridola (*Tr., Ven., Fiume*).
Menoloto, Ghirsa, Garizzo, Menola bianca (*Ven.*).
Croat., Oblica biela, Mendula biela, Milvica (?), Oštruja, Cicavica. Oštruja (*female*), Perč (*male*) (*Spalato*).
Habit. General.
Season. Common in summer.
Quality. 3.

71. *SMARIS ALCEDO,* C. & V.
Menola alcedine (*It.*).
Vulg., Menola (*Tr., Ven.*), Garizzo (*Ven.*).
Croat., Oblica.
Modrulj (*Spalato*).
Habit. General.
Season. February, May; not so common as the foregoing sp.
Quality. 3.

72. *SMARIS MAURII,* Bp.
Menola del Mauri (*It.*).
Vulg., Menola (*Tr., Ven., Spalato*).
Habit. Trieste, Venice, Spalato.
Season. August, October; rare.
Quality. 3.

73. *SMARIS GRACILIS,* Bp.
Menola gracile (*It.*).
Vulg., Agon or Agone d'Istria, Maridola (*Ven., Fiume*).
Croat., Oliga.
Habit. Has a southern extension.
Season. April, May, February, September; rare.
Quality. 3; best of the genus.

Fam. II. MULLIDÆ—Red Mullets.
Gen. MULLUS, *L.*

74. *MULLUS BARBATUS,* L.
The Red Mullet, or Surmullet.
Le Mulle Rouget, le Rouge Barbet.
Die rothe Meerbarbe, der Rothbart.
Triglia minore (*It.*).
Vulg., Barbon (*Ven., Tr., Fiume, Cattaro*).
Cavazioi (young) (*Ven.*).
Croat., Barbun, Trlja, Bĕrkavica.
Pujoglavica (*Spalato*).
Habit. General.
Season. Always common; best in March, April, August, September, December.
Quality. 1.

75. *MULLUS SURMULETUS,* L.
The Striped Surmullet.
Le Surmullet.
Die gestreifte Meerbarbe.
Der grosse Rothbart.
Triglia maggiore (*It.*).
Vulg., Triglia, Tria (*Ven., Tr., Fiume, Cattaro*).
Barbon de nassa (*Fiume*).
Croat., Trlja. Sgrčenice (*Spalato*).
Habit. General.
Season. Always common; best in January, March, October, September. Probably not a distinct species, but the female of the preceding.
Quality. 1.

Fam. III. SPARIDÆ—Sea Breams.
Group I. *Cantharina.*
Gen. I. CANTHARUS, *Cuv.*

76. *CANTHARUS VULGARIS,* C. & V.
The Sea Bream, Old-Wife, the Black Bream.
La Sarde Grise.
Der braune Brassen.
Cantaro comune (*It.*).
Vulg., Cantera, Cantara (*Tr., Ven., Fiume*).

Cantarina, Cantarina de aspreo, Cantarella (*Ven.*).
Croat., Kantar (*Spalato*).
Habit. General.
Season. Common in winter.
Quality. 3.

77. *CANTHARUS BRAMA*, C. & V.
Habit. Dalmatia, Trieste; an Adriatic species.
Season. Not so common as the foregoing sp.; autumn.
Quality. 3.

78. *CANTHARUS ORBICULARIS*, C.&V.
Cantaro orbicolare (*It.*).
Vulg., Cantara, Ociada.
Croat., Kantar (*Spalato*).
Habit. General.
Season. November, March, July, October.
Quality. 2 ; best of the genus.

Gen. II. Box, *Cuv.*
79. *BOX VULGARIS*, C. & V.
Sparus boops, *L.*
The Bogue, Ox-eye.
Le Bogue commun.
Der Gelbstriemen.
Boba comune (*It.*).
Vulg., Boba, Bobba (*Tr.*, *Ven.*, *Fiume*, *Cattaro*).
Croat., Bugva (*Dalmatia*).
Buba (*Fiume*).
Bukva (*Spalato*).
Habit. General.
Season. Midst of winter; common.
Quality. 2.

80. *BOX SALPA*, C. & V.
Sparus salpa, *L.*
Der Goldstriemen.
Boba salpa (*It.*).
Vulg., Salpa (*Ven.*, *Tr.*, *Fiume*, *Cattaro*).
Croat., Salpa.

Habit. General.
Season. Always common.
Quality. 3.

Gen. III. OBLATA, *Cuv.*
81. *OBLATA MELANURA*, L.
Der Brandbrassen.
Obbiada codanera (*It.*).
Vulg., Occiada, Occhiada, Ochiä, Albero bastardo (*Ven.*).
Occhiada (*Tr.*, *Fiume*, *Cattaro*).
Croat., Ušata, Osata, Crnorep.
Habit. General.
Season. Always common.
Quality. 2.

Group II. *Sargina.*
Gen. IV. SARGUS, *Klein.**
82. *SARGUS VULGARIS*, Geoffr.
Sargus Salviani, C. & V.
Der gemeine Geissbrassen.
Salvian's Geissbrassen.
Sargo del Salviani (*It.*).
Vulg., Sparo (*Ven.*).
Spizzo (*Tr.*, *Fiume*, *Cattaro*).
Croat., Pič (*Croat. littoral*).
Fratrić, Oluz (*Spalato*).
Habit. Dalmatia, Cherso, Trieste.
Season. June, July, January, March; rare.
Quality. 2.

83. *SARGUS RONDELETII*, C. & V.
Der grössere Geissbrassen.
Sargo del Rondelezio (*It.*).
Vulg., Sargo (*Tr.*, *Fiume*, *Cattaro*).
Sparo (*Ven.*).
Sparetto (*Tr.*).
Croat., šarg, fratar ; šarag (*Spalato*).
Habit. General.
Season. Summer; common.
Quality. 2.

* *Sargus vetula.* (*See No.* 359.)

84. **SARGUS ANNULARIS**, L.
 Der kleine Geissbrassen.
 Sargo annulare (*It.*).
 Vulg., Sparo, Sparetto (*Tr.*, *Fiume*, *Cat.*).
 Sparo, Sparolo (*Ven.*).
 Croat., Špar.
 Habit. General.
 Season. Common in summer; best in Sept.
 Quality. 2.

 Gen. V. CHARAX, *Risso*.
85. **CHARAX PUNTAZZO**, C. & V.
 Puntazzo.
 Der schwarzgebändete Brassen.
 Carace acuto (*It.*).
 Vulg., Spizzo, Spizzo bastardo (*Tr.*).
 Sargo d'Istria (*Ven.*).
 Pesce morti, Magna morti (*Fiume*).
 Croat., Pič.
 Habit. General.
 Season. Autumn and winter; common.
 Quality. 3.

 Group III. *Pagrina.*
 Gen. VI. PAGRUS, *Cuv.**
86. **PAGRUS VULGARIS**, C. & V.
 The Braize or Becker, Pandora, King of the Sea Bream.
 Der röthliche Goldbrassen, der grosse Rothbrassen.
 Pagro vulgare (*It.*).
 Vulg., Pagaro, Tabaro, Sparo d'Istria, Alboro pagnesco (*generic term*) (*Ven.*).
 Cantarella (*Tr.*).
 Croat., Pagar, Pagrun.
 Habit. General, but scarce.
 Season. May, June, October.
 Quality. 1.

87. **PAGRUS ORPHUS**, C. & V.
 Couch's Sea Bream.

 * *Pagrus Ehrenbergii.* (*See No.* 360.)

 Le pagre Orphe.
 Note.—A very rare sp.

 Gen. VII. PAGELLUS, *C. & V.*
88. **PAGELLUS ERYTHRINUS**, C. & V.
 The Erythrinus, the Red, or Spanish Sea Bream.
 Der rothe Goldbrassen, der kleine Rothbrassen.
 Pagello fragolino (*It.*).
 Vulg., Ribon, Ribone (*Tr.*).
 Arboro (*Fiume*, *Cattaro*).
 Madagia, Madagiola, Arboro, Alboro, Alboretto (*Ven.*).
 Croat., Arbun.
 Habit. General and common.
 Season. Most common in September; best in March and May.
 Quality. 1.

89. **PAGELLUS CENTRODONTUS**, C. & V.
 The common Sea Bream, the Sharp-toothed Sea Bream, the Red Gilt-head.
 Pagello rosso (*It.*).
 Habit. A southern species; Dalmatia, Venice; Rarely met with in the north of the gulf.

90. **PAGELLUS BOGARAVEO**, C. & V.
 Pagello bogaraveo (*It.*).
 Croat., Grbić (*Spalato*).
 Habit. General, but scarce, on rocky beds.

91. **PAGELLUS MORMYRUS**, C. & V.
 Der Marmorbrassen.
 Pagello mormora (*It.*).
 Vulg., Mormoro, Mormiro, Mormora* (*Tr.*, *Ven.*, *Fiume*).
 Croat., Ovca (*Croat. littoral*).

 * Not to be confused with *Gadus minutus*, which is also known by this name.

Arkaj, Ovčica (*Spalato*).
Habit. General, but scarce; common at Spalato at all seasons.
Quality. 2.

PAGELLUS ACARNE, Cuv.
Questionable as belonging to the Adriatic fauna; at any rate very rare. (*See* No. 361.)

Gen. VIII.   CHRYSOPHRYS, *Cuv.*
92. *CHRYSOPHRYS AURATA,* C. & V.
The Gilt-head.   Spare Dorade.
Der gemeine Goldbrassen.
Orada comune (*It.*).
Vulg., Orada, Dorada.
Croat., Ovrata, Lovrata, Lovratica, Podlanica.
Komarča (*Spalato*).
Habit. General and common.
Season. Most common in summer and autumn.
Quality. 1.

Fam. IV.   SCORPÆNIDÆ—Scorpions.
Gen. I.   SEBASTES, C. & V.
93. *SEBASTES IMPERIALIS,* C. & V.
Sebastes dactylopterus, *De la Roche.*
Sebaste imperiale (*It.*).
Vulg., Scorfano de funnale (*Naples*).
Habit. General, but very scarce; Dalmatia, Cherso, Trieste; inhabits great depths.

Gen. II.   SCORPÆNA, *Artedi.*
94. *SCORPÆNA PORCUS,* L.
Der kleine, oder braune Drachenkopf.
Scorpena nera (*It.*).
Vulg., Scarpena, Scarpena negra, Scarpon (*Tr.*, *Ven.*, *Fiume*, *Cat.*).
Croat., Cèrni škarpoč.
Cèrna škarpena (*Fiume* and *littoral*).
škarpun, bodeljka (*Spalato*).

Habit. General and common.
Season. Always; particularly April to June, September and October.
Quality. 2.

95. *SCORPÆNA SCROFA,* L.
Der grosse Drachenkopf.
Der rothe Drachenkopf.
Scorpena rossa (*It.*).
Vulg., Scarpena, Scarpena di sasso (*Tr.*, *Fiume*).
Scarpena rossa (*Ven.*).
Croat., Cèrveni škarpoč, cèrjena škarpena (*Croat. littoral*).
škarpina, bodeljka (*Spalato*).
Habit., *Season,* and *Quality.* Same as the foregoing sp.

Fam. V.   SCIÆNIDÆ—Meagres.
Gen. I.   UMBRINA, *Cuv.*
96. *UMBRINA CIRRHOSA,* L.
The Umbrina.
L'Ombre.
Der Bart-umber.
Ombrina corvo (*It.*).
Vulg., Corbo (*Tr.*, *Ven.*, *Fiume*).
Ombrella, Corbel* (*Tr.*).
Corbetto, Ombrela (*Ven.*).
Croat., Kurben, Kurbeš (*Fiume*), Havba (*Croat. littoral*).
Kèrb, Grb, Crnelj (*Spalato*).
Habit. General and common; brackish waters.
Season. Spring and summer.
Quality. 2.

Gen. II.   SCIÆNA, *Art.*
97. *SCIÆNA AQUILA,* Lac.
The Maigre, Meagre, Shade-fish.
Le Maigre, Poisson royal.

---

* Nardo applies the name *Ombrella* to the young, and *Corbo* to the mature sp.

Der Sceadler.
Sciena aquila (*It.*).
Vulg., Ombra, Ombria (*Ven.*).
Croat., Grb. Kèrb (*Spalato*).
Habit. General; brackish waters, mouths of rivers; Venice.
Season. April; rare.
Quality. 2.

Gen. III. CORVINA, *Cuv.*
98. *CORVINA NIGRA*, Cuv.
Sciæna umbra, *L.*
Le Corbeau.
Der schwarze Schattenfisch.
Corvina locca, Corvo di fortiera (*It.*).
Vulg., Corbo di sasso (*Ven.*, *Fiume*).
Corbel, Corbel di sasso, Ombrella (*Tr.*).
Ombrela (*Ven.*).
Cavalla.
Croat., Kurben, Kurbeš, Kurben od kamena (*Croat. littoral*).
Kavala (*Spalato*).
Habit., *Season*, *Quality*. Same as the Umbrina.

Fam. VI. XIPHIIDÆ—Sword-fishes.
Gen. I. XIPHIAS, *Art.*
99. *XIPHIAS GLADIUS*, L.
The Sword-fish, the common or Sicilian Sword-fish.
Espadon.
Der gemeine Schwertfisch.
Pesce Spada (*It.*).
Vulg., Pesce Spada (*Tr.*, *Ven.*, *Fiume*, *Cat.*), Spadon (*Tr.*, *Ven.*).
Croat., Riba sablja, Jaglun, Obična sablja (*Croat. littoral*).
Habit. General, but rare in the north.
Season. June, August, September.
Quality. 2.

Gen. II. HISTIOPHORUS, *Lac.*
100. *HISTIOPHORUS BELONE*, C. & V.
Tetrapterus belone, *Raf.*
Tetrapturo muso corto (*It.*).
Vulg., Acura imperiale (*Taranto*).
Croat., Jaglun (*Spalato*).
Habit. Very rarely met with; is occasionally caught at Spalato at all seasons of the year; Canale delle Castella.

Fam. VII. TRICHIURIDÆ.*
Gen. I. LEPIDOPUS, *Gouan.*
101. *LEPIDOPUS CAUDATUS*, Euphr.
Trichiurus ensiformis, *Vand.*
The Scabbard-fish, Scale-foot.
Der Degenfisch.
Lepidopo argentino (*It.*).
Vulg., Spada argentina (*Tr.*, *Fiume*).
Arzentin, Serpentin, Spada arzentina, Spada di arzento (*Ven.*).
Croat., Riba sablja, Zmijičnjak (*Croat. littoral*).
Zmijicà morska (*Spalato*).
Habit. General, but very rare; Venice, Zaole, Trieste, Spalato.

Gen. II. TRICHIURUS, *L.*
102. *TRICHIURUS LEPTURUS*, L.
The Hair-tail, Silvery Hair-tail, Blade-fish.
Habit. Quite accidental; a sp. is in the Trieste Museum, caught off the Dalmatian coast.

Fam. VIII. CARANGIDÆ.†
Gen. I. TRACHURUS, C. & V.
103. *TRACHURUS TRACHURUS*, L.
Scomber Trachurus, *L.*
Caranx Trachurus, *C. & V.*

---

* *Thyrsites pretiosus*. (*See* No. 362.)
† *Temnodon saltator*. (*See* No. 363.)

The Scad, or Horse Mackerel.
Der gemeine Stöker.
Die bastard Makreele.
Trachuro comune (*It.*).
Vulg., Suro (*Tr.*, *Fiume*, *Ven.*).
Saron (*Tr.*, *Fiume*).
Suero (*Tr.*).
Cantarini, Musicanti (*Fiume*).
Croat., šur, širun (*Croat. littoral*).
Snjur (*Spalato*).
Habit. General and common.
Season. July, August.
Quality. 2.

Gen. II. CARANX, *Cuv.*

104. *CARANX DENTEX*, Bl., Schn.
Selenia luna, *Bp.*
Carange luna (*It.*).
Vulg., Pei Suvareou (*Nice*).
Habit. Dalmatia, but very rare.
Season. April, September, October.
Quality. 1.

Gen. III. SERIOLA, *Cuv.*

105. *SERIOLA DUMERILII*, Risso.
Yellow-tails (*generic*).
Seriola del Dumeril (*It.*).
Vulg., Lissa bastarda.
Croat., Bilizna (*Croat. littoral*).
Manjak (*young*), Gof (*mature*), (*Spalato*).
Habit. General, but rare; inhabits great depths; Venice, Trieste, Ragusa, Spalato.
Season. Winter.

Gen. IV. NAUCRATES, *Cuv.*

106. *NAUCRATES DUCTOR*, L.
Naucrates indicus, *C. & V.*
The Pilot-fish.
Le Pilote.
Der Lootsenfisch.
Der gemeine Lootsenfisch.
Pesce pilota (*It.*).

Vulg., Fanfano (*Tr.*, *Ven.*, *Fiume*, *Cat.*).
Croat., Fanfan (*Fiume*).
Riba od pjene (*Croat. littoral*).
Habit. General; at times not uncommon.
Season. August to October.
Quality. 1.

Gen. V. LICHIA, *Cuv.*

107. *LICHIA AMIA*, L.
Scomber amia, *L.*
Der bunte Lootsenfisch.
Der bunte Grünzling.
Lizza amia (*It.*).
Vulg., Lissa (*Tr.*).
Lizza (*Ven.*, *Fiume*, *Cat.*).
Croat., Lica, Bilizna, Pastirica (*Croat. littoral*).
Bilizna, Bitinica, Bjelica (*Spalato*).
Habit. General and common.
Season. July, August.
Quality. 1.

108. *LICHIA GLAUCA*, L.
Scomber glaucus, *L.*
The Derbio.
Lampuge.
Lizza glauca (*It.*).
Vulg., Lizza bastarda (*Tr.*, *Ven.*, *Fiume*, *Cat.*).
Croat., Pastirica (*Croat. littoral*).
Bilizna (*Spalato*).
Habit. Trieste, Dalmatia; rare.
Season. September.
Quality. 1.

109. *LICHIA VADIGO*, Risso.
Lizza fasciata (*It.*).
Habit, Season, Quality. Same as foregoing sp.

Gen. VI. CAPROS, *Lac.*

110. *CAPROS APER*, Lac.
The Boar-fish.
Le Sanglier.

Caprisco aspro (*It.*).
Vulg., Tariolo (*Sicily*).
Habit. Fiume, Spalato; very rare.

Fam. IX. CYTTIDÆ—John Dorys.
    Gen. ZEUS, *Art.*
111. *ZEUS FABER*, L.
The Dory, John Dory.
Dorée, Poule de mer. Zée forgeron. Janitor (*Latin*) the door-keeper, *i.e.*, Saint Peter.
Der gemeine Sonnenfisch oder Spiegelfisch.
Pesce San Pietro (*It.*).
Vulg., Sanpiero, Pesce Sanpiero (*Tr.*, *Ven.*, *Fiume*, *Cat.*).
Croat., Petar (*Croat. littoral*).
Kovač (*Spalato*).
Habit. General and common.
Season. Always.
Quality. 2.

112. *ZEUS PUNGIO*, C. & V.
Habit. Dalmatia.
Remark. Considered by many authors to be identical with the foregoing species.

Fam. X. STROMATEIDÆ—Black-fish.
    Gen. I. STROMATEUS, *Art.*
113. *STROMATEUS FIATOLA*, L.
Der gemeine Pampel oder Deckfisch.
Lampuga dorata (*It.*).
Vulg., Figo (*Tr.*, *Fiume*, *Cat.*).
Pesce figa (*Ven.*).
Croat., Smokvača, Piška od mora (*Croat. littoral*).
Smokva (*Spalato*).
Habit. General and not uncommon.
Season. Summer.
Quality. 3.

114. *STROMATEUS MICROCHIRUS*, Bp.
Der gestreifte Pampel oder Deckfisch.
Lampuga fasciata (*It.*).
Vulg., Figo (*Tr.*, *Fiume*, *Cat.*).

Pesce figa (*Ven.*).
Habit, Season, Quality. As the foregoing sp.

    Gen. II. CENTROLOPHUS, *Lac.*
115. *CENTROLOPHUS POMPILUS*, C. & V.
The Black-fish, Black Ruffe, Black Perch, Pompilus.
Merle, Serran de Provence.
Holocentre noir.
Centrolofo pompilo (*It.*).
Vulg., Figa (*Tr.*).
Fanfano (*Ven.*).
Habit. Brackish waters, mouths of rivers, lagoons of Venice; Dalmatia, Trieste.
Season. July, August; rare.
Quality. 3.

116. *CENTROLOPHUS CRASSUS*, C. & V.
Centrolofo grosso (*It.*).
Season. April; very rare.

Fam. XI. CORYPHÆNIDÆ—Dolphins.*
    Gen. I. CORYPHÆNA, *Art.*
117. *CORYPHÆNA HIPPURUS*, L.
Dolphin, by misapplication.
Corifena cavallina (*It.*).
Vulg., Cataluzzo (*Tr.*).
Croat., Lančeska (*Croat. littoral*).
Habit. General, but rare.
Season. Single specimens sometimes caught in June, July, August.
Quality. 2.

118. *CORYPHÆNA PELAGICA*, L.
Habit. Trieste; very rare; summer.

    Gen. II. BRAMA, *Risso.*
119. *BRAMA RAII*, Bl. & Schn.
Ray's Sea-bream, Rayan Gilt-head, Ray's Toothed Gilt-head.
Spare castagnole.

---

* *Schedophilus Botteri.* (See No. 364.)

Der gemeine Bramen.
Der Seebrassen des Ray.
Brama occhiuta (*It.*).
Vulg., Cataluzzo, Castagnola (*Tr.*).
Ociada bastarda, Nodola (*Ven.*).
Croat., Lančeska.
Habit. Dalmatia, Trieste; a rare sp.
Season. Summer.
Quality. 1.

Gen. III. AUSONIA, *Risso.*
120. *AUSONIA CUVIERI*, Risso.
Luvarus imperialis, *Raf.*
Der Hahnenfisch.
Ausonia del Cuvier (*It.*).
Vulg., Pesce Gallo (*Tr.*).
Remark. A very rare sp.; occasionally caught in the Gulf of Trieste; has been caught at Spalato.

Fam. XII. SCOMBRIDÆ.
Gen. I. SCOMBER, *Art.*
121. *SCOMBER SCOMBER*, L.
The common Mackerel.
Le Macquereau.
Die gemeine Makreele.
Scombro comune (*It.*).
Vulg., Scombro (*Tr., Fiume, Cattaro*).
Sgombro, Garzariol (*young*) (*Ven.*).
Pesce blu (*family term*).
Croat., Lokarda, Skuša, Skuš, Vèrnut (*Croat. littoral*).
Golčić (*young*).
Skuša, Sguša pastrica (*Spalato*).
Habit. General and common.
Season. April to October.
Quality. 1.

122. *SCOMBER PNEUMATOPHORUS*, Delar.
Die grossäugige oder blasentragende Makreele.
Vulg., Lanzardo (*Tr.*).
Garzariola (*Ven.*).
Remarks. On the authority of Bp., Grube, Plucar, Canestrini requires confirmation; at all events only occasional.

123. *SCOMBER COLIAS*, L.
The Spanish or Coly Mackerel.
Die mittelländische Makreele.
Scombro macchiato (*It.*).
Vulg., Lanzardo (*Tr., Ven., Fiume, Cat.*).
Croat., Plavica (*Croat. littoral*).
Lokarda, Skuša bilica (*Spalato*).
Habit. General, but rare; common at Spalato.
Season. July to September.
Quality. 2; inferior to the common mackerel.

Gen. II. THYNNUS, *C. & V.*
124. *THYNNUS VULGARIS*, C. & V.
Scomber Thynnus, *L.*
The common Tunny.
Scombre Thon.
Der gemeine Thunfisch.
Tonno comune (*It.*).
Vulg., Ton, Pesce Ton, Tonina (*Tr., Ven., Fiume, Cattaro*).
Pompilo, Pompin, Trompeto, Trompilo, Trompin (*Ven.*).
Croat., Tuna, Tun, Tunina (*Croat. littoral*).
Tunj, Trup ili tunj (*Spalato*).
Habit. General and common.
Season. Summer.
Quality. 1.

125. *THYNNUS THUNNINA*, C. & V.
Tonno tonnina (*It.*).
Vulg., Tonnina (*Tr., Fiume*).
Carcàna (*Ven.*).
Croat., Tunina (*Croat. littoral*).
Habit. General and common.
Season. September, October.
Quality. 1.

126. *THYNNUS PELAMYS*, C. & V.
Scomber pelamys, *L.*
The Bonito.
Scombre Bonite.
Der Bonit, der atlantische Bonit.
Tonno palamida (*It.*).
Vulg., Palamida (*Tr., Ven., Fiume, Cat.*).
Palamia (*Ven.*).
Croat., Palanda, Polanda (*Croat. littoral*).
Palamida (*Spalato*).
Habit. Trieste.
Remark. An Atlantic sp. which is only occasionally met with in the Adria.
Quality. 1.

127. *THYNNUS ALALONGA*, Risso.
Scomber alalonga, *L.*
The Germon, or Long-finned Tunny.
Le Germon, Alilonghi.
Aile-longue.
Tonno alalunga (*It.*).
Habit. Frequents deep water, seldom approaching the shore.
Season. September; but only accidentally met with.
Quality. 1.

Gen. III. PELAMYS, *C. & V.**
128. *PELAMYS SARDA*, C. & V.
Scomber pelamys, *Brünn.*
Scomber Sarda, *Bloch.*
The Pelamid.
La Pélamide.
Der mittelländische Bonit.
Palamida sarda (*It.*).
Vulg., Palamida (*Tr., Ven., Fiume, Cat.*).
Croat., Polanda (*Croat. littoral*).
Polandra (*Spalato*).
Habit. Not uncommon in Dalmatia, Spalato; in other waters it is rare.
Season. August to October.
Quality. 2.

* *Pelamys unicolor.* (See No. 365.)

Gen. IV. AUXIS, *C. & V.*
129. *AUXIS VULGARIS*, C. & V.
Scomber rochei, *Risso.*
The Plain Bonito.
Tambarello comune (*It.*).
Vulg., Sgionfetto (*Tr.*).
Tambarello (*Ven.*).
Tombarello (*Fiume*).
Goffo, Letterato.
Croat., Tumbarel (*Fiume*).
Trup (*Croat. littoral, Spalato*).
Habit. General, but rare.
Season. September, October.
Quality. 1.

Gen. V. ECHENEIS, *Art.**
130. *ECHENEIS REMORA*, L.
The Sucking-fish, Remora, Mediterranean Remora.
Le Remora.
Der kleine Schildfisch.
Echeneide remora (*It.*).
Croat., Ustavica (*Croat. lit.*).
Habit. General, but rare; Trieste.
Quality. 0.

Fam. XIII. TRACHINIDÆ.
Group I. *Uranoscopina.*
Gen. I. URANOSCOPUS, *L.*
131. *URANOSCOPUS SCABER*, L.
The common Star-gazer.
Der gemeine Sternseher.
Uranoscopo scabro (*It.*).
Vulg., Bocca in cao (*Tr., Fiume, Ven., Cat.*).
Bocca in capo (*Tr.*).
Toti, Chiachia (*Ven.*).
Croat., čač, čač muški (*Fiume*).
Bezmek, Batofina (*Spalato*).
Habit. General and common.
Season. Always; January, May to July, September.
Quality. 2.

* *Echeneis scutata.* (See No. 366.)

Group II. *Trachinina.*
Gen. II. TRACHINUS, *Art.*
132. *TRACHINUS DRACO*, L.
The Great Weever, Sting-Bull, Sea-Cat.
Die gemeine Queisen, das Petermännchen.
Trachine dragone (*It.*).
Vulg., Ragno (*Tr.*, *Fiume*, *Cat.*).
Ragno bianco, R. di mar (*Fiume*).
Varagno bianco, Varagnolo (*Ven.*).
Croat., Ranje, Ranje biele, Ranjen.
Pauk (*Spalato*).
Habit. General and common.
Season. Always; May, September, and October.
Quality. 2.

133. *TRACHINUS ARANEUS*, C. & V.
Die mittelländische Queisen.
Das mittelländische Petermännchen.
Trachino ragno (*It.*).
Vulg., Ragno, Ragno pagano (*Tr.*).
Ragno nero, R. di grotta (*Fiume*).
Varagno negro (*Ven.*).
Croat., Ranjen (*generic*).
Habit. General and not uncommon.
Season. Always; August.
Quality. 2; best of the genus.

134. *TRACHINUS RADIATUS*, C. & V.
Trachino raggiato (*It.*).
Vulg., Ragno, R. pagano (*Tr.*).
Varagno pagán (*Ven.*).
Croat., Pauk (*Spalato*).
Habit. General and common.
Season. Always; March to June, September.
Quality. 2.

135. *TRACHINUS VIPERA*, C. & V.
The common Weever.
The Viper Weever.
The lesser Weever.
Black-fin, Sting-fish, Adder-pike, Otter-pike.
Trachino vipera (*It.*).

Vulg., Ragno (*Tr.*).
Varagnola (*Ven.*).
Habit. Trieste.
Season. April, May, August; rare.
Quality. 2.

Fam. XIV. PEDICULATI—Anglers.
Gen. I. LOPHIUS, *Art.*
136. *LOPHIUS PISCATORIUS*, L.
The Angler, Common Angler, The Sea-devil, Toad-fish, Fishing-frog, Frog-fish.
Der gemeine Froschfisch.
Froschteufel, Seeteufel.
Lophie baudroie, Baudroie pécheresse.
Lofio piscatore (*It.*).
Vulg., Rospo, Pesce Rospo, Rospo di mar, Rospo di fango, Diavolo di mar (*Tr.*, *Ven.*, *Fiume*).
Croat., žaba, vražić, čača, hudobina, morski djavol, vrag morski, vukodlak (*Croat. littoral*).
Grdobina (*Spalato*).
Habit. General and common.
Season. Always; especially summer.
Quality. 3.

137. *LOPHIUS BUDEGASSA*, Spin.
Lofio martino (*It.*).
Note. Less common than the foregoing sp.; though sometimes very common at Fiume; smaller and preferable eating to the foregoing.

Fam. XV. COTTIDÆ.
Gen. I. COTTUS, *Art.*
138. *COTTUS GOBIO*, L.
The Miller's Thumb, The Bull Head, Tommy Logge.
Le chabot de rivière, chabot tétard, Séchot, La cotte chabot, Tête d'Aze, Le Chapsot.
Der Kaulkopf, Dickkopf, Die Mühlkoppe Rotz Kolbe, Groppe, Gruppe, Koppe, Der Kautzenkopf, Die Kaulquappe.

Scazzone, Ghiozzo (*It.*).
Vulg., Marson, Cavedon (*Trentino*).
Magnarone, Magnerone (*Verona*).
Marzion, Marsion, Marson (*Treviso*).
Chiavedon (*Gorizia*).
Sloven, Menkišek, Kápč (*Carniola*).
Croat., Balavac, Peš, Peša.
Habit. Fresh-water courses of northern and central Italy; Trentino, Adige, Izonso, Garda.
Quality. 2.

Gen. II. LEPIDOTRIGLA, *Gthr.*

139. *LEPIDOTRIGLA ASPERA*, C. & V.
Trigla aspera, *C. & V.*
Trigla cavillone, *Lac.*
Capone caviglione (*It.*).
Vulg., Anzoletto (*generic*) (*Tr.*).
Anzuletta (*generic*) (*Fiume*).
Turchello insanguinà (*Ven.*).
Croat., Ankulete, Anzuleta (*generic*) (*Croat. littoral*); čučina (*Spalato*).
Habit. General; not common.
Season. January, February, April to June, August, September.
Remark. One of the smallest sp. of the genus.
Quality. 3.

Gen. III. TRIGLA, *Art.*

140. *TRIGLA PINI*, Bl.
Triglia cuculus, *L.*
The Elleck, The Red, or Cuckoo-Gurnard.
Capone imperiale (*It.*).
Vulg., Anzoletto (*Tr.*).
Anzoleto, A. commune, A. piccolo (*Ven.*).
Croat., Ankulete, Anzuleta.
Habit. General; common.
Season. Always; March.
Quality. 3.

141. *TRIGLA LINEATA*, L.
T. lastoviza, *Brünn.*
T. adriatica, *L.*

The streaked Gurnard, French or rock Gurnard.
Rouget camard.
Der gestreifte See- oder Knurr-hahn.
Capone ubbriaco* (*It.*).
Vulg., Anzoletto, Angioletto, Ubriago, Musoduro (*Tr.*).
Anzoleto, Musoduro (*Ven.*).
Anzoletta, Testa grossa, Testa dura (*Fiume*).
Croat., Lastavica, Glavuje (?) Kokot.
Habit., Season, Quality. Same as foregoing sp.; very common.

142. *TRIGLA HIRUNDO*, Bl. & L.
Lucerna Venetorum, *Will.*
Trigla corax, *Bp.*
The Tubfish, The Sapphirine Gurnard.
Trigle hirondelle.
Der grosse See- oder Knurr-hahn.
Die Meerschwalbe.
Capone galinella (*It.*).
Vulg., Anzoletto, Lucerna † (*Tr., Ven., Fiume*).
Maziola (*Ven.*).
Laterna,† Fanale† (*Lig.*).
Croat., Lučenka, Lučerna, Prasica (*Croat. littoral*).
Habit. General and common.
Season. Always; best in January, May, August; the most common of the genus in Spalato waters.
Quality. 2; best of the genus.

143. *TRIGLA GURNARDUS*, L.
The Grey Gurnard.
Capone gorno (*It.*).
Vulg., Anzoletto (*Tr., Ven.*).
Croat., Lastavica.
Habit. General; rare; Trieste.
Quality. 3.

* Signifies "inebriated," owing to its reddish hue.
† Owes these names to the great phosphorescence it produces.

144. **TRIGLA CUCULUS**, Bl.
T. milvus, *Lac.*
Bloch's Gurnard.
Die Seeweihe.
Capone caviglia (*It.*).
Vulg., Anzoletto (*Tr., Ven.*).
Anzoletto grande (*Ven.*).
Croat., Lastavica.
Habit. General; not uncommon.
Season. Best in January, May, August.
Quality. 3.

145. **TRIGLA LYRA**, L.
The Piper, Lyra, Crowner, Sea-hen.
Die Meerleyer.
Capone organo (*It.*).
Vulg., Anzoletto (*Tr.*).
Turchello, Succhetto (*Ven.*).
Anzoletto grande (*Ven.*).
Turchello (*Fiume*).
Croat., Lučerna (*Croat. littoral*).
Kokot (*Spalato*).
Habit. Istria, Dalmatia; rather rare.
Season. April, March, October.
Quality. 3.

Fam. XVI. CATAPHRACTI—Flying Gurnards.
Gen. I. PERISTETHUS, *Kaup.*

146. **PERISTETHUS CATAPHRACTUM**, L.
Peristedion cataphractum, C. & V.
Trigla cataphracta, L.
The Mailed Gurnard.
Le Malarmat.
Der Gabelfisch.
Der gabelige, See- oder Knurr-hahn.
Peristedione forcuto (*It.*).
Vulg., Anzoletto, Angioletto del mare, o di mar, Forcato (*Tr.*).
Anzoleto della Madonna (*Ven.*).
Croat., Turčin (*Spalato*).

Habit. General; Dalmatia, Cherso; inhabits great depths; rare in the north.
Season. Common at Spalato in winter.
Quality. o.

Gen. II. DACTYLOPTERUS, *Lac.*
147. **DACTYLOPTERUS VOLITANS**. C. & V.
Trigla volitans, L.
Der Flughahn.
Pesce rondine (*It.*).
Vulg., Pesce barbastrillo, o barbastella, Rondinela (*Ven.*).
Rondinella (*Fiume*).
Croat., Lastavica, Leteći kokot (*Croat. littoral*).
Poletuša, Lastavica prava (*Spalato*).
Habit. General, but rare; Dalmatia, Lissa, Trieste.
Season. April to July, September.
Quality. o.

Fam. XVII. GOBIIDÆ.
Gen. I. GOBIUS, *Art.**
148. **GOBIUS NIGER**, L.
The Black Goby, Rock-fish, Rock Goby.
Gobie boulerot.
Die schwarze Meergrundel.
Ghiozzo nero (*It.*).
Vulg., Guatto (*generic term*).
Guatto giallo (*Tr., Fiume*).
Paganello di mar (*Ven.*).
Croat., Glavoč (*generic term*).
žuti gulj, glavoč od rupa (*Croat. littoral*).
Glamoč žuti (*Spalato*).
Habit. General and common.
Season. Always.
Quality. 3; *Minutaja* (mixed fish).

149. **GOBIUS AURATUS**, Risso.
The Yellow Goby, *Couch.*

* *Gobius Lesueuri, G. Buchichii, G. Zebra, G. pusillus.* (See Nos. 367—370.)

Ghiozzo dorato (*It.*).
Vulg., Guatto (*Tr.*, *Fiume*).
Marsion (*Ven.*).
Croat., Glamoč žutac (*Spalato*).
Habit. General, but rare; Dalmatia, Lésina, Spalato, Trieste.

150. **GOBIUS JOZO**, L.
Die blaue Meergrundel, Blaugrundel, Seestint.
Ghiozzo comune (*It.*).
Vulg., Guatto, Guatto di fango (*Tr.*, *Fiume*).
Paganello di mar, Paganello bianco, Gô, Menuaja mora (*Ven.*).
Croat., Gulj od blata, Cèrnjak, Glavoč cèrni (*Croat. littoral*).
Batovina, Glamoč bilac, Glamoč lučni (*Spalato*).
Habit. General and common.
Season. Always.
Quality. 3; *Minutaja* (mixed fish).

151. **GOBIUS MARTENSII**, Gthr.
Gobius Bonelli, *Nardo.*
Gobius Fluviatilis, *C. & V.*
The Fresh-water Goby.
Ghiozzo comune (*It.*).
Vulg., Marsion d'aqua dolce (*Ven.*).
Bottola (*Trentino*, *Verona*).
Lardel, Lardello, Goffo (*Treviso*).
Habit. Tagliamento, Isonzo, Adige, Treviso, Garda; common.
Season. February, March, September, October.
Quality. 2.

152. **GOBIUS PANIZZÆ**, Verga.
Ghiozzo del Panizza (*It.*).
Vulg., Marsion (*Ven.*).
Marsionsini (*Treviso*).
Habit. Brackish waters and lagoons; Venice, Comacchio; watercourses of Venice; common.
Season. April.
Quality. 2.

153. **GOBIUS PUNCTATISSIMUS**, Canestr.
Ghiozzo punteggiata (*It.*).
Habit. Same as foregoing; Tagliamento, Sile.
Season. February, April, May.
Quality. 2.

154. **GOBIUS QUAGGA**, Heck.
Habit. Spalato.
Season. June; very rare.

155. **GOBIUS KNERII**, Steind.
Habit. Zaole (Trieste), Lésina (Dalmatia).
Note. An Adriatic species.
Season. May; rare.

156. **GOBIUS PAGANELLUS**, L.
Paganellus Venetorum, *Will.*
The Paganellus.
Die Paganell-Grundel.
Ghiozzo paganello (*It.*).
Vulg., Guatto, G. di sasso (*Tr.*, *Fiume*).
Paganello (*Ven.*, *Tr.*, *Fiume*).
Paganello de porto, Paganello vergà (*Ven.*).
Croat., Gulić, Kamenski gulj (*Croat. littoral*).
Plahut* (*Fiume*).
Glamoč, Pornpujak (*Spalato*).
Habit. General; common.
Season. Always.
Quality. 2; *Minutaja* (mixed fish).

157. **GOBIUS OPHIOCEPHALUS**, Pall.
Gobius lota, *C. & V.*
Die marmorirte Meergrundel.
Ghiozzo gò (*It.*).
Vulg., Guatto (*Tr.*, *Fiume*).
Gò (*Ven.*). Guatto giallo (*Spalato*).
Croat., Gulj (*Croat. littoral*).
Glamoč purićaš (*Spalato*).
Habit. General; common.
Season. Always.
Quality. 2; *Minutaja* (mixed fish).

---

* Denotes timidity.

158. *GOBIUS CRUENTATUS*, Gm.
Die blutrothe Meergrundel.
Ghiozzo insanguinato (*It.*).
Vulg., Guatto di mar (*Tr.*, *Fiume*).
Paganello di mar (*Tr.*).
Paganello insanguinà (*Ven.*).
Croat., Morski gulj, Glavoč (*Croat. littoral*).
Glamoč žudij (*Spalato*).
Habit. General, but rare; not uncommon at Spalato on zostera beds.
Season. April, May, August, September.
Quality. 2; *Minutaja* (mixed fish).¹

159. *GOBIUS GENIPORUS*, C. & V.
Ghiozzo geniporo (*It.*).
Vulg., Guatto (*Tr.*, *Fiume*).
Marsion (*Ven.*).
Habit. General, but rare; Dalmatia, Trieste.
Season. August.
Quality. 2; *Minutaja* (mixed fish).

160. *GOBIUS CAPITO*, C. & V.
Ghiozzo testone (*It.*).
Vulg., Guatto (*Tr.*, *Fiume*).
Gó di mar (*Ven.*).
Croat., Glavoč, Glamoč.
Glamoč pločar (*Spalato*).
Habit. General and common.
Season. Always.
Quality. 2; the largest and most common sp.; does not belong to the class of *Minutaja*.
Variety of the above sp. :—
Gobius guttatus, *C. & V.*
Habit. Lésina (Dalmatia).
Season. March, September; very rare.

161. *GOBIUS MINUTUS*, L.
Gobius quadrimaculatus, *C. & V.*
Gobius unipunctatus, *Parn.*
The Freckled or Spotted Goby, the One-spotted Goby (*Parn*), the Polewig, Pollybait.
Buhotte, Boulerau blanc.
Ghiozzo macchiato (*It.*).
Vulg., Guatto (*Tr.*, *Fiume*).
Marsion, Marsion di mar (*Ven.*).
Croat., Glamoč (*Spalato*).
Habit. General and common.
Season. Always.
Quality. 2; *Minutaja* (mixed fish).

162. *GOBIUS RUTHENSPARRI*, Euph.
The Doubly-spotted Goby.
Vulg., Scagioto (*Ven.*).
Habit. Trieste, Venice; very rare.

163. *GOBIUS QUADRIVITTATUS*, Steind.
Gobio fasciato (*It.*).
Habit. An Adriatic sp. found near Lésina, Dalmatia, in 1863; also at Zaole and the Canale delle Castella; very rare.

164. *GOBIUS MINUTUS*, Penn.
Pennant's Spotted Goby.
Ghiozzo minuto (*It.*).
Vulg., Guatto (*Tr.*, *Fiume*).
Marsion (*Ven.*).
Habit. General; rare.

165. *GOBIUS ELONGATUS*, Canestr.
Habit. Venice; accidental.
Season. April.

Gen. II. LATRUNCULUS, *Gthr.**

166. *LATRUNCULUS ALBUS*, Parn.
Gobius albus, *Parn.*
The White Goby.
Ghiozzo bianco (*It.*).
Habit. Ragusa; very rare.

Gen. III. CALLIONYMUS, *L.*†
167. *CALLIONYMUS LYRA*, L.
Callionymus dracunculus, *L.*

* *Latrunculus pellucidus.* (See No. 371.)
† *Callionymus fasciatus.* (See No. 372.)

The Dragonet, Fox, Skulpin, Sordid Dragonet, Gemmeous Dragonet, Yellow Skulpin.
Die Goldgrundel.
Fuchsgrundel.
Callionimo lira (*It.*).
Habit. Trieste.
Season. Quite exceptionally met with in summer, if not, indeed, altogether questionable.

168. *CALLIONYMUS MACULATUS*, Raf.
Callionimo macchiato (*It.*).
Vulg., Guatto (*Tr.*, *Fiume*).
Lodra, Lodrin (*Ven.*, *Tr.*).
Croat., Miš (*Spalato*).
Habit. Rare at Trieste and Venice; common at Spalato.
Season. March, July to September.
Quality. 3.

169. *CALLIONYMUS FESTIVUS*, Pall.
Callionymus dracunculus, *Risso*.
Callionimo dragoncello (*It.*).
Vulg., as foregoing sp.
Habit. General, but rare; Venice.

170. *CALLIONYMUS BELENUS*, Risso.
Die Belen.
Callionimo belenno (*It.*).
Vulg. as foregoing sp.; also Schilin (*Ven.*).
Croat., Miš, Žabarić (*Spalato*).
Habit. Venice, Trieste, Spalato, Ravenna; pretty general and common.
Quality. 3; *Minutaja* (mixed fish).

171. *CALLIONYMUS MORISSONII*, Risso.
Habit. Trieste, Venice; very rare.
Season. Summer.
Remark. Identity questionable; Perugia cites this as a distinct sp.; Canestrini considers it to be identical with C. Belenus (*Risso*); whereas Bonap. and Günther consider it identical with C. festivus (*Bp.* not *Pall.*), synonymous with C. phaëton (*Gthr.*)

Fam. XVIII. CEPOLIDÆ—Band-fishes.
Gen. CEPOLA, *L.*
172. *CEPOLA RUBESCENS*, L.
The Band-fish, Red Band-fish, Red Snake fish.
Der gemeine Bandfisch, Rother Bandfisch.
Cepola rosseggiante (*It.*).
Vulg., Pesce cordéla (*Tr.*, *Fiume*).
Pesce spada, Spada rossa (*Tr.*).
Spada da Quarnero, Lanspada (*Ven.*).
Croat., Ugoraća (*Croat. littoral*), Mačinac (*Spalato*).
Habit. General.
Season. Common at all seasons.
Quality. 3.

Fam. XIX. BLENNIIDÆ—Blennies.
Gen. I. BLENNIUS, *Art.**
173. *BLENNIUS GATTORUGINE*, Bl.
The Gattoruginous Blenny.
Der gestreifte Schleimfisch.
Bavosa gattorugine (*It.*).
Vulg., Strega, Gattorusola (*Tr.*), Gattarozola (*Ven.*), Baba (*Fiume*) (*generic terms*).
Croat., Kokot, Baba (*Croat. littoral*) (*generic terms*).
Barbir, Babak (*Spalato*).
Habit. General and common; enters brackish waters; lagoons of Venice.
Season. Always.
Quality. 3.

174. *BLENNIUS TENTACULARIS*, Brünn.
Der Meerhirsch.

* *Blennius Cauevæ* and *B. trigloides*. (*See* Nos. 373, 374.)

Bavosa cornuta (*It.*).
Croat., Babica, Barbaroga (*Spalato*).
The same remarks apply to this as to the foregoing sp.; belongs to the class of *Minutaja*.

175. *BLENNIUS ROUXI*, Cocco.
Vulg., Bausa janca (*Sicily*).
Croat., Kraljica (*Spalato*).
Habit. Not uncommon at Spalato in the spring; not found in the north.

176. *BLENNIUS VULGARIS*, Pollini.
The Fresh-water Blenny.
Cagnetto comune (*It.*).
Vulg., Cagnetto, Cabazza (*Lomb.*).
Croat., Babuka (*Spalato*).
Habit. Izonso, Adige (?), Lake of Vrana (Dalmatia, not Cherso), River Giadro, near Salona, Lake Bačina (Dalmatia); is also found in the sea.
Quality. 1.

177. *BLENNIUS VARUS*, Bp.
Cagnetto varo (*It.*).
Habit. Fresh-water courses of Venice.
Remark. Canestrini holds this to be a variety of the foregoing sp.

178. *BLENNIUS PALMICORNIS*, C. & V.
Blennius sanguinolentus, *Pall.*
Bavosa palmicorne (*It.*).
Croat., Balavica (*Spalato*).
The remarks on *B. tentacularis* apply to this sp.
Habit. General and common; Spalato, Lésina, Rimini.

179. *BLENNIUS BASILISCUS*, C. & V.
Habit. Very rarely met with in the Adriatic.

180. *BLENNIUS SPHYNX*, C. & V.
Habit. Lésina (Dalmatia), Trieste, Zaole; rare.

181. *BLENNIUS PAVO*, Risso.
Bavosa cristata (*It.*).
Vulg., Gallo, Gattarozola marina (*female*).
Gattarozola colla cresta (*Ven.*).

Croat., Pivac, Baba krunašica (*Spalato*).
The remarks on *B. tentacularis* apply equally to this species.

182. *BLENNIUS OCELLARIS*, L.
Ocellated Blenny, Butterfly-fish.
Papillon de mer, Blennie Lièvre.
Der geäugelte Schleimfisch.
Schmetterlingfisch.
Bavosa occhiuta (*It.*).
Vulg., Strega, Gattorusola d'aspreo, G. di mar, Lampusa (*Tr.*).
Gattorozola dall'occhiâl, Pesce occhial, Gattina piccola (*Ven.*).
Smida (*Fiume*).
Croat., Baba, Kokot.
Babica od dubine (*Spalato*).
The same remarks apply to this sp. as to *B. gattorugine*.

183. *BLENNIUS GALERITA*, L.
Montagu's Blenny, Diminutive Blenny.
Habit. Dalmatia (Lésina, Lissa, Curzola); but very rare.

184. *BLENNIUS PHOLIS*, L.
Phocis lævis, *Flem.*
The Smooth Blenny, the Shanny, Shan, Smooth Shan.
Die Meerlerche.
Der kleinste Schleimfisch.
Vulg., Gattorusola senza cresta (*Tr.*, *Ven.*).
Lampusa (*Tr.*).
Gattarozola bavosa, o chiossa (*Ven.*).
Remark. Canestrini and other authors are not satisfied as to the identity of this species, although it is cited by Perugia, Martens, and others. In any case, it seems doubtful whether it is the *Shanny* of British waters, or a southern representative variety of this fish.*

---

* See "Martens' Reise nach Venedig," ii. p. 419; and "Catalogo dei Pesci dell' Adriatico," by Alberto Perugia, p. 16, No. 190.

Gen. II. CRISTICEPS, *C. & V.*
185. *CRISTICEPS ARGENTATUS,* Risso.
Blennius variabilis, *Raf.*
Clinus variabilis, *Canestr.*
Der silberne Schleimfisch.
Clino variabile (*It.*).
Vulg., Spirolottu, Sperdetto, Spirda (*Sicily*).
Habit. Dalmatia, Trieste; southern extension.
Season. Summer; very rare.

Gen. III. TRIPTERYGIUM, *Risso.*
186. *TRIPTERYGIUM NASUS,* Risso.
Tritterigio caponero (*It.*).
Croat., Pivčić (*Spalato*).
Habit. General; Spalato, Lésina (Dalmatia), Trieste, &c.
Season. Common in summer.
Quality. 3; *Minutaja* (mixed fish).

Fam. XX. SPHYRÆNIDÆ.
Gen. I. SPHYRÆNA, *Art.*
187. *SPHYRÆNA VULGARIS,* C. & V.
Esox Sphyræna, *L.*
Sphyræna spet, *Lac.*
The Spet.
Der Pfeilhecht.
Sfirena comune (*It.*).
Vulg., Luzzo di mar (*Tr., Ven.*).
Merluzzo salvatico (*Tr.*).
Pesce schermo (*Fiume*).
Croat., Jaglunić, Skaram (*littoral*).
Skaran (*Spalato*).
Habit. General and common.
Season. Summer.
Quality. 3.

Fam. XXI. ATHERINIDÆ—Atherines or Sand-smelts.
Gen. ATHERINA, *Art.*
188. *ATHERINA HEPSETUS,* L.
The Smelt, Atherine, Sand-Smelt.
Le Sanclet Cabassons de Provence.

Der gemeine Achrenfisch.
Latterino sardaro (*It.*).
Vulg., Anguèla, Gerao, Jaral, Garal (*Tr.*).
Anguèla, Anguèla agonada, Agonà, Acquadela (*Ven.*).
Croat., Gavon, Gavun (*Croat. littoral* and *Dalm.*).
Girica (*generic*).
Gaun pravi (*Spalato*).
Habit. General and common, particularly in summer; frequents brackish waters and the lagoons; it is the most common of the genus.
Quality. 3.

189. *ATHERINA BOYERI,* Risso.
Boier's Atherine, *Couch.*
Latterino capoccione (*It.*).
Vulg., Anguèla (*Tr., Ven.*).
Croat., čiga (*Croat. littoral*).
Gaun batelj (*Spalato*).
Habit., Season, Quality. As above.

190. *ATHERINA MOCHON,* C. & V.
Der kleine Achrenfisch.
Latterino comune (*It.*).
Vulg., as above.
Croat., Gaun hrskavac (*Spalato*).
Habit., Season, Quality. As above.

Fam. XXII. MUGILIDÆ—Mullets.
Gen. MUGIL, *Art.**
191. *MUGIL CEPHALUS,* Cuv.
The Grey Mullet.
Le Mulet-Cabot.
Die gemeine Meerüsche.
Der Harder.
Muggine cefalo (*It.*).
Vulg., Volpina, Cievolo (*young*) (*Tr., Fiume*).
Mecchiarini, Mecchiati, Volpina, Cievolo Ceolo, Magna, Magnariazo, Orbeti, Topi, Volpinetti (*Ven.*).

* *Mugil labeo.* (See No. 375.)

Croat., Mulj, Muljal (*Croat. littoral*).
Babaš, Ciepa, čipal glavotni (*Spalato*).
Habit. General and common; frequents brackish waters.
Season. All seasons; particularly in winter; the most prevalent sp. of the genus.
Quality. 2.

192. *MUGIL CAPITO*, Cuv.
Le Meuille blanc.
Muggine calamita (*It.*).
Vulg., Caostello (*Tr.*, *Ven.*, *Fiume*).
Cavostello (*Tr.*).
Caustello, Botolo, Batauro (*Ven.*).
Mazinette (*Fiume*).
Croat., Stirjaš (*Croat. littoral*).
Balavac (*Spalato*).
Habit., *Season*, *Quality.* As above; common.

193. *MUGIL AURATUS*, Risso.
Long-finned Grey Mullet, Golden Mullet.
Muggine orifrangio (*It.*).
Vulg., Lotregan, Dotregan (*Tr.*, *Ven.*).
Croat., Zlatoperac (*Spalato*).
Habit., *Season*, *Quality.* As above.

194. *MUGIL SALIENS*, Risso.
Muggine musino (*It.*).
Vulg., Verzelata (*Tr.*, *Ven.*).
Croat., Mržnjak. Bavuš (*Spalato*).
Habit., *Season*, *Quality.* As above.

195. *MUGIL CHELO*, Cuv.
The thick-lipped Grey Mullet, lesser Grey Mullet.
Le Mulet chaluc.
Muggine chelone (*It.*).
Vulg., Bosega, Boseghe, *plural* (*Tr.*, *Ven.*).
Croat., Putnik (*Spalato*).
Habit. As above; ascends the rivers, and can live in the lakes, but spawns in the sea.
Season, *Quality.* As above.

Fam. XXIII. GASTEROSTEIDÆ—Sticklebacks.
Gen. GASTEROSTEUS, *Art.*

196. *GASTEROSTEUS ACULEATUS*, L..
The Stickleback, Prickleback.
L'Epinoche.
Der gemeine Stichling, Stachelbarsch, Stachelfisch, Schärfling, Stachbüttel.
Spinarello (*It.*).
Vulg., Spin, Spinarola, Spinarella (*Ven.*).
Spinariola (*Treviso*).
Pesce Spin, Roncone (*Lombardy*).
Croat., Gèrgeč, Koljuška, Zet.
Habit. Tagliamento, Adige, Garda, Monfalcone, Venice; brackish waters.
Season. February, May, June.
Quality. o.

197. *GASTEROSTEUS BRACHYCENTRUS*, C. & V.
The Three-spined Stickleback.
Spinarola (*It.*).
Vulg., Spinariola (*Treviso*).
Habit. Has a southern extension; Gorizia, Treviso, Lake of Garda, Venice, Istria; brackish waters.
Season. October.
Quality. o.

Fam. XXIV. CENTRISCIDÆ.
Gen. CENTRISCUS, *L.*

198. *CENTRISCUS SCOLOPAX*, L.
The Trumpet-fish, Sea-snipe, Bellows-fish, Snipe-nosed Trumpet-fish, Woodcock fish, Snipe-fish.
Centrisque becasse.
Der Schnepfenfisch.
Pesce trombetta (*It.*).
Vulg., Galinazza, Pesce trombetta (*Tr.*, *Ven.*, *Fiume*).
Croat., Morska šljuka.

Habit. General; rare; sp. from Dalmatia, Venice, Fiume.
Season. Spring and summer.
Quality. o.

Fam. XXV. GOBIESOCIDÆ—Suck-fishes.
 Gen. I. LEPADOGASTER, *Gouan.*
199. *LEPADOGASTER GOUANII*, Lac.
 The Small Suck-fish, Cornish Sucker, Ocellated Sucker, Jura Sucker.
 Le Barbier, Porte-Ecuelle.
 Der Bauchschild.
 Lepadogastro del Gouan (*It.*).
 Vulg., Taccasasso (*Tr.*).
 Pesce ranin (*Ven.*).
 Sporcello di sasso, Porchetti (*generic term*) (*Fiume*).
 Croat., Riba prasica, Pizdin-prilipak (*generic terms*) (*Croat. littoral*).
 Prilipak, Svićica, Babka (*Spalato*).
Habit. General; not uncommon; Venice, Lissa, Spalato, Zaole, Trieste, Fiume.
Season. March to June, September.
Quality. 3; *Minutaja* (mixed fish).

200. *LEPADOGASTER LISTELLUS*, Nardo.
 Vulg., Listello, Sfrizin (*Ven.*).
Habit. Venice; *Minutaja* (mixed fish).

201. *LEPADOGASTER BROWNII*, Risso.
Habit. A few sp. caught off Lésina (Dalmatia).

202. *LEPADOGASTER ACUTUS*, Canestr.
 Lepadogaster elegans, *Nardo.*
 Der rothe Bauchschild.
 Lepadogastro acuto (*It.*).
 Vulg., Porchetti (*Ven.*, *Fiume*).
 Pesce ranin (*Ven.*).
 Taccasasso (*Tr.*, *Fiume*).
 Croat. As No. 199.
Habit. Rare; sp. from Trieste.

203. *LEPADOGASTER CANDOLLII*, Risso.
 Mirbelia Decandollii, *Canestr.*
 The Connemara Sucker.
 Vulg., *Croat.* As No. 199.
Habit. General; common; sp. from Venice, Trieste, Spalato.
Season. Winter; in summer it retreats to deep waters.

204. *LEPADOGASTER BIMACULATUS*, Flem.
 Lepadogaster Desfontainii, *Risso.*
 Mirbelia Desfontainii, *Canestr.*
 The Bimaculated Sucker, Doubly-spotted Sucker.
Nomenclature. As above.
Habit. Common and general.
Season. June, September.
Quality. 3; *Minutaja.*

 Gen II. LEPTOPTERYGIUS, *Trosch.*
205. *LEPTOPTERYGIUS PIGER*, Nardo.
 Gouania piger, *Bp.*
 Gouania prototypus, *Nardo.*
 Gouania tipo (*It.*).
Habit. A southern sp. occasionally found in the Adriatic; specimens from Lésina (Dalmatia), Trieste, Venice; is not uncommon at the northern head of the island of Bua (Dalmatia).

Fam. XXVI. LOPHOTIDÆ.
 Gen. LOPHOTES, *Giorna.*
206. *LOPHOTES CEPEDIANUS*, Giorna.
 Lophote Cepediano (*It.*).
Habit. Very rare—in fact, accidental; has been met with at Lésina on the Dalmatian coast.

Fam. XXVII. TRACHYPTERIDÆ—Ribbon-fishes.
 Gen. TRACHYPTERUS, *Gouan.*
207. *TRACHYPTERUS TÆNIA*, Bl. & Sch.
 Falx Venetorum, *Bellon.*

Ribbon-fish.
Der gemeine Sensenfisch, der weisse Bandfisch.
Trachittero tenia (*It.*).
Vulg., Falce, Pesce Falce (*Ven.*, *Tr.*).
Spada argentina (*Tr.*).
Spada d'arzento (*Ven.*).
Croat., Mač (*Croat. littoral*).
Riba vlasuja (*Spalato*).
Habit. General, though rare; Trieste, Venice, Dalmatia.

Season. Summer.
Quality. Flesh said to be excellent, and is much consumed at Naples, where it is much esteemed.

208. *TRACHYPTERUS REPANDUS*, Costa.
Trachittero ritorto (*It.*).
Habit. Has been fished in the Gulf of Trieste, and in the Dalmatian Archipelago off Lissa and Lésina, but is very rare.

Order—ACANTHOPTERYGII PHARYNGOGNATHI.

Fam. I. POMACENTRIDÆ—Coral-fishes.

Gen. HELIASTES, *C. & V.*
209. *HELIASTES CHROMIS*, L.
Der Rabenfisch.
Castagnola (*It.*).
Vulg., Fabbro, Pesce fabbro (*Tr.*, *Fiume*).
Caligher, Fabretto, Favaretto (*Tr.*).
Pesce scarpolero, pesce pestafero (*Ven.*).
Croat., Crnjelj, Crnej.
Habit. General and common at all seasons.
Quality. 3; little eaten.

Fam. II. LABRIDÆ—Wrasses.
Gen. I. LABRUS, *Art.*
210. *LABRUS TURDUS*, L.
Der grüne Lippfisch.
Labro tordo (*It.*).
Vulg., Liba (*generic term*) (*Tr.*).
Donzela (*generic*) Papagà (*Ven.*).
Papagallo verde (*Ven.*, *Fiume*).
Verdon (*Fiume*).
Croat., Usnače, Vrana (*generic terms*), Lenica, Zeleni papagal (*Fiume*). Orfanić, Vrana zelena (*Spalato*).
Habit. General, but rare.
Season. Spring and autumn.
Quality. 3; *Minutaja* (mixed fish).

211. *LABRUS MACULATUS*, Bl.
Labrus bergylta, *Ascan.*
The Ballan Wrasse, Ancient Wrasse, Old Wife.
La Vieille.
Das alte Weib.
Vulg., Liba, Pinco (*Tr.*).
Habit. Trieste; one of the rarest sp. of this genus; identity questionable.

212. *LABRUS FESTIVUS*, Risso.
Labro festivo (*It.*).
Vulg., Liba (*Tr.*).
Donzela, Papagà (*Ven.*).
Croat., Drozak, čvrljak (*Spalato*).
Habit. General, but rare; common at Spalato.
Season. Common in autumn.
Quality. 3.

213. *LABRUS MERULA*, L.
Der braune Lippfisch.
Dunkler Lippfisch.
Die Meerschleihe.
Labro merlo (*It.*).
Vulg., Liba (*Tr.*).
Donzela, Papagà (*Ven.*).
Tenca di mar (*Tr.*, *Ven.*).

Croat., Luceta morska, Vrana (*Spalato*).
Habit. General and common at all seasons.
Quality. 3.

214. *LABRUS RETICULATUS*, Lowe.
Labrus nereus, *Risso.*
Vulg., Liba (*Tr.*).
Habit. General, but rare.

215. *LABRUS MIXTUS*, L.
The striped Wrasse, Red Wrasse, Cuckoo Wrasse, the Cook Wrasse.
Labre melé.
Der gefleckte Lippfisch.
Meerjunker.
Labro pavone (*It.*).
Vulg., Liba, Donzella di grotta, Donzella di sasso (*Tr.*, *Fiume*).
Donzella, Papagá, Donzella de Quarnero, Cragnisso (*Ven.*).
Croat., Figa (*Spalato*).
Habit. General at all seasons, but rare; not uncommon at Spalato.
Quality. 3.

Female of the above sp.
Labrus carneus, *Ascan.*
The Red Wrasse, trimaculated or three-spotted Wrasse, Flesh-coloured Wrasse.
Der fleischrothe Lippfisch, Vierfleck.
Habit. General and common at all seasons.

Variety of female.
Labrus bimaculatus, *L.*
The Bimaculated Wrasse.
Der zweigefleckte Lippfisch.
Note. A rare species.

Gen. II. CRENILABRUS, *Cuv.*

216. *CRENILABRUS PAVO*, C. & V.
Paon de mer.
Der buntfärbige Lippfisch.
Der Meerpfau.
Crenilabro pavone (*It.*).
Vulg., Liba, Donzella (*Tr.*).
Donzella, Papagà, Pesce spuzza (*Ven.*), Lepa (*Chioggia*), Verdon (*Fiume*).
Croat., Lenica (*Fiume*).
Lumbrak (*Spalato*).
Boculjava gušavica (*Spalato*).
Jebac (*masc.*), Solnjača (*fem.*), Smokva (*generic*).
Habit. General and common at all seasons.
Quality. 3.

217. *CRENILABRUS MEDITERRANEUS*, C. & V.
C. boryanus, *Risso.*
Der borische Lippfisch.
Crenilabro mediterraneo (*It.*).
Vulg., Liba, Leppa, Donzella (*Tr.*).
Donzella, Papagà, Smergo, Gardelin, Pesce cavalier (*Ven.*).
Croat., Knez. Podujka (*Spalato*).
Habit. General and not uncommon at Spalato.
Season. Winter and spring.
Quality. 3.

218. *CRENILABRUS MELANOCERCUS*, Risso.
Croat., Modri Irnac (*Spalato*).
Habit. A rare sp.; specimens from Trieste and the islands of Lésina, Solta, Bua, and the Canale delle Castella (Dalmatia).

219. *CRENILABRUS CÆRULEUS*, Nardo (Risso?).
Habit. Trieste, Lésina, Spalato; a rare sp., represented in the Trieste Museum.

220. *CRENILABRUS MELOPS*, Cuv.
The Corkwing, Connor or Golden Maid, Golden Wrasse, Gilt-head, Goldsinny, Goldfinny.
Der blaue Lippfisch.
Croat., Smokvica, Spirka (*Spalato*).

Habit. Venice, Dalmatia; very rare; a specimen from Dalmatia is in the British Museum. (*See* Günther's Catalogue of Fishes in the British Museum, Vol. IV. p. 82.)
Season. April, May, September.

221. *CRENILABRUS ROISSALI*, Risso.
C. quinquemaculatus, *Bl.*
Der fünfgefleckte Lippfisch.
Crenilabro macchiato (*It.*).
Vulg. As No. 212.
Croat., Kraška.
Kosirica (*Spalato*).
Habit. Dalmatia, Trieste, Venice; pretty common.
Quality. No. 3.

222. *CRENILABRUS GRISEUS*, L.
C. massa, *Risso.*
Der grüne Lippfisch.
Crenilabro grigio (*It.*).
Croat., Inac (*Spalato*).
Vulg. As above.
Habit. Venice, Dalmatia; pretty common.
Season. March to June.
Quality. Miuutaja (mixed fish).

223. *CRENILABRUS OCELLATUS*, Forsk.
C. littoralis, *Risso.*
Crenilabro occhiato (*It.*).
Vulg. As above.
Croat., Hinjuša.
Pavlinka (*Spalato*).
Habit. General and common.
Season. Summer.
Quality. 3.

224. *CRENILABRUS ROSTRATUS*, Bl.
Coricus rostratus, *C. & V.*
Crenilabro rostrato (*It.*).
Vulg. As above.
Luzziolo (*Ven.*).
Croat., Dugonosica.

Habit. General and common; amongst the rocks in shallow water.
Season. Summer.
Quality. 3.

225. *CRENILABRUS TINCA*, Brünn.
Crenilabro tenca (*It.*).
Vulg. As No. 212.
Croat., Inac (*Spalato*).
Habit. General, but rare; Lésina (Dalmatia); not uncommon at Spalato.

Gen. III. ACANTHOLABRUS, *C. & V.*

226. *ACANTHOLABRUS PALLONII*, Risso.
Acantolabro roseo (*It.*).
Vulg., Pesce spuzza, Pesce nello (*Ven.*).
Croat., Mačin (*Spalato*).
Habit. A rare sp. found amongst the rocks in shallow water; specimens from Venice, Trieste, Spalato; not uncommon in spring off the island of Solta in Dalmatia.

Gen. IV. NOVACULA (XYRICHTHYS), *C. & V.*

227. *NOVACULA CULTRATA*, C. & V.
Pecten romæ, *Aldrov.*
Pesce pettine (*It.*).
Habit. One of the rarest sp.; southern extension; Dalmatia.

Gen. V. JULIS, *C. & V.*

228. *JULIS PAVO*, C. & V.
Julis turcica, *Risso.*
Donzella turca (*It.*).
Vulg., Pesce leone (*Sicily*).
Note. A very rare sp.; southern extension.

Gen. VI. CORIS, *Gthr.*

229. *CORIS JULIS*, L.
Julis vulgaris, *Flem.*
Julis mediterranea, *Risso.*
The Rainbow Wrasse.

Indented-striped Wrasse.
La Girelle.
Der Regenbogenfisch.
Meerjunker.
Donzella zigurella (*It.*).
Vulg., Donzella, Girella (*Tr.*, *Ven.*), Papagà (*Ven.*).
Croat., Knez, Dugnjača, Vladikinja (*Spalato*).
Habit. General and common; amongst the rocks covered with *algæ*.
Season. Summer.
Quality. 3.

Variety. Julis speciosus, *Risso*.
Note. Has been met with in Dalmatia.

230. *CORIS GIOFREDI,* Risso.
Julis Giofredi, *Risso*.
Der Meerjunker.
Donzella del Giofredi (*It.*).
Vulg., Donzella, Girella (*Tr.*, *Ven.*).
Croat. As No. 229.
Habit. Pretty general, but rare; specimens from Fiume, Trieste, Venice, Lésina.
Season. Summer.
Quality. 3; probably the same as the foregoing.

Order—ANACANTHINI.

Fam. I. GADIDÆ—Cod Tribe.

Gen. I. GADUS, *Art.**

231. *GADUS EUXINUS,* Nordm.
Der südliche Schellfisch.
Gado pontico (*It.*).
Vulg., Molo, Molo da parangolo.
Croat. Ugotica dugonosica (*Spalato*).
Habit. A sp. of the Black Sea, occasionally found in the Adriatic: Venice, Fiume, Zara; it has never been caught in the Mediterranean. Professor Kolombatović says that in summer, at Spalato, it is more common than No. 233. A specimen from Dalmatia is in the British Museum.

232. *GADUS MERLANGUS,* L.
Merlangus vulgaris, *Cuv.*
Merlangus vernalis, *Risso.*
The Whiting, Le Merlan, Der Merlan.
Merlango comune (*It.*).
Vulg., Molo, Molo da parangolo (*Tr.*, *Ven.*, *Fiume*), Falso molo, Molloso (*Ven.*).
Croat., Pišmolj od parangala.

Habit. Common in the northern waters; Trieste, Fiume.
Season. August to September.
Quality. 2.

233. *GADUS MINUTUS,* L.
The Poor, Capelan, Power Cod.
Der Zwergdorsch.
Gado minuto (*It.*).
Vulg., Pesce mollo (*Tr.*, *Fiume*, *Cattaro*).
Mormoro, Molmolo (*Tr.*).
Molo, Mormora (*Ven.*).
Croat., Pišmoj, Pišmolj (*generic*), Busbana (*Croat. littoral*).
Tovarčić, Ugotica (*Spalato*).
Habit. Common in the north; Trieste, Fiume, Zara and Spalato.
Season. September to April.
Quality. 2.

234. *GADUS LUSCUS,* L.
The Bib, Pout, Whiting-Pout.
Le Tacaud.
Der Steinbolk.
Gado barbato (*It.*).

---

* *Gadus poutassou.* (See No. 376.)

Habit. Trieste (Giglioli).
Note. Quite accidental. Two specimens in the Florence Museum of Vertebrates.

Gen. II. MERLUCCIUS, *Cuv.*
235. *MERLUCCIUS VULGARIS*, Flem.
The Hake, Common Hake.
Le Grand Merlus.
Der mittelländische Stockfisch.
Merluzzo comune (*It.*).
Vulg., Merluzzo (*Tr., Ven., Fiume, Cattaro*).
Asinello (*Tr., Fiume*).
Lovo (*Tr., Ven.*).
Branzin croato (*Fiume*).
Pesce prete (*Ven.*).
Croat., Oslić, Osal, Tovar morski (*Croat. littoral*). Tovar, Konj morski (*Spalato*).
Habit. General and common at all seasons.
Season. Best in winter.
Quality. 2.

Gen. III. PHYCIS, *Cuv.*
236. *PHYCIS BLENNIOIDES*, Brünn.
Phycis tinca *Bl., Schn.*
The Forked Hake, Greater Forked Beard.
Le Merlu barbu, Barbu.
Fico argentino (*It.*).
Vulg., Figo (*Ven.*).
Sorzo, Sorzo salvatico (*Tr.*).
Habit. Venice, Trieste, Fiume; according to Ninni, it is not so very scarce at Venice.
Season. July, August.

237. *PHYCIS MEDITERRANEUS*, Delar.
Die südliche Meerschleihe.
Fico mediterranco (*It.*).
Vulg., Sorzo, Tenca (*Tr., Fiume*), Figo (*Ven.*).
Croat., Tabinja (*Croat. littoral, Spalato*).
Habit. Fiume, Zara, Trieste, Spalato, Lésina, Venice ; rather rare, if not accidental, in the north ; deep water ; abounds off Lésina.
Season. July, August, September.

Gen. IV. LOTA, *Cuv.**
238. *LOTA VULGARIS*, Cuv.
The Burbot, Burbolt, Eel-pout.
La Lotte.
Die Aalrutte, Aalraupe, Aalquappe.
Bottatrice (*It.*).
Vulg., Bottrisa (*Lombardy*).
Sloven, Menĕk.
Hung., Menyhal.
Habit. In running courses, lakes, and ponds, in depths of thirty to forty fathoms in Lombardy, Lake of Garda, Lake of Zirknitz (Carniola), etc.
Quality. 1.

Gen. V. MOTELLA, *Cuv.*
239. *MOTELLA TRICIRRATA*, Bl.
M. communis, *Costa.*
M. vulgaris, *Cuv.*
M. fusca, *Risso & Swainson.*
Galea Venetorum, *Bellon.*
The Three-bearded Rockling, Rockling, Three-bearded Cod or Gade, Whistler, Whistle-fish.
Gade Mustelle.
Die Meertrüsche.
Motella conunc (*It.*).
Vulg., Sorze, Sorcio (*Tr.*).
Sorze, Pesce Sorze, Mare dei gronghi (*Ven.*).
Madre dei gronghi (*Fiume*).
Croat., Grunjeva mati, Tabinja (*Croat. littoral*).
Miš morski, Mater od ugorâ (*Spalato*).
Habit. More or less general, and pretty common at all seasons ; Trieste, Venice, Rimini, Fiume, Spalato.
Season. Summer.
Quality. 2.

---

* *Lota argentea*, Bp. (*See* No. 377.)

240. *MOTELLA MACULATA*, Risso & Sw.
Note. A mere variety of the above sp., to which the foregoing remarks equally apply; a specimen from Dalmatia in the British Museum.

241. *MOTELLA MUSTELA*, Nilss.
Gadus mustela, *L.*
The Five-bearded Rockling or Cod.
Note. Appears in Perugia's list of the Trieste Museum, though not represented there; mentioned by Nardo as having been observed on the Dalmatian coast. Identity questionable; almost identical with the two former sp.

Fam. II. OPHIDIIDÆ.
Gen. I. PTERIDIUM, *Scopoli.*
242. *PTERIDIUM ATRUM*, Risso.
Pteridio nero (*It.*).
Habit. Almissa, Zirona, Lésina (Dalmatia); very rare; inhabits great depths.

Gen. II. OPHIDIUM, *Art.*
243. *OPHIDIUM BARBATUM*, L.
The Bearded Ophidium.
Ophidie barbu.
Das Bartmännchen.
Ofidio barbato (*It.*).
Vulg., Galiotto, Galera (*Tr.*, *Ven.*), Galia (*Ven.*).
Croat., Huj, Hulj.
Habit. General, and not uncommon.
Season. August, October.
Quality. 3.

244. *OPHIDIUM BROUSONETII*, Müll.
Note. Very similar to the foregoing species.
Habit. Spalato; rare.

245. *OPHIDIUM ROCHII*, Müll.
Note. Very similar to the foregoing sp.
Habit. Southern range; San Benedetto del Tronto.

246. *OPHIDIUM VASSALLI*, Risso.
Habit. Venice, Istria, Spalato; rare.

Gen. III. FIERASFER, *Cuv.**
247. *FIERASFER ACUS*, Brünn.
Der Schlangenaal.
Fiasfero ago (*It.*).
Vulg., Galiotto (*Tr.*, *Ven.*).
Croat., Strmorinac (*Spalato*).
Habit. Lives inside the *Holothuriæ;* Spalato, Bocche di Cattaro; rare.

Gen. IV. AMMODYTES, *Art.*
248. *AMMODYTES SICULUS*, Swains.
Sand-eel, Sand-launce.
Le lançon.
Der Sand-aal, die Schmelte.
Ammodite (*It.*).
Vulg., Cicirelli (*Sicily*).
Habit. Makarska (Dalmatia); very rare at Venice.

Fam. III. MACRURIDÆ.
Gen. MACRURUS, *Bl.*
249. *MACRURUS CŒLORHYNCUS*, Risso.
Macrouro camuso (*It.*).
Vulg., Pesce sorice (*Sicily*).
Habit. Southern coast of Dalmatia (?); very rare.

Fam. IV. PLEURONECTIDÆ—Flat-fish Tribe.
Gen. I. RHOMBUS, *Klein.*
250. *RHOMBUS MAXIMUS*, Cuv.
The Turbot.
Le Turbot.
Die Steinbutte, Dornbutte.
Rombo chiodato (*It.*).
Vulg., Rombo (*Tr.*, *Ven.*, *Fiume*, *Cat.*).
Rombo di sasso (*Ven.*).
Croat., Rumbac, Oblić (*Croat. littoral*).
Oblić (*Spalato*).
Habit. General and common.

* *Fierasfer dentatus.* (See No. 378.)

Season. Winter.
Quality. 1.

251. *RHOMBUS LÆVIS*, Rond.
The Brill.
La Barbue.
Die Glattbutte.
Rombo liscio (*It.*).
Vulg., Suazo, Sfazo, Soazo (*Tr. Ven., Fiume, Cat.*).
Croat., Svac.
Habit. General and common at all seasons.
Season. Best in November.
Quality. 1.

Gen. II. PHRYNORHOMBUS, *Günth.*

252. *PHRYNORHOMBUS UNIMACU-LATUS*, Risso.
Bloch's Topknot.
La petite Limandelle.
Die punctirte Scholle.
Rombo di grotta (*It.*).
Vulg., Peloso, Peloso di grotta (*Tr.*).
Rombetto (Peloso) di grotta (*Ven.*).
Croat., Kosmate šfoljice, Kosmate od grota, šfolja kosmata.
Habit. Rocks and cavities in the rocks, hence its Italian name ; Trieste, Zara ; not uncommon at Spalato, in other waters it is rare.
Season. January, September, October.
Quality. 3 ; *Minutaja* (mixed fish).

Gen. III. ARNOGLOSSUS, *Blkr.**

253. *ARNOGLOSSUS LATERNA*, Walb.
The Megrim, Scald-fish, Smooth Sole.
Die nackte Scholle.
Suacia cianchetta (*It.*).
Vulg., Sanchetto (*Tr., Fiume*).
Pataraccia (*Tr., Ven.*). Misapplied to this species.
Croat., Sankete, Sanketice.

* *Arnoglossus boscii.* (See No. 379.)

Habit. General and more or less common ; rare at Trieste, common at Venice and Spalato.
Season. Summer.
Quality. 3 ; *Minutaja* (mixed fish).

254. *ARNOGLOSSUS CONSPERSUS*, Canestr.
Suacia macchiata (*It.*).
Habit. Ravenna ; rare.
Season. June, August, October.

255. *ARNOGLOSSUS GROHMANNI*, Bp.
Suacia fosca (*It.*).
Vulg., Pataraccia (*Tr., Ven.*).
Pataraccia mora (*Ven.*).
Sfojo (*Fiume*).
Croat., šfolj.
Habit. As No. 253.
Season. Two specimens caught at Trieste in August.
Quality. 3 ; *Minutaja* (mixed fish).

Gen. IV. CITHARUS, *Blkr.*

256. *CITHARUS LINGUATULA*, L.
Suacia comune (*It.*).
Vulg., Pataraccia (*Tr., Ven., Fiume*).
Croat., Patarace.
Habit. General and common.
Season. Summer.
Quality. 2.

Gen. V. RHOMBOIDICHTYS, *Blkr.*

257. *RHOMBOIDICHTYS PODAS*, Delar.
Rombo poda (*It.*).
Habit. Coast of Dalmatia ; very rare.

258. *RHOMBOIDICHTYS MANCUS*, Risso.
Rombo passero (*It.*).
Habit. The same as the foregoing species.
Note. Costa considers this to be the female of *R. podas*.

Gen. VI. PLEURONECTES, *Art.*

259. *PLEURONECTES PLATESSA*, L.
Platessa vulgaris, *Bp.*
The Plaice.
Habit. Two specimens were found by Professor Trois in the fish-market at Venice; these appear to be the only ones hitherto caught in these seas.

260. *PLEURONECTES ITALICUS*, Gthr.
Platessa passer, *Bp.*
The Italian Flounder.
Le Flet.
Der Flunder.
Pianuzza passera (*It.*).
Vulg., Passera, Passara (*Tr., Fiume, Ven., Cat.*).
Passarin, Latesiol (*Ven.*).
Passariello (*Lésina*).
Croat., Pasera, Pasara (*Croat. littoral*).
Plosnatica, Iverak (*Spalato*). Kalkan (*Narenta*).
Habit. An Adriatic, not Mediterranean species; general, and common in brackish waters, and ascends the rivers; Narenta.
Season. Best in May, June.
Quality. 2.

Gen. VII. SOLEA, *Cuv.*

261. *SOLEA VULGARIS*, Quensel.
The Sole.
La Sole.
Die Zunge, Zungenscholle.
Sogliola volgare (*It.*).
Vulg., Sfoja, Sfoglia (*Tr., Fiume, Cat.*).
Sfogio, Sfogio nostran, Sfogio de sasso, Zentil (*Ven.*).
Croat., sfolja, svoja (*Croat. littoral*).
Tabinja ili list, Zalistak (*Spalato*).
Habit. General and common; deep sea-beds.
Season. Best in winter.
Quality. 1.

262. *SOLEA OCELLATA*, L.
La Pégouse.
Sogliola occhiuta (*It.*).
Habit. Common at Spalato in deep water; very rare in the north of the Gulf.

263. *SOLEA KLEINII*, Risso.
Sogliola turca (*It.*).
Vulg., Sfogio turco (*Ven.*).
Sfoja (*Tr.*).
Habit. Venice, Trieste, Spalato, on *algæ* sea-beds; rare.

264. *SOLEA LASCARIS*, Risso (*not* Bp.).
Habit. Trieste, Spalato, on sandy bed; not uncommon.
Note. Many authors confuse this species with *S. lascaris* (Bp.), synonymous with *S. impar** (Benn. and Gthr.), and *S. nasuta* (Nordm.); Günther cites the two as distinct species; Costa considers it a variety of *S. vulgaris*; Canestrini does not cite it at all.

265. *SOLEA VARIEGATA*, Donov.
Solea mangili, *Risso.*
The Variegated Sole, Thickback, Bastard Sole, Red-backed Flounder.
Sfogliola fasciata (*It.*).
Vulg., Sfogietto (*generic for all small soles*); Sfogietto peloso (*Ven.*). Peloso (*Tr.*).
Habit. Venice, Trieste, Zara, Spalato; not uncommon at Spalato.
Season. April, September.
Quality. 3; *Minutaja* (mixed fish).

266. *SOLEA LUTEA*, Risso.
Sogliola gialla (*It.*).
Vulg., Sfogietto, Peloso.
Habit. Ravenna, Trieste, Spalato, Dalmatia; rare.
Season. June.
Quality. 3.

---

* *Solea impar.* (*See* No. 380.)

267. *SOLEA MINUTA*, Parn.
   Little Sole.
   La Solenette.
   Sogliola minuta (*It.*).
   Vulg., Sfogio menuo (*Ven.*).
   Habit. Venice, Trieste; rare.
   Season. September.
268. *SOLEA MONOCHIR*, Bp.
   Die einflossige Scholle.
   Sogliola pelosa (*It.*).
   Vulg., Peloso, Pataraccia (*Tr.*).
   Sanchetto peloso (*Fiume*).

Peloso, Sfogietto peloso (*Ven.*).
Croat., Kosmate sfoljice.
Habit. General, and not uncommon in summer.
Quality. 3.

Gen. VIII. AMMOPLEUROPS, *Gthr.*
269. *AMMOPLEUROPS LACTEUS*, Bp.
   Plagusia lactea, *Bp.*
   Croat., Golica (*Spalato*).
   Note. Is met with every winter on the southern coast of Dalmatia; it frequents great depths; it does not appear in the north of the Gulf.

Order—PHYSOSTOMI.

Fam. I. SCOPELIDÆ.

Gen. I. SAURUS, *C. & V.*
270. *SAURUS GRISEUS*, Lowe.
   Saurus lacerta, *C. & V.*
   Tarantola Romæ, *Will.*
   Sauro lacerta (*It.*).
   Croat., Manjur (*Spalato*).
   Habit. Has a southern extension; Lésina (Dalmatia), where, according to Prof. Kolombatović, it is common, and off the islands Zirona and Solta.

Gen. II. AULOPUS, *Cuv.*
271. *AULOPUS FILAMENTOSUS*, Bl.
   Saurus lacerta, *Risso.*
   Aulopo filamentoso (*It.*).
   Habit. Found in Sicilian waters; a specimen caught in the Bocche di Cattaro is in the Trieste Museum.

Fam. II. CYPRINIDÆ.
   Gen. I. CYPRINUS, *L.*
272. *CYPRINUS CARPIO*, L.
   The Carp, common Carp.
   La Carpe, Carpe vulgaire.
   Der Karpfen, gemeine Karpfen.

Carpa (*It.*).
Vulg., Raina (*Tr.*, *Ven.*).
Carpione (*Fiume*).
Carpione maschio (*Tr.*).
Bulbero, Carpa (*Trentino*).
Gobbo, Gobato, Bulbero (*Ven.*).
Gobbo, Raina, Rainotto (*young*), (*Treviso*).
Croat., Karpiun, Krap obični, šaran.
Sloven, Karf (*Carniola*).
Habit. Venetian watershed: Trentino, Isonzo; attains to a length of thirty-two inches and upwards, and, if reared, up to thirty-five to forty pounds' weight; is best in winter; the flesh of the lake and river carp is preferable to that of ponds and stagnant waters, which retains a disagreeable taste and smell.

273. *CYPRINUS KOLLARII*, Heck.
   La Carpe blanche, Carpe batardée, le Carreau, la Carouche blanche.
   Die Karpf-Karausche, der Karausch Karpfen.
   Note. A hybrid of the common Carp and *Cypr. carassius*, varying according to whether bred by the female of the one or the other kind.
   Habit. Occurs in the Adige.

Gen. II. BARBUS, *Cuv.*

274. *BARBUS FLUVIATILIS*, Ag.
The Barbel.
Le Barbeau.
Die Barbe, Steinbarbe.
Barbo fluviatile (*It.*).
Sloven, Mrena, Pohra, Poharža (*young*) (*Carniola*).
Habit. River Sala, a tributary of the Isonzo, river Piave, river Santerno; this appears to be its southernmost limit; further south, the following species takes its place.

275. *BARBUS PLEBEJUS*, Val.
Barbus eques, *Heck & Kner.*
Barbo comune (*It.*).
Vulg., Barbo, Barbio, Balbio, Barbolo, Balb, Barb, Barbol.
Croat., Mrena (*Dalm.*).
Habit. This is the *southern* Barbel, found in lakes and rivers of Italy and Dalmatia: the Adige, Osbo, or Ospo (near Trieste), Tagliamento, Sile (Treviso), Knin and Xegar (Dalmatia); spawns in April and May; its roe is said to be poisonous; length twelve inches. *B. eques* is cited by Heck. and Kner as a distinct species, but Gthr. considers them identical; it is not found in northern Italy, and in Dalmatia it has hitherto only been found in the river Zermagna; it is smaller than *B. plebejus*—only five inches long.

276. *BARBUS CANINUS*, Cuv.
Barbo canino (*It.*).
Habit. Tributaries of the Isonzo, and in Istria.

Gen. III. AULOPYGE, *Heck.*

277. *AULOPYGE HUGELI*, Heck.
Croat., Uklja ostrulja (*Dalm.*).
Ostrulj (*Livno*).
Habit. Sign (Dalmatia), and in the rivers Cettina, Ricka, Sabljak, Starba; it is five inches long, and is good eating.

Gen. IV. GOBIO, *Cuv.*

278. *GOBIO FLUVIATILIS*, Flem.
The Gudgeon.
Le Goujon.
Die Grundel, Gressling, Kressling, Gründling.
Gobione (*It.*).
Vulg., Gobione, Temalo (*Trentino*).
Veccie, Temalo (*Verona*).
Veccio, Vecez, Variolo (*Treviso*).
Brocciolo, Vanà (*Bologna*).
Sloven, Krašorka, Gründele, Globoček (*Carniola*).
Habit. River Sala (tributary of the Isonzo) in Carniola; Trentino, Adige, Garda, Sile (Treviso), Bologna, and, generally speaking, the watershed of the north of Italy; it attains to a length of four to five inches, and spawns April, May, and June; its flesh is very good and much prized.

279. *GOBIO URANOSCOPUS*, Ag.
The Wapper.
Le Goujon uranoscope.
Die Steinkresse, Steingressling.
Sloven, špice (*Carniola*).
Habit. Sala (tributary of the Isonzo).

Gen. V. LEUCISCUS, *Rond.* (White-fish).

280. *LEUCISCUS AULA*, Bonap.
Der weisse Scharl.
Triotto (*It.*).
Vulg., Pessata (*Trentino*).
Bruffolo, Brussolo (*Ven.*).
Brussolo (*Treviso*).
Croat., Maženica (*Dalmatia*).
Habit. More or less general and common in running courses and stagnant waters: lake of Garda, the rivers Trentino, Treviso, Tagliamento, and in Dalmatia.
Quality. Nowhere valued, and therefore little fished for.

Varieties or synonymous:—
  a. Leuciscus pauperum *de Fil.*
    Sbroffone (*It.*).
    Vulg., Brussolo (*Treviso*).
    Bruffolo (*Verona*).
  b. Leuciscus rubella, *Heck. & Kner.*
    Croat., Peškvela (*Dalm.*).
Habit. Has a southern range; it is found at Treviso, in Istria, and in Dalmatia, where it is common in the Narenta, the marshes of Norin, Imosky, and Carin; two to six inches long.
  c. Leuciscus basak, *Heck. & Kner.*
    Croat., Bazak (*Vergoras*).
    Plotice (*generic term*).
Habit. Peculiar to Dalmatia: at Vergoraz and in the lake of Drusino near Imosky; three to six inches long.

281. **LEUCISCUS ADSPERSUS**, Heck.
  Croat., Gaovica (*Dalm.*).
Habit. Peculiar to Dalmatia; found in the small lake Jezero Rosso, near Imosky; two to four inches long.

282. **LEUCISCUS PIGUS**, de Fil.
  Vraw-fish.
  Der Frauenfisch, Nerfling.
  Pigo, Salione (*It.*).
  Vulg., Pigo (*Trentino*).
  Orada, Sajon (*Ven.*).
  Encobia (*Lake of Como*).
  Sajon, Sajon colle broche (*Treviso*).
  Orada dell' Adese (*Verona*).
Habit. Venetian water-courses: Adige, Bacchiglione, Sile, and peculiar to the lakes of north Italy; it attains to a length of sixteen inches and a weight of three pounds; it spawns in spring; its flesh is white and savorous, and when full grown it is one of the most esteemed fishes of its kind.

283. **LEUCISCUS CEPHALUS**, L.
  The Chubb, Skelly.
  Le Chevanne, Meunier, Vilain, Testard.
  Der Altel, Altl, Alse.
  Squaglio (*It.*).
  Hung., Dobáncs.
  Sloven, Klénéč (*Carniola*).
Habit. Has a northern extension; its southernmost limit in this part of Europe appears to be the river Sala in Carniola, a tributary of the Isonzo, and the Tagliamento; flesh of no value; used as food for other fish in fish-ponds.

Varieties or synonymous:—
  a. Leuciscus cavedanus, *Bonap.*
    Der Alten (*Bozen*).
    Lasca cavedo, Cavedano (*It.*).
    Vulg., Trotta bastardo, Temolo bastardo.
    Squal (*Trentino, Treviso*).
    Cavezzale, Cavedano (*Lombardy*).
    Cavazzino (*Lombardy, Verona*).
    Cavedo (*Bologna*).
Habit. The southern representative of the *Chub*, described by Heck. and Kner as a distinct species or variety; Gthr. and Canestrini cite it as synonymous; found all over Italy, in the Trentino, rivers Pô, Isonzo, Sile (Treviso); frequents deep but quiet waters; flesh of little or no value.
  b. Squalius albus, *Bp., Heck., & Kner.*
Habit. River Kerka, near Scardona, Dalmatia.

284. **LEUCISCUS SVALLIZE**, Heck. & Kner.
  Croat., Svalica (*Dalm.*).
Habit. This is the southern representative of *L. vulgaris* (Gthr)., the Dace, or Graining, La Vandoise (French), Der Hasel (German), found in Dalmatia in the lakes near Vergoraz and the marshy Narenta.

2 G

285. **LEUCISCUS ILLYRICUS**, Heck. & Kner.
Croat., Klen, Klenčić (*Dalm.*).
Habit. Rivers Isonzo and Cettina (Dalmatia); attains to a length of thirteen inches.

286. **LEUCISCUS ERYTHROPHTHALMUS**, L.
The Rudd, Red-eye.
Le Rotengle, la Rosse.
Das Rothauge, die Rothfeder, Rother Scharl, Rothschweif.
Scardola comune, Piotta, Pesce del diavolo (*It.*).
Vulg., Scardola, Sgardola.
Coc-rosse (*Trentino, Ven.*).
Scardola, Scardoloto del Sil (*Treviso*).
Croat., Krupatka (*Dalm.*).
Habit. All Europe, and has both a northern and a southern extension; found all over Italy, in the Trentino and Venetian watersheds; river Tagliamento, lake of Vrana (island of Cherso); frequents marshy waters and the ditches of rice-fields; spawns in April, May; flesh of little value, eaten only by the poor, or used as food for other fish; ten to twelve inches long and one and a half pound weight.

Varieties or synonymous:—
a. Scardinius dergle, *Heck. & Kner.*
Croat., Drlje (*Dalm.*).
Habit. Rivers Kerka and Zermagna in Dalmatia; like the foregoing species, it is little esteemed as food.

b. Leuciscus scardafa, *Bonap.*
Cavezzal (*It.*).
Croat., Peškelj, Keljavac (*Dalm.*).
Habit. An Italian species, found also in Dalmatia, in the marshes of the Narenta, near Fort Opus.

c. Scardinius plotizza, *Heck. & Kner.*
Croat., Plotica (*Dalm.*).

Habit. Jezero Grande near Vergoraz and near Imosky in Dalmatia; fourteen inches long.

287. **LEUCISCUS HEEGERI**, Ag.
Habit. Found in the water-courses of parts of Istria, whence it is brought to market at Fiume, although not much valued as food.

288. **LEUCISCUS MUTICELLUS**, Bonap.
Telestes Savignyi, *Bp.*
Telestes Agassizii, *Heck.*
Die Langen, Laube.
Vairone (*It.*).
Vulg., Vairone (*Trentino, Verona, Lomb.*).
Mozzetta (*Trentino*).
Varone (*Verona*).
Fregarola (*Treviso*).
Habit. Running courses of Italy; Trentino, Sile, etc.; length, four to five inches; flesh insipid and little valued.
Note. Heck. and Kner cite *T. Savignyi* and *T. Agassizii* as different sp., of which the former would appear to be the southern representative; Gthr. cites them as identical.

289. **LEUCISCUS UKLIVA**, Heck.
Habit. River Cettina near Sign, Lake of Imoschi, both in Dalmatia; six inches long.

290. **LEUCISCUS TURSKYI**, Heck.
Habit. Stream Ciccola, near Drnis (Dalmatia); six inches long.

Varieties, or synonymous:—
a. Squalius microlepis, *Heck.*
b. Squalius tenellus, *Heck.*
Croat., Maklja (*Vergoraz*).
Habit. Narenta, near Vergoraz, Lake of Dusino, near Imosky, both in Dalmatia; seven to eight inches long, seldom twelve inches.
Note. Probably not specifically distinct from *L. Turskyi*, according to Gthr.; Canestrini considers *L. ukliva, turskyi, microlepis*, and *tenellus* as identical.

291. *LEUCISCUS PHOXINUS*, L.
The Minnow, Pink.
Le Véron, Véron lisse.
Die Pfrille, Pfrill, Elritze.
Sanguinerola (*It.*).
Vulg., Bressanella, Varone (*Trentino, Verona*).
Lanfresca (*Treviso*).
Fregarola (*Lombardy*).
Hung., Küsz, Csetri.
Sloven, Trigle (*Carniola*).
Croat., Uklja (*Knin*).
Uklja mečica (*Sign*).
Koravica, Tupčić.
Habit. Streams, torrents, rivers, and lakes of the north of Italy; Klincizza (near Trieste), Idria, Treviso; rivers Isonzo, Tagliamento, Adige, Trentino, etc.; in Dalmatia, from Knin, Sign, Xegar, Lake Rastak, island of Veglia (Quarnero); three to four inches long; spawns in spring; flesh little valued as food.

Gen. VI. PARAPHOXINUS, *Blkr.*

292. *PARAPHOXINUS ALEPIDOTUS*, Heck.
Croat., Uklja mečica, Mečica.
Habit. Rivers Cettina and Narenta (Dalmatia); very similar to the Minnow.

293. *PARAPHOXINUS CROATICUS*, Steindachner.
Croat., Piur.
Habit. Lika, in Croatia.

Gen. VII. TINCA, *Cuv.*

294. *TINCA VULGARIS*, Cuv.
The Tench.
La Tanche.
Die Schleihe, Schley, Schlein.
Tinca, Tenca (*It.*).
Vulg., Tinca, Tenca (*Trentino, Ven., Treviso*), Tencoto (*young*) (*Treviso*).

Hung., Czigányhal, Czompó.
Sloven, Karpoz, šlajn (*Carniola*).
Croat., Cvičenica, Linjak, Linj (*Dalmatia*).
Habit. Found all over Italy: Trentino, Lake of Garda, Sile (Treviso), Ravenna, Timao (near Duino), River Sala, Lake Zirknitz (Carniola); general and common; frequents stagnant waters on muddy beds, never strong currents; flesh unhealthy and indigestible, said to produce fever.

Gen. VIII. CHONDROSTOMA, Ag.

295. *CHONDROSTOMA SOETTA*, Bonap.
Savetta, Lasca (*It.*).
Vulg., Savel, Soëtta, Savetta.
Croat., šljivar (*Dalm.*).
Habit. Venetian water-shed, but not common; River Piave (Treviso); attains to a length of twelve to sixteen inches; flesh little prized.
Note. This is the southern representative of *Chr. nasus* (Ag.), die Nase, or Näsling, of Germany, le Nez of France.

296. *CHONDROSTOMA GENEI*, Bonap.
Lasca del Gené (*It.*).
Vulg., Strilot (*Trentino*).
Strigio (*Verona*).
Strillo, Mercandola, Fregata (*Treviso*).
Stria (*Lombardy*).
Habit. Northern and central Italy, Trentino, Tagliamento, Adige, Po, Ticino; length, seven to eight inches; flesh of little or no value.

297. *CHONDROSTOMA KNERII*, Heck.
Croat., Podustva (*Dalm.*).
Habit. Dalmatia, in the Narenta, near Metcovic and Norin; Istria (?).
Note. Similar to No. 296; six to seven inches long.

298. *CHONDROSTOMA PHOXINUS*, Heck.
Habit. Sign (Dalmatia).

Gen. IX. ABRAMIS, *Cuv.* (Breams.)

299. *ABRAMIS BIPUNCTATUS*, Bl.
Alburnus bipunctatus, *Heck. & Kner.*
L'able Eperlan, Le Platet.
Die Laube, Steinlaube.
Habit. Imoschi (Dalmatia).
Note. A species of central Europe, resembling *Alburnus lucidus* (Heck. & Kner) (the Bleak, or Blick), but smaller; it does not exceed four inches in length.

Gen. X. ALBURNUS, *Gthr.*

300. *ALBURNUS ALBURNELLUS*, Martens.
Alburnus alborella, *Heck. & Kner.*
Alburnus fracchia, *Heck. & Kner.*
Der Sonnenfisch.
Avola (*It.*).
Vulg., Alborella, Avola (*Lomb., Trentino*), Aspio (*Trentino*), Avola, Aola, Pincie (*Ven.*), Pincia (*Treviso*).
Croat., Uklja svitloka (*Dalmatia*).
Habit. The southern representative of the Bleak (*A. lucidus*); its northernmost limit is Bozen (south of Tyrol); it inhabits the Lake of Garda, the rivers Isonzo, Tagliamento, Treviso, and generally the whole of north and central Italy; also Dalmatia: the Lake of Dusino, near Imoschi: at Obrovac, Vergoraz, the Narenta, etc.; found in shoals in lakes and rivers; spawns in June, July; length, four inches; flesh of little or no value, excepting as bait for pike and other fishes.

301. *ALBURNUS SCORANZA*, Heck.
Croat., Skoranza (*Dalm.*).
Habit. Lake of Scutari (Albania).

Gen. XI. NEMACHILUS, *Van Hasselt.*

302. *NEMACHILUS BARBATULUS*, L.
Cobitis barbatula, *L.*

The Loach, Beardie.
La Loche, Loche franche.
Die Grundel, Bartgrundel.
Cobite barbatello (*It.*).
Vulg., Strega (*Trentino, Verona*).
Forapiere, Foraprie, Forasassi, Forasecchi (*Treviso*).
Hung., Kövi-Csik.
Sloven, Grúdel (*Carniola*).
Croat., čikov, piškor.
Habit. North of Italy: Adige, Lake of Garda, Trentino; in clear running courses; length, four to five inches; spawns in spring; flesh delicate, and valued as food; rare.

Gen. XII. COBITIS, *Art.*

303. *COBITIS TÆNIA*, L.
The Spinous or Spined Loach, the Groundling.
Der Steinbeisser, Steingrundel, Dorngrundel.
Cobite fluviale (*It.*).
Vulg., Cagnola (*Trentino*).
Pesseta, Pessucola (*Treviso*).
Cagnola, Foraguarda, Lamprcola (*Verona*).
Ussellina (*Lomb.*).
Lampreda (*Dalmatia*).
Hung., Pavágó, Kircza.
Sloven, Stajngeljni (*Carniola*).
Croat., Lizibaba, Legbaba, Govedar.
Habit. North of Italy: Trentino, Lake of Garda; rivers Adige, Tagliamento, Isonzo, Sala (Carniola); Istria; also in Dalmatia, at Sign (river Cettina), Imosky, the Narenta; in lakes, rivers, streams, and ditches, on muddy beds, mostly imbedded in the mud; spawns in April, May; seldom exceeds three inches in length; is only eaten by the poor; makes a curious noise when taken out of the water. *Cobitis elongata* is a variety described by Heckel and Kner, found in the

Sala, near Idria (Carniola); measures five to six inches.

Fam. III. CYPRINODONTIDÆ.
Gen. I. CYPRINODON, *Lac.*
304. *CYPRINODON CALARITANUS*, C. & V.
Lebias calaritana, *Bonelli.*
Lebia calaritana (*It.*).
Vulg., Nonno, Nani, Nano (*Ven.*).
Habit. Venice, Zaole; in brackish waters, mouths of rivers, which they ascend for a considerable distance; in the lagoons they are common all the year round; length, three inches.
Quality. Flesh bad, and of no value.

Fam. IV. SCOMBRESOCIDÆ — Gar-pikes and Flying-fishes.
Gen. I. BELONE, *Cuv.*
305. *BELONE ACUS*, Risso.
The Gar-fish, Gar-pike, Long-nose, Hornbeak.
L'orphie, Bélone, Broche.
Der Hornfisch, Hornhecht, Schneffel, Nadelhecht, die Meernadel.
Aguglia comune, Aguja (*It.*).
Vulg., Angusigola (*Tr.*, *Ven.*, *Fiume*, *Cattaro*).
Croat., Igla, Iaglica.
Habit. General and common; attains to a length of twenty inches and above.
Season. July to September.
Quality. 2.

Gen. II. SCOMBRESOX, *Lac.*
306. *SCOMBRESOX RONDELETII*, C. & V.
Sayris camperi, *Bonap.*
The Saury, Skipper, Skipper-pike, Saury-pike, Bill-fish.

Sairide del Camperi (*It.*).
Croat., Kusača (*Spalato*).
Habit. Sicilian and Neapolitan waters; has been observed on the Dalmatian coast; very rare.

Gen. III. EXOCŒTUS, *Art.*
307. *EXOCŒTUS VOLITANS*, L.
The Flying-fish.
Hirondelle de mer.
Der Italienische Flederfisch, Fliegenderfisch.
Rondinella chiara (*It.*).
Vulg., Rondinella (*Tr.*).
Pesce barbastrillo (*Ven.*).
Croat., Lastavica (*Croat. littoral*).
Poletuša (*Spalato*).
Habit. Rare.
Season. Summer.

308. *EXOCŒTUS RONDELETII*, C. & V.
Vulg., Rondinella.
Croat., Letica, Lastavica (*Spalato*).
Habit. More common than the above, with which this sp. is often confused; Trieste, Fiume, Spalato.
Season. Summer.

Fam. V. ESOCIDÆ—Pikes.
Gen. Esox, *Cuv.*
309. *ESOX LUCIUS*, L.
The Pike, Jack, Luce, Gedd.
Le Brochet.
Der Hecht, gemeiner Hecht.
Luccio (*It.*).
Vulg., Luzzo, Lusso.
Hung., Csuka.
Sloven, šuka (*Carniola*).
Croat., štuka (*Dalm.*).
Habit. General and common; Lake of Garda, Adige, Udine, Tagliamento, Ravenna, Lake of Zirknitz (Carniola), Lake of Vrana (island of Cherso), etc.; enters brackish waters, and has been observed in the Venetian lagoons.

Fam. VI. SALMONIDÆ—Salmon Tribe.
Gen. I. SALMO, *Art.**

310. *SALMO FARIO AUSONII*, Val.
Trutto fario, *L.*
Salar ausonii (*Heck. & Kner*).
The Trout, Common Trout.
La Truite.
Die Forelle, Steinforelle.
Trota, Trutta, Truta (*It.*).
Vulg., Trutta, Forella (*Fiume*).
Sloven, Postern (*Carniola*).
Croat., Postrva (*Croat. littoral*).
Truta (*Illyr.*).
Pastrva (*Spalato*).
Habit. Fresh-water courses, seldom large rivers; found in almost all fresh-water courses of the Julian Alps: Fiume; spawning commences in October, and lasts till January; ascends the rivers to deposit its spawn.

311. *SALMO DENTEX*, Heck.
The Great Dalmatian Trout.
Croat., Pastrva, Bistranga, Pastèrmka.
Habit. A non-migratory sp. from the rivers of Dalmatia; in the river Kerka, near Knin, in the river Cettina, near Sign, and in the Narenta, between Metcovic and Fort Opus; attains to a length of thirty-six inches; Canestr. mentions it as being found also in the Isonzo.

312. *SALMO GENIVITTATUS*, Heck. & Kner.
Habit. Known from a single specimen only, eighteen inches in length, caught in the river Sala, a tributary of the river Isonzo.

313. *SALMO OBTUSIROSTRIS*, Heck.
River Trout of Dalmatia.
Vulg., Trotta.
Croat., Pastrva, Mladica.
Pastrva pirgasica (*Spalato*).

---

* *Salmo trotta.* (*See* No. 381.)

Habit. A non-migratory sp. from the Dalmatian rivers Zermagna, Giadro (Salona), and Verlica, near Imosky, and from the Tiber; rarely exceeding a foot in length.

314. *SALMO CARPIO*, L.
Trutta Benaci lacus, *Aldrov.*
Trout of the Lake of Garda.
Carpione, Trutta del lago (*It.*).
Vulg., Trutta rossa (*Treviso*).
Habit. Lakes of Lombardy and Venice, descends the rivers and enters the sea; river Tagliamento; attains to a length of twenty inches; formerly held to be peculiar to the Lake of Garda (*Lac. Benacus*), after which it has been called, and where it is still best known (as Carpione); flesh much esteemed; spawns in December.

Gen. II. THYMALLUS, *Cuv.*

315. *THYMALLUS VULGARIS*, Nilss.
Thymallus vexillifer, *Ag.*
The Grayling, Umber.
L'Ombre.
Der Asch, die Æsche, Æschling.
Temolo, Temola (*It.*).
Hung. Tomolika. *Sloven*, Lipan (*Carniola*).
Croat., Lipan, Lipljen.
Habit. Rivers of Lombardy and Venice, Carniola and Istria: Tagliamento, Sala, Isonzo, Adige, etc.; clear and shallow streams; attains from one to one and a half pound weight; flesh excellent.

Gen. III. ARGENTINA, *Art.*

316. *ARGENTINA SPHYRÆNA*, L.
The Argentine.
Der toscanische Silberfisch.
Argentina sfirena (*It.*).
Vulg., Arzentin (*Tr., Ven.*).
Croat., Srebèrnica (*Spalato*).

Habit. A deep-sea fish rarely met with in the north of the Adriatic; more common in the Mediterranean; it is common at Spalato in winter.

Fam. VII. CLUPEIDÆ—Herring Tribe.
  Gen. I. ENGRAULIS, *C. & V.*
317. *ENGRAULIS ENCRASICHOLUS*, L.
  The Anchovy.
  L'Anchois.
  Der Anschovi.
  Sardella comune, Anciuga (*It.*).
  Vulg., Sardon(*Tr., Fiume, Cat.*).
  Sardon, Anchio (*Ven.*),—*the name* Sardella *is sometimes misapplied to this sp.*
  Croat., Minćion, Inćun.
  Brgljun (*Spalato*).
Habit. General and common.
Season. May to September.
Quality. 1.

  Gen. II. CLUPEA, *Cuv.*
318. *CLUPEA AURITA*, *C. & V.*
  Sardinella aurita, *C. & V.*
  Sardinella dorata (*It.*).
Habit. Occasionally, but rarely, found on the coast of Dalmatia; generally mistaken for the Sardine; common in the Mediterranean.
Quality. Inferior; its flesh has a bad flavour.

319. *CLUPEA ALOSA*, L.
  Alosa communis, *Yarr.*
  The Shad, Allis-Shad.
  L'Alose commune.
  Die Alse, Else, Maifisch, Mutterhäring.
  Alosa comune (*It.*).
  Vulg., Sardena (*Trentino, Verona*).
  Ceppa (*p*), Cheppia (*Ven., Tr.*).
  Ciepa (*p*), Sardella salvatica (*Fiume*).
  Ceppa (*p*), Agone, Scarabina (*Verona*).
  Ceppa (*p*) (*Treviso*).
  Ceppa (*p*), Agone (*f*), Ceppino (†), Aciuga (*p*) (*Lomb.*).
  Agon de Como (*f*).
  Missoltini (*Lake Como, in a salted state*).
  Croat., čepa, čipa.
Note. Marked thus (*p*) applied to mature sp.; marked thus (*f*) applied to the half mature sp.; marked thus (†) to the fry.
Habit. Frequents the sea and ascends the rivers in spring, entering the lakes for spawning; is caught in the lakes of north Italy in May, June; attains to a length of twelve to sixteen inches; flesh good, excepting at the season of spawning, and in October and November.
Note. This and the *C. finta* are very similar, and they have been generally confused with one another. In fact they have been described as one species by many authors. It therefore becomes doubtful whether it is the *Alosa* proper (the better of the two) we have to deal with here; Garcis doubts the identity, and considers it the less valuable *C. finta* which frequents the *eastern* shores of the Adriatic; these remarks may, therefore, apply equally to the one or the other of these two species.

320. *CLUPEA FINTA*, Cuv.
  The Twaite-Shad, Maid.
  La Feinte, Alose Feinte.
  Die Finte, der kleine Maifisch.
Nomenclature and Remarks. See above (No. 319).
Note. The species hitherto found at Trieste and represented in the Trieste Museum are all *C. finta.*
Habit. Common in summer at Trieste; at Spalato it makes its appearance in October, and is fished during the winter, and chiefly so in spring, disappearing altogether in summer.

321. *CLUPEA PILCHARDUS*, Walb.
Clupea sprattus, *Brünn*.
Clupea sardina, *Cuv*.
The Pilchard, Sardinia of Commerce, Gipsy or Crue Herring.
La Sardine, le Céléron.
Der Pilchard, die Sardelle.
Sardina comune (*It*.).
Vulg., Sardella (*Tr*., *Fiume*, *Ven*., *Cat*.).
Sardèle, Sardeline (*Ven*.).
Croat., Srdela, Srdjela, Srdjelica.
Habit. General and common; attains to a length of six inches.
Season. May, June, August, September; at Spalato also in the winter.
Quality. 1.

322. *CLUPEA PAPALINA*, Bp.
Clupanodon phalerica, *Risso*.
Die Melet.
Sardina papalina (*It*.).
Vulg., Papalina (*Tr*., *Ven*., *Fiume*, *Cat*., *Spalato*).
Sardellina (*Fiume*).
Croat., šarak, šarakina.
Habit. General and common.
Season. As No. 321.
Quality. Equally as good as No. 321, but smaller; attains to a length of four inches.
Note. Dr. Günther does not cite this sp., which is, however, common in these seas. His nearest description is *C. aurita*, which he gives as synonymous with *C. phalerica* (Risso), but neither the figure of Val., nor the description of Günther, viz., "lower jaw slightly projecting beyond the upper," corresponds with our common *Papalina*, whose lower jaw *strongly* projects beyond the upper. I am indebted to Dr. de Marchesetti, Director of the Trieste Museum of Natural History, for the above description. Canestrini cites *C. phalerica* as synonymous with this species.

Fam. VIII. MURÆNIDÆ—Eel Tribe.
Gen. I. ANGUILLA, *Cuv*.
323. *ANGUILLA VULGARIS*, Flem.
Anguilla latirostris, *Risso*.
The Eel, common Eel. Elvers (*fry*).
L'Anguille. Cives, Pibales (*fry*).
Der Aal, gemeiner Aal. Elvers (*fry*).
Anguilla, Inguilla (*It*.).
Vulg., Anguilla, Bisatto (*Tr*., *Ven*., *Fiume*).
Buratello (*fry*).
Teston (*Ven*.).
Croat., Ogor, Ugor, Angulja, Jegulja, Jamarica, Punjeglavica, Gruj, Gor, Mala jegulja (*fry*).
Habit. General and common; chiefly in the lagoons of Venice and Comacchio and the mouths of rivers; Fiume, Noghera (near Trieste), Timavo (near Duino), etc.; ascend the rivers in January and February (*Montata*), and descend the rivers and enter the sea for spawning from October to December (*Calata*); are reared in the *valli* of the lagoons.
Quality. Those of rivers and lakes are preferable to those of the lagoons.

324. *ANGUILLA EURYSTOMA*, Heck. & Kner.
Croat., Capor (*Dalmatia*).
Note. A variety found in the Narenta (Dalmatia).

Gen. II. CONGER, *Kaup*.
325. *CONGER VULGARIS*, Cuv.
Conger niger, *Risso*.
The Conger Eel.
Le Congre, Der Meeraal.
Grongo vulgare (*It*.).
Vulg., Grongo (*Tr*., *Ven*., *Fiume*).
Grongo di grotta (*Fiume*).
Croat., Grum, Grunj (*Croat. littoral*).
Ugor (*Spalato*).

Habit. General and common.
Season. Particularly in the autumn.
Quality. 2.

Gen. III. MYRUS, *Kaup.*
326. *MYRUS VULGARIS*, Kaup.
Conger myrus, *Cuv.*
Grongo muro (*It.*).
Vulg., Grongo (*Ven.*, *Tr.*, *Fiume*).
Grongo di sabbia (*Fiume*).
Croat., Morska zmija (*Spalato*).
Habit. General; rare; Quarnero, Trieste, Spalato.
Quality. Inferior to No. 325.

Gen. IV. OPHICHTHYS, *Gthr.**
327. *OPHICHTHYS SERPENS*, L.
Muræna serpens, *L.*
Ophisurus serpens, *Lac.*
Ofisuro serpente (*It.*).
Habit. General, but rare; Almissa (Dalmatia), Trieste; the specimen caught at Almissa measured 2·29 mètres; it has been caught at Trieste in December.

328. *OPHICHTHYS IMBERBIS*, Delar.
Sphagebranchus imberbis, *Delar.*
Sphagebranchus oculatus, *Risso.*
Sfagebranco sbarbato (*It.*).

Habit. Very rare; it has been observed on the Dalmatian coast; length, twelve to sixteen inches; flesh excellent.

Gen. V. MURÆNA, *Gthr.*
329. *MURÆNA HELENA*, L.
The Murry.
La Murène.
Die Muräne.
Murena elena.
Vulg., Murena, Morena, Bisatto tegrà, Bisatto indevisa (*Ven.*).
Croat., Ugor šari, Murina, Gruj (*Croat. littoral*).
Ugorova majka, Mrina (*Spalato*).
Habit. A rare species in the north of the Adriatic,—Trieste, Zara; frequents the rocky beds, and has a southern extension; it is common off the islands in the open sea, as Lagosta and Lésina, and is also caught off the islands of Solta and Zirona, near Spalato.
Season. Winter.
Quality. Flesh white and savoury.

330. *MURÆNA UNICOLOR*, Delar.
Murena monaca (*It.*).
Habit. Southern Adriatic; specimen from Otranto; smaller than No. 329.

Order—LOPHOBRANCHII.

Fam. SYNGNATHIDÆ--Pipe-fishes.

Gen. I. SIPHONOSTOMA, *Kaup.*
331. *SIPHONOSTOMA TYPHLE*, L.
Syngnathus typhle, *L.*
Broad-nosed Pipe-fish.
Der gemeine Nadelfisch, die Scenadel.
Sifonostomo tifle (*It.*).
Vulg., Angusigola falsa, Angusigola salvatica, Ago di mar, *generic terms* (*Tr.*, *Ven.*, *Fiume*).

* *Ophichthys cæcus.* (*See* No. 382.)

Croat., Igla diva, Igla morska, šilo, *generic.*
Habit. General and common; Sebenico, Spalato.
Season. February, September.
Quality. 0.

332. *SIPHONOSTOMA RONDELETII,* Delar.
Syngnathus viridis, *Risso.*
Habit. Rare; not uncommon at Spalato.
Season. January, March, May, September.
Note. Very similar to No. 331; Dr. Günther considers them synonymous.

333. *SIPHONOSTOMA ROTUNDATUM*, Michah.
Der abgerundete Nadelfisch.
Habit. Venice; rare; eight inches in length.
Season. March, August.

Gen. II. SYNGNATHUS, *Art.*

334. *SYNGNATHUS ACUS*, L.
Syngnathus tenuirostris, *Rath.*
The Great Pipe-fish or Needle-fish, Tangle-fish.
Signato tenuirostre (*It.*).
Vulg., Pesce ago (*Ven.*).
Croat., šilo, *generic.*
Habit. General and common; sixteen inches in length.
Season. Summer.

335. *SYNGNATHUS RUBESCENS*, Risso.
Signato rossastro (*It.*).
Habit. General and common.
Season. March, May, September.
Note. Dr. Günther holds this sp. to be synonymous with No. 334; attains to twelve inches in length.

336. *SYNGNATHUS TÆNIONOTUS*, Can.
Signato fasciato (*It.*).
Habit. Confined to the Venetian lagoons.

337. *SYNGNATHUS ABASTER*, Risso.
Signato cristato (*It.*).
Habit. Venice; rare; attains to five inches in length.
Season. May, August.

338. *SYNGNATHUS AGASSIZII*, Michah.
Syngnathus muræna, *Kaup.*
Signato dell' Agassiz (*It.*).
Habit. Venice; rare; six inches in length.
Season. July to September.

339. *SYNGNATHUS BREVIROSTRIS*, H. & E.
Signato brevirostre (*It.*).
Habit. General and common; length, five to six inches.

Gen. III. NEROPHIS, *Kaup.*

340. *NEROPHIS OPHIDION*, Kaup.
Syngnathus ophidion, *L.*
The Straight-nosed Pipe-fish.
Nerofide cristata (*It.*).
Habit. Has a southern extension; Spalato, Dalmatia; rare; length, seven to eight inches.
Season. May.

341. *NEROPHIS PAPACINUS*, Risso.
N. maculata, *Raff.*
Nerofide macchiata (*It.*).
Habit. Rarer than No. 340; Trieste, Spalato; length, eleven to twelve inches.
Season. Summer.

Gen. IV. HIPPOCAMPUS, *Cuv.*

342. *HIPPOCAMPUS BREVIROSTRIS*, Cuv.
Hippocampus antiquorum, *Leach.*
The Sea-horse, Short-snouted Hippocampus.
Cheval marin.
Das Seepferdchen.
Pferdeförmiger Nadelfisch.
Hippocampo brevirostre (*It.*).
Vulg., Caval marin (*Tr.*, *Ven.*).
Cavalo storno (*Ven.*).
Caval di mar (*Fiume*).
Croat., Konj morski, Konj od mora (*Croat. littoral*), Konjić morski (*Spalato*).
Habit. General, and common at Trieste; length, six inches; rare at Spalato.
Season. Summer.
Quality. o.

343. *HIPPOCAMPUS GUTTULATUS*, Cuv.
Hippocampo comune (*It.*).
Vulg. As No. 342.
Croat. As No. 342.
Habit. General, and more common than No. 342.

Order—PLECTOGNATHI.

Fam. I. SCLERODERMI—File-fishes.

Gen. BALISTES, *Cuv.*

344. *BALISTES CAPRISCUS*, Gm.
The File-fish, Mediterranean File-fish, Pig-faced Trigger-fish.
Le poupon noble.
Der Hornfisch, Seebock, Schiessfisch.
Balista caprisco (*It.*).
Vulg., Pesce balla, pesce balestra (*Tr.*, *Ven.*, *Fiume*).
Croat., Mihača.
Habit. General; Venice, Trieste; rare; not uncommon in the south (Spalato).
Season. Summer.
Quality. o.

Fam. II. GYMNODONTES—Sun-fishes.

Gen. ORTHAGORISCUS, *Bl. Schn.*

345. *ORTHAGORISCUS MOLA*, L.
Tetrodon mola, *L.*
The Molebut, Sun-fish.
Le Mole.
Der Mondfisch, Klumpfisch.
Ortagorisco luna (*It.*).
Vulg., Pesce luna, pesce balla (*Tr.*), pesce balla, pesce barila (*Fiume*), pesce luna, pesce rioda, pesce rioda ruvido, (*Ven.*).
Mjesečarka, butac, bucàt mjesečara (*Croat.*).
Habit. General, but rare; sp. from Venice, Trieste, Spalato.
Season. July, August.
Quality. o; attains to a length of upwards of three feet.

346. *ORTHAGORISCUS TRUNCATUS*, Retz.
Truncated Sun-fish.
Der Mondfisch.
Ortagorisco del Planco (*It.*).
Vulg., Girasol (*Fiume*).
Pesce luna, Pesce balla (*Tr.*).
Pesce rioda liscio (*Ven.*).
Croat. As No. 345.
Habit. General, but rare; sp. from Trieste, Curzola, St. Pietro della Brazza, Neum, Czirquenicza, off the island of Solta.
Season. Occasionally caught in July, August, and April.
Quality. o; attains to a length of twenty inches.

Sub-Class—CYCLOSTOMATA.

Fam. PETROMYZONTIDÆ—Lampreys.

Gen. PETROMYZON, *Art.*

347. *PETROMYZON MARINUS*, L.
The Lamprey, Sea Lamprey, Spotted Lamprey.
La Lamproie de mer, la grande Lamproie.
Die Seelamprete, das Neunauge, die Pricke, Meerpricke.
Lampreda marina (*It.*).
Vulg., Lampreda, Lampreda di mar (*Tr.*, *Ven.*, *Fiume*).
Magna (Mangia) pegola* (*Tr.*, *Fiume*).
Croat., Lamprida, Paklena.
Paklara (*Spalato*).
Habit. General, though rare; ascends the rivers in spring; found in most rivers flowing into the Adriatic; also in Dalmatia (Narenta).
Season. Summer.
Quality. Flesh savoury.

---

* *i.e.* "Pitch-eater."

348. *PETROMYZON FLUVIATILIS*, L.
The River Lamprey
Lamproie de rivière.
Das Flussneunauge.
Lampreda di fiume (*It.*).
Vulg., Lampreda, Lampredone, Lampreda d'argento (*Ven.*), Lampreda di sasso, (*Treviso*).
Hung., Orsóhal.
Sloven, Piškúr (*Carniola*).
Croat., Lamprida, zmijulica. Piškor, potočni piškor.
Habit. Lake of Garda, river Ticino, and, generally speaking, in lakes, rivers, streams, and stagnant waters; also in the lagoons of Venice; further south it becomes very rare; length, twelve to eighteen inches.

349. *PETROMYZON PLANERI*, Bl.
Petromyzon branchialis, *L.* (*the young*).

The Fringe-lipped Lampern, Planer's Lamprey.
La petite Lamproie.
Das kleine Neunauge, die kleine Pricke.
The Young:—
The Pride, Sand-piper, Small Lamprey, Mud Lamprey, Sandpride, Sandprey.
Le Lamprillon.
Die Uhle.
Piccola Lampreda (*It.*).
Vulg., Lampreda piccola, Lampreda di sasso, (*Treviso*).
Sloven, Pohkaža, *young* (*Carniola*).
Croat., Obloustka, potočni piškor.
Habit. All over Italy, watershed of the Adria; Lake of Garda, Monfalcone; the most common of the genus.
Quality. Flesh good when mature; young used as bait; attains seven to nine inches in length.

Sub-Class—LEPTOCARDII.

Fam. CIRROSTOMI.
Gen. BRANCHIOSTOMA, *Costa.*
350. *BRANCHIOSTOMA LANCEOLATUM*, Pall.
Branchiostoma lubricum, *Costa.*

The Lancelet.
Croat., Suličica.
Habit. Appears to be very rare in the Adria; has been caught off the island of Lésina (Dalmatia).

NEW FISHES OF THE ADRIATIC.*

Fam. CARCHARIIDÆ.
Gen. CARCHARIAS.
351. *CARCHARIAS LAMIA*, Risso.
Prionodon lamia, *Risso.*
Habit. Two specimens have been caught in Dalmatian waters, of which one is in the

Trieste Museum. (*See* "La Pesca," by Dr. Carlo de Marchesetti, Trieste, 1882, p. 137.)
352. *CARCHARIAS GLYPHIS*, M. & H.
Prionodon glyphis, *M. & H.*
Habit. One specimen in the Trieste Museum was caught in Dalmatian waters. (*See* as above, No. 351.)

Fam. LAMNIDÆ.
Gen. ODONTASPIS.
353. *ODONTASPIS TAURUS*, Raf.
Habit. Two specimens were fished in Dalmatian

* *See* the "Elenco dei Pesci dell' Adriatico" di Alberto Perugia, Milano, 1881, and "Fische welche in den Gewässern von Spalato beobachtet und überhaupt im Adriatischen Meere registrirt wurden" von Prof. George Kolombatović, Spalato, 1882, and "La Pesca lungo le coste Orientali dell' Adria" del Dr. Carlo de Marchesetti, Trieste, 1882.

waters in the summer of 1881. (*See* Kolom., "Fische," p. 56.)

Fam. SCYLLIIDÆ.
Gen. SCYLLIUM.

354. *SCYLLIUM ACANTHOMOTUM*, De Fil.
Dr. Günther considers this a fœtal example of *S. stellare*, or *canicula*.
Habit. One specimen, one decimètre long, found in the market at Spalato, March 30, 1882.—STEINDACHNER. (*See* Kolombatović, "Fische," p. 56.)

Fam. ACIPENSERIDÆ.
Gen. ACIPENSER.

355. *ACIPENSER STELLATUS*, Pall.
Habit. A specimen is in the Museum at Trieste, caught in the waters of Zara; hence it may be presumed that it inhabits the rivers of Dalmatia. (*See* Perugia's "Elenco," No. 211.)

Fam. PERCIDÆ.
Gen. SERRANUS.

356. *SERRANUS ACUTIROSTRIS*, C. & V.
Habit. A single specimen from the Istrian coast; not uncommon at Taranto. (*See* Perugia's "Elenco," No. 7, and Plate I.)

Gen. DENTEX.

357. *DENTEX FILOSUS*, Va.
Habit. Steindachner found a specimen at Spalato, December 7, 1881, and the fishermen say that it is not the first time this species has been caught there. (*See* Kolom., "Fische," p. 11.)
Note. Hitherto not mentioned in the Adriatic, nor by Canestrini in Italian waters; Doderlein found two specimens at Palermo.

358. *DENTEX MACROPHTHALMUS*, C. & V.
Habit. Not uncommon at Spalato in autumn and winter; probably to be found in other waters too; is easily overlooked by its outward resemblance to *Pagellus erythrinus*. Risso found it at Nice, Canestrini at Genoa, so it is probably common to the Mediterranean. (*See* Kolom., "Fische," p. 12.)

Fam. SPARIDÆ.
Gen. SARGUS.

359. *SARGUS VETULA*, C. & V.
Habit. Very rare, from two sp. of the Southern Adriatic. (*See* Perugia's "Elenco," No. 26.)

Gen. PAGRUS.

360. *PAGRUS EHRENBERGII*, C. & V.
Croat. Pagar prljaš (*Spalato*).
Habit. One specimen found by Professor Kolombatović in the fish-market at Spalato in 1873, and one specimen caught in Cattaro waters by the Italian cutter "Violante" in September, 1880. (*See* "Pesci delle Acque di Spalato" by Professor G. Kolombatović, Spalato, 1881.)

Gen. PAGELLUS.

361. *PAGELLUS ACARNE*, C. & V.
The Axillary Bream.
Croat., Grbić (*Spalato*).
Habit. Not common; every autumn some specimens are caught at Spalato, and sometimes a large number.—STEINDACHNER. (*See* Kolom., "Fische," p. 16.)

Fam. TRICHIURIDÆ.
Gen. THYRSITES.

362. *THYRSITES PRETIOSUS*, Cocco.
Habit. A specimen is mentioned by Professor Kalombatović as having been found in April, 1875, alive on the beach of the island of

Solta, where it had been washed ashore. This is supposed to be the first fish of this species which has been caught in these waters.

Fam. CARANGIDÆ.
Gen. TEMNODON.

363. *TEMNODON SALTATOR*, Bl.
Skipjack.
Habit. In the winter 1879-80 ten specimens were caught in the channel off Almissa (Dalmatia), and one specimen was found in the same year in the Trieste fish-market.— STEINDACHNER, GIGLIOLI. (*See* " Pesci di Spalato," by Prof. Kolombatović.)

Fam. CORYPHÆNIDÆ.
Gen. SCHEDOPHILUS, *Cocco*.

364. *SCHEDOPHILUS BOTTERI*, Steindachner.
S. Berthelotii, *Val.*
Habit. From a single specimen from Lésina in the Viennese Museum. (*See* Perugia's "Elenco," No. 73.)

Fam. SCOMBRIDÆ.
Gen. PELAMYS.

365. *PELAMYS UNICOLOR*, Gthr.
Habit. Very rare; a dried specimen in the Museum at Trieste. (*See* Perugia's "Elenco," No. 61.)

Gen. ECHENEIS.

366 *ECHENEIS SCUTATA*, Gthr.
Habit. From a single specimen described by Perugia in his "Elenco," No. 65, and Plate II., now in the Florence Collection of Vertebrates.

Fam. GOBIIDÆ.
Gen. GOBIUS.

367. *GOBIUS LESUEURI*, Risso.
Croat. Popauk (*Spalato*).

Habit. Common at Spalato; inhabits deep water on muddy beds (KOLOMBATOVIĆ); also common in the waters of Istria.—STEINDACHNER & NINNI.

368. *GOBIUS BUCHICHII*, Steindachner.
Croat. Glamočić (*Spalato*).
Habit. This new and quite distinct sp. is common (at Spalato) amongst the rocks on muddy beds partly covered with shingle.— KOLOMBATOVIĆ.

369. *GOBIUS ZEBRA*, Risso.
Croat. Glamoč (*Spalato*).
Habit. Not uncommon in spring along the shores of Spalato.—STEINDACHNER. Common at Trieste.—PERUGIA.

370. *GOBIUS PUSILLUS*, Can.
Habit. Zaole; rare. (*See* Perugia's "Elenco," No. 93.)

Gen. LATRUNCULUS.

371. *LATRUNCULUS PELLUCIDUS*, Nardo.
Croat. Mlič (*Spalato*).
Habit. Common along the coast from Traü, the Riviera delle Castella, as far as Vranjica, where the sea-water is tempered by the sweet water of the river Giadro.—KOLOMBATOVIĆ.
Season. Common from the commencement of spring to the end of summer; rare during the rest of the year.

Gen. CALLIONYMUS.

372. *CALLIONYMUS FASCIATUS*, C. & V.
Vulg., Guatta.
Habit. First cited by Ninni in the Adriatic; a specimen is in the Trieste Museum from Istria. (*See* Perugia's "Elenco," No. 103.)

Fam. BLENNIIDÆ.
Gen. BLENNIUS.
373. *BLENNIUS CANEVÆ*, Vinciguerra.
Croat. Prhna ribica (*Spalato*).
Habit. A new sp. recently described by Dr. Vinciguerra (Genoa) according to a specimen caught in the Gulf of Genoa. Since found in 1881 by Dr. Kolombatović in the Canale delle Castella, near Spalato; frequents the cavities of large rocks.
Season. Spring, summer, and autumn.
374. *BLENNIUS TRIGLOIDES*, C. & V.
Habit. Lésina.—GIGLIOLI. (*See* Perugia's "Elenco," No. 114.)

Fam. MUGILIDÆ.
Gen. MUGIL.
375. *MUGIL LABEO*, Cuv.
Habit. Rare; Ragusa.—GIGLIOLI. (*See* Perugia's "Elenco," No. 127.)

Fam. GADIDÆ.
Gen. GADUS.
376. *GADUS POUTASSOU*, Risso.
Merlangus albus, *Yarrell.*
Couch's Whiting, *Yarrell.*
Habit. Very rare. Ninni, *loco cit.* (*See* Perugia's "Elenco," No. 152.)

Gen. HYPSIPTERA.
377. *HYPSIPTERA ARGENTEA*, Gthr.
Lota argentea, *Bp.*
Habit. Professor Stossich mentions this sp. as having been met with at Trieste.

Fam. OPHIDIIDÆ.
Gen. FIERASFER.
378. *FIERASFER DENTATUS*, Cuv.
Drummond's Echiodon.
Habit. Two specimens of this species have been caught at Venice, and one at Spalato; two are in the Trieste Museum.—KOLOMBATOVIĆ.

Fam. PLEURONECTIDÆ.
Gen. ARNOGLOSSUS.
379. *ARNOGLOSSUS BOSCII*, Risso.
Habit. Lower Adriatic; quoted by Ninni, "Anacantini Basso Adriatico." (*See* Perugia's "Elenco," No. 168.)

Gen. SOLEA.
380. *SOLEA IMPAR*, Benn.
Solea lascaris, *Bp.*
Solea nasuta, *Nordm.*
Sogliola dal porro (*It.*).
Vulg., Sfogio dal porro (*Ven.*).
Habit. According to Ninni this sp. is very common in the lagoons of Venice and in the sea.
Season. June to October; rarely in winter.
Quality. Inferior to *S. vulgaris.*
Note. This sp. is entirely distinct from *Solea lascaris*, Risso (No. 264). (*See* Günther's "Catalogue of Fishes in the British Museum," also Professor Ninni's "Gli Anacantini del Mare Adriatico," and Professor Kolombatović's "Pesci delle Acque di Spalato.") Professor Stossich does not cite this sp.

Fam. SALMONIDÆ.
Gen. SALMO.
381. *SALMO TRUTTA*, L.
Habit. A specimen weighing three kilos was caught on the 24th December, 1879, off Vranjica, near Spalato.—GIGLIOLI. According to Professor Kolombatović it appears that, hitherto, no other author has mentioned this sp. as having been found in Mediterranean waters.

Fam. MURÆNIDÆ.
Gen. OPHICHTHYS.
382. *OPHICHTHYS CÆCUS*, L.
Habit. A specimen was caught off Zirona in October, 1881; the first one cited in the Adriatic. (*See* Kolombatović, "Fische," p. 50.)

PART IV.—SPECIAL LISTS OF FISHES.

A. List of Fresh-water Fishes.

Ref. No. in Syst. List	Fresh-water Fishes. English Names.	Fresh-water Fishes. Scientific Names.	Flesh Value	Venetian Watershed	Dalmatian Watershed	Special Habitat and Notes	Trentino	Lombardy	Found in most Fresh-water Courses	Found only in certain Fresh-water Courses	Enter the Sea	Found in Quiescent Waters and Running Streams	Found only in Running Streams	Prefer Brackish Waters, but do not enter the Sea
		a. GANOIDEI												
50	The Adriatic Sturgeon	Acipenser Naccarii	1											
51		,, Nardoi	1											
52	The broad-nosed Sturgeon	,, nasus	1											
53		,, huso	1											
54		,, Heckelii	1											
55	The common Sturgeon	,, sturio	1											
355		,, sichlaus	1			Zara								
		b. ACANTHOPTERYGII.												
56	The freshwater Perch	Perca fluviatilis	2											
58	The Pike-Perch	,, lucioperca	1	*a.* Rare										
158	The Miller's Thumb	Cottus gobio	2			*a.* According to De Betta								
151	The freshwater Goby	Gobius fluviatilis	2											
152		,, panizzæ	2											
153	The freshwater Blenny	Blennius vulgaris punctatissimus	2											
176		,, varus	2											
177	The Stickleback	Gastrosteus aculeatus	0											
196	Three-spined Stickleback	,, brachycentrus	0			Istria								
		c. ANACANTHINI.												
238	The Burbot	Lota vulgaris	2			Carniola								
		d. PHYSOSTOMI.												
381	The Salmon-Trout	Salmo trutta	1		*a.*	(*a.* Vranjica, near Syalato, according to Giglioli)								
310	The common Trout	,, fario ausonii	1											
311	Great Dalmatian Trout	,, dentex	1			River Isonzo (?)								
312		,, genivittatus	1			River Sala								
313	River Trout of Dalmatia	,, obtusirostris	1											
314	Trout of the Lake of Garda	,, carpio	1			{ Istria								
315	The Grayling	Thymallus vulgaris	2			{ Carniola								
272	The common Carp	Cyprinus carpio												

234

SYSTEMATIC LIST OF THE FAUNA.

1	2	3	4	5	6	7. According to Ic Betta	8	9	10	11	12	13	14	15
273	The Barbel	" kollarii	—	—	—		—	—	—	—	—	—	—	—
274		Barbus fluviatilis	2	—	—	River Isonzo	—	—	—	—	—	—	—	—
275		" plebejus	2	—	—	River Isonzo / Istria	—	—	—	—	—	—	—	—
276		" caninus	2	—	—		—	—	—	—	—	—	—	—
277	The Gudgeon	Audopyge Illugelii	—	—	—		—	—	—	—	—	—	—	—
278	The Wapper	Gobio fluviatilis	0	—	—		—	—	—	—	—	—	—	—
279		" uranoscopus	3	—	—		—	—	—	—	—	—	—	—
280		Leuciscus aula	3	—	—	River Sala	—	—	—	—	—	—	—	—
281		" adspersus		—	—		—	—	—	—	—	—	—	—
282		" pigus		—	—		—	—	—	—	—	—	—	—
283	The Vraw-fish	" cephalus	3	—	—	R. Tagliamento / River Sala	—	—	—	—	—	—	—	—
284	The Rudd	" svallize		—	—		—	—	—	—	—	—	—	—
285		" illyricus	3	—	—	River Isonzo	—	—	—	—	—	—	—	—
286		" erythrophthalmus	3	—	—	Cherso	—	—	—	—	—	—	—	—
287		" Ilcegeri	3	—	—	Istria	—	—	—	—	—	—	—	—
288		" muticellus		—	—		—	—	—	—	—	—	—	—
289		" Knerii		—	—		—	—	—	—	—	—	—	—
290		" ukliva		—	—		—	—	—	—	—	—	—	—
291	The Minnow	" turakyi	3	—	—		—	—	—	—	—	—	—	—
292		" phoxinus		—	—		—	—	—	—	—	—	—	—
293		Paraphoxinus alepidotus	3	—	—	Croatia	—	—	—	—	—	—	—	—
294	The Tench	" croaticus	2	—	(?)	In quiescent waters	—	—	—	—	—	—	—	—
295		Tinca vulgaris	3	—	—		—	—	—	—	—	—	—	—
296		Chondrostoma soëtta	3	—	—		—	—	—	—	—	—	—	—
297		" Genei		—	—		—	—	—	—	—	—	—	—
298		" Knerii	3	—	—	Istria (?)	—	—	—	—	—	—	—	—
299		" phoxinus		—	—		—	—	—	—	—	—	—	—
300		Abramis bipunctatus		—	—		—	—	—	—	—	—	—	—
301		Alburnus alburnellus	3	—	—		—	—	—	—	—	—	—	—
302	The Loach	" scoranza	2	—	—	Lake Scutari	—	—	—	—	—	—	—	—
303	The Spinous Loach	Nemachilus barbatulus	3	—	—		—	—	—	—	—	—	—	—
304		Cobitis taenia	0	—	—	Carniola / Istria	—	—	—	—	—	—	—	—
305		Cyprinodon calarianus	2	—	(?)	Zaole	—	—	—	—	—	—	—	—
309	The Pike, Jack	Esox lucius	2	—	—	Cherso / Carniola	—	—	—	—	—	—	—	—
319	The Allis-Shad	Clupea alosa	2	—	—	Lake Garda	—	—	—	—	—	—	—	—
320	The Twaite-Shad	" finta	3	—	—		—	—	—	—	—	—	—	—
323	The common Eel	Anguilla vulgaris	2	—	—	Narenta	—	—	—	—	—	—	—	—
324		" euryxtoma	2	—	—		—	—	—	—	—	—	—	—

c. CYCLOSTOMATA.

1	2	3	4	5	6	7	8	9	10	11	12	13	14	15
347	The Sea Lamprey	Petromyzon marinus	0	—	—		—	—	—	—	—	—	—	—
348	The River Lamprey	" fluviatilis	2	—	—		—	—	—	—	—	—	—	—
349	Planer's Lamprey	" Planeri	2	—	—		—	—	—	—	—	—	—	—

N. B.—The sign (—) in this table denotes that the heading applies to the fish opposite to which it appears.

B. LIST of BRITISH FISHES which are common to the ADRIATIC FAUNA.

24 FRESH-WATER FISHES.

The Sturgeon (*Acipenser sturio*), the Fresh-water Perch, the Bullhead, 2 Sticklebacks, the Burbot, the Carp, the Barbel, the Gudgeon, the Chubb, the Rudd, the Minnow, the Tench, the Loach, the Groundling, the Pike, the Trout, the Grayling, 2 Shads, the Eel, 3 Lampreys.

126 SEA FISHES.

14 *Sharks*, viz.: the Blue Shark, the Tope, the Hammer-head, the Smooth-hound, the Porbeagle, the Fox, the Basking Shark, the Grey Notidanus, 2 Spiny Dogs, 3 Dog-fishes, and the Angel-fish.

10 *Rays*, viz.: 2 Electric Rays, 5 Rays, 1 Sting Ray, and 2 Eagle Rays.

66 *Acanthopterygii*, viz.: the Basse, the Stone-basse, 2 Serranus, the Dentex, 1 Mendole, 2 Red Mullets, the Black Sea-bream, the Bogue, the Braize, Couch's Sea-bream, the Spanish Sea-bream, the Common Sea-bream, the Gilt-head, the Axillary Bream, the Umbrina, the Meagre, the Sword-fish, the Hair-tail, the Horse Mackerel, the Derbio, the Pilot-fish, the Boar-fish, the John Dory, the Black-fish, Ray's Sea-bream, 2 Mackerels, the Tunny, the Bonito, the Germon, the Pelamid, the Plain Bonito, the Remora, 2 Weevers, the Angler, 6 Gurnards, 1 Flying Gurnard, 7 Gobies, 1 Dragonet, the Band-fish, 4 Blennies, 1 Atherine, 3 Grey Mullets, the Trumpet-fish, 3 Suck-fishes.

4 *Acanthopterygii Pharyngognathi*, viz.: 4 Wrasses.

18 *Anacanthini*, viz: the Whiting, the Poor, the Bib, Couch's Whiting, the Hake, the Forked Hake, 2 Rock Lings, the Bearded Ophidium, Drummond's Echiodon, the Turbot, the Brill, the Topknot, the Scald-fish, the Plaice, 3 Soles.

6 *Physostomi*, viz.: the Gar-pike, the Saury-pike, the Anchovy, the Pilchard, the Conger-eel, the Murry.

4 *Lophobranchii*, viz.: 3 Pipe-fishes, 1 Sea-horse.

3 *Plectognathi*, viz.: 1 File-fish, 2 Sun-fishes.

1 *Leptocardii*, viz.: the Lancelet.

C. LIST of FIVE FISHES *belonging exclusively to the* ADRIATIC FAUNA.

Reference No. to Systematic List.	Description.	Reference No. to Systematic List.	Description.
42	Trygon thalassia.	163	Gobius quadrivittatus.
77	Cantharus brama.	260	Pleuronectes italicus.
155	Gobius Knerii.		

D. LIST of THIRTY-ONE FISHES *which are only quite accidentally met with in the Adriatic.*

Reference No. to Systematic List.	Description.	Reference No. to Systematic List.	Description.
11	Odontaspis ferox.	122	Scomber pneumatophorus.
353	,, taurus.	126	Thynnus pelamys.
13	Selache maxima.	127	,, alalonga.
354	Scyllium acanthomotum.	366	Echeneis scutata.
24	Echinorhinus spinosus.	165	Gobius elongatus.
37	Raja radula.	167	Callionymus lyra.
45	Pteroplatea altavela.	184	Blennius pholis (?).
49	Dicerobatis Giornæ.	206	Lophotes cepedianus.
355	Acipenser stellatus.	211	Labrus maculatus.
356	Serranus acutirostris.	234	Gadus luscus.
360	Pagrus Ehrenbergii.	377	Hypsiptera argentea.
93	Sebastes imperialis.	241	Motella mustela.
102	Trichiurus lepterus.	259	Pleuronectes platessa.
362	Thyrsites pretiosus.	271	Aulopus filamentosus.
364	Schedophilus Botteri.	381	Salmo trutta.
120	Ausonia Cuvieri.		

E. List of Fourteen Fishes which belong more especially to the Venetian Fauna.

Reference No. to Systematic List.	Description.	Reference No. to Systematic List.	Description.
33	Raja asterias.	259	Pleuronectes platessa.
34	,, fullonica.	380	Solea impar.
68	Mræna jusculum.	304	Cyprinodon calaritanus.
165	Gobius elongatus.	333	Siphonostoma rotundatum.
200	Lepadogaster listellus.	336	Syngnathus tænionotus.
376	Gadus poutassou.	337	,, abaster.
246	Ophidium vassalli.	338	,, Agassizii.

F. List of Forty-eight Fishes which belong more especially to the Dalmatian Fauna.

Reference No. to Systematic List.	Description.	Reference No. to Systematic List.	Description.
351	Carcharias lamia.	154	Gobius quagga.
352	,, glyphis.	155	,, Knerii.
9	Lamna Spallanzanii.	160	,, guttatus.
353	Odontaspis taurus.	163	,, quadrivittatus.
354	Scyllium acanthomotum.	368	,, Buchichii.
23	Spinax niger.	166	Latrunculus albus.
48	Rhinoptera marginata.	371	,, pellucidus.
355	Acipenser stellatus.	175	Blennius rouxi.
60	Anthias sacer.	183	,, galerita.
62	Serranus cabrilla.	373	,, Canevræ.
66	Dentex gibbosus.	374	,, trigloides.
357	,, filosus.	201	Lepadogaster Brownii.
358	,, macrophthalmus.	206	Lophotes cepedianus.
69	Mræna zebra.	230	Julis speciosus.
82	Sargus vulgaris.	241	Motella mustela.
360	Pagrus Ehrenbergii.	244	Ophidium Broussonetii.
361	Pagellus acarne.	257	Rhomboidichtys podas.
93	Sebastes imperialis.	258	,, mancus.
102	Trichiurus lepturus.	381	Salmo trutta.
362	Thyrsites pretiosus.	318	Clupea aurita.
104	Caranx dentex.	328	Ophichthys imberbis.
112	Zeus pungio.	382	,, cræcus.
128	Pelamys sarda.	329	Muræna helena.
147	Dactylopterus volitans.	350	Branchiostoma lanceolatum.

G. List of Twenty-nine Fishes *which have hitherto been caught only on the south coast of Dalmatia.*

Reference No. to Systematic List.	Description.	Reference No. to Systematic List.	Description.
8	Lamna cornubica.	242	Pteridium atrum.
26	Squatina oculata.	245	Ophidium Rochii.
65	Apogon imberbis.	247	Fierasfer acus.
359	Sargus vetula.	248	Ammodytes siculus.
89	Pagellus centrodontus.	249	Macrurus cœlorhyncus.
100	Histiophorus belone.	379	Arnoglossus boscii.
364	Schedophilus Botteri.	262	Solea ocellata.
175	Blennius rouxi.	269	Ammopleurops lacteus.
185	Cristiceps argentatus.	270	Saurus griseus.
375	Mugil labeo.	271	Aulopus filamentosus.
205	Leptopterygius piger.	306	Scombresox Rondeletii.
208	Trachypterus repandus.	316	Argentina sphyræna.
225	Crenilabrus tinca.	330	Muræna unicolor.
227	Novacula cultrata.	340	Nerophis ophidion.
228	Julis pavo.		

H. List of Fishes *which belong to the class of* Minutaja, *or* Misto, *i.e., Fishes which are thrown together, and sold as one class.*

Reference No. to Systematic List.	Description.	Reference No. to Systematic List.	Description.
59	Centropristis hepatus.	210	Labrus turdus.
148–166	Gobius sp., excepting G. capito.	222	Crenilabrus griseus.
167–171	Callionymus sp.	252	Phrynorhombus unimaculatus.
173–185	Blennius sp., excepting B. gattorugine and B. ocellaris.	253	Arnoglossus laterna.
		255	,, Grohmanni.
186	Tripterygium nasus.	265	Solea variegata.
199–205	Lepadogaster sp.		

I. TABLE of the FRESH-WATER and SEA FISHES, showing the number of Species belonging to each Family.

	Names of Families.	Fresh-water Fishes.			Sea Fishes.			TOTAL.		
		Family.	Genus.	Species.	Family.	Genus.	Species.	Family.	Genus.	Species.
	CHONDROPTERYGII—SHARKS.									
1	Carchariidæ (Blue Shark, Tope, Hammerhead, Hound)	...	...	...	1	4	9	1	4	9
2	Lamnidæ (Porbeagle, Fox-Shark, Basking-Shark)	...	...	...	1	5	7	1	5	7
3	Notidanidæ	...	...	...	1	1	3	1	1	3
4	Scylliidæ (Dog-fishes)	...	...	...	1	2	4	1	2	4
5	Spinacidæ (Spiny Dogs)	...	...	...	1	4	5	1	4	5
6	Rhinidæ (Angel-fish)	...	...	...	1	1	2	1	1	2
	TOTAL	...	...	...	6	17	30	6	17	30
	RAYS.									
1	Torpedinidæ (Electric Rays)	...	...	...	1	1	3	1	1	3
2	Rajidæ (Rays and Skates)	...	...	...	1	1	12	1	1	12
3	Trygonidæ (Sting-Rays)	...	...	...	1	2	4	1	2	4
4	Myliobatidæ (Eagle-Rays)	...	...	...	1	3	4	1	3	4
	TOTAL	...	...	...	4	7	23	4	7	23
	GANOIDEI.									
1	Sturgeons	1	1	7	...	...	...	1	1	7
	ACANTHOPTERYGII.									
1	Percidæ (Perch tribe) / Pristipomatidæ	1	2	2	1	6 / 3	9 / 10	1	8 / 3	11 / 10
2	Mullidæ (Red Mullets)	...	...	...	1	1	2	1	1	2
3	Sparidæ (Sea-breams)	...	...	...	1	8	20	1	8	20
4	Scorpænidæ (Scorpions)	...	...	...	1	2	3	1	2	3
5	Sciænidæ (Meagres)	...	...	...	1	3	3	1	3	3
6	Xyphiidæ (Sword-fishes)	...	...	...	1	2	2	1	2	2
7	Trichiuridæ (Scabbard-fishes, Hair-tails)	...	...	...	1	3	3	1	3	3
8	Carangidæ (Horse Mackerels, Pilot-fish, Boar-fish)	...	...	...	1	7	9	1	7	9
9	Cyttidæ (John Dory)	...	...	...	1	1	2	1	1	2
10	Stromateidæ	...	...	...	1	2	4	1	2	4
11	Coryphænidæ (Dolphins)	...	...	...	1	4	5	1	4	5
12	Scombridæ (Mackerel, Tunny, Bonito, Remora)	...	...	...	1	5	12	1	5	12
13	Trachinidæ (Weevers, Star-gazers)	...	...	...	1	2	5	1	2	5
14	Pediculati (Anglers)	...	...	...	1	1	2	1	1	2
15	Cottidæ (Gurnards, Bull-heads)	1	1	1	1	2	7	1	3	8
16	Cataphracti (Flying Gurnards)	...	...	...	1	2	2	1	2	2
17	Gobiidæ (Gobies, Dragonets)	1	1	3	1	3	27	1	3	30
18	Cepolidæ (Band-fishes)	...	...	...	1	1	1	1	1	1
19	Blenniidæ (Blennies)	1	1	2	1	3	14	1	3	16
20	Sphyrænidæ (Spet)	...	...	...	1	1	1	1	1	1
21	Atherinidæ (Atherines)	...	...	...	1	1	3	1	1	3
22	Mugilidæ (Mullets)	...	...	...	1	1	6	1	1	6
23	Gasterostidæ (Sticklebacks)	1	1	2	...	...	...	1	1	2
24	Centriscidæ (Trumpet-fish)	...	...	...	1	1	1	1	1	1
25	Gobiesocidæ (Suck-fishes)	...	...	...	1	2	7	1	2	7
26	Lophotidæ	...	...	...	1	1	1	1	1	1
27	Trachypteridæ (Ribbon-fishes)	...	...	...	1	1	2	1	1	2
	TOTAL	5	6	10	26	69	163	27	73	173
	Carried forward	6	7	17	36	93	216	38	98	233

SYSTEMATIC LIST OF THE FAUNA.

INDEX to *Fresh-water Fishes and Sea Fishes* (continued).

Names of Families.	Freshwater Fishes.			Sea Fishes.			Total.		
	Family.	Genus.	Species.	Family.	Genus.	Species.	Family.	Genus.	Species.
Brought forward ...	6	7	17	36	93	216	38	98	233
ACANTHOPTERYGII PHARYNGO-GNATHI.									
1 Pomacentridæ (Coral-fishes) ...	...	...	...	1	1	1	1	1	1
2 Labridæ (Wrasses) ...	...	...	...	1	6	21	1	6	21
Total ...	...	...	...	2	7	22	2	7	22
ANACANTHINI.									
1 Gadidæ (Cod tribe) ...	1	1	1	1	5	12	1	6	13
2 Ophidiidæ (Sand-Eels, &c.) ...	...	...	...	1	4	8	1	4	8
3 Macruridæ ...	...	...	...	1	1	1	1	1	1
4 Pleuronectidæ (Flat-fishes) ...	...	...	...	1	8	22	1	8	22
Total ...	1	1	1	4	18	43	4	19	44
PHYSOSTOMI.									
1 Scopelidæ	...	...	...	1	2	2	1	2	2
2 Cyprinidæ (Carp tribe)...	1	12	32	...	...	...	1	12	32
3 Cyprinodontidæ...	1	1	1	...	...	...	1	1	1
4 Scombresocidæ (Gar-pike, Saury, Flying-fish)	...	...	...	1	3	4	1	3	4
5 Esocidæ (Pike) ...	1	1	1	...	...	...	1	1	1
6 Salmonidæ (Salmon) ...	1	2	7	1	1	1	1	3	8
7 Clupeidæ (Herring tribe)	1	1	2	1	2	4	1	2	6
8 Murænidæ (Eel tribe) ...	1	1	2	1	4	7	1	5	9
Total ...	6	18	45	5	12	18	8	29	63
LOPHOBRANCHII.									
1 Sygnathidæ (Pipe-fishes, Sea-Horses)	...	...	...	1	4	13	1	4	13
PLECTOGNATHI.									
1 Scleroderml (File-fishes) ...	...	...	...	1	1	1	1	1	1
2 Gymnodontes (Sun-fishes) ...	...	...	...	1	1	2	1	1	2
Total ...	...	...	...	2	2	3	2	2	3
CYCLOSTOMATA.									
1 Petromyzontidæ (Lampreys) ...	1	1	3	...	...	...	1	1	3
LEPTOCARDII.									
1 Cirrostomi (the Lancelet) ...	...	...	...	1	1	1	1	1	1
Grand Total ...	14	27	66	51	137	316	57	161	382

Part V.—LIST OF INVERTEBRATA.*

MOLLUSCA.

Class I. CEPHALOPODA.

Fam. Octopodidæ.

Gen. Octopus, *Cuv.*

1. *OCTOPUS VULGARIS*, Lamark.
   The Poulp or Octopus.
   La Poulpe.
   Gemeiner Vielfuss, grosser Tintenfisch, grosse Sprutte.
   Vulg., Folpo, Folpo todero, Polpo. Folpi toti (*Ven.*).
   Croat., Mèrkačić, Hobot, Karakatnica, Hobotnica, Ubotnica.
   Muzgavac (*Spalato*).
   Habit. General and common, but not much prized.

Gen. Eledone, *Leach.*

2. *ELEDONE MOSCHATA*, Risso.
   Die Bisamsprutte, Bisam Tintenfisch.
   Vulg., Folpo, Folpo da risi (*Ven.*), Muscardino, Muscarolo, (*Ven.*).
   Croat., Mèrkač, Hobotnica, Pèrč.
   Habit. General and common; much prized by the poor.

Fam. II. Loligidæ.

Gen. Loligo, *Lam.*

3. *LOLIGO VULGARIS*, Lam.
   The Squid.
   Calmar, Rautenförmiger Tintenfisch.
   Vulg., Calamajo, Calamaro, Kalimar, Kalamar, Totano.
   Croat., Liganj.
   Lignja ili obična crna kraka (*Spalato*).
   Pocuranac (*Fiume*).
   Habit. General and common; the most valued of the Cephalopods.

4. *LOLIGO SAGITTATA*, Lam.
   Pfeilförmiger Tintenfisch.
   Vulg., Calamaro todero, Calamar toto.
   Habit. Not common and little prized; Gulf of Venice.

Gen. Sepiola, *Rond.*

5. *SEPIOLA RONDELETII*, Leach.
   Kleine Sprutte, Kleiner Tintenfisch.
   Vulg., Sepiola, Sepolina, Zottolina, Zottolo, Calmaretto, Seppetta.
   Croat., Sipica.
   Habit. General and common, and prized as food.

Fam. III. Sepiadæ, *d'Orb.*

Gen. Sepia, *L.*

6. *SEPIA OFFICINALIS*, L.
   Cuttle-fish, Black-fish.
   La Seiche.

---

* This list comprises only the more important kinds, viz., those which have a commercial value, or boast of a local name.

Der Tintenfisch, Sepia, Sprutte.
Vulg., Seppa, Sépa, Seppia.
Croat., Sipa.
Habit. General and common.

Class II. CEPHALOPHORA.
  Fam. I. MURICIDÆ, *Adams.*
    Gen. MUREX, *Lam.*

7. *MUREX BRANDARIS*, L.
  Brandhornschnecke.
  Vulg., Garùsolo, Garùsolo mascio.
  Bullo maschio, Murice, Scoglio brandare (*Ven.*).
  Croat., Moruzga, Volak, Volina.
  Habit. General and common; on muddy beds in fifteen fathoms at all seasons, and is eaten by the lower classes.

8. *MUREX TRUNCULUS*, L.
  Leistenschnecke, Purpurschnecke, Stumpfe Leistenschnecke.
  Vulg., Garùsolo, Garusolo feména, Porpora, Porco, Garusa, Bullo femmina, Murice, Scoglio troncato.
  Croat., Kravica.
  Habit. As above, but inferior as food.

  Fam. II. BUCCINIDÆ, *Deshayes.*
    Gen. BUCCINUM, *L.* (Nassa, *Lam.*).

9. *NASSA RETICULATA*, L.
  A Whelk.
  Vulg., Berolla del tenero.
  Croat., Iskra.
  Habit. Cherso, Trieste; general and common.

10. *CYCLOPE NERITEA*, L.
  Little whelk.
  Gemeines Wellenhorn.
  Vulg., Buligone.
  Croat., Klapunice.
  Habit. Trieste, Fiume, Cherso; common.

Fam. III. CASSIDACEA, *Adams.*
  Gen. CASSIDARIA, *Lam.*

11. *CASSIDARIA ECHINOPHORA*, L.
  Knotenhorn.
  Cassidaria tuberculosa (*It.*).
  Vulg., Porcelletta, Porcelletta.
  Croat., Kačiga.
  Habit. Off the coast of Grignano, Pirano, Capo d'Istria; also at Venice, Ravenna, Cherso, Zara, Lésina; rare in seventeen to twenty-five fathoms.

Fam. IV. DOLIIDÆ.
  Gen. DOLIUM, *Lam.*

12. *DOLIUM GALEA*, L.
  Vulg., Porcella.
  Habit. Deep water; Gulf of Trieste; rare in the Quarnero; more common in Dalmatia at Zara, Spalato, Ragusa, Lissa, Lésina.

Fam. V. CERITHIIDÆ.
  Gen. CERITHIUM, *Brug.*

13. *CERITHIUM VULGATUM*, Brug.
  Gemeine Nadelschnecke.
  Ceritio comune (*It.*).
  Vulg., Caragolo longo (*Ven.*), Campanari (*Tr.*).
  Croat., Vretenača, Krapulj.
  Habit. Common in the lagoons of Venice, where it is much eaten by the poor; also found in the salines of Zaole and Pirano in one to five feet of water, and in greater depths on muddy beds; Quarnero.

Fam. VI. STROMBIDÆ, *d'Orb.*
  Gen. APORRHAIS, *Aldrov.*

14. *APORRHAIS PES PELECANI*, Dill.
  Der Pelicansfuss.
  Pié di pellicano (*It.*).
  Vulg., Zamarugolo.

Habit. Sometimes caught in large quantities and brought to market; inhabits depths of twenty-five fathoms on muddy beds; Trieste, Quarnero; general.

Fam. VII. TURRITELLIDÆ, *Clarck.*
Gen. TURRITELLA, *Lam.*
15. *TURRITELLA COMMUNIS*, Risso.
Thurmschnecke, Thurmschraube.
Vulg., Campanile.
Croat., Bumburak, bamburač, Tornjić, Kampanil.
Habit. Common in the greater depths (twenty-five to thirty fathoms) on muddy beds; Trieste, Quarnero.

Fam. VIII. TROCHIDÆ, *Adams.*
Gen. I. TROCHUS, *L.*
16. *TROCHUS CONOLUS*, L.
Top-shells.
Eckmund.
Vulg., Caragolo (*generic*).
Croat., Narikle, čigraši (*generic*).
Habit. In twenty-five fathoms; Grignano, Punta Grossa, Pirano, Rovigno, Trieste, Quarnero, Dalmatia; not uncommon.

17. *TROCHUS BIASOLETTI*, Phil.
Kreiselschnecke.
Caragolo tondo (*It.*).
Vulg., Trottolo bianchiccia.
Croat., Nanarica, Nanarić.
Habit. Common on the limestone beds in six to ten fathoms off Sestiane; Quarnero, Zara.

18. *TROCHUS ADRIATICUS*, Phil.
Adriatischer Kreisel.
Caragolo (*It.*).
Vulg., Caragoletti da galanterie (*Ven.*).
Habit. Littoral univalves found on *algæ* in the salines of Zaole, Capo d'Istria, Pirano; shells used as women's ornaments.

19. *TROCHUS VARIUS*, L.
Geschneckter Eckmund.
Caragolo tondo (*It.*).
Vulg., Naridola.
Habit. Zaole, Barcola, Rovigno, Quarnero; rare.

20. *TROCHUS UMBILICARIS*, L.
Caragolo tondo di mar (*It.*).
Habit. Rare; Rovigno, Quarnero, Dalmatia.

21. *TROCHUS ZIZYPHINUS*, L.
Jujuben Kreisel.
Caragolo, Naridola grande (*It.*).
Habit. Rare; on sandy beds in twenty fathoms; Capo d'Istria, Pirano, Venice, Zara.

Gen. II. MONODONTA, *Lam.*
22. *MONODONTA FRAGAROIDES*, Lam.
Trochus tessellatus, *Gm.*
Bunte Kreiselschnecke.
Naridola (*It.*).
Habit. Littoral univalves found more or less all along the coast adhering to stones; edible.

23. *MONODONTA ARTICULATA*, Lam.
Grüne Kreiselschnecke.
Naridola (*It.*).
Habit. As above; Isola, Trieste, Venice, Zara, Curzola.

Gen. III. TURBO, *L.*
24. *TURBO RUGOSUS*, L.
Runzeliger Rundmund.
Vulg., Occhio di Santa Lucia.
Habit. Common on limestone beds in eight to ten fathoms; Quarnero, Isola, Pirano; little eaten; shells used as women's ornaments.

Fam. IX. HALIOTIDÆ.
Gen. HALIOTIS, *L.*
25. *HALIOTIS TUBERCULATA*, L.
Seeohr, Meerohr, gemeines Meerohr.

SYSTEMATIC LIST OF THE FAUNA. 245

Vulg., Orecchio di San Pietro.
Croat., Zlatinka, Puzlatka (*Spalato*).
Habit. Attached to stones in shallow water; Pirano, Zaole; common in the south of Istria; Quarnero.

Fam. X. FISSURELLIDÆ.
Gen. FISSURELLA, *Brug.*
26. *FISSURELLA COSTARIA*, Desh.
Spaltschnecke, Schlitzschnecke.
Vulg., Pantalena, Santalena.
Croat., Priliepak, Razporka, čupka (*Spalato*).
Habit. Isola, Pirano, Rovigno, Dalmatia; edible and pretty common in medium depths, attached to stones.

Fam. XI. PATELLIDÆ.
Gen. PATELLA, *L.*
27. *PATELLA VULGATA*, L.
Common Limpet.
Gemeine Schüsselschnecke, Napfschnecke.
Vulg., Pantalena, Santalena.
Croat., Priliepak, Lupar, Bljudica.
Habit. Quarnero.

Fam. XII. CHITONIDÆ.
Gen. CHITON, *L.*
28. *CHITON SICULUS*, Gray.
Käferschnecke.
Vulg., Salissoni cape.
Croat., Babuška, Priliepak.
Habit. Found attached to stones and *Pinnæ*, off Zaole, Capo d'Istria, Pirano, Quarnero; in one to eight fathoms.

Fam. XIII. DENTALIDÆ, *d'Orb.*
Gen. DENTALIUM, *L.*
29. *DENTALIUM ENTALIS*, L.
Der Wolfszahn.
Croat., Slonov zub.
Habit. Rare; Pirano, Quarnero, Dalmatia.

Fam. XIV. BULLIDÆ.
Gen. BULLA, *L.*
30. *BULLA LIGNARIA*, L.
Meerblasenschnecke.
Vulg., Berolla di mar.
Croat., Zlatenka.
31. *BULLA HYDATIS*, L.
Vulg., Oliva. ·
Croat., Michurača.
Habit. Near Trieste, amongst *zostera* and *algæ* on limestone beds; Quarnero, Dalmatia.

Fam. XV. APLYSIIDÆ.
Gen. APLYSIA, *L.*
32. *APLYSIA DEPILANS*, L.
Sea-hare.
Der Seehase, die Seelunge.
Lepre marino (*It.*).
Vulg., Coghe de mar.
Croat., Morski zec, Zečac.
Habit. Barcola, Servola, in shallow waters; Quarnero, Venice.

Fam. XVI. HELICIDÆ, *Gray.*
Gen. HELIX, *L.*
Gen. CLAUSILIA, *Drap.*
Snail-shells.
Vulg., Buovoli.
Croat., Puži, Pužići, Spuži, *generic* (*Spalato*).
33. *HELIX SECERNENDA*, Rossm.
Croat., Glevoć.
Habit. Castelli di Spalato.
34. *HELIX VERMICULATA*, Müller.
Croat., Puž, Spuž.
Habit. Castelli di Spalato.
35. *HELIX APERTA*, Born.
Croat., Kravica.
Habit. Castelli di Spalato.

2 K 2

36. *HELIX PONZOLZI*, Michel.
   Croat., Crni spuž, Zenski spuž, Pizdarica.
   Habit. Ragusa.
37. *HELIX SETIGERA*, Ziegler.
   Croat., Gubavac.
   Habit. Ragusa.
38. *HELIX SETOSA*, Ziegler.
   Croat., Runjavac.
   Habit. Montano di Zara.
39. *ZONITES ACIES*, Partsch.
   Croat., Magavetàs.
   Habit. Castelli di Spalato.
40. *ZONITES ALBANICUS*, Ziegler.
   Croat., Pasjak.
   Habit. Duave, near Almissa.
41. *HYALINA CELLARIA*, Müll.
   Croat., Poljski slemak.

Class III. ACEPHALA.
   Fam. I. OSTREIDÆ, Brod.
       Gen. OSTREA, L.
   The Oyster.
   L'huitre.
   Die Auster.
   Ostrica.
42. *OSTREA ADRIATICA*, Lam.
   Ostrea stentina, *Payeandeau.*
   Ostrica dell' Adriatico (*It.*).
   Vulg., Ostrica di palo.
   Habit. Limestone beds; not in the lagoons or oyster-ponds.
43. *OSTREA LAMELLOSA*, Brocchi.
   Ostrea Cyrnusii, *Payeandeau.*
   Vulg., Ostrica a lamelle (*It.*).
   Habit. Reared in ponds; attains to large dimensions, and is much prized; Trieste.
44. *OSTREA EDULIS*, L.
   Croat., Oštriga; Kamenica (*Spalato*), generic terms.

Varieties:—
   a. Depressa, *Phillipi.*
       Ostrica comune depressa (*It.*).
       Vulg., Ostrichino.
   Habit. Lagoons of Venice and Zaole, attached to wood and the mussels *Pinna* and *Mytilus*; a small sp., but very savoury and much liked.
   b. Cristata, *Auct.* (?), *Born.* (?).
       Ostrica comune cristata (*It.*).
   Habit. Lagoons, ponds, harbours; on limestone and muddy beds; is the only kind which is found in the Quarnero.
   c. Falcata, *Chiereghin.*
       Ostrica comune falcata (*It.*).
   Habit. As above.

Fam. II. PECTINIDÆ, L.
       Gen. I. PECTEN, L.
45. *PECTEN JACOBÆUS*, L.
   Scallop.
   Pilgermuschel, Jacobsmuschel.
   Capa santa, (*It.*).
   Pellegrina di San Giacomo.
   Croat., Pokrovača, Jakovska kapica (*Spalato*).
   Habit. Grado, Pirano, Quarnero; much sought for on account of the shells, which are exported; general and common.
46. *PECTEN OPERCULARIS*, L.
   Pettine operculare (*It.*).
   Vulg., Canestrello (*generic*).
   Croat., Pokrovača poklopita.
   Habit. Formerly much more common than at present; lagoons of Venice; edible; one of the most elegant of the genus; Quarnero, Trieste.
47. *PECTEN GLABER*, L.
   Glatte Kamm-muschel.
   Pettine vario (*It.*).

Vulg., as above.
Croat., Pokrovača gladka, Kapica, Migavica.
Habit. Common in the Trieste market mixed with No. 49; Quarnero.

48. *PECTEN VARIUS*, L.
Gescheckte Kamm-muschel.
Pettine vario (*It.*).
Vulg., Canestrello de mar, C. da una recia (*Ven.*), Capa santa piccola.
Habit. Common in the lagoons, and at Zaole, Capo d'Istria, Pirano, Cherso, etc., in shallow water amongst sponges, on muddy beds; Quarnero.

49. *PECTEN POLYMORPHUS*, Brown.
Vulg., Canestrello.
Habit. Common in the lagoons and on sandy beds on the Istrian coast, amongst *zostera*, *algæ*, and sponges; off Zaole, Pirano, etc.; Quarnero.

Gen. II. LIMA, *Brug.*

50. *LIMA INFLATA*, Lam.
Feilenmuschel, Raspelmuschel.
Vulg., Sorbolo di mar.
Croat., Pilača.
Habit. Deep limestone beds (twenty-five fathoms), also on the sandy beds off Zaole, Capo d'Istria, Pirano; edible, but not much prized; general and common.

Gen. III. SPONDYLUS, *Lam.*

51. *SPONDYLUS GÆDEROPUS*, L.
Gemeine Klappmuschel, Lazarus Klappe.
Vulg., Gaidero, Copiza, Iardon.
Croat., Kopito, Kopitnjak.
Habit. Zaule, Capo d'Istria, Pirano, Rovigno, in two to four fathoms; general and common, particularly in the south of Istria on limestone beds.

52. *SPONDYLUS ACULEATUS*, Delle Chia.
Nomenclature. As 51.
Habit. Rovigno, Quarnero; rare; both sp. are edible, but seldom come to market.

Fam. III. AVICULIDÆ, *Swainson*.

Gen. PINNA, *L.*

53. *PINNA NOBILIS*, Weinkauff.
Steckmuschel.
Pinna nobile (*It.*).
Vulg., Astóra, Astúra, Lastúra, Ostúra, Astúra, Stura, Palóstrega di porto (*Ven.*), Piede de caval (*Fiume*).
Croat., Butovka, Ljuštura, Peritska (*Spalato*).
Habit. Lagoons of Venice and elsewhere on muddy beds; Quarnero; this and other sp. of Pinna, such as *P. rudis* (L.), and *P. squamosa* (Gm.), are little eaten.

Fam. IV. MYTILIDÆ, *Flem.*

Gen. I. MYTILUS, *L.*

54. *MYTILUS EDULIS*, L.
Common Mussel.
Moule of the French.
Gemeine Miesmuchel.
Mitilo commestibile (*It.*).
Vulg., Pedocchio, Pedocchio di mar, Pecocchio, Peocio.
Croat., Kokošica, Klapunica. Šenac (*Fiume*). Daguja (*Novigrad*), Klapavica (*Spalato*).
Habit. On muddy and sandy beds in the lagoons of Venice (those hailing from the Royal Arsenal at Venice being especially prized), and very numerous between Grado and the mouth of the river Tagliamento in a depth of thirteen to fifteen fathoms and about nine miles distant from the shore, also off the reefs (*Scogli*) of Istria. *M. flavius* (Poli) is not

uncommon in these waters, and *M. minimus* (Poli) is common everywhere, and is found attached to rocks, oysters, *modiola*, etc.

Gen. II. LITHODOMUS, *Lam.*
55. *LITHODOMUS LITHOPHAGUS*, Lam.
The Date-shell.
See- oder Stein-dattel.
Litodomo litofago (*It.*).
Vulg., Dattolo di pietra, Dattolo di mar, Dattero di mar (*Ven.*).
Pevarone (*Ven.*).
Croat., Pèrstenac, Prstenci, Prstići (*Spalato*).
Habit. Pretty general and common in the south of Istria and the Quarnero, and on the eastern coast of the Adriatic; rare on the western coast of Istria, and not known at Venice; found imbedded in the limestone rock; is much esteemed as food.

Gen. III. MODIOLA, *Lam.*
56. *MODIOLA BARBATA*, L.
Bärtige Miesmuschel.
Modiola barbata (*It.*).
Vulg., Mussolo, Muzzolo, Pedocchio peloso, Peocio peloso (*Ven.*).
Habit. General and common on muddy and sandy beds; little esteemed as food, and only eaten by the poor.

Fam. V. ARCACIDÆ, *d'Orb.*
Gen. I. ARCA, *L.*
57. *ARCA NOÆ*, L.
Noah's Ark, Noah's Lighter.
Arche de Noë.
Noah's Arche, Das Schiffchen.
Arca di Noè (*It.*).
Vulg., Coffano di grotta (*Ven.*), Mussolo (*Tr.*, *Fiume*).
Croat., Kunjka, Mušul, Pizdica; školjak (*Ragusa*).

Habit. Pretty general and common; has a disagreeable flavour and is only eaten by the poor.

58. *ARCA BARBATA*, L.
Fringed Ark.
Bart Arche, Bärtige Arche.
Arche barbue.
Arca barbata (*It.*).
Vulg., Cofano del duro.
Habit. Fissures of rocks; Venice, Cherso, Salvore, Lussin, Dalmatia.

Gen. II. PECTUNCULUS, *Lam.*
59. *PECTUNCULUS GLYCIMERIS*, L.
Orbicular Ark.
Veränderliche Sammtmuschel, glatte Arche, Gogelhöpflein.
Arche glycyméride, Bignet, Vovan.
Arca liscia (*It.*).
Vulg., Pié d'asino.
Croat., Konjina, čaška.
Habit. Pretty common on muddy and sandy beds; Isola, Pirano, Pago; rare at Ragusa and Lésina.

Gen. III. NUCULA, *Lam.*
60. *NUCULA MAGARITACEA*, Lam.
Vulg., Fave, Sangue de Turco (*It.*).
Habit. Venice, Trieste, Muggia, Pirano, Cherso, Unie, Val Cassione, Zara, etc., on muddy bed; rare.

Fam. VI. CHAMIDÆ.
Gen. I. CHAMA, *L.*
61. *CHAMA GRYPHOIDES*, L.
Gienmuschel.
Vulg., Ostreghetta del duro.
Habit. Pretty common and general; Quarnero.

Fam. VII. CARDIIDÆ, *Brod.*
Gen. I. CARDIUM, *L.*
62. *CARDIUM EDULE*, L.
Common Cockle.

Essbare Herzmuschel.
Cardium commestibile (*It.*).
Vulg., Capa tonda (*Ven.*).
Croat., Kunjka, čančica; Srčavka (*Spalato*).
Habit. General and common, on muddy and sandy beds in shallow water, imbedded in the mud or sand; is the best of the genus, and forms the object of profitable fishing, especially in the lagoons of Venice; it is best in the winter.

63. *CARDIUM CLODIENSE*, Renier.
Cardio di Chioggia (*It.*).
Vulg., Capa tonda di valle.
Habit. Lagoons of Venice.

64. *CARDIUM RUSTICUM*, L.
Runzelige Herzmuschel.
Vulg., Capa tonda rigata, Cocciola.
Croat., Kapica, Solinarka.
Habit. One of the most common of the genus at Trieste; found in shallow water on muddy beds at Zaole, Capo d'Istria, Pirano, etc.

65. *CARDIUM TUBERCULATUM*, L.
Höckerige Herzmuschel.
Vulg., Capa tonda di mar (*It.*).
Croat., Kapica obla, Morska srčavka (*Spalato*).
Habit. Rather rare; Venice, Sestiane, Capo d'Istria, Pirano, Quarnero, Zara, Curzola, Lésina.

66. *CARDIUM CILIARE*.
Habit. Common at Trieste, Zaole, Capo d'Istria, Pirano, Portoré, Cherso, Veglia, Zara, etc.
Note. Other sp., such as *C. aculeatum* (L.), *C. echinatum* (L.), *C. papillosum* (Poli), *C. parvum* (Phil.), are more or less rare.

Gen. II. ISOCARDIA, *Lam.*
67. *ISOCARDIA COR*, Lam.
Heart-shell.
Vulg., Bibaron de mar.
Croat., čanča.

Habit. Common at Zara and Spalato; a single sp. from Promontore in Istria; Quarnero.

Fam. VIII. VENERIDÆ, *Leach.*
Gen. I. VENUS, *L.*
68. *VENUS GALLINA*, L.
Strahlige Gienmuschel.
Venere gallina (*It.*).
Vulg., Bibarazza, Pevarazza.
Habit. Very common on sand-banks and along the shore of the gulfs of Venice, and Trieste, and in Dalmatia; less common in the Quarnero; it is found imbedded in the sand, and is caught by hand or the *voleghetta*, and in deep water by the *cassa*; is good eating, but is only eaten by the poorer classes.

69. *VENUS VERRUCOSA*, L.
Wartzige Gienmuschel.
Vulg., Bibarazza di mar, Caparozzolo.
Croat., Prnjavica, Ladinka.
Habit. Common all along the coast on sandy beds.

Gen. II. CYTHEREA, *Lam.*
70. *CYTHEREA CHIONE*, L.
Spielmuschel.
Citerea chione (*It.*).
Vulg., Issolon, Issolone.
Croat., Klapun, Klapunica.
Habit. The most common sp. of the genus in the lagoons of Venice and on the sand-banks of Grado; rare on the deeper sand-banks off the coast of Istria (Pirano, Rovigno), and in the Quarnero; Unie, Zara, Lésina; not inferior eating to the other sp.; shells are large, and are exported for miniature painting.

Gen. III. TAPES, *Mühlf.*
71. *TAPES EDULIS*, Chemn.
Jungfern Gienmuschel.
Venere commestibile (*It.*).
Vulg., Caparon, Longon.
Croat., Lisanka (*Fiume*).

Pužica (*Novigrad*).
Habit. Common in the lagoons of Venice, imbedded in the muddy or sandy beds; is indigestible, like the other sp. of this genus, and only eaten by the poorer classes.

72. *TAPES DECUSSATUS*, L.
Gegitterte Gienmuschel.
Clovissa of France.
Venere incrocicchiata (*It.*).
Vulg., Caparozzolo (*Trieste*), Caparozzolo dal scorzo grosso (*Ven.*), Capa tonda di mar.
Croat., Kućica, Gajun (*Veglia*), Pripelanka.
Habit. On mixed clay and sand beds, amongst stones in the lagoons of Venice and the Gulf of Trieste and the Quarnero; the best of the genus, and is much esteemed as food at Venice and Trieste, as also in France, especially in the Provence, where it is known by the name of *clovissa*.
Note. *T. aureus* (Gm.) (*vulg.* Longón), and *T. geographicus* (L.), are also sp. which are common, and are prized as food for the lower classes, especially at Venice.

Fam. IX. TELLINIDÆ, *Latreille.*
Gen. I. DONAX, *L.*

73. *DONAX TRUNCULUS*, L.
Gemeine Dreieck-Muschel.
Donace troncata (*It.*).
Vulg., Cazzonello, Calzinei (*Ven.*).
Habit. Common along the littoral of the Gulfs of Venice and Trieste; rare on the eastern coast; Cherso; lives on the sand close to the shore, and is left dry by the receding tide; is little eaten.

Gen. II. TELLINA, *L.*

74. *TELLINA EXIGUA*, Poli.
Croat., Crljene kućice, Crljenice.
Habit. Sands of Grado, Cherso, Lésina, Curzola.

Gen. III. SCROBICULARIA, *Schum.*

75. *SCROBICULARIA PIPERITA*, Schum.
Ottermuschel.
Scrobicularia peverina (*It.*).
Vulg., Caparozzolo sottile, C. dal scorzo sottile (*Ven.*).
Loca, Loca di fango (*Tr.*).
Habit. Common in the Gulfs of Venice and Trieste on clay and mud beds in shallow water, or on the shore, which is only watered at flood tide, as in the salines of Zaole; lives imbedded in the mud, whence it establishes communication with the outer world by means of two siphons, about six inches in length, which extend through the mud; at ebb-tide it is caught by hand or the *voleghetta*, or is dug out with a spade; common in the markets of Trieste and Venice, where it is valued as food, making a good soup; Quarnero, Zara, Spalato, Ragusa.

Fam. X. MACTRIDÆ, *Fleming.*
Gen. I. MACTRA, *L.*

76. *MACTRA LACTEA*, Poli.
Milchweisse Trogmuschel.
Madia candida (*It.*).
Vulg., Bibaron di marina (*Ven.*).
Habit. Inhabits the sand and is often left dry by the receding tide; is little eaten, although not bad food; Venice, Grado, Zaole.

77. *MACTRA STULTOSUM*, Auct.
Mactra corallina, *L.*
Gefärbte Trogmuschel.
Madia corallina (*It.*).
Vulg., Bibaron colorito, B. di marina (*Ven.*).
Croat., Kopanjica.
Habit. As above; Capo d' Istria, Veglia, Zara, Meleda, Curzola, Spalato, Almissa.

Gen. II. LUTRARIA.

78. *LUTRARIA ELLIPTICA*, Lam.
Croat., Skipa (*Novigrad*).

Fam. XI. SOLENIDÆ.
Gen. SOLEN, *L.*
79. *SOLEN VAGINA,* L.
Weisse Rinne, gemeine Messerscheide.
Soleno manicajo, Soleno coltellajo.
Vulg., Capa longa nostrana, Capa da dito, Manico da coltello (*Ven.*), Capa da deo (*Tr.*), Capa lunga, Capa lunga bianca (*Ven.*).
Croat., šljanak, šljanci, krastavica (*Spal.*).
Habit. On sandy and muddy bed, which it penetrates to a depth of three feet and above, rising to the surface in calm weather; lagoons of Venice, Monfalcone, Capo d'Istria, Pirano; common at Venice and Trieste, where it is much eaten by the lower classes; Zara, Curzola.

80. *SOLEN SILIQUA,* L.
Ensis siliqua, *L.*
Gefärbte Rinne, Hülsenformige Messerscheide.
Soleno siliqua (*It.*).
Vulg., Capa longa marina (*Ven.*), Capa longa colorita.
Tabachina, Capa tabachina (*Chioggia*).
Habit. As above; inferior to No. 79. Trieste, Brevilaqua, Zara, Spalato, Ragusa.

Fam. XII. PHOLADIDÆ.
Gen. PHOLAS, *L.*
81. *PHOLAS DACTYLUS,* L.
Dactylina dactylus, *L.*
Bohrmuschel, Steinbohrer, Steinfinger muschel.
Folade dattilo (*It.*).
Vulg., Dattolo, Dattolo di mar, Dattolo di sabion, Dattero di mar (*Ven.*).
Croat., Obični kamotoč (*Spalato*).
Habit. Found all along the littoral in the rock, and in pieces of submerged wood; it is very good eating; abounds at Ancona, where it is not eaten; has entirely disappeared from the lagoon of Chioggia since fresh water has been conducted into it. Trieste, Pirano, Brevilaqua, Zara.

Fam. XIII. TEREDININÆ.
Gen. TEREDO, *L.*
82. *TEREDO NAVALIS,* L.
Calamitas navium, *L.*
Capanus, Dry-rot Worm.
Le Taret.
Die Pfahlmuschel.
Teredine commune (*It.*).
Vulg., Brumo, Bissa dei legni, Verme dei legni.
Croat., Glistice, Glista drva, Obični Šašanj, Ladjar.
Habit. Penetrates wood, submerged piles, and the bottoms of uncoppered wooden vessels; is the curse of some harbours; abounds at Sebenico.

Class IV. TUNICATA.
Gen. CYNTHIA, *Sav.*
83. *CYNTHIA PAPILLOSA,* L.
Vulg., Limone di mar (*It.*).
Habit. Portoré.

84. *CYNTHIA MICROCOSMUS,* Cuv.
See-scheide.
Vulg., Uovi di mar (*It.*), Ovi di mar (*Fiume*).
Croat., Jaja od mora.
Habit. Trieste, Quarnero.

Gen. POLYCLINUM.
85. *POLYCLINUM FICUS,* Cuv.
Vulg., Figo di mar, Tartuffolo (*It.*).

Class V. BRYOZOA.
Gen. RETEPORA, *Lam.*
86. *RETEPORA CELLULOSA,* L.
Neptun's Manschette.
Vulg., Rosa di mar (*It.*).
Croat., Šeputnjača (*generic*).
Habit. Trieste, Quarnero.

CRUSTACEA.

Gen. STENORRHYNCHUS, *Lam.*

87. *STENORRHYNCHUS PHALAN-GIUM*, Lam.
   Vulg., Zanzaloro (*It.*).
   Habit. Venice, Trieste, Pirano, Quarnero, Dalmatia.

Gen. INACHUS, *Leach.*

88. *INACHUS SCORPIO*, Fabr.
   Vulg., Selmo delle grancéole (*It.*).
   Habit. General and pretty common on limestone beds.

Gen. MAIA, *Latr.*

89. *MAIA SQUINADO*, Latr.
   Sea Spider.
   Araignée de mer, Grampelle.
   Spinnen-Krebs, Seespinne, gemeiner See-Krebs.
   Vulg., Granzon, Granzon falso d'aspreo (*male*), Granzéola (*female*) (*It.*).
   Croat., Rakovica, Račnjak, Morski pauk.
   Habit. General and common; Trieste, Quarnero.

Gen. LAMBRUS, *Leach.*

90. *LAMBRUS MEDITERRANEUS*, Leach.
   Vulg., Granzo compasso (*It.*).
   Croat., Rakovica, šestilo, krugalo.

Gen. IAXEA.

91. *IAXEA NOCTURNA*, Chier., Nard.
   Vulg., Granzo di notte (*It.*).
   Croat., Rakovica, Noćno krugalo.

Gen. XANTHO, *Leach.*

92. *XANTHO FLORIDUS*, Leach.
   Schwarzscheerige Strandkrabbe.
   Vulg., Forfetula (*It.*).

Habit. Venice, Trieste, Pirano, Lussin, Quarnero, Dalmatia.

93. *XANTHO RIVOLOSUS*, Risso.
   Vulg., Poréssa salvatica (*It.*).
   Habit. Quarnero, Venice, Pirano, Lussin, Dalmatia.

Gen. PILUMNUS, *Leach.*

94. *PILUMNUS HIRTELLUS*, Leach.
   Vulg., Grancipol, Grancipoletto (*It.*).
   Croat., Strigljača.
   Habit. Trieste, Portoré, Cherso, Lussin, Dalmatia.

Gen. ERIPHIA, *Latr.*

95. *ERIPHIA SPINIFRONS*, Desm.
   Italienischer Taschenkrebs.
   Vulg., Taska, Grancipóro (*male*), Poressa (*female*) (*It.*).
   Croat., Grmalj.
   Habit. Venice, Rimini, Trieste, Cherso, Pirano, Dalmatia.

Gen. CARCINUS, *Leach.*

96. *CARCINUS MÆNAS*, Leach.
   Common Shore-crab, Harry-crab.
   Crabe commun, Cr. enragé, Ménade.
   Gemeine Krabbe, Gemeiner Seekrebs.
   Vulg., Granzo, Spiantano (*male*), Masanetta, Masinetta (*female*), Molecca, Molecche (*with the soft shell*) (*It.*).
   Croat., Rak, obična rakovica, gola rakovica (*Spalato*).
   Habit. General and common; Venice, Trieste, Cherso, Dalmatia.

Gen. PORTUNUS, *Fabr.*

97. *PORTUNUS DEPURATOR*, Leach.
   Ruderkrabbe.

Vulg., Gambero dell' ala, Granžćola, Granzevolo (*It.*).
Croat., Rakovica, Strigjača.
Habit. Venice, Trieste, Quarnero, Dalmatia.

Gen. PINNOTHERUS, *Latr.*
98. *PINNOTHERUS VETERUM*, Bosc.
Erbsenkrabbe, Erbsenschild, Steckmuschelkrebs.
Vulg., Granzetto d' ostriga (*It.*).
Croat., Račić od ostrige.
Habit. Venice, Trieste, Quarnero, Dalmatia.

99. *PINNOTHERUS PISUM.*
Muschelwächter.
Vulg., Piso (*It.*).
Habit. Venice, Trieste, Quarnero, Dalmatia.

Gen. GONOPLAX, *Leach.*
100. *GONOPLAX RHOMBOIDES*, Fabr.
Vulg., Azzalino, Contrapasso (*It.*).
Habit. On limestone beds; Venice, Trieste, Quarnero, Dalmatia.

Gen. GRAPSUS, *Lam.*
101. *GRAPSUS VARIUS*, Latr.
Schwarzer Taschenkrebs.
Vulg., Granzo piato, Grancipóro (*male*), Poressa (*female*) (*It.*).
Croat., Urak.
Habit. Trieste, Lussin, Dalmatia.

102. *GRAPSUS MARMORATUS*, Fabr.
Marmorirte Viereckskrabbe.
Vulg., Granzo piato (*It.*).
Croat, Urak.
Habit. Trieste, Quarnero.

Gen. ILIA, *Leach.*
103. *ILIA NUCLEUS*, Herbst.
- *Vulg.*, Zucchetto (*It.*).
Habit. Fiume, Cherso, Dalmatia.

Gen. DROMIA, *Fabr.*
104. *DROMIA RUMPHII*, Bosc.
Kugelkrebs.
Vulg., Facchino (*It.*).
Croat., Kosmač, Prug (*Spalato*).
Habit. Venice, Trieste, Pirano, Portoré, Lussin, Dalmatia.

Gen. DORIPPE, *Fabr.*
105. *DORIPPE LANATA*, Latr.
Vulg., Facchino piccolo (*It.*).
Habit. Rimini, Ravenna, Venice, Trieste, Quarnero, Spalato.

Gen. CORISTES, *Latr.*
106. *CORISTES DENTALUS*, Latr.
Vulg., Scarpion di grotta (*It.*).
Croat., Scarpion.
Habit. Very rare; Venice, Quarnero, Lésina.

Gen. PAGURUS, *Fabr.*
107. *PAGURUS MACULATUS*, Roux.
The Great Crab.
Grosser rother Taschenkrebs.
Vulg., Granzipóro (*male*), Poressa (*female*) (*It.*).
Habit. Trieste, Pirano, Quarnero, Dalmatia.

108. *PAGURUS BERNHARDUS*, L.
Sp. of *Pagurus* in shells of *Murex.*
Hermit-crab.
L'Ermit, Le Soldat.
Einsiedlerkrebs.
Pagurus Arten in Gehäusen von Murex.
Vulg., Bulli (Bule) col granzo (*It.*).
Croat., Bramburači, Rak-samac.
Habit. Trieste, Pirano, Dalmatia.

Gen. PORCELLANA, *Lam.*
109. *PORCELLANA LONGICORNIS*, Lam.
Vulg., Scarpion de sabbion, Scarpione de sabionao (*It.*).

2 L 2

Habit. Venice, Trieste, Pirano, Cherso, Lussin, Dalmatia.

Gen. GALATHEA, *Fabr.*
110. *GALATHEA RUGOSA*, Fabr.
Vulg., Scampo morte, Scampa falsa a man lunghe (*It.*).
Croat., Smèrt.
Habit. Rimini, Pirano, Quarnero, Dalmatia.

111. *GALATHEA STRIGOSA*, Fabr.
Vulg., Scampa salvàtica (*It.*).
Habit. Venice, Trieste, Pirano, Quarnero, Dalmatia.

112. *GALATHEA SCAMPARELLA*, Chier.
Vulg., Scamparello, Scampetto (*It.*).
Croat., Kozlica, Skila, Hlapić.

Gen. PALINURUS, *Fabr.*
113. *PALINURUS VULGARIS*, Latr.
The Rock-lobster, Spiny Lobster.
Languste (von Locusta), Heuschreckenkrebs.
Vulg., Grillo di mar (*It.*).
Langusta, Agusta, Agosta, Ragosta, Aragosta (*Ven.*).
Astice (*Dalmatia*).
Croat., Prug, Pizdoklep, Čerčak.
Habit. Dalmatia; not north of Lussin.

Gen. GEBIA, *Leach.*
114. *GEBIA LITTORALIS*, Leach.
Vulg., Córbola, Scardóbola (*It.*).
Croat., Karlić.
Habit. Venice, Trieste, Cherso, Ossero, Dalmatia, Taranto.

Gen. ASTACUS, *Fabr.*
115. *ASTACUS FLUVIATILIS*, Fabr.
The Crayfish.
Süsswasserkrebs.
Gámbero d'acqua dolce (*It.*).
Croat., Vodni rak, Potočni rak.
Habit. Lake of Vrana (Cherso).

Gen. HOMARUS, *Edw.*
116. *HOMARUS VULGARIS*, Edw.
The Lobster.
Der Hummer.
Astice, Astese, Astise (*It.*).
Croat., Astić, Jastog.
Habit. Trieste, Cherso; general and common.

Gen. NEPHROPS, *Leach.*
117. *NEPHROPS NORVEGICUS*, L.
The Norway Lobster.
Norwegischer Krebs, Buchstabenkrebs.
Vulg., Scampo (*Fiume, Trieste*).
Croat., Rak.
Habit. Common in the Quarnero; not found elsewhere in the Adriatic.

Gen. CRANGON.
118. *CRANGON VULGARIS*, Fabr.
The Shrimp.
Garnele, Graue Garnele.
Vulg., Schila, Squilla, Skila (*It.*).
Croat., Obični račić.
Habit. Venice, Trieste, Pirano, Dalmatia.

Gen. SCYLLARUS.
119. *SCYLLARUS ARCTUS*, Fabr.
Vulg., Cigala di mar (*It., Fiume*).
Croat., Žežalo (*Fiume*).
Habit. Quarnero, Dalmatia.

120. *SCYLLARUS LATUS*, Latr.
Croat., Kuka.
Habit. Lésina.

Gen. PALÆMON, *Fabr.*
121. *PALÆMON SQUILLA*, Fabr.
The Prawn.
Salicoques of France.
Garnat, Garnele, Glashelle Garnele.
Vulg., Gambero, Gambaro, Gambaretto d'acqua salsa, Skilla.
Croat., Kostica, Morski rak, Rak (*Spalato*).
Habit. Trieste, Fiume, Dalmatia.

Gen. LYSIANASSA, *Edw.*
122. *LYSIANASSA SPINICORNIS*, Cost.
Vulg., Granzéola piccola (*It.*).
Habit. Trieste, Cherso, Dalmatia.

Gen. SQUILLA, *Rond.*
123. *SQUILLA MANTIS*, Rond.
Goger, Gemeine Goger.
Vulg., Canócchia, Canóccia (*It.*).
Croat., Kanoće, Vabić.
Habit. General and common; Trieste, Quarnero, Dalmatia.

Gen. ORCHESTIA.
124. *ORCHESTIA LITTOREA*, Leach.
Vulg., Saletto de fosso (*It.*).
Habit. Quarnero, Dalmatia, Otranto.

Gen. LIGIA, *Fabr.*
125. *LIGIA ITALICA*, Leach.
Vulg., Sallizzoni delle rive (*It.*).
Habit. General and common.

Gen. CORONULA.
126. *CORONULA TESTUDINARIA*, Lam.
Vulg., Cappa delle galene (*It.*).
Croat., želvin zvončić.

Gen. CHTHAMALUS, *Ranz.*
127. *CHTHAMALUS STELLATUS*, Ranz.
Vulg., Capa de palo (*It.*).

Capa delle piere.
Habit. General and common; Quarnero.

Gen. ANATIFA.
128. *ANATIFA LÆVIS*, Brug.
Vulg., Caparozzoletti di mar (*It.*).
Croat., Obični lupar, Cicala.

Class. II.—VERMES—Annulata.
Gen. SERPULA, *L.*
129. *SERPULA*, sp.
Vulg., Bisse delle cape, Bisse delle sassi, Cannelle.
Croat., škoravi cievnjak, svirale od mora, cievnjak sviják.

Gen. ARENICOLA, *Lam.*
130. *ARENICOLA PISCATORUM*, Cuv.
Lug-worm.
Vulg., Vescola (*It.*).
Croat., škorak, pjeskožil.

Gen. APHRODITE, *L.*
131. *APHRODITE HYSTRIX*, Sav.
Aphrodite.
Chenille de mer.
Die Aphrodite Seeraupe.
Vulg., Afrodita, Bruco di mar (*It.*).
Croat., Pustenka, dlakuša.
Habit. Trieste, Portoré.

ECHINODERMATA.

Gen. HOLOTHURIA, *L.*
132. *HOLOTHURIA TUBULOSA*, Gthr.
Sea-slugs.
Seewalzen.
Vulg., Cazzo del mar, Caz marin, Cucumero de mar (*It.*).

Croat., Pestelj (*Spalato*), tèrpen, trp, morski kurac, brizgavac.
Habit. Trieste, Portoré, Cherso.

Gen. CUCUMARIA, *Blainv.*
133. *CUCUMARIA DOLIOLUM*, Grube.
Cucumbers.

Concombres, Cornichons de mer, Meergurken.
Vulg., Cucumero de mar (*It.*).
Habit. Trieste, Portoré.

Gen. ECHINUS, *L.*

134. *ECHINUS MICROTUBERCULATUS*, Blainv.
Sea-urchins.
See-Igel.
Vulg., Castagne de mar, Tartuffoli (*It.*).
Croat., Ježić.
Habit. Trieste, Quarnero.

135. *ECHINUS BREVISPINOSUS*, Risso.
Vulg., Rizzo di mar, Castagna commun de mar (*It.*).
Croat., Ježina.
Habit. Trieste, Quarnero.

136. *ECHINUS LIVIDUS*, Deslong.
Stein See-igel.
Vulg. As No. 135 (*It.*).
Croat., Jež, Morski jež.
Habit. Trieste. Quarnero.

137. *ECHINUS MELO*, Lmck.
Vulg., Melon de mar, Rizzo melon (*It.*).
Croat. As No. 136.
Habit. Dalmatia, Quarnero.

Gen. ASTERACANTHION, *M. Tr.*

138. *ASTERACANTHION, SP.*
Sea-pads, Sea-star, Finger-fish, Star-fish.
Etoiles de mer.
See-sterne.
Stelle marine (*It.*).
Croat., Morska zviezdica.

139. *ASTERACANTHION RUBEUS*, M. Tr.
Stella rossa (*It.*).
Croat., Kèrstiješ, Kèrstača.

Gen. ASTERISCUS. *M. Tr.*

140. *ASTERISCUS MEMBRANACEUS*, M. Tr.
Vulg., Pie d'occha (*It.*).
Croat., Guskina noga, Nejasitka (*Spalato*).

141. *ASTERISCUS VERRICULATUS*, M. Tr.
Vulg., Stelletta (*It.*).
Croat., Križalina.
Habit. Portoré.

Gen. ASTROPECTEN, *Lmck.*

142. *ASTROPECTEN AURANTIACA*, L.
Vulg., Stellon, Stella (*It.*).
Habit. Portoré.

Gen. OPHIODERMA, *M. Tr.*

143. *OPHIODERMA LONGICAUDA*, M. Tr.
Vulg., Selmo a compasso (*It.*).
Habit. Trieste, Portoré.

Gen. SCHIZASTER, *Ag.*

144. *SCHIZASTER CANALIFERUS*, Lam.
Vulg., Peto de dolfin (*It.*).
Croat., Dupinska pèrsa.
Habit. Zaole, Quarnero.

Gen. OPHIOTHRIX, *M. Tr.*

145. *OPHIOTHRIX FRAGILIS*, Müll.
Vulg., Selmo (*It.*).
Habit. Trieste, Quarnero.

POLYPI.

Gen. ANEMONIA.
146. *ANEMONIA, SP.*
Sea Anemones.
Anémone de mer.
See Anemone.
Anemonia di mare (*It.*).
Croat., Moruzga, vlasulja (*generic terms*).

Gen. ACTINIA, *L.*
147. *ACTINIA*, Sp.
Actinia, Blubber.
Actinie.
See-rose, Aktinie.
Attinia, Rosa di mar, Madrona, Marona (*It.*).
Croat., Vlasulja, cvjetulja, vjetrenica, moruzga.

148. *ACTINIA VIRIDIS*, L.
Attinia verde (*It.*).
Croat., Moruzga zelena.
Habit. Quarnero.

149. *ACTINIA RUBRA*, Brug.
Wrinkled Actinia.
Actinie ridée.
Rothe Aktinie.

Attinia rossa, A. porporina, Anemolo rosso marino (*It.*).
Croat., Moruzga, vlasulja crvena.

150. *ACTINIA EFFŒTA*, L.
Enervated Actinia.
Actinie épuisée, anguleuse, blanche.
Die Seeblume.
Attinia angulosa, bianca (*It.*).
Habit. Attached to *Murex brandaris*; Trieste.

Gen. RHIZOSTOMUM, *Cuv.*
151. *RHIZOSTOMUM CUVIERI*, Lam.
Vulg., Potta di mar, Potta marina (*It.*).
Croat., Modra morska pluća.
Habit. Trieste.

Gen. PENNATULA, *L.*
152. *PENNATULA PHOSPHOREA*, Ell.
Sea-pen.
Vulg., Penna di mar, Pennacchiera (*It.*).
Croat., Perulja.
Habit. Quarnero.

153. *PENNATULA RUBRA.*
Vulg., Pennacchiera rossa (*It.*).
Croat., Perulja rumena.

Appendix to the List of Invertebrates.
A. Mollusks of the Adriatic enumerated by Professor M. Stossich.

a. 13 CEPHALOPODS, *viz.:*

- 3 Octopus.
- 2 Eledone.
- 1 Argonauta.
- 1 Ommastrephes.
- 2 Loligo.
- 2 Sepiola.
- 2 Sepia.

b. 371 GASTROPODS, *viz.:*

- 10 Murex.
- 1 Typhis.
- 8 Fusus.
- 1 Euthria.
- 1 Triton.
- 1 Ranella.
- 1 Pisania.
- 3 Pollia.
- 9 Nassa.
- 1 Cyclope.
- 1 Fasciolaria.
- 1 Voluta.
- 10 Mitra.
- 4 Columbella.
- 4 Marginella.
- 1 Dolium.
- 1 Cassis.
- 2 Cassidaria.
- 2 Lamellaria.
- 8 Natica.
- 4 Scalaria.
- 8 Turbonilla.
- 14 Odostomia.
- 1 Eulimella.
- 3 Aclis.
- 6 Eulima.
- 3 Leiostraca.
- 2 Solarium.
- 4 Cerithiopsis.
- 1 Conus.
- 1 Turbo.
- 1 Collonia.
- 1 Cyclostrema.
- 1 Adeorbis.
- 3 Clanculus.
- 1 Craspedotus.
- 2 Monodonta.
- 12 Zizyphinus.
- 13 Trochus.
- 1 Anatomus.
- 2 Haliotis.
- 2 Lachesis.
- 13 Raphitoma.
- 3 Mangelia.
- 8 Defrancia.
- 1 Chenopus.
- 2 Cyprœa.
- 3 Trivia.
- 1 Erato.
- 3 Ovula.
- 9 Cerithium.
- 1 Triforis.
- 1 Littorina.
- 6 Fossarus.
- 1 Rissoina.
- 28 Rissoa.
- 12 Alvania.
- 2 Setia.
- 3 Cingula.
- 2 Amnicola.
- 2 Hydrobia.
- 1 Barleeia.
- 3 Turritella.
- 6 Vermetus.
- 1 Siliquaria.
- 1 Cæcum.
- 2 Calyptræa.
- 2 Crepidula.
- 1 Capulus.
- 1 Neritina.
- 4 Phasianella.
- 1 Scaphander.
- 1 Philine.
- 1 Gasteropteron.
- 6 Aplysia.
- 7 Pleurobranchus.
- 1 Umbrella.
- 2 Tylodina.
- 8 Doris.
- 1 Polycera.
- 2 Idalia.
- 2 Tritonia.

GASTROPODS (*continued*).

- 3 Fissurella.
- 6 Emarginula.
- 1 Gadinia.
- 6 Patella.
- 2 Acteon.
- 7 Cylichna.
- 1 Volvula.
- 2 Bulla.
- 2 Haminea.
- 4 Akera.
- 1 Tethys.
- 1 Doto.
- 3 Æolis.
- 1 Elysia.
- 1 Truncatella.
- 1 Auricula.
- 2 Melampus.
- 1 Assemínia.
- 7 Chiton.
- 8 Dentalium.

c. 190 CONCHIFERS, *viz.:*

- 2 Pholas.
- 4 Teredo.
- 1 Gastrochæna.
- 1 Clavagella.
- 1 Solen.
- 2 Ensis.
- 1 Pharus.
- 5 Solecurtus.
- 2 Saxicava.
- 1 Corbula.
- 1 Lyonsia.
- 7 Thracia.
- 1 Neæra.
- 2 Dosinia.
- 12 Venus.
- 2 Venerupis.
- 1 Cypricardia.
- 1 Petricola.
- 12 Cardium.
- 2 Lævicardium.
- 1 Isocardia.
- 3 Chama.
- 6 Lucina.
- 2 Loripes.
- 3 Modiola.
- 1 Lithodomus.
- 1 Avicula.
- 4 Pinna.
- 5 Arca.
- 3 Pectunculus.
- 2 Nucula.
- 1 Pandora.
- 4 Mactra.
- 2 Lutraria.
- 11 Tellina.
- 1 Gastrana.
- 2 Lucinopsis.
- 3 Psammobia.
- 1 Strigilla.
- 5 Donax.
- 5 Scrobicularia.
- 4 Erycina.
- 1 Mesodesma.
- 3 Cytherea.
- 1 Scacchia.
- 1 Diplodonta.
- 5 Kellia.
- 1 Thyasira.
- 1 Montacuta.
- 2 Galeomma.
- 1 Solemya.
- 1 Astarte.
- 4 Cardita.
- 4 Mytilus.
- 2 Crenella.
- 2 Leda.
- 10 Pecten.
- 1 Vola.
- 5 Lima.
- 1 Spondylus.
- 8 Anomia.
- 5 Ostrea.

d. 7 BRACHIOPODS, *viz.:*

- 1 Terebratulina.
- 1 Megerlea.
- 4 Argiope.
- 1 Crania.

B. CRUSTACEANS *of the Adriatic enumerated by* PROFESSOR M. STOSSICH.

a. 126 MALACOSTRACA, *viz.*:

- 2 Stenorhynchus.
- 1 Achæus.
- 4 Inachus.
- 1 Herbstia.
- 6 Pisa.
- 1 Lissa.
- 2 Maja.
- 1 Acanthonyx.
- 1 Eurynome.
- 2 Lambrus.
- 1 Cancer.
- 1 Pirimela.
- 4 Xantho.
- 2 Pilumnus.
- 2 Eriphia.
- 1 Lupa.
- 5 Portunus.
- 1 Carcinus.
- 1 Platyonychus.
- 1 Gelasimus.
- 1 Gonoplax.
- 1 Heterograpsus.
- 1 Pachygrapsus.
- 1 Nautilograpsus.
- 2 Pinnotheres.
- 1 Ilia.
- 4 Ebalia.
- 1 Calappa.
- 2 Atelecyclus.
- 1 Corystes.
- 1 Dorippe.
- 1 Cymopolia.

- 1 Ethusa.
- 1 Dromia.
- 1 Homola.
- 13 Pagurus.
- 2 Porcellana.
- 3 Galathea.
- 1 Munida.
- 2 Scyllarus.
- 1 Palinurus.
- 2 Callianassa.
- 1 Gebia.
- 1 Calliaxis.
- 1 Homarus.
- 1 Nephrops.
- 5 Crangon.
- 4 Alpheus.
- 2 Pontonia.
- 1 Typton.
- 1 Caridina.
- 1 Nika.
- 1 Athanas.
- 4 Palæmon.
- 1 Gnathophyllum.
- 3 Anchistia.
- 3 Hyppolyte.
- 2 Pandalus.
- 1 Lysmata.
- 1 Sicyonia.
- 2 Penæus.
- 2 Mysis.
- 3 Squilla.
- 1 Gonodactylus.

b. 151 ARTHROSTRACA, *viz.*:

- 1 Tanais.
- 2 Apseudes.
- 2 Anthura.
- 1 Praniza.
- 3 Anceus.
- 4 Cymothoa.
- 3 Anilocra.
- 2 Nerocila.
- 1 Æga.
- 4 Rocinela.
- 1 Cirolana.
- 8 Sphæroma.

- 2 Cymodocea.
- 1 Nesæa.
- 6 Idotea.
- 3 Jæra.
- 1 Limnoria.
- 1 Bopyrus.
- 1 Gyge.
- 1 Ione.
- 1 Ligia.
- 1 Tylos.
- 8 Caprella.
- 1 Chelura.

ARTHROSTRACA (*continued*).

- 2 Corophium.
- 1 Cyrtophium.
- 2 Cratippus.
- 1 Icridium.
- 2 Microdeutopus.
- 2 Cerapus.
- 5 Podocerus.
- 4 Amphitoë.
- 1 Talitrus.
- 4 Orchestia.
- 3 Allorchestes.
- 11 Nicea.
- 1 Atylus.
- 3 Protomedeia.
- 1 Pherusa.
- 5 Dexamine.

- 2 Iphimedia.
- 1 Isæa.
- 1 Ampelisca.
- 1 Kroyera.
- 1 Eusirus.
- 1 Leucothoë.
- 6 Gammarus.
- 3 Melita.
- 7 Mæra.
- 1 Eurystheus.
- 1 Amathilla.
- 7 Lysianassa.
- 2 Probolium.
- 2 Ichnopus.
- 7 Anonyx.
- 1 Callisoma.

c. 1 LEPTOSTRACA, *viz.*:
- 1 Nebalia.

d. 91 ENTOMOSTRACA, *viz.*:

- 2 Cypridina.
- 1 Lepas.
- 1 Conchoderma.
- 1 Scalpellum.
- 1 Chthamalus.
- 1 Chelonobia.
- 1 Balanus.
- 2 Peltogaster.
- 1 Parthenopea.
- 1 Sacculina.
- 1 Lichomolgus.
- 1 Sabelliphilus.
- 1 Staurosoma.
- 2 Bomolochus.
- 1 Nicothoe.
- 1 Ergasilus.
- 1 Medesicaste.
- 7 Chondracanthus.
- 5 Caligus.
- 2 Lepeoptheirus.
- 1 Lütkenia.
- 1 Trebius.
- 1 Elytrophora.
- 1 Dinematura.
- 1 Cecrops.

- 1 Læmargus.
- 1 Perissopus.
- 1 Anthrosoma.
- 5 Lernanthropus.
- 1 Dichelestium.
- 1 Kröyeria.
- 1 Clavella.
- 2 Nemesis.
- 1 Ergasilina.
- 1 Cycnus.
- 1 Eudactylina.
- 5 Philichthys.
- 2 Sphærifer.
- 2 Pennella.
- 3 Lernæenicus.
- 1 Tripaphylus.
- 1 Lernæolophus.
- 1 Naobranchia.
- 1 Charopinus.
- 1 Achtheres.
- 6 Brachiella.
- 10 Anchorella.
- 1 Notopterophorus.
- 1 Peltidium.
- 1 Hersilia.

C. VERMES of the ADRIATIC, *enumerated by* PROFESSOR M. STOSSICH.

a. 168 ANNELIDES.

1 Tomopteris.
2 Eteone.
5 Eulalia.
1 Carobia.
5 Phyllodoce.
1 Oxydromus.
1 Ophiodromus.
3 Podarke.
1 Peribœa.
1 Fallacia.
4 Procerœa.
2 Grubea.
1 Sphærosyllis.
2 Ptérosyllis.
1 Trypanosyllis.
1 Eurysyllis.
1 Eusyllis.
2 Odontosyllis.
1 Ehlersia.
1 Syllides.
9 Syllis.
1 Sylline.
4 Glycera.
1 Nephthys.
10 Nereis.
2 Marphysa.
4 Eunice.
1 Onuphis.
1 Lysidice.
2 Nematonereis.
4 Lumbriconereis.
1 Arabella.
1 Staurocephalus.
1 Spinther.
2 Euphrosyne.
1 Chrysopetalum.
2 Sigalion.
1 Leanira.
1 Acholoë.
1 Hermadion.
1 Lepidonotus.
1 Lepidasthenia.
1 Lagisca.
6 Polynoe.
1 Hermione.
1 Aphrodite.
6 Serpula.
2 Eupomatus.

ANNELIDES (*contd.*).

1 Placostegus.
1 Spirorbis.
1 Filograna.
3 Vermilia.
1 Pomatocerus.
3 Protula.
10 Sabella.
1 Spirographis
1 Lagis.
1 Pectinaria.
1 Melinna.
1 Sabellides.
1 Terebellides.
1 Polycirrus.
1 Myxicola.
15 Terebella.
1 Siphonostomum.
1 Chætopterus.
3 Heterocirrus.
2 Cirratulus.
1 Maldane.
4 Clymene.
1 Arenicola.
1 Dasybrancus.
1 Notomastus.
1 Armandia.
1 Polyophthalmus.
1 Enchytræus.
1 Pontobdella.

b. 8 GEPHYREA.

1 Sipunculus.
4 Phascolosoma.
1 Aspidosiphon.
1 Bonellia.
1 Thalassema.

c. 42 NEMATHEL-MINTHES.

11 Echinorhynchus.
11 Ascaris.
2 Acanthocheilus.
1 Heterakis.
2 Leeanocephalus.
3 Agomonematodum.
3 Agomonema.
1 Thominx.
1 Stelmius.
1 Echinocephalus.

NEMATHELMINTHES (*contd.*)

2 Ichthyonema.
1 Spiroptera.
1 Enchelidium.
2 Enoplus.

d. 92 PLATELMINTHES.

5 Cerebratulus.
1 Meckelia.
2 Tubulanus.
1 Micrura.
1 Polystemma.
1 Valencinia.
3 Nemertes.
1 Tetrastemma.
1 Borlasia.
1 Gyrator.
1 Stylochus.
1 Leptoplana.
2 Thysanozoon.
1 Proceros.
1 Polycelis.
1 Opisthomum.
1 Proporus.
1 Otocelis.
1 Sidonia.
2 Monotus.
3 Turbella.
2 Vortex.
1 Trigonostomum.
1 Vorticeros.
1 Celidotis.
1 Stenostomum.
26 Distomum.
1 Holostomum.
1 Monostomum.
1 Gasterostomum.
1 Onchocotyle.
3 Tetrarhynchobothrium.
2 Orygmathobothrium.
1 Tetrabothrium.
2 Echeneibothrium.
1 Phyllobothrium.
2 Anthobothrium.
1 Polyonchbothrium.
2 Calliobothrium.
3 Dibothrium.
1 Amphicotyle.
4 Rhyncobothrium.
2 Caryophyllæus.

APPENDIX I.

ALPHABETICAL INDEX to the Scientific Names.

a. MAMMALIA AND REPTILES.

(The numbers opposite the names refer to the Systematic List, p. 177.)

Chelonia *sp.*, 1, 2.	Grampus griseus, 5.	Phoca vitulina, 1.
Delphinus *sp.*, 3–5.	Pelagius monachus, 2.	Physeter *sp.*, 6, 7.
Emys Lutaria, 3.	Phoca monachus, 2.	

b. PISCES.

(The numbers opposite the names refer to the Systematic List, p. 179.)

Abramis bipunctatus, 299.	Cantharus *sp.*, 76–78.	Dactylopterus volitans, 147.
Acanthias *sp.*, 21, 22.	Capros aper, 110.	Dasibatis *sp.*, 30–32.
Acantholabrus Pallonii, 226.	Caranx dentex, 104.	Dentex *sp.*, 66, 357, 358.
Acipenser *sp.*, 50–55, 355.	,, trachurus, 103.	Dicerobatis giornæ, 49.
Alburnus *sp.*, 299–301.	Carcharias *sp.*, 1, 2, 351, 352.	Echineis *sp.*, 130, 366.
Alopias vulpes, 12.	Carcharodon Rondeletii, 10.	Echinorhinus spinosus, 24.
Alosa communis, 319.	Centrina Salviani, 20.	Engraulis encrasicholus, 317.
Ammodytes siculus, 248.	Centriscus scolopax, 198.	Esox belone, 305.
Ammopleurops lacteus, 269.	Centrolophus *sp.*, 115, 116.	,, lucius, 309.
Anguilla *sp.*, 323, 324.	Centropristis hepatus, 59.	,, sphyræna, 187.
Anthias sacer, 60.	Cephaloptera giorna, 49.	Exocœtus *sp.*, 307, 308.
Apogon imberbis, 65.	Cepola rubescens, 172.	Falx Venetorum, 207.
,, rex mullorum, 65.	Charax puntazzo, 85.	Fierasfer *sp.*, 247, 378.
Argentina sphyræna, 316.	Chondrostoma *sp.*, 295–298.	,, dentatus, 360.
Arnoglossus *sp.*, 253–255, 379.	Chrysophrys aurata, 92.	Gadus *sp.*, 231–234, 376.
Atherina *sp.*, 188–190.	Citharus linguatula, 256.	Galeus canis, 3.
Aulopus filamentosus, 271.	Clinus variabilis, 185.	Gasterosteus *sp.*, 196, 197.
Aulopyge Hügeli, 277.	Clupanodon phalerica, 322.	Gobio *sp.*, 278, 279.
Ausonia Cuvieri, 120.	Clupea *sp.*, 318–322.	Gobius *sp.*, 148–166, 367–370.
Auxis vulgaris, 129.	Cobitis *sp.*, 302, 303.	Gouania piger, 205.
Balistes capriscus, 344.	Conger *sp.*, 325, 326.	Heliastes chromis, 209.
Barbus *sp.*, 274–276.	Coricus rostratus, 224.	Heptanchus cinereus, 15.
Belone acus, 305.	Coris *sp.*, 229, 230.	Hippocampus *sp.*, 342, 343.
Blennius *sp.*, 173–185, 373, 374.	Corvina nigra, 98.	Histiophorus belone, 100.
	Coryphæna *sp.*, 117, 118.	Hypsiptera, 377.
Box *sp.*, 79, 80.	Cottus gobio, 138.	Julis *sp.*, 228–230.
Brama Raji, 119.	Crenilabrus *sp.*, 216–225.	Labrax lupus, 57.
Branchiostoma lanceolatum, 350.	Cristiceps argentatus, 185.	Labrus *sp.*, 210–215.
	Cyprinodon calaritanus, 304.	Lamna *sp.*, 8, 9.
Callionymus *sp.*, 167–171, 372.	Cyprinus *sp.*, 272, 273.	Latrunculus *sp.*, 166, 371.

2 M 2

THE ADRIATIC GULF.

Lebias calaritana, 304.
Lepadogaster *sp.*, 199–204.
Lepidopus caudatus, 101.
Lepidotrigla aspera, 139.
Leptopterygius piger, 205.
Leuciscus *sp.*, 280–291.
Lichia *sp.*, 107–109.
Lophius *sp.*, 136, 137.
Lophotes cepedianus, 206.
Lota vulgaris, 238.
„ argentea, 359.
Lucerna Venetorum, 142.
Lucioperca Sandra, 58.
Luvarus imperialis, 120.
Macrurus cœlorhyncus, 249.
Mæna *sp.*, 67–69.
Merluccius vulgaris, 235.
Mirbelia *sp.*, 203, 204.
Motella *sp.*, 239–241.
Mugil *sp.*, 191–195, 375.
Mullus *sp.*, 74, 75.
Muræna *sp.*, 329, 330.
Mustellus *sp.*, 6, 7.
Myliobatis *sp.*, 46, 47.
Myrus vulgaris, 326.
Naucrates ductor, 106.
Nemachilus barbatulus, 302.
Nerophis *sp.*, 340, 341.
Notidanus *sp.*, 14–16.
Novacula cultrata, 227.
Oblata melanura, 81.
Odontaspis *sp.*, 11, 353.
Ophichthys *sp.*, 327, 328, 382.
Ophidium *sp.*, 243–246.
Ophisurus serpens, 327.
Orthagoriscus *sp.*, 345, 346.
Paganellus Venetorum, 156.
Pagellus *sp.*, 88–91, 361.
Pagrus *sp.*, 86, 87, 360.

Paraphoxinus *sp.*, 292, 293.
Pelamys *sp.*, 128, 365.
Perca fluviatilis, 56.
Peristedion cataphractum, 146.
Peristethus cataphractum, 146.
Petromyzon *sp.*, 347–349.
Pholis lævis, 184.
Phrynorhombus unimaculatus, 252.
Phycis *sp.*, 236, 237.
Plagusia lactea, 269.
Platessa passer, 260.
Platessa vulgaris, 259.
Pleuronectes *sp.*, 259, 260.
Polyprion cernium, 64.
Pristiurus melanostomus, 19.
Pteridium atrum, 242.
Pteroplatea altavela, 45.
Raja *sp.*, 30–41.
Rhina *sp.*, 25, 26.
Rhinoptera marginata, 48.
Rhomboidichtys *sp.*, 257, 258.
Rhombus *sp.*, 250, 251.
Salar ausonii, 310.
Salmo *sp.*, 310–314, 381.
Sardinella aurita, 318.
Sargus *sp.*, 82–84.
Saurus *sp.*, 270, 271.
Sayris Camperi, 306.
Scardinius *sp.*, 286.
Schedophilus Botteri, 364.
Sciæna aquila, 97.
Scomber *sp.*, 121–123.
Scombresox rondeletii, 306.
Scorpæna *sp.*, 94, 95.
Scyllium *sp.*, 17, 18, 354.
Sebastes imperialis, 93.
Selache maxima, 13.
Seriola Dumerilii, 105.

Serranus hepatus, 59.
Serranus *sp.*, 61–63, 356.
Siphonostoma *sp.*, 331–333.
Smaris *sp.*, 70–73.
Solea *sp.*, 261–268, 380.
Sphagebranchus *sp.*, 328.
Spinax niger, 23.
Sphyræna vulgaris, 187.
Squalius albus, 283.
Squatina oculata, 26.
Stromateus *sp.*, 113, 114.
Syngnathus *sp.*, 334–339.
Tarantola Romæ, 270.
Telestes *sp.*, 288.
Temnodon saltator, 363.
Tetrapterus belone, 100.
Tetrodon mola, 345.
Thymallus vulgaris, 315.
Thynnus *sp.*, 124–127.
Thyrsites pretiosus, 362.
Tinca vulgaris, 294.
Torpedo *sp.*, 27–29.
Trachinus *sp.*, 132–135.
Trachurus trachurus, 103.
Trachypterus *sp.*, 207, 208.
Trichiurus *sp.*, 101, 102.
Trigla *sp.*, 139–145.
„ cataphracta, 146.
„ volitans, 147.
Tripterygium nasus, 186.
Trutta *sp.*, 310–314.
Trygon *sp.*, 42–44.
Umbrina cirrhosa, 96.
Uranoscopus scaber, 131.
Xiphias gladius, 99.
Xirichthys cultrata, 227.
Zeus *sp.*, 111, 112.
Zygæna *sp.*, 4, 5.

c. INVERTEBRATES.

(The numbers opposite the names refer to the Systematic List, p. 242.)

Actinia *sp.*, 147–150.
Anatifa lœvis, 128.
Anemonia *sp.*, 146.
Aphrodite hystrix, 131.
Aplysia depilans 32.

Aporrhais pes pelicani, 14.
Arca *sp.*, 57, 58.
Arenicola piscatorum, 130.
Astacus fluviatilis, 115.
Asteracanthion *sp.*, 138, 139.

Asteriscus *sp.*, 140, 141.
Astropecten aurantiaca, 142.
Bulla *sp.*, 30, 31.
Calamitas navium, 82.
Carcinus mœnas, 96.

Cardium *sp.*, 62–66.
Cassidaria echinophora, 11.
Cerithium vulgatum, 13.
Chama gryphoides, 61.
Chiton siculus, 28.
Chthamalus stellatus, 127.
Coristes dentalus, 106.
Coronula testudinaria, 126.
Crangon vulgaris, 118.
Cucumaria doliolum, 133.
Cyclope neritea, 10.
Cynthia *sp.*, 83, 84.
Cytherea chione, 70.
Dentalium entalis, 29.
Dolium galea, 12.
Donax trunculus, 73.
Dorippe lanata, 105.
Dromia Rumphii, 104.
Echinus *sp.*, 134–137.
Eledone moschata, 2.
Eriphia spinifrons, 95.
Fissurella costaria, 26.
Galathea *sp.*, 110–112.
Gebia littoralis, 114.
Gonoplax rhomboides, 100.
Grapsus *sp.*, 101, 102.
Haliotis tuberculata, 25.
Helix *sp.*, 33–38.
Holothuria tubulosa, 132.
Homarus vulgaris, 116.
Hyalina cellaria, 41.

Iaxea nocturna, 91.
Ilia nucleus, 103.
Inachus scorpio, 88.
Isocardia cor, 67.
Lambrus mediterraneus, 90.
Ligia italica, 125.
Lima inflata, 50.
Lithodomus lithophagus, 55.
Loligo *sp.*, 3, 4.
Lutraria elliptica, 78.
Lysianassa spinicornis, 122.
Mactra *sp.*, 76, 77.
Maia squinado, 89.
Modiola barbata, 56.
Monodonta *sp.*, 22, 23.
Murex *sp.*, 7, 8.
Mytilus edulis, 54.
Nassa reticulata, 9.
Nephrops norvegicus, 117.
Nucula margaritacea, 60.
Octopus vulgaris, 1.
Ophioderma longicauda, 143.
Ophiotrix fragilis, 145.
Orchestia littorea, 124.
Ostrea *sp.*, 42–44.
Pagurus *sp.*, 107, 108.
Palæmon squilla, 121.
Palinurus vulgaris, 113.
Patella vulgata, 27.
Pecten *sp.*, 45–49.
Pectunculus glycimeris, 59.

Pennatula *sp.*, 152, 153.
Pholas dactylus, 81.
Pilumnus hirtellus, 94.
Pinna nobilis, 53.
Pinnotherus *sp.*, 98, 99.
Polyclinum ficus, 85.
Porcellana longicornis, 109.
Portunus depurator, 97.
Retepora cellulosa, 86.
Rhizostomum Cuvieri, 151.
Schizaster canaliferus, 144.
Scrobicularia piperita, 75.
Scyllarus *sp.*, 119, 120.
Sepia officinalis, 6.
Sepiola Rondeletii, 5.
Serpula, *sp.*, 129.
Solen *sp.*, 79, 80.
Spondylus *sp.*, 51, 52.
Squilla mantis, 123.
Stenorrhynchus phalangium, 87.
Tapes *sp.*, 71, 72.
Tellina exigua, 74.
Teredo navalis, 82.
Trochus *sp.*, 16–21.
Turbo rugosus, 24.
Turritella communis, 15.
Venus *sp.*, 68, 69.
Xantho *sp.*, 92, 93.
Zonites *sp.*, 39, 40.

Appendix II.

Alphabetical Index to the English Names.

a. FISHES.

(The numbers opposite the names refer to the Systematic List, p. 179.)

Adder-pike, 135.
Adriatic Sturgeon, 50.
Allis-Shad, 319.
Anchovy, 317.
Angel-fish, Angel Shark, 25.
Angler, the common, 136.
Argentine, 316.
Atherine, 188.
,, Boier's, 189.
Axillary Bream, 361.
Balance-fish, 4.
Band-fish, 172.
,, the Red, 172.
Barbel, 274.
Basse, 57.
,, Stone Basse, 64.
Beardie, 302.
Becker, 86.
Bellows-fish, 198.
Bib, 234.
Bill-fish, 306.
Black Bream, 76.
Black-fin, 135.
Black-fish, 115.
Black-mouthed Dog-fish, 19.
Black Perch, 115.
Black Ruffe, 115.
Blade-fish, 102.
Blenny, the Diminutive, 183.
,, the Freshwater, 176.
,, the Gattoruginous, 173.
,, Montagu's, 183.
,, the Ocellated, 182.
,, the Smooth, 184.
Boar-fish, 110.
Bogue, 79.

Boier's Atherine, 189.
Bone-dog, 21.
Bonito, 126.
,, the Plain, 129.
Bounce, 18.
Braize, 86.
Brill, 251.
British Torpedo, 27-29.
Bullhead, 138.
Burbot, Burbolt, 238.
Burton Skate, 40.
Butterfly-fish, 182.
Cackarel, 67.
Capelan, 233.
Carp, 272.
Cat-fish, 18.
Chub, 283.
Cod, the Three-bearded, 239.
,, the Five-bearded, 241.
Comber, 62.
Conger-eel, 325.
Connor Maid, 220.
Coral-fish, 209.
Corkwing, 220.
Couch's Polyprion, 64.
,, Sea Bream, 87.
Cramp-fish, 29.
Crowner, 145.
Crue Herring, 321.
Dentex, 66.
Derbio, 108.
Devil-fish, 46-49.
Dog-fish, 17-19, 21, 22.
Dolphin, 117, 118.
Dory, 111.
Dragonet, 167.

Dragonet, the Gemmeous, 167.
,, the Sordid, 167.
Eagle-Ray, 46.
Echiodon, Drummond's, 378.
Eel, the common, 323.
,, the Conger, 325.
Eel-pout, 238.
Electric Ray, 27-29.
Erythrinus, 88.
Eyed Dog-fish, 19.
File-fish, 344.
,, the Mediterranean, 344.
Fire Flaire, Fiery-Flaw, 44.
Fishing Frog, 136.
Flounder, the Italian, 260.
,, the Red-backed, 265.
Flying-fish, 307, 308.
Fox, 12, 167.
Freshwater Perch, 56.
Frog-fish, 136.
Gade, the Three-bearded, 239.
Gar-fish, Gar-pike, 305.
Gedd, 309.
Germon, 127.
Gilt-head, 92, 220.
,, the Rayan, 119.
,, Ray's Toothed, 119.
,, the Red, 89.
,, the Toothed, 66.
Gipsy Herring, 321.
Goby, the Black, 148.
,, the Doubly-spotted, 162.
,, the Freshwater, 151.
,, the Paganellus, 156.
,, Pennant's Spotted, 164.
,, the White, 166.

Goby, the Yellow, 149.
Golden Maid, 220.
Goldfinny, Goldsinny, 220.
Grayling, 315.
Grey Mullet, 191–195.
   „   the Golden, 193.
   „   the Long-finned, 193.
   „   the Thick-lipped, 195.
Grey Notidanus, 14.
Groundling, 303.
Gudgeon, 278.
Gurnard, Bloch's, 144.
   „   the Cuckoo, 140.
   „   the Elleck, 140.
   „   the Flying, 147.
   „   the French, 141.
   „   the Grey, 143.
   „   the Lanthorn, 142.
   „   the Mailed, 146.
   „   the Piper, 145.
   „   the Red, 140.
   „   the Rock, 141.
   „   the Sapphirine, 142.
   „   the Streaked, 141.
Hair-tail, 102.
Hake, 235.
   „   the Forked, 236.
Hippocampus, the Short-snouted, 342.
Hornbeak, 305.
Horse Mackerel, 103.
Hound-fish, 21.
   „   the Rough, 17.
Huso, 53.
Jack, 309.
John Dory, 111.
King of the Sea Bream, 86.
Lampern, the fringe-lipped, 349.
Lamprey, 347.
   „   Planer's, 349.
   „   the River, 348.
   „   the Sea, 347.
   „   the Spotted, 347.
Lancelet, 350.
Large Spotted Dog-fish, 18.
Lesser „   „   17.
Loach, 302.

   „   the Spinous or Spined, 303.
Long-nose, 305.
Luce, 309.
Lyra, 145.
Mackerel, the Coly, 123.
   „   the common, 121.
   „   the Horse, 103.
   „   the Spanish, 123.
Maid, 320.
Maigre, Meagre, 97.
Mediterranean Remora, 130.
Megrim, 253.
Mendole, 67.
Miller's Dog, 3.
   „   Thumb, 138.
Minnow, 291.
Molebut, 345.
Monk, Monk-fish, 25.
Morgay, 17.
Mullet, the Grey, 191–195.
   „   the Red, 74.
Murry, 329.
Needle-fish, 334.
Numb-fish, 29.
Nurse-hound, 18.
Notidanus, 14.
Old Wife, 76, 211.
Ophidium, the Bearded, 243.
Otter-pike, 135.
Ox-eye, 79.
Ox-Ray, 49.
Paganellus, 156.
Pandora, 86.
Pelamide, 128.
Penny-Dog, 3.
Perch, 56.
   „   the Dusky, 63.
Picked Dog-fish, 21.
Pike, 309.
Pike-perch, 58.
Pilchard, 321.
Pilot-fish, 106.
Pink, 291.
Pipe-fish, the Broad-nosed, 331.
   „   the Great, 334.
   „   the Straight-nosed, 340
Piper, 145.
Plaice, 259.
Pompilus, 115.

Poor, 233.
Porbeagle, 8.
Pout, 234.
Power Cod, 233.
Prickleback, 196.
Rays, 27, 49.
Ray, the Bordered, 38.
   „   the Cuckoo, 37, 41.
   „   the Eagle, 46.
   „   the Electric, 27–29.
   „   the Fuller, 31.
   „   the Homelyn, 31.
   „   the Horned, 49.
   „   the Ox, 49.
   „   the Painted, 31.
   „   the Rough, 30.
   „   the Sand, 31.
   „   the Sandy, 37, 41.
   „   the Shagreen, 34.
   „   the Spotted, 31.
   „   the Sting, 44.
   „   the Whip, 46.
Rayan Gilt-head, 119.
Ray's Sea-bream, 119.
   „   Toothed Gilt-head, 119.
Ray-mouthed Dog, 7.
Red-eye, 286.
Red Gilt-head, 89.
Red Mullet, 74.
Red Snake-fish, 172.
Remora, 130.
Ribbon-fish, 207.
Robin Huss, 17.
Rock Dog-fish, 18.
Rock-fish, Rock Goby, 148.
Rock Ling, 239.
   „   the Three-bearded, 239.
   „   the Five-bearded, 241.
Rough Hound, 17.
Rudd, 286.
Sail-fish, 13.
Sand-eel, 248.
Sand-launce, 248.
Sapphirine Gurnard, 142.
Sardine, 321.
Saury, Saury-pike, 306.
Scabbard-fish, 101.
Scad, 103.

Scald-fish, 253.
Scale-foot, 101.
Scorpions, 93-95.
Sea-Ape, 12.
„ Bream, 76.
„ „ the common, 89.
„ „ Couch's, 87.
„ „ King of the, 86.
„ „ Ray's, 119.
„ „ the Red, or Spanish, 88.
„ „ the Sharp-toothed, 89.
„ Cat, 132.
„ Devil, 46, 49, 136.
„ Eagle, 46.
„ Fox, 12.
„ Hen, 145.
„ Horse, 342.
„ Perch, 61.
„ Snipe, 198.
Serranus, the Dusky, 63.
„ the Smooth, 62.
Shad, 319.
Shade-fish, 97.
Shanny, Shan, Smooth Shan, 184.
Sharks, 1-26.
Shark, the Angel, 25.
„ the Basking, 13.
„ the Beaumaris, 8.
„ the Blue, 1.
„ the Dog-fish, 17, 18.
„ the Fox, 12.
„ the Great Blue, 10.
„ the Hammer-headed, 4.
„ the Long-tailed, 12.
„ the Notidanus, 14.
„ the Picked, 21.
„ the Porbeagle, 8.
„ the Six-gilled, 14.
„ the Skate-toothed, 7.
„ the Smooth-hound, 7.
„ the Spinous, 24.
„ the Spotted, 17.
„ the Tope, 3.
Shark Ray, 25.
Silvery Hair-tail, 102.
Six-gilled Shark, 14.
Skelly, 283.

Skipjack, 363.
Skipper, Skipper-pike, 306.
Skulpin, 167.
„ the Yellow, 167.
Smelt, Sand Smelt, 188.
Snipe-fish, 198.
Sole, the Bastard, 265.
„ the common, 261.
„ the Little, 267.
„ the Smooth, 253.
„ the Variegated, 265.
Sparus, 66.
„ the Four-toothed, 66.
Spet, 187.
Spiny Dog-fish, 21, 22.
Spotted Dog-fish, 17, 18.
Star-gazer, 131.
Stickle-back, 196.
„ the Three-spined, 197.
Sting Bull, 132.
„ -fish, 135.
„ Ray, 44.
Stinkard, 7.
Stone-Basse, 64.
Sturgeons, 50-55.
„ the Adriatic, 50.
„ the Blunt-nosed, 53.
„ the Broad-nosed, 53.
Suck-fish, the Small, 199.
Sucker, the Bimaculated, 204.
„ the Connemara, 203.
„ the Cornish, 199.
„ the Jura, 199.
„ the Ocellated, 199.
Sucking-fish, 130.
Sun-fish, 13, 345.
„ the Truncated, 346.
Surmullet, 74, 75.
„ the Striped, 75.
Sword-fish, 99.
Tangle-fish, 334.
Tench, 294.
Thickback, 265.
Thornback, 30.
Thornhound, 21.
Thrasher, Thresher, 12.
Toad-fish, 46, 136.
Tommy Logge, 138.

Toothed Gilt-head, 66.
Tope, Toper, 3.
Topknot, Bloch's, 252.
Trigger-fish, the Pig-faced, 344.
Trout, the common, 310.
„ the Great Dalmatian, 311.
„ River Trout of Dalmatia, 313.
„ of the Lake of Garda, 314.
Trumpet-fish, 198.
„ the Snipe-nosed, 198.
Trygon, 44.
Tubfish, 142.
Tunny, the Bonito, 126.
„ the common, 124.
„ the Long-finned, 127.
Turbot, 250.
Twaite-Shad, 320.
Umbrina, 96.
Viper Weever, 135.
Wapper, 279.
Weevers, 132-135.
Weever, the common, 135.
„ the Great, 132.
„ the Lesser, 135.
„ the Viper, 135.
Whip Ray, 46.
Whistler, Whistle-fish, 239.
Whiting, 232.
„ Pout, 234.
„ Couch's, 376.
Woodcock-fish, 198.
Wrasse, the Ancient, 211.
„ the Ballan, 211.
„ the Cook, 215.
„ the Cuckoo, 215.
„ the Flesh-coloured, 215.
„ the Golden, 220.
„ the Indented-striped, 229.
„ the Rainbow, 229.
„ the Red, 215.
„ the Striped, 215.
„ the Three-spotted, 215.
„ the Trimaculated, 215.
Wreck-fish, 64.
Yellow Goby, 149.
Yellow-tail, 105.

b. INVERTEBRATES.

(The numbers opposite the names refer to the Systematic List, p. 242.)

Actinia, 147.
Black-fish, 6.
Blubber, 147.
Capanus, 82.
Cockle, 62.
Cray-fish, 115.
Cucumbers, 133.
Cuttle-fish, 6.
Date-shell, 55.
Dry-rot Worm, 82.
Fringed Ark, 58.
Great Crab, 107.
Harry Crab, 96.
Heart-shell, 67.
Hermit Crab, 108.
Limpet, 27.
Lobster, the common, 116.
Lug-worm, 130.
Mussels, 54.
Noah's Ark, 57.
Norway Lobster, 117.
Orbicular Ark, 59.
Oyster, 42–44.
Poulp, 1.
Prawn, 121.
Rock Lobster, 113.
Scallop, 45–49.
Sea-anemone, 146.
Sea-hare, 32.
Sea-pad, 138.
Sea-pens, 152.
Sea-slugs, 132.
Sea-spider, 89.
Sea-star, 138.
Sea-urchin, 134.
Shore Crab, 96.
Shrimp, 118.
Snail-shells, 33–38.
Spiny Lobster, 113.
Squid, 3.
Top-shells, 16–21.
Whelk, 9, 10.

Appendix III.

Reference Index *to the Italian Local and Vulgar Names of the Adriatic Fauna on the Austro-Hungarian Seaboard and Venetian Estuary.*

Acquadela .... Atherina hepsetus.
Adano, Adello, Adilo ... Acipenser sturio.
Afrodita .... Aphrodite hystrix.
Ago di mar .... { Siphonostoma and Syngnathus *sp*.
Agon, Agone d'Istria ... Smaris gracilis.
Agonà .... Atherina hepsetus.
Agone, Agon de Como ... Clupea alosa and finta.
Agosta, Agusta .... Palinurus vulgaris.
Albero bastardo .... Oblata melanura.
Alboro pagnesco .... Pagrus vulgaris.
Alborella .... Alburnus alburnellus.
Anchio .... Engraulis encrasicholus.
Anemolo rosso marino ... Actinia rubra.
Anguilla .... Anguilla vulgaris.
Anguéla .... Atherina *sp*.
  ,,   agonada ...... ,, hepsetus.
Angusígola .... Belone acus.
  ,,   falsa ...... } Siphonostoma and Syngnathus *sp*.
  ,,   salvatica... }
Anzoletta, Anzuletta ... Trigla *sp*.
Anzoletto comune ... } Trigla pini.
  ,,   piccolo ... }
  ,,   grande ...... ,, cuculus.
  ,,   di mar...... } Peristethus cataphractum.
  ,,   della madonna. }
Aragosta .... Palinurus vulgaris.
Arbon .... Pagellus erythrinus.
Arboro, Alboro, Alboretto. } ,, ,,
Arzentin .. .. { Argentina sphyræna. Lepidopus caudatus.
Asiá, Asiar, Asial ... { Acanthias vulgaris and Blainvillii.
Asinello .... Merluccius vulgaris.
Aspio .... Alburnus alburnellus.

Ástice, Ástese, Astise { Homarus vulgaris. Palinurus vulgaris.
Astóra, Astára, Astúra ... Pinna nobilis.
Attinia .... Actinia *sp*.
  ,,   angulosa ...... } ,, effœta.
  ,,   bianca .... }
  ,,   rossa .... } ,, rubra.
  ,,   porporina...... }
Avola, Avla .... Alburnus alburnellus.
Azzalino . ... Gonoplax rhomboides.
Babba .... Blennius gattorugine.
Baicolo .... Labrax lupus (*fry*).
Baile .... Zygæna malcus.
Balestra .... Balistes capriscus.
Barácola .... { Raja clavata.
                            ,, punctata.
                            ,, fullonica.
  ,,   alba .... } ,, punctata.
  ,,   bianca ...... }
Baracoletta .... { ,, ,,
                          ,, marginata.
Barbo, Barbio, Barb, } Barbol, Barbolo, } Barbus plebejus. Barbio, Balb, Balbio }
Barbon .... Mullus barbatus.
  ,,   de nassa .... ,, surmuletus.
Batauro, Botolo .... Mugil capito.
Bavosa, Baosa .... Raja marginata.
Berolla del tenero ...... Nassa reticulata.
  ,,   di mar............ Bulla lignaria.
Bibaron colorito .... Mactra stultosum.
  ,,   di mar .... Isocardia cor.
  ,,   di marina ... { Mactra lactea. ,, stultosum.
Bibarazza .... Venus gallina.
Bibarazza di mar .... Venus verrucosa.

Bisatto	Anguilla vulgaris.
„ tegrà	} Murœna helena.
„ indevisa	
Bisse delle cape	} Serpula *sp*.
„ „ sassi	
Boba, Bobba	Box vulgaris.
Bocca in cao	} Uranoscopus scaber.
„ capo	
Bon	One of the Mugil *sp*.
Bosega, Boseghe	Mugil chelo.
Branzin	Labrax lupus.
„ croato	Merluccius vulgaris.
Bressanella	Leuciscus phoxinus.
Bruco di mar	Aphrodite hystrix.
Bruffolo, Brussolo	{ Leuciscus aula.
	„ pauperum.
Brumo, Bisse dei legni	} Teredo navalis.
Bufalo de aspreo	Mæna zebra.
Bulbero	Cyprinus carpio.
Buligone	Cyclope neritea.
Bulli (Bule) col granzo	Pagurus Bernhardus.
Bullo maschio	Murex brandaris.
„ femena	„ trunculus.
Buovoli	Helix *sp*.
Buratello	Anguilla vulg. (*Elvers*).
Caecchia, Cagnea	Carcharias Milberti.
Cagnia	{ Selache maxima.
	Notidanus griseus.
	„ cinereus.
	Lamna cornubica.
	„ Spallanzanii.
	Carcharodon Rondeletii.
	Odontaspis ferox.
Cagnetto	{ Mustelus lævis and vulgaris.
Cagnizza	{ Carcharias glaucus and other large sharks.
„ glauca	Carcharias glaucus.
„ nasuta	Lamna Spallanzanii.
„ vera	Carcharodon Rondeletii.
Cagnola	Cobitis tænia.
Calamajo, Calamaro	Loligo vulgaris.
„ todero	} „ sagittata.
„ toto	
Caligher	Heliastes chromis.
Campanari	Cerithium vulgatum.
Campanile	Turritella communis.
Can	{ Generic term for all sharks.
Can barbaro	Notidanus barbarus.
„ bianco	Mustelus vulgaris.
„ da denti	{ Carcharias glaucus Galeus canis. Odontaspis ferox.
Can macchia	} Mustelus vulgaris.
„ pontisà	
„ senza denti	
„ negro	Galeus canis.
„ turchin	Carcharias glaucus.
Canestrello	Pecten *sp*.
„ di mar	} Pecten varius.
„ da una recia	
Cànissi, Cànizzi, Cragnizi	} Serranus cabrilla.
Cannelle	Serpula *sp*.
Canòcchia, Canoccia	Squilla mantis.
Cantarella	{ Pagrus vulgaris. Cantharus vulgaris.
Cantarini	Trachurus trachurus.
Cantara, Cantera, Cantarina, Cantarina de aspreo	} Cantharus vulgaris.
Cao da oglio	} Lamna cornubica.
Cavo d'ojo	
Caostello, Cavostello Caustello	} Mugil capito.
Capa da deo	} Solen vagina.
„ da dito	
„ de palo	} Chthamalus stellatus.
„ delle piere	
„ „ galene	Coronula testudinaria.
„ lunga	
„ „ nostrana	} Solen vagina.
„ „ bianca	
„ „ colorita	
„ „ marina	} „ siliqua.
„ tabachina	
„ santa	Pecten jacobæus.
„ „ piccola	„ varius.
„ tonda	Cardium edule.
„ „ di mar	{ „ tuberculatum. Tapes decussatus.
„ „ rigata	Cardium rusticum.
Caparon	Tapes edulis.
Caparozzolo	{ „ decussatus. Venus verrucosa.
„ dal scorzo grosso	} Tapes decussatus.

Caparozzolo dal scorzo sottile, Caparozzolo sottile	Scrobicularia piperita.
Caparozzoletti de mar	Anatifa lævis.
Caragolo	Trochus *sp.*
„ longo	Cerithium vulgatum.
Caragoletti da galanterie	Trochus adriaticus.
Carcána	Thynnus thunnina.
Carpa, Carpione, C. maschio	Cyprinus carpio.
Carpione	Salmo carpio.
Castagne commun de mar	Echinus brevispinosus.
Castagne de mar	{ „ microtuberculatus.
Castagnola	Brama raji.
Cataluzzo	{ „ „ Coryphæna hippurus.
Caval marin	
„ de mar	Hippocampus *sp.*
Cavalo storno	
Cavalla	Corvina nigra.
Cavazioi	Mullus barbatus (*fry*).
Cavedo, Cavedano	Leuciscus cavedanus.
Cavedon, Chiavedon	Cottus gobio.
Cavezzal	Leuciscus scardafa.
Cavezzale, Cavazzino	Leuciscus cavedanus.
Caz marin, Cazzo del mar	Holothuria tubulosa.
Cazzonello, Calzinei	Donax trunculus.
Ceppa, Ceppino, Cheppia, Ciepa	Clupea alosa and finta.
Cherne, Chierne	Serranus gigas.
Chiachia	Uranoscopus scaber.
Cievolo, Ceolo	Mugil cephalus.
Cigala de mar	Scyllarus arctus.
Cocciola	Cardium rusticum.
Coc-rosse	{ Leuciscus erythropthalmus.
Coffano del duro	Arca barbata.
„ di grotta	„ Noæ.
Coghe de mar	Aphysia depilans.
Colombo	{ Myliobatis aquila. Trygon pastinaca.
„ de mar	Myliobatis aquila.
„ vescovo	„ noctula.
Contrapasso	Gonoplax rhomboides.
Copiza	Spondylus gaederopus.
Coppése, Copése	Acipenser *sp.*
Corbo, Corbel, Corbetto	Umbrina cirrhosa.
Corbo di sasso, Corbel di sasso	Corvina nigra.
Córbola	Gebia littoralis.
Cortesan de caorle	Serranus cabrilla.
Cragnisso	Labrus mixtus.
Cucumero de mar	{ Holothuria *sp.* Cucumaria *sp.*
Dattolo, Dattolo di mar, Dattolo di Sabion, Dattero di mar	Pholus dactylus.
Dattolo di pietra, Dattolo di mar, Dattero di mar	{ Lithodomus. Lithophagus.
Dental	Dentex vulgaris.
Dentale della corona	„ gibbosus.
Diavolo di mar	Lophius piscatorius.
Donzella	{ Serranus scriba. Labrus *sp.*
Donzella di grotta, Donzella di sasso, Donzella di Quarnero	Labrus mixtus.
Dorada	Chrysophrys aurata.
Dotregan	Mugil auratus.
Fabbro, Fabretto, Favaretto	Heliastes chromis.
Facchino	Dromia Rumphii.
„ piccolo	„ lanata.
Falce	Trachypterus tænia.
Falso molo	Gadus merlangus.
Fanale	Trigla hirundo.
Fanfano	{ Naucrates ductor. Centrolophus pompilus.
Fave	Nucula magaritacea.
Figo	{ Stromateus *sp.* Centrolophus pompilus. Phycis *sp.*
„ di mar	Polyclinum ficus.
Folpo, Folpo todero, Folpo toti	Octopus vulgaris.
Folpo, Folpo da risa	Eledone moschata.
Foraguarda	Cobitis tænia.
Forapiere, Forasassi, Forasecchi	Nemachilus barbatulus.
Forcato	{ Peristethus cataphractum.
Forella	Salmo fario.
Forfetula	Xantho floridus.

Fregarola	{ Leuciscus muticellus. " phoxinus.	Go di mar	Gobius capito.
Fregata	Chondrostoma genei.	Gobato, Gobbo	Cyprinus carpio.
Gaidero	Spondylus gaederopus.	Gobione	Gobio fluviatilis.
Galinazza	Centriscus scolopax.	Goffo	Auxis vulgaris.
Galiotto, Galera	{ Ophidium barbatum. Fierasfer acus.	Grancipóro	{ Grapsus varius. Eriphia spinifrons. Pagurus maculatus.
Gambaro, Gambero, Gambaretto d'acqua salsa	Palæmon squilla.	Grancipol, Grancipoletto	Pilumnus hirtellus.
		Granzetto d'ostriga	Pinnotherus veterum.
Gambero d'acqua dolce	Astacus fluviatilis.	Granzéola piccola	Lysianassa spinicornis.
		Granzévola, Granzéola	Portunus depurator.
Gambero dell' ala	Portunus depurator.	Granzo	Carcinus mænas.
Ganzarioi	Scomber scomber.	" compasso	Lambrus mediterraneus.
Ganzariola	" pneumatophorus.	" di notte	Iaxea nocturna.
Gardelin	{ Crenilabrus mediterraneus.	" piato	{ Grapsus varius and marmoratus.
Garizzo	{ Smaris vulgaris and alcedo.	Granzon, Granzéola, Granzon falso d'aspreo	Maia squinado.
Garusa	Murex trunculus.		
Garúsolo	" sp.	Grillo de mar	Palinurus vulgaris.
" maschio	" brandaris.	Grongo	Conger sp.
" feména	" trunculus.	" di grotta	" vulgaris.
Gatta	Scyllium sp.	" di sabbia	Myrus vulgaris.
" d'aspreo " de Quarnero	" canicula.	Guatto	{ Gobius and Callionymus sp.
" nostrana " schiava	" stellare.	" di fango	Gobius jozo.
Gattorusola, Gattarozola	Blennius gattorugine.	" giallo	" niger.
		" di sasso	" paganellus.
Gattorusola colla cresta	Blennius pavo (male).	Iaral	Atherina hepsetus.
		Iardon	Spondylus gaederopus.
Gattorusola marina, Gallo	" " (female).	Issolon, Issolone	Cytherea chione.
		Kalimar, Kalamar	Loligo vulgaris.
Gattorusola bavosa " chiossa " senza cresta	" pholis.	Ladano	Acipenser huso.
		Lampreda " di mar	Petromyzon marinus.
Gattorusola d'aspreo " di mar " dall'occiàl	" ocellaris.	Lampreda " d'argento " di sasso	" fluviatilis.
		Lampredone	
Gattina piccola		Lampreda piccola " di sasso	" Planeri.
Gatton brunno	Notidanus griscus.		
" grigio	" cinereus.	Lampreda, Lampreola	Cobitis tænia.
Gerao, Garal, Gavon	Atherina hepsetus.	Lampusa	{ Blennius ocellaris and pholis.
Ghirsa	Smaris vulgaris.		
Girasol	Orthagoriscus Planci.	Lanfresca	Leuciscus phoxinus.
Girella	Coris Julis and Giofredi.	Langusta	Palinurus vulgaris.
Gò	{ Gobius ophiocephalus and other Gobius sp.	Lanspada	Cepola rubescens.
		Lanzardo	{ Scomber colius. " pneumatophorus.

Lasca	Chondrostoma soëtta.
Lastúra	Pinna nobilis.
Laterna	Trigla hirundo.
Latesiol	Pleuronectes italicus.
Lepa, Leppa	{ Crenilabrus pavo. „ mediterraneus.
Letterato	Auxis vulgaris.
Liba	Labrus *sp*.
Limone de mar	Cynthia papillosa.
Listello	Lepadogaster listellus.
Lizza	Lichia *sp*.
„ bastarda	„ glauca.
Loca	} Scrobicularia piperita.
„ di fango	
Lodra, Lodrin	Callionymus *sp*.
Longon	Tapes edulis.
Lotregan	Mugil auratus.
Lovo	Merluccius vulgaris.
Lucerna	Trigla hirundo.
Luzziolo	Crenilabrus rostratus.
Luzzo, Lusso	Esox lucius.
„ di mar	Sphyræna vulgaris.
Madagia, Madagiola	Pagellus erythrinus.
Madre dei gronghi, Mare dei gronghi	} Motella tricirrata.
Madrona, Marona	Actinia *sp*.
Magna, Magnariazo	Mugil capito.
Magna morti	Charax puntazzo.
„ pegola	Petromyzon marinus.
Magnarone	Cottus gobio.
Manico da coltello	Solen vagina.
Maride, Maridole	Smaris *sp*.
Marsion	{ Gobius auratus, Panizzæ, and other *sp*.
Marson, Marsion	Cottus gobio.
Marsion d'acqua dolce	Gobius fluviatilis.
„ de mar	„ minutus.
Martello	Zygæna malleus.
Matán, Matana	{ Trygon *sp*. Myliobatis aquila.
Mazanetta, Masinetta	Carcinus mænas.
Mazinette	Mugil capito.
Maziola	Trigla hirundo.
Mechiati, Mechiarini	Mugil cephalus.
Melon de mar	Echinus melo.
Menole	Mæna and Smaris *sp*.
Menola schiava (chiava)	} Mæna vulgaris and other *sp*.
Menoloto	Smaris vulgaris.
Menuaja mora	Gobius jozo.
Mercandola	Chondrostoma genei.
Merlo de mar	Serranus scriba.
Merluzzo	Merluccius vulgaris.
„ salvatico	Sphyræna vulgaris.
Molecca, Molecche	Carcinus mænas.
Molloso	Gadus merlangus.
Molo	„ *sp*.
„ da parangolo	{ „ euxinus and merlangus.
Moretta	Galeus canis.
Mormoro, Mormora, Mormiro	} Pagellus mormyrus.
Mormoro, Mormora, Molmolo	} Gadus minutus.
Moro	Raja macrorhynchus.
Mozzetta	Leuciscus muticellus.
Muccio, Mucchio	Trygon pastinaca.
Murena, Morena	Muræna helena.
Murice	{ Murex brandaris and trunculus.
Muscardino, Muscarolo	} Eledone moschata.
Musicanti	Trachurus trachurus.
Musoduro	Trigla lineata.
Mussolo, Muzzolo	{ Modiola barbata. Arca Noæ.
Naridola	{ Trochus varius and other *sp*.
„ grande	Trochus zizyphinus.
Nodola	Brama raji.
Nonno, Nano	Cyprinodon calaritanus.
Occiada, Occhiada, Ochiá	} Oblata melanura.
Ociada	Cantharus orbicularis.
„ bastarda	Brama raji.
Occhio di Santa Lucia	} Turbo rugosus.
Oliva	Bulla hydatis.
Ombra, Ombria	Sciæna aquila.
Ombrela, Ombrella	{ Umbrina cirrhosa. Corvina nigra.
Orada	{ Chrysophrys aurata. Leuciscus pigus.
Orada dell' Adese	„ „
Orbetti	Mugil cephalus.
Orecchio di San Pietro	Haliotis tuberculata.
Ostreghetta del duro	Chama gryphoides.
Ostrica a lamelle	Ostrea lamellosa.
„ comune cristata	} „ edulis, *var*. cristata.

Ostrica comune depressa, Ostrichino	Ostrea edulis, *var.* depressa.
Ostrica comune falcata	Ostrea edulis, *var.* falcata.
Ostrica di palo	Ostrea adriatica.
Ostura	Pinna nobilis.
Ovi di mar	Cynthia microcosmus.
Paganello	
" di porto	Gobius paganellus.
" verga	
" bianco	" jozo.
" di mar	" niger and jozo.
" insanguinà	" cruentatus.
Pagaro	Pagrus vulgaris.
Palamida, Palamia	Thynnus pelamys. / Pelamys sarda.
Palóstrega di porto	Pinna nobilis.
Pantalena	Fissurella and Patella *sp.*
Papagà	Labrus *sp.* / Serranus scriba.
Papagallo verde	Labrus turdus.
Papalina	Clupea papalina.
Passara, Passera, Passarin, Passariello	Pleuronectes italicus.
Pataraccia	Arnoglossus *sp.* / Citharus linguatula. / Solea monochir.
" mora	Arnoglossus Grohmanni.
Pedocchio, Peocchio, Peocio, Peocio di mar	Mytilus edulis.
Peocio peloso	Modiola barbata.
Pellegrina di San Giacomo	Pecten jacobæus.
Peloso	Solea variegata. / " monochir.
Peloso	Phrynorhombus unimaculatus.
" di grotta	
Penna di mar, Pennacchiera	Pennatula *sp.*
Perga	Serranus scriba.
" dalmata	" cabrilla.
Perha	" scriba and cabrilla.
Perso di fiume	Perca fluviatilis.
Persico, Persego	" "
Pesce ago	Syngnathus acus.
" baile	Zygæna malcus.
" balla	Balistes capriscus. / Orthagoriscus mola.
Pesce bandiera	Alopias vulpes.
" barbastrillo	Exocœtus volitans.
" barbastella	Dactylopterus volitans.
" barila	Orthagoriscus mola.
" blu	Scomber and Thynnus *sp.*
" can	Generic term for sharks.
" " spinarol	Acanthias vulgaris and Blainvillii.
" cavalier	Crenilabrus mediterraneus.
" colombo	Myliobatis aquila. / Trygon pastinaca.
" cordéla	Cepola rubescens.
" fabbro	Heliastes chromis.
" falce	Trachypterus tænia.
" figa	Stromateus *sp.*
" gallo	Ausonia Cuvieri.
" luna	Orthagoriscus mola.
" manzo	Notidanus griseus.
" martello	Zygæna malcus.
" mollo	Gadus *sp.*
" morti	Charax puntazzo.
" nello	Acantholabrus Pallonii.
" occhial	Blennius ocellaris.
" pantofola	Zygæna tudes.
" perseghin	Perca fluviatilis.
" pestafero	Heliastes chromis.
" pettine	Novacula cultrata.
" porco	Centrina Salviani.
" prete	Merluccius vulgaris.
" ranin	Lepadogaster *sp.*
" rioda	Orthagoriscus mola.
" " liscio	" Planci.
" " ruvido	" mola.
" rospo	Lophius piscatorius.
" sanpietro	Zeus faber.
" scarpolero	Heliastes chromis.
" schermo	Sphyræna vulgaris.
" sorcio	Centrina Salviani.
" sorze	Motella tricirrata.
" spada	Xiphias gladius. / Cepola rubescens.
" spin	Gasterosteus *sp.*
" spuzza	Crenilabrus pavo. / Acantholabrus Pallonii.
" ton	Thynnus *sp.*
" tremolo	Torpedo *sp.*
" trombetta	Centriscus scolapax.
" violin	Rhina squatina.
" volpe	Alopias vulpes.

Pesseta, Pessucola	Cobitis tænia.	Rombo	} Rhombus maximus.
Peto de dolphin	Schizaster canaliferus.	„ di sasso	
Pevarazza	Venus gallina.	Rondinella	{ Exocœtus volitans. Dactylopterus volitans.
Pevarone	Lithodomus lithophagus.		
Piè d'asino	Pectunculus glycimeris.	Rosa di mar	{ Retepora cellulosa. Actinia *sp.*
„ d'occha	{ Asteriscus membranaceus.		
		Rospo	
Piede de caval	Pinna nobilis.	„ di mar	} Lophius piscatorius.
Pigo	Leuciscus pigus.	„ di fango	
Pincia, Pincie	Alburnus alburnellus.	Sacchetto	Centropristis hepatus.
Pinco	Labrus maculatus.	Sagri, Sagrin	Squatina oculata.
Piso	Pinnotherus pisum.	Sajon	} Leuciscus pigus.
Polpo	Octopus vulgaris.	„ colle broche	
Pompilo, Pompin	Thynnus vulgaris.	Saletto de fosso	Orchestia littorea.
Pontio	Mœna vulgaris.	Salissoni cape	Chiton siculus.
Porcella	Dolium galea.	„ delle rive	Ligia italica.
Porcelletta, Porzelletta	Cassidaria echinophora.	Salpa	Box salpa.
Porchetti	Lepadogaster *sp.*	Sanchetto	Arnoglossus laterna.
Poréssa	{ Pagurus maculatus. Eriphia spinifrons. Grapsus varius.	„ peloso	Solea monochir.
		Sangue de Turco	Pectunculus glycimeris.
		Sanpiero	Zeus faber.
„ salvatica	Xantho rivolosus.	Santalena	Fissurella and Patella *sp.*
Porpora, Porco	Murex trunculus.	Sardella, Sardéle, Sardeline	} Clupea pilchardus.
Porzella, Porzellata	Acipenser sturio (*fry*).		
Potta di mar	} Rhizostomum Cuvieri.	Sardelina	„ papalina.
„ marina		Sardella salvatica, Sardena	} „ alosa and finta.
Quattro occhio	} Raja miraletus.		
Quattr' occhio		Sardon	Engraulis encrasicholus.
Ragno	{ Trachinus draco. Labrax lupus.	Sargo	Sargus Rondeletii.
		„ d'Istria	Charax puntazzo.
„ bianco	} Trachinus draco.	Saron, Suro, Suero	Trachurus trachurus.
„ di mar		Savetta, Savel, Soëtta	Chondrostoma soëtta.
„ nero	{ „ arancus.	Scagiotto	Gobius Ruthensparri.
„ di grotta		Scampa salvatica	Galathea strigosa.
„ pagano	{ „ radiatus.	Scamparello, Scampetto	} „ scamparella.
Ragnola	Trachinus vipera.	Scampo morte	} „ rugosa.
Ragosta	Palinurus vulgaris.	Scampa falsa a man lunghe	
Raina, Rainotto	Cyprinus carpio.		
Rasa	Raja *sp.*	Scampo	Nephrops norvegicus.
„ spinosa	„ clavata.	Scarabina	Clupea alosa and finta.
„ di sabbia	„ macrorhyncus.	Scardóbola	Gebia littoralis.
Rasetta	{ „ punctata and other small rays.	Scardola, Sgardola, Scardoloto del Sil	} Leuciscus erythropthalmus.
Ribon, Ribone	Pagellus erythrinus.	Scarparo	Raja miraletus.
Rizzo de mar	{ Echinus lividus and brevispinosus.	Scarpena	Scorpæna *sp.*
		„ negra, Scarpon	} „ porcus.
„ melon	Echinus melo.		
Rombetto di grotta	{ Phrynorhombus unimaculatus.	Scarpena de sasso	} „ scrofa.
		„ rossa	

APPENDIX III.

Scarpena salvatica, di sasso	} Polyprion cernium (?).
Scarpion di grotta	Coristes dentalus.
„ di sabbion, del sabionao	} Porcellana longicornis.
Schiavon	Serranus cabrilla.
Schila, Skila, Squilla	{ Cranzon vulgaris. Palæmon squilla.
Schilin	Callionymus belenus.
Scoglio brandare	Murex brandaris.
„ troncato	„ trunculus.
Scombro, Sgombro	Scomber scomber.
Selmo	Ophiothrix fragilis.
„ a compasso	Ophioderma longicauda.
„ delle grancéole	Inachus scorpio.
Sepiola, Sepiolina	Sepiola Rondeletii.
Seppa, Sépa, Seppia	Sepia officinalis.
Serpentin	Lepidopus caudatus.
Sfogietto	Solea lutea.
Sfogietto	} „ variegata.
„ peloso	„ monochir.
Sfogio dal porro	„ impar.
„ menuo	„ minuta.
„ turco	„ Kleinii.
Sfoja, Sfoglia, Sfogio, „ nostran, „ di sasso	} Solea vulgaris.
Sfojo	Arnoglossus Grohmanni.
Sfrizin	Lepadogaster listellus.
Sgardobola falsa	Calianassa subterranea.
Sgarzanel	Donax trunculus.
Sgionfetto	Auxis vulgaris.
Sgramfo	Torpedo marmorata.
Smergo	{ Crenilabrus mediterraneus.
Smida	Blennius ocellaris.
Sorbola di mar	Lima inflata.
Sorzo	Phycis mediterraneus.
„ Sorcio, Sorze	Motella tricirrata.
„ salvatico	Phycis blennioides.
Spada argentina, „ arzentina, „ di argento	} Lepidopus caudatus. / Trachypterus tænia.
„ rossa, „ de Quarnero	} Cepola rubescens.
Spadon	Xyphias gladius.
Sparetto	{ Sargus Rondeletii and annularis.
Sparo	Sargus sp.
Sparo bastardo	Mæna zebra.
Sparo d'Istria	Pagrus vulgaris.
Sparolo	Sargus annularis.
Speardo	Acipenser sturio.
Sperga	{ Serranus scriba and cabrilla.
Spiantano	Carcinus mænas.
Spin, Spinarola, Spinariola, Spinarella	} Gasterosteus sp.
Spizzo	{ Sargus vulgaris. Charax puntazzo.
„ bastardo	„ „
Sporcella, Sforzella	Acipenser sp. (fry).
Sporcello di sasso	Lepadogaster sp.
Squæna, Squalena	Rhina squatina.
Squal	Leuciscus cavedanus.
Stella rossa	Asteracanthion rubens.
„ marina	„ sp.
Stelletta	{ Asteriscus verriculatus.
Stellon, Stella	Astropecten aurantiaca.
Storion, Sturione	Acipenser sturio.
Strega	{ Blennius sp. Nemachilus barbatulus.
Stura	Pinna nobilis.
Suazo, Soazo, Sfazo	Rhombus lævis.
Succhetto	Trigla lyra.
Tabaro	Pagrus vulgaris.
Tabacchina	Solen siliqua.
Taccasasso	Lepadogaster sp.
Tambarello, Tombarello	} Auxis vulgaris.
Tartuffolo	{ Polyclinum ficus. Echinus microtuberculatus.
Taska	Eriphia spinifrons.
Temalo	Gobio fluviatilis.
„ bastardo	Leuciscus cavedanus.
Tenca	Phycis mediterraneus.
„ di mar	Labrus merula.
Testa dura, „ grossa	} Trigla lineata.
Teston	Anguilla vulgaris.
Tinca, Tenca, Tencoto	} Tinca vulgaris.
Ton, Tonina	Thynnus vulgaris.
Tonina	„ thunnina.
Topi	Mugil cephalus.
Totano	Loligo vulgaris.
Toti	Uranoscopus scaber.
Tremolo, Tremola	Torpedo sp.

2 O

Tremolo occià	} Torpedo narce.	Varagnolo	{ Trachinus draco and vipera.
„ a macchie negre		Varolo, Variolo	Labrax lupus.
Triglia, Tria	Mullus surmuletus.	Veccio, Veccie, Vecez	Gobius fluviatilis.
Trompeto, Trompilo, Trompin	} Thynnus vulgaris.	Verdon	{ Labrus turdus. Crenilabrus pavo.
Trotta bastarda	Leuciscus cavedanus.	Vermi dei legni	Teredo navalis.
Trottolo bianchiccia	Trochus Biasoletti.	Verzelata	Mugil saliens.
Trutta	Salmo fario.	Vescola	Arenicola piscatorum.
„ rossa	„ carpio.	Violin	Rhina squatina.
Turchello	Trigla lyra.	Volpe	Alopias vulpes.
„ insanguinà	Lepidotrigla aspera.	Volpina, Volpinetti	Mugil cephalus.
Ubriago	Trigla lineata.	Zamarugolo	Aporrhais pes pelicani.
Uovi di mar	Cynthia microcosmus.	Zanzaloro	{ Stenorrhynchus phalangium.
Vairone, Varone	{ Leuciscus muticellus. „ phoxinus.	Zentil	Solea vulgaris.
Varagno bianco	Trachinus draco.	Zottolo	} Sepia Rondeletii.
„ nero	„ araneus.	Zottolina	
„ pagán	„ radiatus.	Zucchetto	Ilea nucleus.

Key to the Pronunciation of Croatian Words.

The c is pronounced like the German z, English *tzet*.
č like *tshay* (English).
ć like the Italian ci, in *cielo*.
š like the English *sh*.
z as in English.
ž like the French j, as in *jour*.
nj like the French gn, in *signal*.
lj like the French l mouillé, or the Italian *gli*.
gje like *je-ay* (Eng), *gie* (Ital.).
gjo like *je-oh* (Eng.), *gio* (Ital.).
gja like *je-ah* (Eng.), *gia* (Ital.).
gju like *je-uh* (Eng.), *giu* (Ital.).
è before an r, as in *cèrna, pèrc*, etc , is not pronounced at all.

Appendix IV.

REFERENCE INDEX *to the Croatian Local and Vulgar Names of the Adriatic Fauna on the Austro-Hungarian Seaboard.*

Agaća	Labrax lupus.
Angulja	Anguilla vulgaris.
Ankulete, Anzuleta	Trigla *sp*.
Arbun	Pagellus erythrinus.
Arkaj, ovčica	Pagellus mormyrus.
Astić	Homarus vulgaris.
Babaš	Mugil cephalus.
Baba	{ Blennius gattorugine. Blennius ocellaris.
Baba krunašica	Blennius pavo.
Babica	Lepodogaster *sp*.
Babica od dubine	Blennius ocellaris.
Babka	Blennius tentacularis.
Babuka	Blennius vulgaris.
Babuška	Chiton siculus.
Balavac	{ Mugil capito. Cottus gobio.
Balavica	Blennius palmicornis.
Barakula	{ Raja clavata and miraletus.
Barakulica	Raja punctata.
Barbaroga	Blennius tentacularis.
Barbir	Blennius gattorugine.
Barbun	Mullus barbatus.
Batofina	Uranoscopus scaber.
Batovina	Gobius jozo.
Bavuš	Mugil saliens.
Bazak	Leuciscus basak.
Berkavica	Mullus barbatus.
Bezmek	Uranoscopus scaber.
Bilizna, Bilizma	{ Seriola Dumerilii. Lichia amia.
Biškup	Myliobatis noctula.
Bistranga, pastrmka	Salmo dentex.
Bitinica	Lichia amia.
Bjelica	Lichia amia.
Bljudica	Patella vulgata.

Boculjava gušavica	Crenilabrus pavo.
Bodeljka	Scorpæna *sp*.
Bramburači	Pagurus Bernhardus.
Brgljun	Engraulis encrasicholus.
Brizgavac	Holothuria tubulosa.
Buča	{ Raja marginata. Trygon *sp*.
Bućát mjesečarka	Orthagoriscus mola.
Bugva, Bukva, Buba	Box vulgaris.
Bulja	Perca fluviatilis.
Bumbarak Bamburač	} Turritella communis.
Busbana	Gadus minutus.
Butac	Orthagoriscus mola.
Butovka	Pinna nobilis.
čač, čač muški	Uranoscopus scaber.
čača	Lophius piscatorius.
čanča	Isocardia cor.
čančica	Cardium edule.
Capor	Anguilla eurystoma.
čaška	Pectunculus glycimeris.
čepa, čipa	Clupea alosa and finta.
čerčak	Palinurus vulgaris.
Cèrna škarpena Cèrni škarpoč	} Scorpæna porcus.
Cèrjena škarpena Cèrveni škarpoč	} Scorpæna scrofa.
Cèrnjak	Gobius jozo.
četiri oči	Raja miraletus.
Cicala	Anatifa lævis.
Cicavica	Smaris vulgaris.
Ciepa čipal glavotni	} Mugil cephalus.
Cievnjak	Serpula *sp*.
čiga	Atherina boyeri.
čigraši	Trochus *sp*.
čikov	Nemachilus barbatulus.

Crljene kućice } Tellina exigua.	
Crljenice }	
Crnelj, crnej	Umbrina cirrhosa.
Crnjelj	Heliastes chromis.
Crni spuž	Helix Ponzolzi.
Crnorep	Oblata melanura.
Ćučina	{ Centropristis hepatus. Lepidotrigla aspera.
Ćuk	Rhina squatina.
Ćupka	Fissurella costaria.
Cvičenica	Tinca vulgaris.
Čvrljak	Labrus festivus.
Cvjetulja	Actinia sp.
Daguja	Mytilus edulis.
Divi	One of the Mugil sp.
„ pišmoj	Gadus minutus.
Dlakuša	Aphrodite hystrix.
Drhtuja	Torpedo sp.
Drlje	Scardinius dergle.
Drozak	Labrus festivus.
Dugnjača	Coris sp.
Dugonosica	Crenilabrus rostratus.
Dupinska pèrsa	Schizaster canaliferus.
Fanfan	Naucrates ductor.
Figa	Labrus mixtus.
Fratar	Sargus Rondeletii.
Fratrić, oluz	„ vulgaris.
Gajun	Tapes decussatus.
Gaovica	Leuciscus adspersus.
Gaun batelj	Atherina Boyeri.
„ hrskavac	„ mochon.
„ pravi	„ hepsetus.
Gavun, gaun, gavon...	{ Atherina hepsetus and other sp.
Gèrgeć	Gasterosteus aculeatus.
Gira } Mæna vulgaris.	
„ oblica }	
Girica	Atherina sp.
Glamoč bilac	Gobius jozo.
„ lučni	„ jozo.
„ pločar	„ capito.
„ purićaš	„ ophiocephalus.
„ žutac	„ auratus.
„ žudij	„ cruentatus.
„ žuti	„ niger.
Glamočić	Gobius Buchichii.
Glavoč, Glamoč, Gulj...	„ sp.
„ cèrni	„ jozo.
„ od ruba	„ niger.
Glavuje	Trigla lineata.
Glevoć	Helix secernenda.
Glista drva } Teredo navalis.	
Glistice }	
Gof	Seriola Dumerilii.
Gola rakovica	Carcinus mœnas.
Golćić	Scomber scomber (fry).
Golica	Ammopleurops lacteus.
Golub	{ Myliobatis noctula. „ aquila.
„ morski	„ „
Govedar	Cobitis tænia.
Grb	{ Umbrina cirrhosa. Sciæna aquila.
Grbić	Pagellus acarne.
Grbić	Pagellus bogaraveo.
Grdobina	Lophius piscatorius.
Grmalj	Eriphia spinifrons.
Grum, Grunj	Conger sp.
Gruj, Gor	Anguilla vulgaris.
Grunjeva mati	Motella tricirrata.
Gubavac	Helix setigera.
Gulić	Gobius paganellus.
Gulj od blata	„ jozo.
Guskina noga	{ Asteriscus membranaceus.
Havba	Umbrina cirrhosa.
Hinjuša	Crenilabrus ocellatus.
Hlapić	Galathea scamparella.
Hobot	Octopus vulgaris.
Hobotnica	{ Eledone moschata. Octopus vulgaris.
Hudobina	Lophius piscatorius.
Huj, Hulj	Ophidium barbatum.
Iaglun	Histiophorus belone.
Igla	Belone acus.
Igla diva } Siphonostoma and Syngnathus sp.	
„ morska }	
Inac	{ Crenilabrus griseus, and tinca.
Inćun	Engraulis encrasicholus.
Iskra	Nassa reticulata.
Iverak	Pleuronectes italicus.
Jaglica	Belone acus.
Jaglun	Xyphias gladius.
Jaglunić	Sphyræna vulgaris.
Jaja od mora	Cynthia microcosmus.
Jakovska kapica	Pecten jacobæus.
Jaram, joron, jorona	Zygæna malleus.
Jastog	Homarus vulgaris.
Jebac	Crenilabrus pavo (*male*).

Jegulja, jamarica..........Anguilla vulgaris.
Jesetra, jesetre ....Acipenser *sp*.
Jež, morski jež ....Echinus lividus & melo.
Ježić .... „ microtuberculatus.
Ježina .... „ brevispinosus.
Kačiga....................Cassidaria echinophora.
Kalkan....................Pleuronectes italicus.
Kamenica .... { Ostrea *sp*.
{ Raja clavata.
Kamenski gulj ....Gobius paganellus.
Kampanil ....Turritella communis.
Kanjac....................Serranus scriba.
Kantar....................Cantharus *sp*.
Kanoće ....Squilla mantis.
Kapica.................. { Pecten glaber.
{ Cardium rusticum.
„ obla............... „ tuberculatum.
Karakatnica.............Octopus vulgaris.
Karlić ....Gebia littoralis.
Karpiun ....Cyprinus carpio.
Kavala...................Corvina nigra.
Keljavac ....Leuciscus scardafa.
Kèrb ....Umbrina cirrhosa.
Kèrna, Kirnja prava ...Serranus gigas.
Kèrstača .... }
Kèrstijež .... } Asteracanthion rubeus.
Kirnja mala.............Apogon imberbis.
Kirnja mala............. }
„ velika .... } Anthias sacer.
Klapavica ....Mytilus edulis.
Klapun, Klapunica......Cytherea chione.
Klapunica ....Mytilus edulis.
Klapunica ....Cyclope nerithea.
Klen, Klenčić...........Leuciscus illyricus.
Klinka.................. { Raja macroryhnchus and
{ oxyrhynchus.
Knez .... { Crenilabrus mediterra-
{ neus.
Knez ....Coris *sp*.
Kokošica................Mytilus edulis.
Kokot .... { Blennius *sp*.
{ Trigla lyra.
{ Trigla lineata.
Koljuška ....Gasterosteus aculeatus.
Komarča ....Chrysophrys aurata.
Konj morski .... { Hippocampus *sp*.
{ Merluccius vulgaris.
Konj od mora, Ko- } Hippocampus *sp*.
njić morski .... }
Konjina ....Pectunculus glycimeris.

Kopanjica ....Mactra stultorum.
Kopit .... }
Kopitnjak .... } Spondylus gædcropus.
Koravica ....Leuciscus phoxinus.
Košćerin ....Acanthias *sp*.
Kosir ....Myliobatis aquila.
Kosirica ....Crenilabrus Roissali.
Koslica ....Galathea scamparella.
Kosmač ....Dromia Rumphii.
Kosmate od grota ... } Phrynorhombus unima-
„ šfoljice ...... } culatus.
Kosmate šfoljice.........Solea monochir.
Kostelj....................Acanthias, *sp*.
Kostelj vlastelin ... .Acanthias Blainvillii.
Kostica ....Palæmon squilla.
Kovač ....Zeus faber.
Kraja ....Serranus gigas.
Králjica ....Blennius rouxi.
Krap obični..............Cyprinus carpio.
Krapulj ....Cerithium vulgatum.
Kraška....................Crenilabrus Roissali.
Krastavica ....Solen vagina.
Kravica .... { Murex trunculus.
{ Helix aperta.
Križalina ....Asteriscus verriculatus.
Krugalo ....Lambrus mediterraneus.
Krupatka............... { Leuciscus erythrophthal-
{ mus.
Kućica...................Tapes decussatus.
Kučina...................Carcharodon Rondeletii.
Kuka ....Scyllarus latus.
Kunjka .... { Arca Noæ.
{ Cardium edule.
Kurben, Kurbeš ...... { Umbrina cirrhosa.
{ Corvina nigra.
Kurben od kamena ... „ „
Kusača ....Scombresox Rondeletii.
Ladinka ....Venus verrucosa.
Ladjar ....Teredo navalis.
Lamprida ....Petromyzon marinus.
Lančeska................Coryphæna hippurus.
Lastavica............... { Trigla *sp*.
{ Exocœtus volitans.
Lastavica prava ....Dactylopterus volitans.
Lenica .... { Serranus scriba.
{ Labrus turdus.
{ Crenilabrus pavo.
Leteći kokot ....Dactylopterus volitans.
Letica, lastavica ....Exocœtus Rondeletii.
Lica ....Lichia amia.

Liganj, Lignja ili obična crna kraka	Loligo vulgaris.
Linj, Linjak	Tinca vulgaris.
Lipan, Lipljen	Thymallus vulgaris.
Lisanka	Tapes edulis.
Lisica	Alopias vulpes.
Lizibaba, Legbaba	Cobitis tænia.
Ljuštura	Pinna nobilis.
Lokarda	Scomber Scomber colias.
Lovrata, Lovratica	Chrysophrys aurata.
Luben, Lubin, Lubanj, Ljubljaj	Labrax lupus.
Lučenka, Lučerna	Trigla hirundo. lyra.
Luceta morska	Labrus merula.
Lumbrak	Crenilabrus pavo.
Lupar	Patella vulgata.
Mač	Trachypterus tænia.
Mačak crni	Scyllium canicula.
Mačak naški	„ stellare.
Mačka	„ canicula.
Mačin	Acantholabrus Pallonii.
Mačinac	Cepola rubescens.
Mačka šargasta	Scyllium stellare.
Magavetás	Zonites acies.
Maklja	Squalius tenellus.
Mala jegulja	Anguilla vulg. (Elvers).
Manjak	Seriola Dumerilii (*fry*).
Manjur	Saurus griseus.
Mater od ugorâ	Motella tricirrata.
Matulić	Apogon imberbis.
Maženica	Leuciscus aula.
Mečica	Paraphoxinus alepidotus.
Mendula biela	Smaris vulgaris.
Mèrkač	Eledone moschata.
Mèrkačić	Octopus vulg.
Metja	One of the Mugil *sp*.
Mjehurača	Bulla hydatis.
Migavica	Pecten glaber.
Mihača	Balistes capriscus.
Milvica	Smaris vulgaris.
Minčion	Engraulis encrasicholus.
Miš	Callionymus maculatus and belenus.
Miš morski	Motella tricirrata.
Mjesečarka	Orthagoriscus mola.
Mladica	Salmo obtusirostris.
Mlič	Latrunculus pellucidus.
Modra morska pluća	Rhizostomum Cuvieri.
Modrak, Modraš	Mæna vulgaris.
Modri Inâc	Crenilabrus melanocercus.
Modrulj	Smaris alcedo.
Morska šljuka	Centriscus scolopax.
„ zmija	Myrus vulgaris.
„ srčavka	Cardium tuberculatum.
„ zviezdica	Asteracanthion *sp*.
Morski djavol	Lophius piscatorius.
„ gulj	Gobius cruentatus.
„ jež	Echinus lividus and melo.
„ kurac	Holothuria tubulosa.
„ pauk	Maia squinado.
„ rak	Palæmon squilla.
„ zec	Aplysia depilans.
Morun, Moruna	Acipenser huso.
Moruzga	Murex brandaris.
Moruzga	Anemonia and Actinia *sp*
Mrena	Barbus plebejus.
Mržnjak	Mugil saliens.
Mulj, Muljal	Mugil *sp*.
Murina, Mrina	Muræna helena.
Mušul	Arca Noæ.
Muzgavac	Octopus vulgaris.
Nanarić, Nanarica	Trochus Biasoletti.
Narikle	Trochus *sp*.
Nejasitka	Asteriscus membranaceus.
Noćno krugalo	Iaxea nocturna.
Obična rakovica	Carcinus mænas.
„ sablja	Xyphias gladius.
Obični kamotoč	Pholas dactylus.
„ lupar	Anatifa lævis.
„ račić	Crangon vulgaris.
„ šašanj	Teredo navalis.
Oblić	Rhombus maximus.
Oblica	Smaris *sp*.
„ biela	„ vulgaris.
Obloustka	Petromyzon Planeri.
Ogor	Anguilla vulgaris.
Oliga	Smaris gracilis.
Oluz	Sargus vulgaris.
Orfanić	Labrus turdus.
Osata	Oblata melanura.
Osal, Oslić	Merluccius vulgaris.
Ostrieš	Perca fluviatilis.
Oštriga	Ostrea *sp*.
Oštruja	Smaris vulgaris (*female*).
Ostrulj	Aulopyge Hügeli.

Ovca, Ovčica	Pagellus mormyrus.
Ovrata	Chrysophrys aurata.
Pagar, Pagrun	Pagrus vulgaris.
Pagar prljaš	„ Ehrenbergii.
Paklena, Paklara	Petromyzon marinus.
Palamida, Palanda, Polanda	{ Thynnus pelamys. / Pelamys sarda.
Pas	Generic term for sharks.
„ butor „ crni „ crnomanjast „ riba „ sa zubi	} Galeus canis.
„ spadun	Alopias vulpes.
„ ženka	Carcharodon Rondeletii.
Pasara, Pasera	Pleuronectes italicus.
Pas bulaš	Mustelus vulgaris.
Pasjak	Zonites albanicus.
Pasnica	{ Carcharias glaucus. / Carcharodon Rondeletii.
Pastèrmka	Salmo dentex.
Pastrva	Salmo sp.
Pastrva pirgasica	„ obtusirostris.
Pastirica	Lichia sp.
Pataračе	Citharus linguatula.
Pauk	Trachinus draco.
Pavlinka	Crenilabrus ocellatus.
Pazdrk	Pteroplatea altavela.
Pèrč	{ Smaris vulgaris (male). / Eledone moschata.
Peritska	Pinna nobilis.
Pèrstenac	Lithodomus lithophagus.
Perulja	Pennatula phosphorea.
Peš, peša	Cottus gobio.
Peškelj	Leuciscus scardafa.
Peškvela	Leuciscus rubella.
Pestelj	Holothuria tubulosa.
Petar	Zeus faber.
Pic	{ Sargus vulgaris. / Charax puntazzo.
Pilača	Lima inflata.
Pinzulić	Centropristis hepatus.
Pirka	{ Serranus cabrilla. / „ scriba.
Piška od mora	Stromateus fiatola.
Piškor	Nemachilus barbatulus.
Piškor, potočni piškor	{ Petromyzon fluviatilis and Planeri.
Pišmoj, Pišmolj	Gadus sp.
Pišmolj od parangala	Gadus merlangus.
Piur	Paraphoxinus croaticus.
Pivac	Blennius pavo.
Pivčić	Tripterygium nasus.
Pizdarica	Helix Ponzolzi.
Pizdica	Arca Noæ.
Pizdin-prilipak	Lepadogaster sp.
Pizdoklep	Palinurus vulgaris.
Pjeskožil	Arenicola piscatorum.
Plahut	Gobius paganellus.
Plavica	Scomber colias.
Plosnatica	Pleuronectes italicus.
Plotica	Leuciscus plotizza.
Plotice	Leuciscus sp.
Pocuranac	Loligo vulgaris.
Podlanica	Chrysophrys aurata.
Podujka	{ Crenilabrus mediterraneus.
Podustva	Chondrostoma Knerii.
Pokrovača	Pecten jacobæus.
„ gladka	„ glaber.
„ poklopita	„ opercularis.
Poletuša	{ Dactylopterus volitans. / Exocœtus volitans.
Polig bieli	Raja punctata.
„ košćati	„ clavata.
Poljski slemak	Hyalina cellaria.
Popauk	Gobius Lesueuri.
Pornpujak	„ paganellus.
Postrva	Salmo sp.
Potočni rak	Astacus fluviatilis.
Prasac „ morski	} Centrina Salviani.
Prasica	Trigla hirundo.
Pravi	One of the Mugil sp.
Pravi jesetar	Acipenser sturio.
Prhna ribica	Blennius canevæ.
Pripelanka	Tapes decussatus.
Prilicpak	{ Fissurella sp. / Patella sp. / Chiton siculus.
Prilipak	Lepadogaster Gouanii.
Prnjavica	Venus verrucosa.
Prstenci Prstići	} Lithodomus lithophagus.
Prug	{ Dromia Rumphii. / Palinurus vulgaris.
Pujoglavica	Mullus barbatus.
Punjeglavica	Anguilla vulgaris.
Pustenka	Aphrodite hystrix.
Putnik	Mugil chelo.

Puži, Pužići	Helix *sp*.
Pužica	Tapes edulis.
Puzlatka	Heliotis tuberculata.
Račić od ostrige	Pinnotherus veterum.
Račnjak	Maia squinado.
Ranje biele	Trachinus draco.
Ranjen	„ *sp*.
Rak	{ Carcinus mænas. Nephrops norvegicus.
Rakovica	{ Maia squinado. Lambrus mediterraneus. Iaxea nocturna. Portunus depurator.
Rak-samac	Pagurus Bernhardus.
Raža	Raja punctata.
Ražica	Raja punctata.
Ražina drnčava	„ clavata.
Razporka	Fissurella costaria.
Riba lesica	Alopias vulpes.
„ od pjene	Naucrates ductor.
„ prasac	Centrina Salviani.
„ prasica	Lepadogaster *sp*.
„ sablja	{ Xyphias gladius. Lepidopus caudatus.
„ vlasuja	Trachypterus tœnia.
Rumbac	Rhombus maximus.
Runjavac	Helix setosa.
Salpa	Box salpa.
Sanketе	Arnoglossus laterna.
Sanketice	{ „ „ Centropristis hepatus.
Šarak, šarakina	Clupea papalina.
Šaran	Cyprinus carpio.
Šarena drhtulja	Torpedo *sp*.
Šarg, šarag	Sargus Rondeletii.
Škarpion	Coristes dentalus.
Skoranza	Alburnus scoranza.
Šenac	Mytilus edulis.
Šeputnjača	Retepora cellulosa.
Šestilo	Lambrus mediterraneus.
Šfoj	Arnoglossus Grohmanni.
Šfolja kosmata	{ Phrynorhombus unimaculatus.
Šfolja, švoja	Solea vulgaris.
Sgrčenice	Mullus surmuletus.
Sguša bilica	Scomber colias.
„ pastrica	„ scomber.
Šiba	{ Trygon thalassia. Myliobatis noctula.
Šilj	Lucioperca sandra.
Šilo	{ Siphonostoma and Syngnathus *sp*.
Sipa	Sepia officinalis.
Sipica	Sepiola Rondeletii.
Skaram, skaran	Sphyræna vulgaris.
Škarpina	Scorpæna scrofa.
Škarpoč	„ *sp*.
Škarpun	„ porcus.
Skila	Galathea scamparella.
Skipa	Lutraria elliptica.
Sklat	Rhina *sp*.
Sklat od purica	Rhina squatina.
Školjak	Arca Noœ.
Škorak	Arenicola piscatorum.
Škoravi cievnjak	Serpula *sp*.
Skuš, skuša, sguša	Scomber scomber.
Šljanak	} Solen vagina.
Šljanci	
Šljivar	Chondrostoma soëtta.
Slonov zub	Dentalium entalis.
Smrt	Galathea rugosa.
Smokva	{ Crenilabrus *sp*. Stromateus fiatola.
Smokvača	{ „ „ Serranus scriba.
Smokvica	Crenilabrus melops.
Smudj	Lucioperca sandra.
Smudut	Labrax lupus.
Sokot, Sklat	Rhina squatina.
Solinarka	Cardium rusticum.
Solnjača	Crenilabrus pavo.
Špar	Sargus annularis.
Špirka	Crenilabrus melops.
Spuži	Helix, *sp*.
Srčavka	Cardium edule.
Srdjela, srdela	} Clupea pilchardus.
Srdjelica	
Srebrnica	Argentina sphyrœna.
Strigljača	{ Pilumnus hirtellus. Portunus depurator.
Štiriun	Acipenser *sp*.
Stirjaš	Mugil capito.
Strmorinac	Fierasfer acus.
Štuka	Esox lucius.
Suličica	{ Branchiostoma lanceolatum.
Sunj	Trygon brucco.
Šur, širun, šnjur	Trachurus trachurus.
Sužanj mačak	Scyllium stellare.
Svač	Rhombus lævis.

Svalica	Leuciscus svallize.	Vabić	Squilla mantis.
Svićica	Lepadogaster Candollii	Velik sunj	Trygon thalassia.
Svirale od mora	Serpula sp.	Vèrnut	Scomber scomber.
Svitloka	Alburnus alburnellus.	Viža	Trygon pastinaca.
Tabinja	{ Phycis mediterraneus. Motella tricirrata.	Vjetrenica	Actinia sp.
		Vladika	Myliobatis noctula.
Tabinja ili list	Solea vulgaris.	Vladikinja	Coris sp.
Tararajka, Tarnjača Tèrn, Tèrnka Tèrnovka	} Torpedo sp.	Vlasulja, cvjetulja	Actinia sp.
		Vodni rak	Astacus fluviatilis.
		Vol, Volina	Notidanus griseus.
Tèrpen, Trp	Holothuria tubulosa.	Volak, volina	Murex brandaris.
Tornjić	Turritella communis.	Volina	{ Raja oxyrhynchus and macrorhynchus.
Tovar, Tovar morski	Merluccius vulgaris.		
Tovarčić	Gadus minutus.	Volinica	Raja marginata.
Tremajuka, Tremavka Trepljivica Trepotnjak	} Torpedo sp.	Vrag morski	Lophius piscatorius.
		Vrana	Labrus sp.
		Vrana zelena	Labrus turdus.
Trlja	Mullus sp.	Vražić	Lophius piscatorius.
Trog	Mæna vulgaris.	Vretenača	Cerithium vulgatum.
Trup ili tunj	Thyanus sp.	Vučić	Centropristis hepatus.
Truta	Salmo fario.	Vukodlak	Lophius piscatorius.
Tumbarel, Trup	Auxis vulgaris.	žaba	Lophius piscatorius.
Tuna, Tun, Tunina	Thynnus sp.	žabarić	Callionymus belenus.
Tupčić	Leuciscus phoxinus.	Zalistac	Solea vulgaris.
Turčin	{ Peristethus cataphractum.	Zečac	Aplysia depilans.
		Zeleni papagal	Labrus turdus.
Ubotnica	Octopus vulgaris.	želvin zvončić	Coronula testudinaria.
Ugor	{ Anguilla vulgaris. Conger vulgaris.	Zenski spuž	Helix Ponzolzi.
		Zet	Gasterosteus aculeatus.
Ugor śari	Muræna helena.	žežalo	Scyllarus arctus.
Ugorača	Cepola rubescens.	Zlatenka	{ Bulla lignaria. Haliotis tuberculata.
Ugorova majka	Muræna helena.		
Ugotica	Gadus sp.	Zlatoperac	Mugil auratus.
Ugotica dugonosica	Gadus Euxinus.	Zmijica morska Zmijičnjak	} Lepidopus caudatus.
Uklja	{ Leuciscus phoxinus. Alburnus alburnellus.		
		Zmijulica	Petromyzon fluriatilis.
Uklja mečica	{ Leuciscus phoxinus. Paraphoxinus alepidotus	Zubac, zubatac	Dentex vulgaris.
		Zubatac od krune " krunaś	} " gibbosus.
Uklja ostrulja	Aulopyge Hügeli.		
Urak	{ Grapsus varius. " marmoratus.	žuti gulj	Gobius niger.
		žutuga	Trygon sp.
Uśata	Oblata melanura.	žutulja	{ Myliobatis aquila. Trygon pastinaca.
Ustavica	Echeneis remora.		
Uznače	Labrus sp.		

GENERAL INDEX.

Adria	page 1
Adriatic gulf, its limits	... 1
„ seal	... 27
Agonera	... 108
Agugliara	... 115
Ali	... 113
Alzana	102, 117
Ancona	... 6
Anchovy, the	29, 85
Anglers, or fishing frogs	30, 79
Anguellera	... 107
Aphyes	... 81
Arbe, island	2, 7
Arctic forms	... 37
Argano	... 100
Argentine, the	... 84
Arte, Arti	... 104
Asturera	... 133
Atherines	15, 26, 38, 80
Atri	... 1
Aulona	... 6
Aussa, river	... 2
Austrian coast, its limits	... 2
Baicolera	... 110
Bait	107, 134
Bait for Sardine fisheries	... 107
Band-fishes	29, 80
Barbonera	... 111
Barca	... 100
„ di Muggia	... 100
Barcola	... 49
Barriaghi	... 129
Basket-traps	... 128
Basse, the	32, 38, 71
Battello	99, 103
Battelletto, Battellazzo ...	... 103
Bed, sea-bed	... 8
Bivalves	... 87
Black-fishes	33, 38, 77
Blennies	26, 38, 80
Boar-fish	28, 76
Bobera	page 108
Boccaporta	... 101
Bocche di Cattaro	... 49
„ false	... 67
„ di Segna	... 3
Bogue, the	28, 38, 74
Bombina	... 110
Bora	... 2
Boreal forms	23, 37
Botarga	... 81
Brackish waters, forms of the ...	... 38
Bragagna, Bragagnello	100, 119
Bragotto, Bragottin di mar ...	... 121
Bragozzo, Bragozzetto ...	101, 103
Brancarella	... 132
Brazza, channel	... 7
„ island	67, 68
Brazzera di Capo d' Istria ...	... 100
Brill, the	38, 83
Brindisi	... 6
Brioni, islands	... 64
Broschetti	114, 138
Buccari	62, 65
Buccarica	... 65
Budello	... 105
Bukvare	... 108
Burchio, Burchiello	103, 129
Burton, Capt. R. F.	41, 88, 90
Buso, cape	... 2
Busto	... 119
Cagnera	... 108
Calamotta, channel	... 67
Calata	... 125
Canapa, Canapin	... 104
Canavaca	... 132
Canna	123, 130
Caorlina	... 103
Capelan, the	29, 82
Capo d' Istria	62, 63
Carlopago	... 2
Carpenter, Dr.	... 7

Cassa	page 120
Castelmuschio	65
Cattaro, channel of	67, 68
Cephalopods	28, 30, 87
Cerbere, Cerberao	109, 110
Cerchietti	119
Cerchio, cerchiello	122
Cetina, river	67
Cevènte	3
Characteristic species of the various zones	34
Chelonia caretta	27
Chiara	119
Chiaroni	109
Chiaviche	124
Chioggia fisheries, value of craft and gear	60
Chioggiotti fishermen	45, 49, 64, 117
Chorology	10
Cievolame	81
Cievolera	108
Cimarol	101
Cio	99
Circle-nets	111, 113
Cittanuova	63
Cladophora	10
Claires	88
Cod tribe, the	29, 82
Cogòlo	117, 123
Complaints against trawling	43
Conger-eel, the	17, 29, 86
Cocchia, coccia	64, 117
Coral fisheries	97, 98, 121
Corallines	12
Coralline zone	20
Cornalia	27
Correnti	3
Corteghe	105
Coscioni	121
Crabs	93
Crapano, island	63
Crustaceans	91
Cucchiaia	120
Currents	3
Curzola, island	67
Cusidura	123
Cystoseira	14, 16, 17
Daïla	63
Dalmatia, its breadth	41
Dalmatian coast, its limits	2
Dandolo	114
Declivity, fishes of the	28
Deep-bed, fishes of the	page 29
Delfinera	133
Dentalà	131
Dente, Punta del	64
Dentex, the	28, 72
Depths	6, 9
Derbio, the	33, 76
Diatomaceæ	12, 17
Distribution of fauna	10
„ "extended"	35
„ "limited"	35
Districts of the Aust.-Hungarian fisheries	62
Division of profits	138
Dobrigno, bay of	15
Dolphins	33, 77
Dosana	3
Dragonets	80
Draw-nets	113
Dražice	2
Drezze	123
Drift-nets	105
„ fisheries	106
Duino	63
Eastern shore of the Adriatic, its limits	1, 2
Ecdysis of the shore-crabs	93, 129
Echinoderms	94, 145
Eckel, G. R. von	96
Eel tribe, the	27, 38, 39
Enea	119
Enteromorpha	10
Epidaurus	67
Esca	134
"Extended" distribution	35
Facies	10
Fango	8
Fasana	64
File-fishes	38, 87
Fiocina, Foscina	133
Fishing gear, value of	129
Fish-market	141
„ ponds, fish-weirs	122, 123
„ reared in the valli chiuse	127
Fisheries, their character	40
„ value of	154, 158
Fishes, recapitulation of	37
Fishing craft	99, 155, 165
„ frog, the	30, 79
„ gear	165

Fishing rights pertaining to the communes
under the Republic of Venice, *page* 47
Fiumara 7
Fiume 2, 62
„ Gulf of 6, 7, 23
Flat-fish tribe 29, 83
Flocco 100
Fluctuations in the yield of the fisheries 43
Flying-fishes 33, 38, 84
Forbes, Professor... ... 10, 11, 17, 24, 27
Forked hake 83
Fossenin, fossenigolo 133
Fountain-fish, the 31
Fraima 125
Fraschiata 134
Fregana 122
Fresh-water fishes... ... ... 37, 39
Frutti di mar 144

GACCIO, Giacchio 122
Gaëta 100, 114
Gar-pike, the 17, 29, 38, 84
Garcis, Anton 97
Gassa 122
Gavonera 108
Giravica 120
Ghirzi 65
Giadro, river 67
Giglioli, E. H. 85
Gilt-head, the 38, 74
Giogo 106
Giuppana 67
Glossa, Cape 1
Gobies 26, 37, 80
Godwin-Austen, R. 23
Gombina 110
Gorghi 124
Gorizia (Görz) 63
Gradisca 63
Grado 6, 62, 63
Grampa, Grampon 133
Graticola 100
Gravosa 62
Grayling, the 84
Grey Mullet, the 15, 32, 38, 81
Grigiuoli Griziole 123
Grippo 99, 117, 119
Grisiolo 104
Groppo 105
Ground-springs 7, 23

Grube, Dr. A. E. ... *page* 13, 14, 18, 19, 22, 31
Guatta 121
Günther, Dr. A. ... 9, 71, 74, 76, 77, 78, 81
Gurnards 28, 38, 79
Guzzo 99

HADRIA 1
Hair-tail, the 76
Hake, the 29, 82, 143
Hand-nets 120
Herring tribe, the... ... ... 32, 85
Heteractis 11
Historical part 40
Holdsworth, E. W. H.: "Sea-fisheries"... 106
Horizontal distribution 10, 35, 36
Horse Mackerel, the 33, 76
Hound, the 34
Hungarian-Croatian littoral 2, 62, 65, 156, 160,
161, 163, 164, 165, 166, 167

IAGLICARA 115
Ice for preserving fish 45
Ichthyoscopi 112
Illuminatore 100, 107
Ima 105
Ima da cortici 105, 113
„ piombo 105, 113
Imports into Italy of fish caught in Aus-
trian-Hungarian territorial waters 52, 168
In fianco 119
Incoronata, island 9
Increase of demand for fish 42
Individual share of fishermen ... 163, 165
Intenzer la rè 104
Invertebrates ... 10–25, 34–37, 87–95
Isola 62, 63
Istria, peninsula of, its limits 2
Italian boats fishing in Austrian-Hun-
garian waters 51
„ their share in the Austrian-
Hungarian fisheries 51, 162
„ individual profits derived
thence 52, 162
„ fishing in foreign waters 59, 60
Italian fauna 39
„ fisheries 58
„ fishing fleet 58
„ flounder 29, 38, 83
„ law regulating the sea-fisheries ... 49

JOHN DORY, the 28, 77

Kerka, river	page 67
Kirzi	65
Knots	105
Koescher	122
Kolombatović, Professor G.	82
Küstenland	2
Lagoons of Venice	86, 123
,, fish reared in the	81
Lagosta, island	62, 68
Laminarian zone	17
Lampreys	32, 38, 39, 87
Lancelet, the	87
Lavoriero	123
Legislation	47
Leme, channel	64
Lenza	131
Lésina, island	62, 67, 68
Leuto	100, 114
Ligazzi	3
"Limited" distribution of fauna	35
Line-fishing	130
Linguetta, Cape	1
Lino	104
Lissa, island	7, 62, 67, 68
Littoral rovers	26
,, squatters	27
,, zone, the exposed	10
,, ,, the submerged	12
Lobsters	17, 92
Lorenz, Dr. J. R.	10, 25, 26
Luksch, Professor J.	5
Luminiero	114
Lussinpiccolo, island	62, 64
Macarska	3, 62, 67
Mackerel, the	32, 38, 77
Maglia	105
Maltempo, channel	3
Mandracchio	2
Marano	63
Marazzi, Vice-Consul Count Antonio	46, 51, 158, 159
Marchesetti, Dr. C. de	57, 85
Marea	3
Mare Adriaticum	1
,, Superum	1
Marotta	129
Meagre, the	75
Megline	62
Meleda, channel	67
Meleda, island	page 9, 67
Mendole	63, 73
Meshes	105
Mezzana	119
Mezzo, channel	67
Migavica	120
Migratory fishes	26, 29, 30
Ministry of Commerce	41, 44
Minutaja, or Misto	135, 142
Molebut, the	34, 38
Mollusks	87
Monfalcone	62
Monk, the	27
Montata	124
Molinello	119
Morlacca, channel	3
Moulting of crabs	93, 129
Mounting the nets	105
Muggia	62, 63
Murry, the	86
Mussels	89
Mussolera	121
Names applied to fishermen	135
,, ,, the various methods of fishing	136
Nappa sottile	109
Narenta, river	67
Nasse	128
Nazádra	99
Nephrops Norvegicus	22
Nets	104
,, where made	104
Ninni, Professor A. P.	52
Nonnati	80
Northern forms, isolated colonies of	23
Norway lobster, the	22, 65, 91, 144
Nudibranchs	90
Nullipores	12, 17
Number of well-defined species of fish and other sea produce which come to market	98, 141
Occhi della catena	101
Octopus, the	28, 30, 87
Oliźnica	120
Ombla, river	67
Opposition to the Chioggiotti	49
Oprara	122
Ordega	121
Ordegno di pesca del corallo	121

GENERAL INDEX.

Organisation of the fisheries	*page* 62
Orsero	62
Oscellaria	11
Ostreghera	120
„ a piombo	121
Ostreoculture	88
Otranto	1
Outliers	23
Oysters	17, 87
Oyster fisheries of Stagno	68
PACCIUGO	107
Palanda	116
Palandara da posta	113
„ tiro	116
Pali	88
Pannola	130
Panza	113
Paper sailor, the	31
Parangale	131
„ a vela	131
Parenzo	62, 64
Pareti	113
Passelera	110
Pastello	107
Pelagic fishes	26, 30
Pelagosa, island	2, 67
Pelamide, the	33
Perch	38
„ tribe, the	71
Pesca a spavento, a ludro	133, 136
„ a volo	115
Pesce bianco	81, 125
„ da strame	81, 127
„ di grotta	28
„ nobile, fino	135, 142
„ novello	121, 124
„ ordinario, salvatico	142
„ populo	83, 135, 142
„ rosso	73
Peschera	65
Pesson	123
Pesto	107
Petter's "Dalmatia"	27
Phoca monachus	27
„ vitulina	27
Pike, the	37, 39, 84
Pilchard, the	29, 32, 85
Pillela, Piela	119
Pilot-fish, the	33, 38, 76
Piombi	105
Pipe-fishes	*page* 17, 29, 38, 86
Pirano	63
Piston, Pobug	133
Plaice, the	84
Planca, promontory	2
Ploča	2
Poklopnica	108
Pola	62, 64
Political conditions of the Adriatic sea-coast	41
Pomo, scoglio	9
Pompilus, the	76
Poor, the	29, 82
Popovnica	110
Portoré	62
Portellata	103
Posta, poste	105, 114
Posta di bobe	108
„ di ton	111
Poverty of the inhabitants of the coast	40
Preluca	65
Produce of the fisheries	69, 161, 166, 169, 170
Promontore, Cape	6, 64
Promontorium Diomedis	2
„ Solentinum	1
Prongs	133
Prostica	108
Proximity of land, its influence on the temperature of the water	4
Punta Croce, channel	23
Punta d' Ostro	6
Puschia	132
QUARNERO	6
Quarnerolo	6, 23
Quatrefages	18
Quieto, river	63
RADAZZE	121
Radiates	94
Ragusa	2, 7, 62, 67, 68
Ragusavecchia	67, 68
Ravenna	6
Rays	29, 70
Ray's Sea-bream	33, 77
Recapitulation of the fauna	34
Red Mullet, the	33, 38, 73
Regulations for fishing under the French	48
„ seine-fishing in Dalmatia	114, 137
Remora, the	33, 78

Resta ... ... *page* 100	Sars, Professor G. O., on the spawning of fishes ... ... *page* 118
Rete 105	Scabbard-fish, the 76
„ a fermo 111	Scald-fish, the 29
„ a strascino (strascico) 117	Scandaglio 100
„ da chiusa 111	Scares 133
„ d' angudella 107	Scattaroni 123
„ di barboni 111	Schiletto 101
„ di can 108	Sciabica (Žabica) 116
„ di capparozzoli 121	Sciassa 123
„ di guatti 111	Scirocco 2
„ d' imbrocco, da incetto 105	Scogli 2
„ d' insacco 109	Scogliani 2
„ da posta 105	Scoglio Sant' Andrea 67
„ di sardelletti 107	Scombrera 108
„ di sfoglie 111	Scorpions 28, 75
„ simplice, nude 105	Scorza de pin mazená 104
„ trammacchiate, tramagliate ... 105, 109	Scuri 137
„ tramezzata 110	Sea-anemones 95
„ vestite 105, 109	Sea-breams 27, 28, 74
Reti raschianti 117	Sea-horses 28, 38, 87
Revest, Consul Dr. Nic. 53	Sea-perches 28, 71
Rezzola, rezzuola 116	Sea-urchins 95
Ribbon-fishes 82	Seals 27
Rights of fishing 46	Seine-nets 113
Rizzajo, Rizzagio, Rizzagno 122	Seine fishing *versus* Drift-net fishing ... 115
Rockling, the 29, 38, 82	Seasons 5
Romagnuoli 64	„ of fishing 68
Rovers 25, 28	Sebenico 66
Rovigno 62, 64	Secche 122
Rovigo 1	Sedentary fishes 8, 25, 26
	Segna (Zengg) 7, 62
Sabaka (Žabaka) 120	„ channel 6, 7
Sabakone (Žabakun) 116	Segnale 131
Sacco 113	Selve, island 2
Saccoleva 121	Selce 62
Salmon tribe, the 84	Senello 108
Saltarello 109	Sepparola 132
Salting of fish 148	Serpents de mer 31
Saltness of water 6, 9	Serragli, Serragie 123
Salvore 63	Serranus, the 28, 29, 72
San Giacomo 65	Set-nets 109, 111
Sand-banks 8	Sfogliante 111
Sand-eel, Sand-launce, the 83	Shad, the 38, 39, 86
Sandoli 99	Sharks 30, 33, 69
Sansego 62	Shore fishes 8, 25
Santa Maria di Leuca 1	Skipjack, the 76
Sardellera 103, 105	Sloke plants 10
Sardines de Nantes 150	Snares 128
Sardine, the 29, 32, 85	Sole, the 29, 38, 83
„ fisheries, the ... 86, 106, 114, 137	Spalato 1, 62, 66
Sardonera 107	

Spanish mackerel, the	page 32, 38, 77	
Spawning of fishes	 44	
Species common to the various zones	... 35	
Species exclusively found in the various zones	 35	
Spedoni	 105	
Spet, the	... ... 29, 80	
Spirone di verzelati	 108	
„ da lotregani	 108	
Sponge fisheries	 63	
Sponges	 96	
Spunteri	... ... 100, 102, 119	
Squadrale	 131	
Squaënera	 108	
Squatters	... ... 26, 29	
Squid, the	... ... 28, 30, 87	
Stagno, channel	... ... 67, 68	
Star-gazers	... ... 29, 78	
Statistics	 154	
„ of Austro-Hungarian craft	... 155	
„ of the imports and exports of fish in the Aust.-Hungarian empire	 168	
„ of fish brought to market at Fiume	... ... 161, 166	
„ of fisheries	 154	
„ of the yield of the fisheries	162, 163	
Sticklebacks	 81	
Stone-basse, the	... ... 28, 72	
Stumigio, Stambul	 133	
Sturgeons	... ... 38, 39, 70	
Submarine springs	... ... 7, 23	
Sub-littoral zone	 15	
Suck-fishes	... ... 26, 81	
Sucking-fish, the, or Remora	 78	
Sugheri	 105	
Sun-fishes	... ... 34, 87	
Super-littoral zone	 10	
Supplies by rail	... ... 42, 156	
Surface waters	 4	
Sustavica	 132	
Sviéarica	 100	
Sword-fish, the	... ... 33, 75	
Syrski, Dr.	 96	
Tanaglia	 133	
Tanning nets	 104	
Tarabara	 110	
Tarantella	 111	
Tartana, Tartanella	... 102, 103, 117, 119	
Tela	 121	
Temperature	... ... page 4
Thynnoscopi	 112
Tides	 3
Titles from which originate fishing rights	46
Togna	 131
Tonnare, Tunere, Tonnere	... 65, 111
Tope, the	 34
Topknot, Bloch's	 29
Toppo	 99
Tortoise, the	... . 27, 147
Trabaccolo	 101
Trada	 104
Traëna, Trajna	 131
Tramata	 134
Trammel-nets	 109
Trappano	... ... 62, 67
Tratta	... ... 64, 113
„ d' angusigole	 115
„ da cievoli	 116
„ da fondo	... ... 117, 120
„ da menole	 120
„ da orate	 116
„ di sardelle	 114
„ da sardoni	 115
„ da scombri	 115
„ di ton	 116
„ grande d' estate	 114
„ piccola d' inverno	 120
Trattisella	 120
Traü	 67
Trawling, Trawlers	... ... 101, 102
Trawling-nets	 117
Tremeti, islands	 6
Treaty rights of the Italian fishermen	... 48
„ with Italy	 46
Tregina	 104
Trieste, Gulf of	... ... 3, 7
„ seaboard, its limits	 2
Tritura di granzetti	 107
Tronto	 1
Trout, the	... ... 39, 84
Trumpet-fish, the	 81
Tunny-fish	... ... 33, 77
„ fisheries	... 65, 78, 111, 164
Tunicates	 90
Turbot, the	... ... 29, 38, 83
Ulvæ	 10
Umago	... ... 62, 63
Umbrina, the	... ... 28, 38, 75
Univalves	 90

VALLI ... page 2, 3, 86, 119, 123	
„ a grigiuoli	124
„ chiuse	124
„ chiuse arginate	124
„ di Brenno	68
„ semi-arginate	124
Valligiani, Vallicultori	123, 124
Vallioni	2
Vallone di Muggia	63
Value of Aust.-Hung. fishing craft, 103, 165, 170	
„ „ „ fishing gear, 129, 165, 170	
Veglia, island	65
Venetian fisheries, fishing craft, &c.	61
Venetian lagoon fisheries ... 86, 123, 127	
„ regulations concerning the fisheries	47
Venice, imports and exports of fish at	60
Verse	128
Vertebrates	25
Vertical currents	7
„ distribution	35
Vivajo, Viera	129
Voiga	105
Volega, Vuoega	122
Vollari	109
Volosca	65
Voyageurs	26
Voz	65
Vrulja, bay	3
WANT of capital	43
„ of markets	42
„ of salt	45
„ of ice	45

Weevers	page 29, 78
Whiting, the	29, 82
Whiting-pout, the	29, 82
Willow basket-traps	128
Winds	3
Wolf, Professor J.	5
Wrasses	17, 26, 28, 82
YARRELL's "British Fishes"	72
Yellow-tails	33
Yield of the valli chiuse	127
„ of the Aust.-Hungarian fisheries, 156, 158	
„ of the fishing by Italian boats on the Aust.-Hungarian coast	159
„ of the fisheries of the Hungarian-Croatian littoral	160
ZARA	62, 66
Zel	121
Zerer	108
Zermagna, river	67
Zlarin, island	63
Zocco	123
Zone I.	10
„ II.	10
„ III.	12
„ IV.	15
„ V.	17
„ VI.	20
„ VII.	25
Zoppolo	99
Zostera	8
Zuri, island	9, 68

THE END.

www.ingramcontent.com/pod-product-compliance
Lightning Source LLC
Chambersburg PA
CBHW030423300426
44112CB00009B/821